Great Places™
Washington

A Recreational Guide to Washington's Public Lands and Historic Places for Birding, Hiking, Photography, Fishing, Hunting, and Camping

Titles Available from Wilderness Adventures Press, Inc.™

Flyfishers Guide to™

Flyfisher's Guide to Alaska

Flyfisher's Guide to Arizona

Flyfisher's Guide to Chesapeake Bay

Flyfisher's Guide to Colorado

Flyfisher's Guide to the Florida Keys

Flyfisher's Guide to Freshwater Florida

Flyfisher's Guide to Idaho

Flyfisher's Guide to Montana

Flyfisher's Guide to Michigan

Flyfisher's Guide to Minnesota

Flyfisher's Guide to Missouri & Arkansas

Flyfisher's Guide to New York

Flyfisher's Guide to the Northeast Coast

Flyfisher's Guide to New Mexico

Flyfisher's Guide to Northern California

Flyfisher's Guide to Northern New England

Flyfisher's Guide to Oregon

Flyfisher's Guide to Pennsylvania

Flyfisher's Guide to Saltwater Florida

Flyfisher's Guide to Texas

Flyfisher's Guide to the Texas Gulf Coast

Flyfisher's Guide to Utah

Flyfisher's Guide to Virginia

Flyfisher's Guide to Washington

Flyfisher's Guide to Wisconsin & Iowa

Flyfisher's Guide to Wyoming

Flyfisher's Guide to Yellowstone National Park

Best Fishing Waters™

California's Best Fishing Waters

Colorado's Best Fishing Waters

Idaho's Best Fishing Waters

Montana's Best Fishing Waters

Oregon's Best Fishing Waters

Washington's Best Fishing Waters

Anglers Guide to™

Complete Anglers Guide to Oregon

Saltwater Angler's Guide to the Southeast

Saltwater Angler's Guide to Southern California

On the Fly Guide to™

On the Fly Guide to the Northwest

On the Fly Guide to the Northern Rockies

Field Guide to™

Field Guide to Fishing Knots

Field Guide to Retriever Drills

Field Guide to Dog First Aid

Fly Tying

Go-To Flies™

Great Places™

Great Places™ Montana

Great Places™ Washington

Great Places™
Washington

A Recreational Guide to Washington's Public Lands and Historic Places for Birding, Hiking, Photography, Fishing, Hunting, and Camping

John Kruse

Great Places™ Series

Wilderness
Adventures
Press, Inc.™

Belgrade, Montana

Great Places™ Series

       Published by Wilderness Adventures Press, Inc.™
       45 Buckskin Road
       Belgrade, MT 59714
       866-400-2012
       Website: www.wildadvpress.com
       email: books@wildadvpress.com

       First Edition

Printed in South Korea.

ISBN: 978-1-932098-69-3

Acknowledgements

My heartfelt thanks go out to:

My father, who taught me to love the outdoors and who has proven to be a wonderful editor for the initial draft of this book.

My wife and children – for standing by me and showing me more patience than I deserved over the last year and a half.

My publisher, Chuck Johnson, for giving me my first book contract and gently guiding me through this process.

The many people in government and private life who looked over these entries, gave suggestions, and helped me through countless hours of research and travel to put this together.

My fellow writers whose advice helped me along the way.

And most importantly, my thanks go up to God for blessing me with all of this and more.

John Kruse
September, 2008

Table of Contents

Introduction

Great Places Washington. So, just what is this book all about, and more importantly, why should you spend your hard-earned money on it? Well, if you're like me, you enjoy the outdoors. I'd imagine you are also interested in more than just one outdoor pursuit. You may be an angler who likes to hike or a bicyclist who also enjoys kayaking. Perhaps you are a hunter with a love for horses who also does a lot of wildlife watching in the off-season, or a rock climber who seeks additional adrenaline from whitewater rafting. The point is – you are probably a multi-faceted outdoors enthusiast.

Unfortunately, most guidebooks are written with only one sport in mind. If you want to go hiking in Washington, you have to buy a book that covers that specific activity. The same goes for fishing, climbing, bicycling, hunting, paddling, etc... That's where this title comes in. Great Places Washington is meant to be your first stop and "go to" reference guide when it comes to recreating outdoors in the Evergreen State. Inside you'll find 76 entries covering Washington's major public lands and another 77 entries focusing on some of the best lodges, resorts, guides and outfitters in the Pacific Northwest. The activities described in each entry run the gamut of what you can do outside; a huge change from the one-sport-at-a-time offering found in most books. Immediately below each entry title you'll find a contact address, phone number, and website where you can get more information.

Every private business listed in this book has, for the lack of a better term, been investigated. All of them have earned a solid reputation and, as of press time, no major changes (to include being sold) are part of their long-term plans. On a related note, nobody bought their way into this book. Some "Best Of..." books are nothing more than a listing of companies that have paid a price to be there. This isn't the case here. We haven't listed every place you can go in Washington; just the ones where we think you'll have a great time!

The public lands cover everything from national parks and recreation areas to state wildlife areas, parks, national forests, and designated wilderness areas. Broken down geographically, you will find a representative sample of places to stay and eat, and adventures to take that you'll remember for years to come. To aid in planning your next trip, each entry has a rundown of what outdoor activities are available. Take a look at the symbols for a quick idea of what you'll find:

Accommodation Symbol

You'll get a roof over your head and a place to sleep here. This could be anything from a 5-star room at a luxury lodge to a yurt in a state park.

Camping Symbol

A place to pitch a tent, and in many instances, hook up a recreational vehicle (RV).

Fishing Symbol

There's fish to be caught here! Clamming and shell fishing for crabs and shrimp are also included with this symbol.

Hunting Symbol

Load up that firearm (safely please). Big game animals, upland birds, or waterfowl can be hunted in places where you see this symbol.

Hiking Symbol

In the mood for a walk? Whether you want to go a long ways or just for an easy stroll, you'll find it here.

Bicycling Symbol

Some places are paved, some are gravel, and some are single-track trails, but whatever it is, it's a good choice for a bike ride.

Horseback Riding Symbol

Saddle up and head out on the trail! The West is still alive and well where you find this symbol.

Climbing Symbol

This is not a detailed climbing guide, but we've got some pretty good ideas of peaks you may want to summit. Many of them require little to no technical expertise.

Paddlesports Symbol

Kayaking, canoeing, rowing a boat, and whitewater rafting. It's all covered here.

Snow Sports Symbol

Nordic skiing and snowshoeing are addressed here. Motorized winter sports are not.

Wildlife Watching Symbol

Bird watchers will find a lot of information in this book, as will those who enjoy seeing everything from butterflies to amphibians to birds and mammals.

Point of Interest Symbol

There are two sides of history covered here. Sometimes this symbol will point to a natural point of interest such as a cave, waterfall, volcano, or a petrified forest. Other times it will direct you towards some piece of human history; examples being the trail blazed by Lewis and Clark, former military forts, or the site of the Whitman Mission.

If you have budgetary constraints (and most of us do) you may want to look at the pricing symbols. Broken down for lodging and for adventures (which can cover trips, rentals and in some cases, the price of admission), you'll find a rough breakdown that looks like this:

$	$$	$$$	$$$$
$0 to $50	$51 to $150	$151 to $250	$250 and up

Finally, we include a little piece about "getting there" at the end of each entry. After all, it wouldn't be fair to tell you where to go and then not tell you how to get there, would it?

So there you have it. A quick introduction to a book that I hope will become your well-worn reference to Washington's outdoors for years to come. Dive in, there's more to do outside in Washington than you could ever imagine!

For Your Information

Nickname	Evergreen State
Population	6,587,600 (2008 estimate)
Capitol	Olympia
Largest City	Seattle (592,800 – 2008 estimate)
Size	71,303 square miles (18th largest state)
Length and Width	360 miles long and 240 miles wide
Highest Point	Mt. Rainier – 14,410 feet above sea level
Lowest Point	Sea level – where Washington borders the Pacific Ocean
Most Annual Rainfall	Forks, Olympic Peninsula – 121.7 inches
Least Annual Rainfall	Desert Aire/Central Washington – 6.84 inches
State Mammal	Orca (killer) whale
State Bird	Willow goldfinch
State Fish	Steelhead trout
State Flower	Coast rhododendron
State Fossil	Columbian mammoth
State Gemstone	Petrified wood
State Grass	Bluebunch wheatgrass
State Tree	Western hemlock
State Insect	Green darner dragonfly
Official State Song	"Washington, My Home"
Unofficial State Song	"Louie, Louie"
State Folk Song	"Roll On, Columbia, Roll On"
State Motto	"Alki" – an Indian word meaning "bye and bye"

The Ten Essentials

If you are going to play outside, you need to be prepared. Nature can be beautiful, but at times weather and conditions can get not only ugly, but unforgiving. It was that knowledge that led The Mountaineers Club in the 1930s to develop a list of "Ten Essentials" that should be carried on any backcountry outing. Here's the list, along with a few editorial comments:

Map	The more detail, the better.
Compass	And the knowledge to use it with a map. GPS systems seem to be taking the place of this item in the 21st Century, but being electronic, they are prone to failure.
Sunglasses and sunscreen	Not just for the desert or lake, but for snowfields as well.
Extra clothing	It gets cold at night and sometimes you get wet and need to change.
Headlamp/flashlight	There are no streetlights in the backcountry.
First-aid supplies	No explanation needed.
Firestarter	A campfire will keep you warm. It will also allow you to cook and signal your presence to others. They are not always easy to start. Carry a little insurance with you – you'll be glad you did.
Matches	It's tough to get that firestarter going without these.
Knife	The ultimate tool in the outdoors.
Extra food and water	They provide the fuel your body needs to survive.

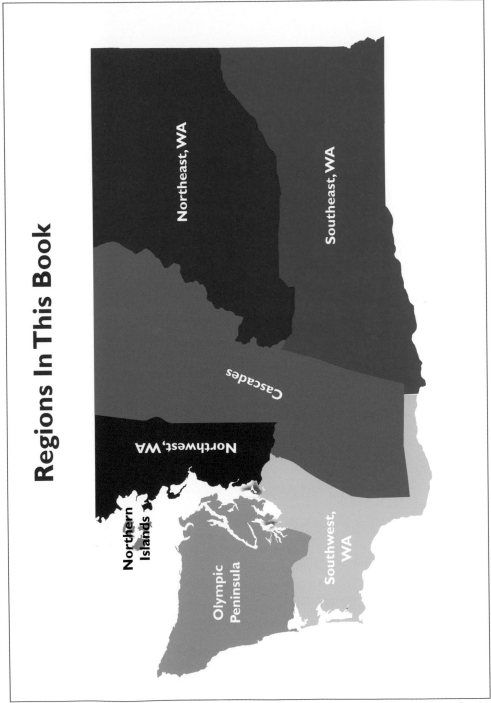

Regions In This Book

Northeast, WA

Southeast, WA

Cascades

Northwest, WA

Northern Islands

Olympic Peninsula

Southwest, WA

Outdoor Recreation in Washington

What can you do outside in Washington? A better question might be, "What can't you do?" There is a no shortage of activities to choose from for the outdoor enthusiast. We don't describe every one of them here, but we'll discuss quite a few in detail. The following is a preview.

Wildlife Viewing

Wildlife viewing is becoming big business. According to a national survey conducted by the U.S. Fish and Wildlife Service in 2006, 46 percent of Washington's population takes part in fishing, hunting, or wildlife watching, the latter activity being far and away the most popular.

There is good reason for this popularity. The different environments found in Washington support a wide variety of wildlife to include 147 different species of mammals, 32 of which are marine mammals. There is also an abundance of birds in the Evergreen State. The Washington Audubon Society has come up with a handy resource titled "The Great Washington State Birding Trail", which is viewable online at http://wa.audubon.org/birds_GreatWABirdingTrail.html and is also available for purchase. The map lists dozens of places of interest to bird watchers along with the species you may see at each location. When you add reptiles, amphibians, and insects like colorful butterflies and dragonflies to the mix, you'll find more than enough wildlife watching opportunities to last a lifetime. To find out exactly what kind of birds and mammals are found in Washington, study the University of Puget Sound's Slater Museum of Natural History checklist toward the end of this book.

Fishing

 Historically, fishing has been a major part of life for Native Americans, commercial fishermen, and sport anglers. That continues today in Washington State. Most people think of the coldwater species when it comes to fishing in the Pacific Northwest. After all, Washington is known nationwide for an abundance of steelhead (winter and summer runs) and salmon (five different native species). Several different types of trout and char can also be found in the state's lakes and streams (rainbow, brown, cutthroat, brook, golden, and bull trout) while whitefish and kokanee also garner some attention.

A variety of other game fish are just as worthy of consideration. Sturgeon are found in several large rivers, providing an incredible trophy angling opportunity. Walleye are becoming an increasingly popular quarry on the Columbia River and in several large eastern Washington lakes. Bass (both largemouth and smallmouth) have a dedicated following while other warmwater species such as perch, crappie, bluegill, bullhead, and catfish provide additional opportunities.

In the saltwater, salmon reign as king but bottomfishing can be very good. Halibut seasons generally run for short periods from May into the summer, and big lingcod provide tasty saltwater fare. Other ocean species of note for anglers are rockfish, cod, greenling, cabezon, piling perch, and surf perch.

Finally, it should be noted that in Washington, not all fishing takes place with a hook and line. Dungeness, rock crab, and shrimp are tasty crustaceans you can catch with a pot or ring in Puget Sound or the Pacific Ocean, while over 2,750 miles of marine beaches yield shellfish such as oysters and steamer clams, as well as northwest delicacies like razor clams and mammoth geoducks. When it comes to shellfishing, some caution is in order. Seasons and beaches close on short notice, sometimes due to health concerns. Be sure to call the Shellfish Safety Hotline (800-562-5632) and Shellfish Rule Change Hotline (866-880-5431) before you go out to get your clams or oysters.

DID YOU KNOW?

Fishing is such an important part of Washington's heritage that a leaping chinook salmon is prominently featured on the Washington State Quarter.

Hunting

 Hunting is another time-honored tradition in the Northwest, and there are ample opportunities for big game, waterfowl, and upland bird hunters. Deer and elk are the most popular big game species hunted, though black bear, coyote and, to a lesser extent, cougar and bobcat also have followings. Every year a few lucky hunters also draw permits to hunt for bighorn sheep, moose, and mountain goat as well.

On the bird side, ducks are a popular quarry with greenhead (drake) mallards being the most sought after target for shotgunners. Canada geese have become especially abundant, to the point of being a nuisance in some areas. Snow geese and brant are hunted in western Washington on a more limited basis.

OCTOBER IS WHEN MOST HUNTERS HEAD AFIELD IN WASHINGTON. WHAT ARE THEY AFTER?

- Deer
- Pheasant
- Waterfowl

The reason why? General seasons for all three start in October, providing the chance for good shooting in nice autumn weather.

Another game bird doing quite well is the wild turkey. Harvested primarily in northeastern Washington, these big birds are establishing themselves throughout the state, much to the delight of hunters. Several species of grouse are also found in the woods, and pheasant hunting remains popular throughout the state. In eastern Washington, quail and chukar provide additional upland bird hunting and dove season offers fast shooting for hard to hit birds at the beginning of September.

Hiking

A glance at the shelves of the local bookstore will let you know that Washingtonians have caught the hiking bug in a big way. The Cascade Mountains are the preferred destination for many, and the beauty found along these alpine trails is a good reason why they are so popular. However, hikers have plenty of other places from which to choose. Spring wildflower hikes in eastern Washington are an option, as are spring through fall hikes in the Blue Mountains or Kettle Range. In southern Washington, there are plenty of places to wander near the Columbia River. To the west there are beaches, dikes, and tidelands to explore near the saltwater, rainforests to trek through in the Olympics, and a host of other options farther inland.

One of the best resources in the state for hikers is found through the Washington Trails Association. Dedicated to the protection and maintenance of Washington's trails, the non-profit organization's website (www.wta.org) has an extensive library of trip reports that can help you decide where to go for your next hike.

Climbing

This isn't a climbing book per se, but there are several good climbing destinations found between the covers of this book. Three of the state's mountains get the most attention (Rainier, Adams, and Baker) but there are several other peaks in the Cascades and Olympics discussed as well. Many of these peaks don't require much in terms of technical skill, but several are clearly meant for climbers with a considerable amount of experience.

While the thrill of obtaining that proverbial mountain-top experience is hard to beat, caution is in order before any climbing expedition. In short, be cognizant of the weather, have the right equipment, be realistic about your own experience level, and call one of the guides found in this book if you want some help or just want to become a better climber.

WHAT IS WASHINGTON'S MOST POPULAR MOUNTAIN TO CLIMB?

Most people would guess Mt. Rainier, but in reality, Mt. Si near North Bend gets the honor. According to the Washington Trails Association, over 80,000 hikers a year make the 4-mile, 4,167-foot climb towards the summit.

Horseback Riding

 In this age of trains, planes, and automobiles, traveling anywhere on a horse seems decidedly antiquated. However, time in the saddle is a wonderful way of spending time outdoors. You won't wear yourself out hiking and the companionship of a horse on the trail makes a great trip even more memorable. Going by horseback is also an efficient way to get deep into the forest for an extended stay, especially if you have some horses, mules, or llamas to pack your gear.

Several outfitters offer pack trips for nature lovers and high-lakes anglers in the summer and big game hunters in the fall. Generally speaking, no experience is required if you go with an established outfitter. The outfitters cater to adults and children alike with short forays into the woods for an hour, day rides, short overnight trips, or multi-day expeditions.

If you don't want to go with an outfitter don't worry; there are plenty of trails to ride on your own. These range from flat, wide and easy trails on one end to challenging paths along high ridgelines in the backcountry at the other extreme. Some of these routes are on old rail lines converted to trails. Innumerable other opportunities await within national forests. Dig further into this book to find out more.

Bicycling

 Bicycling is not only a great way to exercise, but also a wonderful way to experience the outdoors. Whether you want to cycle towards Washington Pass on Highway 20, cycle along an old rail line, explore a seldom traveled country road, or take a mountain bike down a challenging single-track trail, you've got lots of options.

A number of trails (and roads) within national forests are great places for summer biking, while rail-to-trail destinations near Snoqualmie, Yelm, Bellingham, Cheney, Klickitat, Easton, and Cle Elum are great for day (or multi-day) rides. If you find yourself in town for business, or just can't leave town to get away, several cities have some great paved trails perfect for cycling. Some of the better ones are found in (or near) Seattle, Redmond, Spokane, Pullman, Wenatchee, Yakima, and the Tri-Cities.

BICYCLING NIRVANA

The San Juan Islands might qualify. These three islands provide lots of country road cycling in beautiful settings. Lopez is the easiest choice, Orcas has the most varied terrain, and San Juan Island should not be missed.

Cycling opportunities are more limited within national parks, wildlife refuges, and state wildlife areas but are definitely worth checking out. One more option is found near Winthrop and Mazama, where the extensive Methow Valley Sports Trail Association trail system favored by cross-country skiers in the winter becomes a favorite destination for mountain bikers from spring through fall.

Paddlesports

 Paddlesports include kayaking, canoeing, and rowing. All three conjure up images of tranquil waters and scenic settings. This type of paddling is possible on many of Washington's waterways. You can kayak in Puget Sound with views of Mt. Rainier, Mt. Baker, or the Olympics and likely spy the bobbing head of a curious seal along the way. The Columbia River also has lots of kayaking possibilities, particularly near Hanford Reach and near the Julia Butler Hansen National Wildlife Refuge. You can row a boat for exercise or troll for fish on any number of lakes large and small; and setting forth in a canoe for a day trip, or multi-day expedition, is possible in places like Lake Roosevelt, Ross Lake, and Lake Chelan.

On the more exhilarating end of the paddling spectrum is the chance to go whitewater rafting or kayaking. There are several streams where this is possible; most of them emanate from the Cascades, though there are also opportunities on the Olympic Peninsula and on the Snake River. The best time for whitewater fun is in the spring and early summer, when melting snow raises river levels and turns them into watery roller coasters. Two notable exceptions to this rule are the Tieton River (which has a September rafting season) and the White Salmon River in south central Washington, which relies as much on cold springs as it does on snowmelt for its water supply.

CLASS WHAT?? WHITEWATER RATINGS

The International Scale of River Difficulty gives you an idea of how difficult a particular stretch of river is to navigate by dividing the water into six different classes. American Whitewater, a non-profit organization, defines them as follows:

Class I Rapids: Easy – Fast moving water with riffles and small waves. Few obstructions, all obvious and easily missed with little training.
Class II Rapids: Novice - Straightforward rapids with wide, clear channels which are evident without scouting. Occasional maneuvering may be required, but rocks and medium-sized waves are easily missed by trained paddlers.

Class III: Intermediate – Rapids with moderate, irregular waves which may be difficult to avoid and which can swamp an open canoe. Complex maneuvers in fast current and good boat control in tight passages or around ledges are often required; large waves or strainers may be present but are easily avoided.

Class IV: Advanced – Intense, powerful but predictable rapids requiring precise boat handling in turbulent water. Depending on the character of the river, it may feature large, unavoidable waves and holes or constricted passages demanding fast maneuvers under pressure.

Class V: Expert – Extremely long, obstructed, or very violent rapids which expose a paddler to added risk. Drops may contain large, unavoidable waves and holes or steep, congested chutes with complex, demanding routes.

Class VI: Extreme and Exploratory Rapids – These runs have almost never been attempted and often exemplify the extremes of difficulty, unpredictability, and danger.

Snow Sports

 The outdoor fun doesn't end when the snow flies. Downhill skiing and snowmobiling are not addressed in detail in this book, but cross-country skiing and snowshoeing are. As you may imagine, most of these winter sports occur in the Cascades, though mountains in Northeast and Southeast Washington do offer additional choices. The Washington State Parks and Recreation Commission operates several Sno-Parks in these areas, and some are non-motorized parks with groomed trails for cross-country skiers. Several non-profit organizations also maintain trail systems with public access for skiers and snowshoers. They include the Methow Valley Trails Association, the Leavenworth Winter Sports Club, and the Mount Tahoma Trails Association near Ashford. Finally, you'll also find a few lodges in the pages of this book that cater to the cross-country skiing crowd. Some of the notable examples include The Scottish Lakes High Camp, the Sun Mountain Lodge, and the North Cascades Lodge.

Camping and Other Overnight Accommodations

You might want to stay at some of these places for a while. With that in mind, you'll find a number of camping options that may help you decide where to go. There are also a good number of private lodges and resorts in this book. Some of them are simple, family oriented places in great environments. Others have restaurants and yes, some of those restaurants serve up some very good food. Finally, a few lodges fall under the category of luxurious. However, one thing they all share is a decided bent towards the outdoors in terms of offerings, setting, and amenities.

You won't find every one of Washington's lodges and resorts listed in this book. However, you will find the best representative places to stay in each geographical area. How did that determination come about? Primarily through research. In addition to that, every lodge and resort listed in this book had a personal visit, talks with the management took place, and the properties were compared to their neighboring competition.

WILDERNESS LUXURY

Looking for a pampered outdoor getaway? If you really don't want to rough it overnight, try booking a stay at one of these places:

- The Salish Lodge
- Sun Mountain Lodge
- Alderbrook Resort
- Lake Quinault Lodge
- The Lodge at the Lakedale Resort
- Bull Hill Guest Ranch

Points of Interest – Natural and Historical

Finally, you'll find that Washington is full of fascinating history from both a natural and historical point of view. Much of the state's history is tied to the opening of the Western Frontier. The Lewis and Clark Expedition followed the Snake and Columbia Rivers on their way to the Pacific Ocean and later, Marcus and Narcissa Whitman established an ill-fated mission along the Oregon Trail. The military left its mark on the region as well in places like Fort Spokane in Eastern Washington and at coastal fortifications built to defend Seattle and the shipyards within Puget Sound from enemy fleets. Finally, lighthouses built to warn mariners of danger now stand as picturesque historical buildings in a number of scenic seaside settings.

The natural history of the state is every bit as interesting as the human history that made its mark on the land. Mount St. Helens is probably the best example of this. An active volcano that blew up in a big way on May 18, 1980, the eruption left a devastated landscape behind that is still in the process of coming back to life. Mt. Rainier, Mt. Adams, and Mt. Baker are three other points of interest as towering sentinels of the Cascades, and the rainforests of the Olympic Peninsula provide a home for several species of creatures found nowhere else on earth. In eastern Washington there is a petrified forest near Vantage and in the southeast corner of the state you'll find the entrance to Hell's Canyon, North America's deepest gorge. Also in eastern Washington are the channeled scablands, a landscape of basalt scoured by ice-age floods. Dry Falls is one such place the floods ran through. Although the falls are merely a skeleton now, they once roared with water, dwarfing the size of Niagara Falls. Speaking of waterfalls, they represent another point of interest and there are a number of picturesque ones found throughout Washington.

MAGNIFICENT WATERFALLS

Looking for Washington's most spectacular waterfalls? Try visiting these two, especially in May when snowmelt and rain sends torrents of water downstream.

Snoqualmie Falls, Snoqualmie: 268 feet
Palouse Falls, Starbuck: 198 feet

Where to Go – An Overview

There are scores of public lands within Washington where you can recreate. Some of them are administered by the federal government, others by the state, and still others by local counties. A few non-profit organizations get into the mix as well. The following is a brief breakdown of the different entities.

State and County Parks

The Washington State Parks and Recreation Commission manages 120 different parks. Some are day-use areas, but others offer camping and RV sites. These parks generally offer more amenities than federal campgrounds. Restrooms with flush toilets and showers are the norm, as are summer concessionaires, paved boat launches at lakes, and plenty of hook ups for recreational vehicles (RVs). While campsites make up most of the overnight accommodations, several parks offer more. At Dosewallips State Park you can stay in a furnished canvas tent, while other parks offer furnished yurts or cabins with heat and electricity. A select few parks even have furnished vacation homes for rent.

County parks, in contrast, are generally day-use properties and operate on more limited budgets. There are a few notable exceptions, though, where camping is allowed. Two county parks in northwestern Washington (Silver Lake and Kayak Point) offer the same variety of accommodations and amenities found in some of the better state parks. With only a few exceptions (Kayak Point County Park being one of them), state and county parks do not charge day-use fees, though boat launch fees are common.

State Wildlife Areas and Natural Preserves

The Washington State Department of Fish and Wildlife manages 850,000 acres of state land for the purpose of maintaining fish and wildlife habitat and also to provide sustainable outdoors recreational opportunities. Most of this land is grouped within 27 different wildlife management areas. Hunting and fishing are the main attractions in most of the wildlife areas, and an access permit (to be displayed through the windshield of your car) is issued with every license. In recent years, wildlife watching, dog training, hiking, bicycling, horseback riding, and other non-consumptive activities have also become popular on these state lands. These users also need a vehicle use permit, which costs $10 at sporting goods stores throughout the state.

In addition to wildlife areas, the state also manages 51 natural preserves that cover 31,000 acres. Administered by the Department of Natural Resources, these places have been established and are maintained for the conservation of certain plant and animal species (many of them rare). Hiking and wildlife viewing are allowed in designated areas within many of these preserves.

National Forests and Wildlife Refuges

The U.S. Forest Service is responsible for five national forests in Washington. They consist of the 1.1-million acre Colville National Forest in the northeast, the newly combined Okanogan-Wenatchee National Forest that covers much of the eastern Cascades, the Mt. Baker-Snoqualmie National Forest along the western slopes of the same mountain range, the Gifford Pinchot National Forest in south central Washington, and finally the Olympic National Forest that surrounds much of Olympic National Park. These huge tracts of land are managed for multiple uses that include hunting, fishing, hiking, horseback riding, snow sports, and motorized activities like snowmobiling and motorized trail use. Activities in designated wilderness areas within the National Forest Service boundaries are generally limited to non-motorized use and group size is often limited to minimize impacts to the fragile environments found in them.

You'll find a good number of campsites within these national forests. The drive-to campgrounds are often found next to lakes or streams. The amenities are not as nice as you will find in state parks (there are generally no RV hook-ups and vault or pit toilets are often the only restroom facilities), but the locations are often ideal. Other campsites are hike-in or ride-in destinations, where you'll find a place to pitch a tent, start a campfire, and relax after a day on the trail. Unfortunately, federal funding has not kept pace with the budgetary needs of the Forest Service. As a result, there is a huge backlog of maintenance and repair projects that affect everything from roads to bridges, trails, and campgrounds within these forests. To help address this, the Forest Service has instituted a user fee requiring recreational passes to park at many trailheads and other sites in Oregon and Washington. As of 2008, you can buy a day pass for as little as $5 or an annual pass for $30.

You'll also need to pay an entry fee to get into most of the national wildlife refuges within Washington. Administered by the U.S. Fish and Wildlife Service, the 23 different refuges have all been established to protect wildlife and the habitat they live in. Many of them have been founded with birds in mind, and seeing huge flocks of migrating waterfowl and other avian species is possible at places like the McNary, Columbia, Ridgefield, Willapa, and Nisqually Refuges. Other wildlife refuges are oriented towards rare mammals, like the Julia Butler Hansen Refuge for the Columbian white-tailed deer. Not all of them are open to the public, and even those that are often have significant portions of their land closed to protect the animals and habitat.

In a similar vein, recreational uses vary widely. Those refuges open to the public generally allow wildlife viewing, and several also offer hiking and even kayaking opportunities. Surprisingly, hunting is allowed in some refuges, and places like McNary and Ridgefield Refuges have been longtime favorite destinations for waterfowlers. On the other hand, dogs (by and large), are not welcome at wildlife refuges unless they are actively engaged in hunting. The recreation fee to enter most refuges is modest (less than $10) and if you possess a valid federal duck stamp (required for waterfowl hunting) you don't have to pay anything. The same goes for those who possess an America the Beautiful Pass, an $80 annual pass that allows you to recreate in a variety of federal lands including national forests, parks, and refuges.

DUCK STAMPS – DID YOU KNOW?

First issued in 1934 as a federal hunting license for migratory waterfowl, duck stamps today provide millions of dollars for wetlands conservation in national wildlife refuges. Over 700 million dollars have been generated by duck stamp sales since their inception and have been used to purchase or lease 4.5 million acres of habitat.

National Parks, Historical Sites, and Monuments

Three of Washington's most beautiful places have obtained status as national parks. Mt. Rainier National Park surrounds the state's tallest peak. Olympic National Park encompasses the wild Pacific Ocean coast, temperate rainforests, and a mountain range. Meanwhile, the North Cascades National Park Complex is broken down into two units full of peaks and glaciers and two national recreation areas accessing the pristine waters of Ross Lake and Lake Chelan. While the North Cascades National Park Complex does not have an entrance fee, you will have to pay ($15 or less) to enjoy Mt. Rainer or Olympic National Park.

National recreation areas provide a few more options outdoors than national parks. For example, while hunting is not allowed in national parks, it is allowed in national recreation areas. Mountain biking and equestrian options are also limited in national parks compared to these federal lands. National recreation areas do not have entrance fees, though there is usually a fee to use the boat launches found inside their boundaries. In addition to the recreation areas found at Ross Lake and Lake Chelan, the Lake Roosevelt National Recreation Area is also located in Washington. The huge impoundment of the Upper Columbia River is a boater's paradise, with campsites and marinas scattered along the 129-mile long lake.

National monuments do not have the same level of protection as national parks and are not overseen by the National Park Service. The Mount St. Helens Volcanic National Monument is managed by the U.S. Forest Service and focuses on educating the public about this very active volcano that erupted in a spectacular and devastating fashion in 1980. In contrast, the Hanford National Monument is administered by the U.S. Fish and Wildlife Service and is located in south central Washington near a historic nuclear reactor. The dry country that surrounds it and the Columbia River that runs through it support a surprising amount of diverse wildlife.

Finally, there are several national historic sites within the state that are managed by the National Park Service. The San Juan Island National Historic Park preserves land occupied by American and British forces in the middle of the 19th Century. Visit them to learn the story of a war that, fortunately, never occurred. In southeastern Washington, the Whitman National Historic Site has been established at the site where missionaries Marcus and Narcissa Whitman, along with several others, were killed by hostile Cayuse Indians. The story of the attack, along with the tragic events that led to the massacre and those that followed it, is well told in this now peaceful setting near Walla Walla. Both places are wonderful for walking and offer the chance to combine wildlife watching with historical education.

Great Trails

Washington has a number of fantastic long-distance trails worth exploring on foot, bicycle, through skiing, and even afloat.

Pacific Crest National Scenic Trail: The 2,650-mile trail runs all the way from southern California through Oregon and Washington into British Columbia. In Washington, the trail runs 500 miles from the Bridge of the Gods over the Columbia River along the Cascade Mountains to the Canadian border. Several of the entries in the Cascade Mountains section of this book give more details about this popular hiking trail, which is best traveled from July to September.

Cascadia Marine Trail: A favorite among kayakers, this trail connects 55 shoreline campsites throughout Puget Sound. A small fee ($12 to $14 at press time) is required to stay overnight at these sites which are only open to campers in small wind- or human-powered boats. The trail is administered by the Washington State Parks Commission (www.parks.wa.gov).

Columbia Plateau Trail State Park: This Washington State Park trail runs 130 miles through eastern Washington along an old railroad grade. It is still being developed, but some 23 miles of the trail near Cheney are currently open for hikers, bicyclists, and equestrians.

Iron Horse State Park: Another state "Rails to Trails" park, this one goes from North Bend, through a tunnel at Snoqualmie Pass, and then all the way to the Columbia River near Vantage, covering about 110 miles in the process. Used by hikers, bicyclists, horseback riders, and in some portions, by cross-country skiers, it is also known as the John Wayne Pioneer Trail. Both the Columbia Plateau and Iron Horse State Parks are covered in detail in this book.

Methow Valley Sports Trail Association: This non-profit organization maintains a 200-kilometer trail system in northeast Washington's Methow Valley. It is very popular in the winter for cross-country skiers and is used by bicyclists, trail runners, and hikers the rest of the year. See their entry in this book for further information.

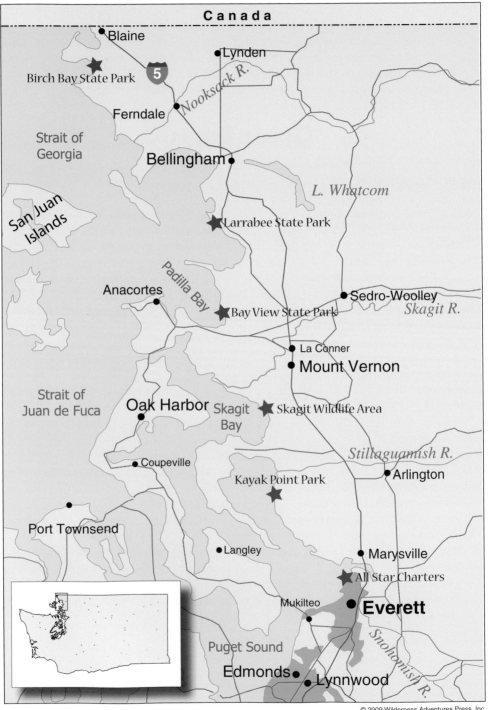

Canada

Blaine

Lynden

Nooksack R.

Birch Bay State Park

5

Ferndale

Strait of
Georgia

Bellingham

L. Whatcom

San Juan
Islands

Larrabee State Park

Padilla Bay

Anacortes

Sedro-Woolley

Skagit R.

Bay View State Park

La Conner

Mount Vernon

Strait of
Juan de Fuca

Oak Harbor

Skagit
Bay

Skagit Wildlife Area

Coupeville

Stillaguamish R.

Kayak Point Park

Arlington

Port Townsend

Langley

Marysville

All Star Charters

Mukilteo

Everett

Puget Sound

Snohomish R.

Edmonds

Lynnwood

Northern Puget Sound

Kayak Point Park

15610 Marine Drive, Stanwood, WA 98292 / 360-652-7992
www1.co.snohomish.wa.us/Departments/Parks/Park_Information/Park_Directory

Lodging Prices

Adventure Pricing

Most county and municipal parks are day-use affairs. It seems that local government, by and large, has left parks with overnight camping in the hands of state and federal agencies. One exception to this rule can be found at Snohomish County's Kayak Point Park. This fabulous park has camp sites, yurts, and even a rental house along with a large day-use area that stretches 3,300 feet along the shoreline of Puget Sound.

Kayak Point is located between Marysville and Stanwood. Upon entering the park you'll first come across the main office and the Kayak Cottage, a three-bedroom, fully furnished house that can be rented for group or family vacations (there is a two-night minimum stay between May 15 and October 15). A few feet from the cottage, a road loops past the campground and Yurt Village. Each of the ten yurts accommodates up to five guests with futons, bunk beds, and tables inside. Pets are not allowed in the Yurt Village but if you rent the single yurt outside the village (which also has an adjoining campsite) you can keep your pet in the camp site area. The park's 30 campsites have electricity and many of them will accommodate small RVs. Water spigots are located at several places in the campground and a restroom with showers is also available. All of the overnight locations are found in a heavily forested part of the park, with red cedar and Douglas fir being the predominant trees. Some of the trees have been around awhile; one giant fir is estimated to be 700 years old.

You can drive (or take a trail) from the upper portion of the park to the expansive day-use area below. Once there, you'll find a long pebble-strewn beach along the shores of Port Susan. You can walk over 0.6 miles of public beach, finding agates, small crabs, and shellfish such as mussels, barnacles, littleneck and butter clams. Even though you aren't allowed to harvest the clams, they are fun to look at and you'll probably get the chance to see some wildlife as well. Eagles frequently soar over the beach, as do more common gulls. Waterfowl swim in the water near shore and seals are known to pop up to see what's going on. On rare occasions in the spring, you may even get the chance to see a migrating gray whale.

A saltwater pier provides a place to view the ocean and Camano Island while you drop a crab ring or go fishing. In the spring, angling for pile perch and other bottomfish can be good and every other autumn, pink salmon are caught in good numbers from the pier and the beach. If you want to venture farther out into the water, there is a small boat launch that can be used at high tide, and at the north end of the day-use area are two camp sites specifically for kayakers who paddle the Cascadia Marine Trail. Launching from here, you'll find Camano Island State Park, Everett, and Mukilteo all within a day's paddle.

As enjoyable as all of these activities are, many visitors content themselves by picnicking at one of the many sites along the beach. Some of the sites are covered, some have fire pits, and there is one covered area suitable for group use. A large grassy area lends itself well to summer play, as does a colorful and uniquely designed playground. If all of this is not enough, the county-owned 18-hole Kayak Point Golf Course is right across Marine Drive and has a full-service restaurant at the clubhouse.

Kayak Point Park is open all year.

There are two local rules that are worth noting. First; there is no alcohol allowed in the park, even for overnight guests. Second; there is a $5 day-use fee for visitors.

Getting There: Take the Smokey Point/Lakewood Exit off of Interstate 5 north of Marysville. Follow State Highway 531 west and continue to Marine Drive. Follow Marine Drive south to the park.

The Kayak Cottage is a furnished three-bedroom home available for rent.

ALL STAR CHARTERS

Gary Krein
720 Waverly Avenue, Everett, WA 98201 / 800-214-1595
www.allstarfishing.com

Lodging Prices: N/A   Adventure Pricing: $$$

If you want to go for a quick and easy fishing trip in the Seattle area, give All Star Charters a call. They offer morning and afternoon saltwater fishing excursions in the sheltered waters of Puget Sound all year long from Seattle and Everett. Captain Gary Krein, the owner, has been a guide since 1983 and is currently the president of the Charter Boat Association of Puget Sound. All Star Charters has two boats: a 28-foot Uniflyte named "The Morningstar" and a brand new 26-foot Wooldridge. Both can fish six guests at a time and each has a covered berth, comfortable seating, and a head (bathroom).

Most of the time you'll be going after salmon, a fish so connected with Washington that you can find its image on the back of the state quarter minted in 2007. If you go out in July you'll be hitting the water at the prime time to catch big king (chinook) salmon in Elliott Bay. Coho (silvers) are also fair game from July through August within view of the Space Needle. Fishing for silvers continues through September, and during odd numbered years there is usually a strong fishery for pinks, smaller salmon that offer lots of fast catching action. From October until early November chum salmon will draw your attention and blackmouth (immature chinook salmon) can be caught from October all the way into April.

Most of the salmon are caught trolling, a popular and effective method that allows you to take in the sights while waiting for your next take. Seals, bald eagles, gulls, and other birds are commonly seen, while passing boats and the urban skyline provide a nice backdrop for your day on the water.

At the beginning of May, the salmon get a break and All Star Charters goes bottomfishing until the middle of June. A typical morning will start by catching some sand dab (flounder) for bait, a fun diversion that some people would like to do all day. However, you're better off going after bigger fish in the sea. Colorful rockfish and bottom-dwelling cabezon are two species frequently caught on these trips, but most anglers have their hearts set on lingcod. These aggressive fish are found in good numbers, and it's not uncommon to have a big one chomp onto a smaller lingcod you have on the end of your line, which results in a bit of a tug of war. You are allowed to keep one lingcod between 26 and 40 inches in length. Bottomfish, like salmon, are very good table fare and All Star Charters will fillet and bag them for you at the dock.

Getting There: All Star Charters operates one boat out of Seattle's Shilshole Marina. For most of the year, the second boat departs from the Port of Everett Marina. Check the website for detailed directions.

Skagit Wildlife Area

Washington Department of Fish and Wildlife
21961 Wylie Road, Mount Vernon, WA 98273 / 360-445-4441
http://wdfw.wa.gov/lands/r4skagit.htm

The Skagit Wildlife Area, a longtime favorite destination for bird hunters and wildlife watchers, is going through some significant changes. The 16,708 acres of state land are easily accessible from Interstate 5 and lie near the small communities of Stanwood and Conway. The wildlife area fronts Skagit Bay on its southeastern end, and other portions are bordered by the North and South Forks of the Skagit River, where a dike system encloses farmland and riparian habitat.

The most popular place to visit is the Headquarters Unit. Located on Fir Island near Conway, you'll find a boat launch, a pheasant release site for fall bird hunting, and 6 miles of trails that run along dikes. These dikes provide walk-in access for waterfowlers who hunt near ponds, intertidal sloughs, and flooded agricultural fields managed by the Washington Department of Fish and Wildlife (WDFW) for the purpose of providing a wintering food resource for birds. This same area is a popular place to hike and go bird watching outside of the October-through-January hunting season.

This Headquarters Unit is getting a major makeover courtesy of the Wiley Slough Restoration Project that is currently underway. Dikes that are part of the 6-mile trail system and protect the agricultural fields are being removed to increase estuarine habitat for threatened chinook salmon. The major recreational impacts are a loss of the agricultural fields and pheasant hunting, along with some opportunities for walk-in duck hunting and extended hiking. However, the WDFW is working to mitigate this with plans to establish new ponds and riparian habitat. They are also pledging to keep several new and existing dikes open for public access at the Headquarters Unit. Finally, the WDFW is working to provide additional hunting opportunities through partnerships with nearby private-property owners.

Other places to get into the Skagit Wildlife Area from north to south are at the North Fork Access at the mouth of the Skagit River, the Jensen Access, the

Hayton Reserve on Fir Island, the old Milltown Access south of Conway, the Big Ditch Access north of Stanwood and the Leque Island Unit (formerly known as Davis Slough or Smith Farm) just west of Stanwood. There is also a Skagit County boat launch at Conway where the bridge crosses the south fork of the Skagit River.

The wildlife is what draws most people here. Massive flocks of snow geese migrate here from Russia's Wrangell Island every winter. They are joined by significant numbers of trumpeter and tundra swans that come every fall to feed in the agricultural fields around the Wildlife Area until early spring. Mallards, wigeon, pintail, green-winged teal, and bufflehead are all ducks that attract human hunters, while bald eagles, owls, falcons, and marsh hawks (northern harriers) are hunters of the winged variety that frequent the region. Other birds to watch for include great blue heron, marsh wren, and a variety of different shorebirds in the intertidal zones while woodland species such as sparrows, woodpeckers, flickers, and northern shrike can be found farther inland. Other animals that live in the wildlife area are black-tailed deer, raccoon, opossum, beaver, cottontail rabbit, muskrat, coyote, and red fox.

Kayaking or canoeing through the sloughs within the wildlife area and in Skagit Bay is worth mentioning. The landscape of dikes, farmlands, marshy flats, and the open bay is quite beautiful and paddling is a great way to see the birds and mammals that call this area home. However, too many paddlers can be problematic. Contrary to what some believe, you can disturb wildlife from small craft, so limiting the size of groups and how close you get to wildlife is important, especially when birds are nesting or molting. Likewise, paddlers would be wise to stay out of the wildlife area during hunting season.

Paddlers and others entering the intertidal zones do need to keep the fluctuating tides and currents in mind. It is easy to get stranded by the incoming tides that quickly and quietly fill up sloughs and canals. Likewise, outgoing tides can easily leave you and your boat on a mudflat if you are not careful. Familiarizing yourself with the tide tables will help in this regard.

The Skagit Wildlife Area is open all year during daylight hours. Hunters who come here need to be selective in their shooting, especially while hunting the farmed island segment and Welts Unit of the wildlife area where you are limited to having only 15 steel shot shells in your possession.

Getting There: Take Exit 221 off Interstate 5 south of Mt. Vernon. Travel 1.5 miles west on Fir Island Road past the small community of Conway and then travel south a mile on Wylie Road to reach the Skagit Wildlife Area's Headquarters Unit.

Wintering snow geese are abundant around the Skagit Wildlife Area.

Padilla Bay and Bay View State Park

Bay View State Park
0901 Bay View-Edison Road, Mt. Vernon, WA 98273 / 360-757-0227
www.parks.wa.gov

Lodging Prices

A shallow saltwater bay near Anacortes provides a quality, low-key outdoors experience with lots of wildlife viewing, trails to explore, an opportunity for education, and a state park to camp in. The bay in question is the Padilla Bay National Estuarine Research Reserve which covers some 11,000 acres. Biologists come here to study water quality and the huge meadows of eelgrass, a critical component of this estuary.

The Breazeale Interpretive Center has a number of indoor exhibits that explain the Padilla Bay eco-system. It's open all year Wednesdays through Sundays from 10:00am to 5:00pm. Besides indoor exhibits, the center has a short path that leads to the bay and a separate 0.8-mile-long trail. Called the Upland Trail, this is a lollipop loop through meadows and trees, starting and ending at the interpretive center. Field guides and binoculars are available on loan to use during your visit.

Another trail of note is the Padilla Bay Shore Trail. You can hike or bike the flat path on top of a dike for 2.25 miles from the small community of Bay View. On one side, you'll see green agricultural fields intersected by canals. Thick blackberry brambles grow close to the dike, giving small birds cover and food. On the seaward side of the dike are several saltwater sloughs and the bay. It's a pleasant place with expansive views of Puget Sound, Mount Baker, and the Cascades.

This specific area is also a great place for bird watching, and over 200 species have been observed around the bay. Great blue heron hunt for small fish along the waterline while raptors like bald eagle, red-tailed hawk, and northern harrier look for waterfowl, mice, and other small birds and animals. Meanwhile, small flocks of shorebirds like sandpiper and dunlin search for

food on the mudflats while various species of gulls, terns, loons, and grebes can be seen swimming on the surface of the shallow bay.

Raptors are not the only hunters here. Waterfowlers are known to use the Padilla Bay Shore Trail to access tidal marsh areas for ducks from October until January. If you have a boat, you can launch at Bay View to target not only ducks, but also brant, an uncommon species of geese that can be hunted for only a short time in January.

If you want to see wildlife in a more civilized environment, head towards La Conner, 8 miles south of Bay View. The heart of the town fronts the saltwater

Rabbits are plentiful at Bay View State Park.

Swinomish Channel. In addition to shops, cafes, and art galleries, you'll also likely see cormorants, waterfowl, gulls, and eagles on or around the water. Seals often come up the channel and in February the town hosts a smelt fishing derby. The wildlife sightings don't stop at the channel. Wild turkey commonly stroll the quiet residential streets of this unique town.

If you are looking for a place to camp, Bay View State Park is a good choice and is less visited than several nearby state parks. In addition to 45 tent sites, there are also 30 utility sites with water and electrical hook ups. Many of these are tucked into the woods and some surround a large grassy playfield. Also worth noting are six newer, cozy cabins. Each sleeps four people, though you'll need to bring your own sleeping bags or linens. The wooden structures also have heat and electricity. A covered porch swing with views of the bay, along with a picnic table and fire pit outside, make these nice places to stay. Restrooms with showers are located close to both the camping and cabin area and the two newest cabins actually have restrooms inside. Cabins can be reserved year round while campsites can be reserved from May 15 through September 15.

Across the road from the campground, you'll find a low grassy bluff with lots of picnic tables and a large enclosed shelter that overlooks the bay. Clamming is not permitted here, but you can certainly walk along the 1,285 feet of park-owned shoreline. Be careful about venturing onto the mud flats while doing this since it's easy to get stuck. Bay View State Park is open all year. Pets are permitted on a leash, but they are not allowed in the cabins.

Getting There: Drive west on State Highway 20 from Interstate 5 at Burlington/Mt. Vernon. Take a right and travel north at Bay View-Edison Road. Travel 0.8 miles north to reach the southern trailhead for the Padilla Bay Shore Trail. Continue 2.5 miles further to reach Bay View State Park and an additional 0.5 miles to visit the Breazeale Interpretive Center.

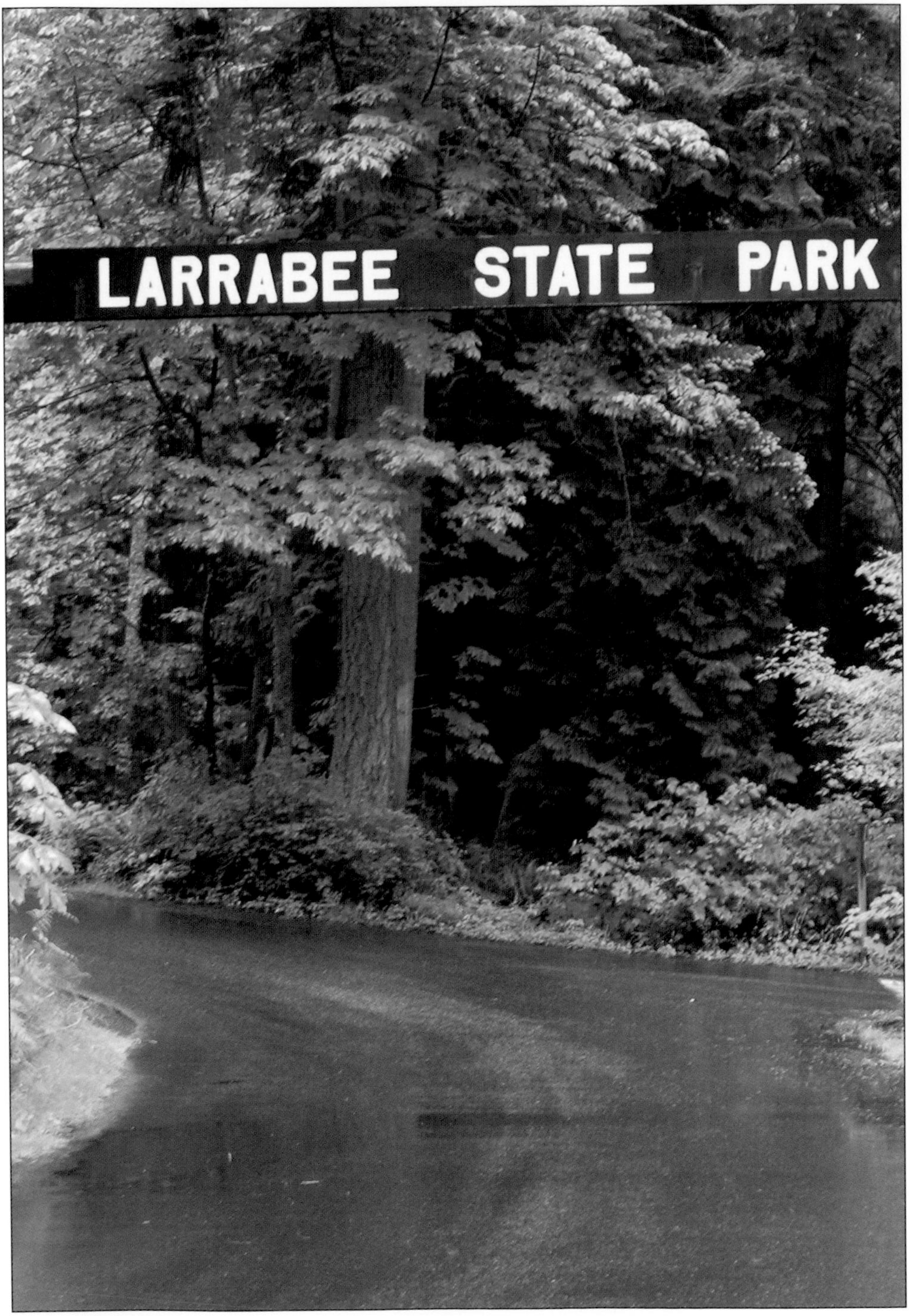
LARRABEE STATE PARK

Larrabee State Park

245 Chuckanut Drive, Bellingham, WA 98229 / 360-676-2093
www.parks.wa.gov

Lodging Pricing

Larrabee State Park has the distinction of being Washington's first state park, thanks to the generous donation of 20 acres of land for this purpose in 1915 by Charles Larrabee. Today, it has grown to 2,683 acres, which also makes it one of the state's ten largest parks. Bordered by Chuckanut Mountain and Samish Bay, you have plenty of recreational options to choose from to include hiking, horseback riding, bicycling, shellfishing, and wildlife watching.

With so much to do, you may want to spend a night (or three). There are 85 campsites within the park, 26 of which have water, power, and sewer hook-ups for RVs. Restrooms with showers provide a place to clean up and a group camp can handle 40 guests at a time. If you are just staying for the day, there are two large picnic shelters, a playground, and a large stage used, at times, for interpretive programs.

Hikers, bicyclists, and equestrians enjoy 14 miles of trails within the park and on Chuckanut Mountain. All three of these groups can travel 6.5 miles (one way) along the Interurban Trail. Taking off from the Clayton Beach Trailhead, the trail sits on a former railroad line used by the Bellingham to Mt. Vernon Interurban Trolley that ran along here between 1912 and 1930. If you like lakes, the Fragrance Lake Trail starts just outside the main entrance of the park. The first half of the 1.9-mile trail is only open to hikers. If you go, take your fishing rod because angling for rainbow and cutthroat trout can be good. Bicyclists and horseback riders do have other options though, since they are allowed to take the main north-south route into the Chuckanut Mountain Trail System. The North Lost Lake Trail goes 4.6 miles to a narrow body of water east of Fragrance Lake. Other multi-use trails around Chuckanut Mountain include the Salal Trail (1.2 miles), the Hemlock Trail

(3.5 miles) and Pine and Cedar Lakes Trail (2 to 3 miles). Several of these trails are co-managed with Whatcom County Parks.

If you like to crab or gather clams, you'll want to walk 0.7 mile to Clayton Beach. In the summer, you can wade among the eelgrass beds to find Dungeness crab and on shore you can use a rake and shovel to get into some cockles and steamer clams. The clamming season is open year round but you should check the Shellfish Safety Hotline for emergency closures (800-562-5632).

Other beach access is possible below the day-use area and at the main boat launch in Wildcat Cove. There is no clamming in the cove due to pollution concerns but you can do some beachcombing and explore the tide pools at low tide for marine life. During your walks through the park, you may find fossilized plant leaves from palm, cyprus, or sycamore trees. Take pleasure in looking at these pieces of natural history, but leave them where you found them.

Finally, a large amount of wildlife can be found in the park. Herons and eagles are two big birds frequently seen here and mammals such as black-tailed deer, raccoon, squirrels, porcupine, and red fox also make appearances within the park and on Chuckanut Mountain.

Larrabee State Park is open all year. Camping reservations can be made from May 15 through September 15 for individual sites. The group camp has to be reserved in advance year round.

Getting There: Larrabee State Park is located 6 miles south of Bellingham along State Highway 11 (Chuckanut Drive).

Eagles are a common sight over the beaches of Northern Puget Sound.

Birch Bay State Park

5105 Helwig Road, Blaine, WA 98230 / 360-371-2800
www.parks.wa.gov

Lodging Pricing

A lovely beach, a quiet creek, and a wooded campground a few miles away from the Canadian border comprise the setting for Birch Bay State Park. Located just south of the small village of Birch Bay, the park fronts 8,000 feet of saltwater shoreline. Picnic tables and ample parking allow you to spend time next to the beach, and steamer clams, cockles, and other shellfish can be harvested from the rocky beach at low tide.

Across the road from the beach you'll find Terrell Creek, a stream that passes through much of the park before flowing into the bay. The northern part of the creek within the park is a game sanctuary frequented by mallard ducks, great blue herons, and eagles along with finches, sparrows, and other common birds that flit among the adjacent brush and trees. Uphill from the creek is another picnic area that includes some covered shelters for groups to huddle under when it rains.

Beyond the picnic area is a campground. Split into two camping areas, you have plenty of campsites to choose from. Most of the 167 sites are set within the woods and 20 of them have hook-ups for RVs. There is also a walk-in camping area. Reservations for campsites are accepted between May 15 and September 15, but for the rest of the year all of the sites are available on a first-come, first-served basis. Finally, near the entrance and park office is the half-mile Terrell Marsh Trail. The interpretive trail is perfect for a nice contemplative stroll after a meal of freshly steamed clams.

Getting There: Take Exit 266 off Interstate 5 north of Ferndale. Travel west on Grandview Road towards Birch Bay and follow the signs a short distance to the park.

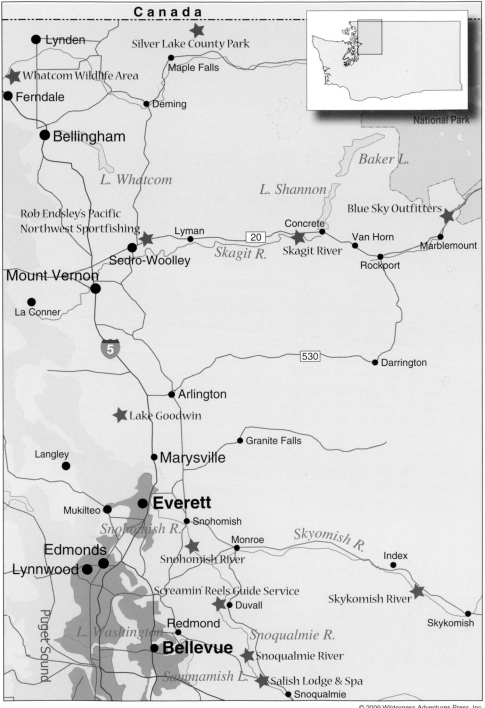

Canada

Lynden

Silver Lake County Park

Maple Falls

Whatcom Wildlife Area

Ferndale

Deming

Bellingham

National Park

Baker L.

L. Whatcom

L. Shannon

Blue Sky Outfitters

Rob Endsley's Pacific
Northwest Sportfishing

Lyman

Concrete

Van Horn

Marblemount

20

Skagit R.

Skagit River

Rockport

Sedro-Woolley

Mount Vernon

La Conner

5

530

Darrington

Arlington

Lake Goodwin

Granite Falls

Langley

Marysville

Everett

Mukilteo

Snohomish

Snohomish R.

Skyomish R.

Monroe

Index

Edmonds

Lynnwood

Snohomish River

Screamin' Reels Guide Service

Skykomish River

Duvall

Redmond

Skykomish

Puget Sound

L. Washington

Snoqualmie R.

Bellevue

Sammamish L.

Snoqualmie River

Salish Lodge & Spa

Snoqualmie

The Interior

Whatcom Wildlife Area

5975 Lake Terrell Road, Ferndale, WA 98248 / 360-384-4723
www.wdfw.wa.gov

The newly formed Whatcom Wildlife Area consolidates six separate land units dedicated primarily to bird hunting, though fishing and wildlife watching are also popular activities. All but one of the units is near Ferndale within Whatcom County.

The Headquarters Unit is found at Lake Terrell. Established as the Lake Terrell Game Range in 1947, the 1,500-acre property's centerpiece is Lake Terrell. Waterfowlers primarily hunt Canada geese, pintails, and mallard ducks along with some teal and wood ducks between October and January. You are limited to hunting from 16 established blinds (one of which is compliant with the Americans with Disabilities Act – ADA) on a first-come, first-served basis. A small boat will come in handy to get to most of the blinds on this 500-acre lake, though a couple of blinds are land based for field hunting. Pheasant hunting is also possible from October until Thanksgiving, thanks to periodic releases by the Department of Fish and Wildlife during this time. If you come for the pheasant hunting, you won't be able to head afield until 8:00am and you have to use non-toxic shot in your shells.

Hunting is not the only game afoot. Bass anglers have discovered Lake Terrell in a big way and it has become a popular spot for local tournaments, despite a no-wake rule that limits the speed of boats on the water. Two-pound bass are common around the lily pads of this lake, and perch, bluegill, and pumpkinseed can also be caught. The best fishing is from a boat, though you can do some fishing from shore near the small boat launch by the wildlife area manager's office. Don't bring your boat for fishing between October 1 and January 31. Boat use by anglers is prohibited at this time of year to limit conflicts with waterfowl hunters.

The BP and Intalco Units are close to Lake Terrell. Both 1,000-acre properties are leased from the companies they're named after. The Intalco Unit is adjacent to the Lake Terrell Unit and has grasslands, forest, and ponds on it while the BP Unit has ponds, sloughs, grasslands, and riparian habitat. Both offer pheasant and waterfowl hunting.

If you didn't get to Lake Terrell in time for a blind, you might want to head to the 627-acre Nooksack Unit off of Slater Road. Recently acquired, this property is considered to be a very good destination for waterfowl hunters. A favorite tactic is to hunker down in planted cornfields and wait for the birds that come here to feed.

Another place to hunt is the Tennant Lake Unit. Found just outside of Ferndale, hunters are allowed to shoot from three established blinds on the lake. You can only access these blinds with a small boat and, like Lake Terrell, the first one to the blind gets it for the morning shoot. Hunters are not the only ones who come to Tennant Lake. There is also an interpretive center here focusing on wetlands wildlife watching and education. Co-managed with Whatcom County Parks, a visit to the Tennant Lake Interpretive Center could include climbing a viewing tower or walking along a 1.4-mile boardwalk loop trail to look at ducks, geese, swans, and perhaps a beaver slapping its tail against the water.

Finally, the 120-acre Pine and Cedar Lake Unit is located not around Ferndale, but at Chuckanut Mountain southwest of Bellingham. There's no hunting here, but you can get a workout hiking 3 miles to the two lakes, enjoying views of Bellingham, Mt. Baker, and the San Juan Islands along the way. Once you reach the lakes, cast a line for the rainbow trout you'll find there.

Getting There: You can get to the Lake Terrell Unit from Ferndale by driving west on Main Street (which becomes Mountain View Road) for 4 miles. Turn right at Lake Terrell Road and follow the road to the Wildlife Area Headquarters.

Mother goose gives her goslings a lesson.

Silver Lake County Park

9006 Silver Lake Road, Maple Falls, WA 98266 / 360-599-2776
www.whatcomcounty.us/parks

Lodging Prices   Adventure Pricing

Drive into Whatcom County's Silver Lake Park and you'll think you are at one of Washington's nicer state parks. Located just a few miles south of the Canadian border near Maple Falls, the park offers both camping and cabins near Silver Lake, a popular place for paddlers, anglers, and equestrians.

In the main campground are 62 campsites, most of which have water and electrical hook-ups for RVs. The campsites are tucked into a lush, wooded area dominated by tall cedar trees and low-growing ferns. There is also a group camp in the park that has 30 hook-up sites and a covered picnic shelter. It's a good idea to reserve an individual campsite in the summer, but it's not required.

If you want something more, there are six 1940s-vintage cabins overlooking the water. The spacious one- and two-bedroom buildings each sleep four to six people. Every cabin has a kitchen with appliances, a fireplace, electricity and heat. Only one cabin, however, has a restroom. Everyone else has to use a vault toilet a short distance away. If you want to take a shower there is a centrally located bath house within the park. Reservations for the cabins are highly recommended and there is a two-night minimum stay requirement during the weekend.

Equestrians will appreciate the horse camp across the road from the main portion of the park. In addition to 28 utility camping sites, you'll find two large stables and two picnic shelters. It's the perfect place to camp overnight before saddling up for a short 2-mile ride (or hike) on a multi-use trail through the park. If you want to ride further, head east up to Red Mountain and explore miles of ridgeline.

There is a day-use area which has a boat launch, a small playground, and lots of picnic tables with barbeques on grassy lawns. The main office building in the park not only houses the registration desk, but also a three-bedroom lodge with a bathroom on the lower floor. Upstairs you'll find a snack bar serving food kids will love (popcorn, candy, soft drinks, and ice cream). If you want to steer the kids away from the sugar for a while, visit the Gerdrum Museum across the road from the park's entrance. Open weekends from noon to 4:00pm, it is named after the man who settled here in the late 1800s and then opened up the Silver Lake Resort at the turn of the century. This resort became the present day county park in 1969.

Paddling is popular along the deep green waters of the lake and you can rent rowboats, canoes, and paddleboats by the hour or for the day. If you brought your own boat, keep in mind you can't use more than a 10-horsepower motor here. This requirement keeps the water skiers and personal watercraft away, making the surroundings more peaceful for everyone.

The scenic 180-acre wood-lined lake is also a good place for wildlife watching. Great blue heron look for fish along the shoreline, eagles and osprey can be seen overhead, and beavers can be heard slapping their tails on the water. Various species of waterfowl visit the lake in the fall and geese with their goslings are common in the spring. Coyote, raccoon, deer, and even river otters are some of the other animals you may see during your visit.

Last but not least, Silver Lake is known as a good place to cast a line. It's open for fishing from the last weekend of April through the end of October. Most anglers come to catch stocked rainbow and cutthroat trout using boats or casting from shore. If you are fishing at the park, spots below the cabins and around the day lodge are known to be good for shore anglers. The average trout is pan sized, though it's not uncommon to catch one up to 15 inches long. If trout fishing is slow, you might want to investigate the shallower waters around the lake for largemouth bass that weigh up to 4 pounds. A worm under a bobber might also attract some bluegill or sunfish for the kids.

The 411-acre park is open all year. However, things are pretty quiet here from November until the middle of April.

Getting There: Drive 28 miles from Bellingham on State Highway 542 to Maple Falls. Turn left and go north for 3 miles on Silver Lake Road to the park.

Boats for rent.

Lake Goodwin

Wenberg State Park
15430 East Lake Goodwin Rd., Stanwood, WA, 98292
www.parks.wa.gov

Lodging Prices

This suburban lake north of Marysville gets lots of traffic from people drawn here by the prospect of a quick boating, swimming, or fishing getaway. Fortunately, a state park, a county park, and two private resorts provide plenty of room for everyone to play.

Wenberg State Park is located on the east side of the lake, off of State Highway 531. Boasting the only public boat launch on the lake, the 46-acre park is a popular place. Just north of the two-ramp launch is a day-use area that includes a large swimming beach, summer concession store, playground, and lots of picnic tables that sit on a grassy peninsula under tall trees. Above the day-use area is a group picnic area that includes a covered kitchen shelter. Also above the lake is the campground. Featuring 30 utility sites (water and electric hook-ups) and 45 tent sites, the camping area offers a place to stay but no real view of the lake.

As this book goes to press, Wenberg State Park is scheduled to be transferred to another public entity. It is not known at this time what agency or group will operate the park or exactly when this transfer will occur. Check the Washington State Parks website for further details.

At the north end of the 545-acre lake off of Lakewood Road, you'll find the Lake Goodwin Community Park. The 12-acre day-use area has a nice beach, a pier that's handy for fishing, a playground, restroom, and a short trail that loops through a small natural preservation area of trees and wetlands. Semi-tame mallards and geese also call the park home.

Next to the community park is a private resort with over 90 RV sites, 11 tent sites, and four cabin rentals. Although half of the RV sites are often rented on a seasonal basis, the amenities of this crowded waterfront resort (full hook ups to include cable, Wi-Fi Internet, two docks for fishing and moorage, a grassy play area for sports, and a gas station with convenience store) make it a place to consider for a stay. Another private resort on the west side of the lake offers additional RV sites and dock space.

In the summer, the lake is abuzz with power boaters and personal watercraft enthusiasts. At other times of year, the lake is a good place to paddle or row in relative serenity. Anglers come to the lake for good bass and trout fishing. Rainbow trout from 12 to 15 inches are the norm, and catching one over 2 pounds is fairly common. Perch are another abundant species, but the lake is perhaps known as a place to catch big bass. Both smallmouth and largemouth bass are present, and bass weighing over 8 pounds have been caught here on several occasions. Some believe the next state record bass will come out of Lake Goodwin. Recently an 11-pound bass (a few ounces short of the state record) was rumored to have been caught and released back into the lake.

Lake Goodwin is open for fishing all year, as are the parks and resorts around the lake.

Getting There: Take Exit 206 (Smokey Point/ Lakewood) off of Interstate 5 north of Marysville. Follow State Highway 531 for 5 miles to the west to reach Lake Goodwin.

Conner and Parker Jones of Everett get in some early spring fun at Lake Goodwin Community Park.

Suburban Rivers

SNOHOMISH, SNOQUALMIE, AND SKYKOMISH

Washington Department of Fish and Wildlife
16018 Mill Creek Boulevard, Mill Creek, WA 98012 / 425-775-1311
www.wdfw.wa.gov

Three rivers in the suburbs of Seattle receive heavy fishing pressure, but still offer a quick and worthwhile break for anglers as well as paddlers looking for extreme whitewater or calm estuary paddling. A dramatic waterfall is an added bonus that is a destination unto itself.

The first of the rivers is the Snoqualmie. Three forks come together near North Bend to form the main stem of the river that flows northwest for 43 miles and joins the Skykomish to become the Snohomish River. Snoqualmie is the English translation for the Salish Indian word "moon", and one of the best places to view the river on a moonlit night – or sunny morning – is at Snoqualmie Falls. The 268-foot waterfall is a popular tourist destination, receiving over 1.5 million visitors a year. You can view the falls from a viewing platform for free or pay to linger longer with a meal or overnight stay at the Salish Lodge and Spa, an upscale place at the top of the falls known for fine dining and elegant accommodations (see entry for further details).

Fishing brings many to the river from nearby urban areas. Above the falls you can cast flies or spinners with barbless hooks for trout. Below the falls you can also catch cutthroat trout, but most are after bigger fish, especially steelhead. Hotspots for bank anglers after these ocean-going rainbow trout are found near Tokul Creek below the falls, by Falls City, and around Carnation where the Tolt River flows into the Snoqualmie. Drift-boat anglers can put in at Plum Landing below Tokul Creek and take out at several boat landings downstream. The peak time for the summer run steelhead is from July to October, while winter runs are most abundant in good numbers in December and January. During good years, the river opens up for salmon as well, with chinook, coho, and chum salmon making up the bulk of the fall migrants you may hook into.

Moving downstream from Carnation you'll find the closest bird hunting opportunities for Seattle area outdoorsmen at the 456-acre Stillwater Wildlife

Area, 3 miles north of Carnation, and the Cherry Creek Wildlife Area north of Duvall. Both are located off of State Highway 203 and offer duck hunting as well as pheasant hunting, with the best waterfowl hunting coinciding with rising river levels and the arrival of migrating northern waterfowl in late November through December. The 110-acre Crescent Lake Wildlife Area, also located near Duvall, offers similar opportunities and, in the off-season, all three places are good destinations for dog training and bird watching.

Another suburban river getting plenty of attention from metropolitan anglers is the Skykomish River. Like the Snoqualmie, salmon and steelhead are big draws. Formed by a number of tributaries on the west side of Stevens Pass, the river flows close to US Highway 2 all the way from Skykomish past Monroe, providing lots of easy access. A steelhead hatchery at Reiter Ponds near Gold Bar provides good numbers of returning fish for anglers who congregate here in January and again in the summer. If you don't like the crowds there are plenty of places to cast from shore, or from a boat, downstream from the hatchery. Meanwhile, anglers can catch chinook in the summer, silvers in the fall, and chum salmon in November and December. During odd years strong runs of pink salmon enter the river, giving you a chance to hook into smaller salmon from August well into September, especially around Monroe. If salmon and steelhead aren't enough, you can also catch cutthroat trout on the Sky as well as the occasional Dolly Varden.

These suburban rivers offer more than fishing. The Skykomish is known as a great whitewater river and has a reputation for being quite challenging. You can run the North Fork of the river in the spring and early summer. After that you drop down into

The Snoqualmie River offers some outstanding whitewater.

the main section of the river below Index and raft the main whitewater to Gold Bar. The highlight of this section is Boulder Drop – a Class IV piece of whitewater. This part of the Skykomish offers great rafting and whitewater kayaking from April through August and again after fall rains cause the river to rise. If you are more into scenery than whitewater you might want to launch a raft or drift boat at Gold Bar or Sultan and take a family float downstream, enjoying the spectacular mountain scenery along the way.

The whitewater of the Skykomish is not something to be taken lightly, and if you choose to embark upon a float here you really should do it the first few times with a guide. One that has been around a while is Shane Turnbull, the owner of Chinook Expeditions (800-241-3451 – www.chinookexpeditions.com). Turnbull also runs a guide school on the Skykomish out of Index, should you become so taken with whitewater rafting that you want to do it full time.

Near the State Highway 522 bridge below Monroe, the Snoqualmie and Skykomish join together to form the Snohomish River. There are no rapids along the Snohomish, just a wide river that flows past Snohomish into Port Gardner Bay at Everett. However, there are subtle holes and runs in this river which do provide good angling for both pink and silver salmon in the fall. A sturgeon fishery between Snohomish and Everett is also becoming better known, though it is nowhere near the fishery found on the Columbia or Snake Rivers. The best way to fish the Snohomish is from a boat, and good launch sites are available in both Everett and Snohomish.

One place you can fish from shore is from the Bob Heirman Wildlife Preserve at Thomas Eddy. The 343-acre Snohomish County Park is 3 miles south of Snohomish on the south bank of the river. The eddy is a well-known steelhead hole and the rest of the area is a managed preserve with nature trails that look out over riparian, wetland, and agricultural habitats. These different areas host up to 80 different bird species. Some that you may see include hairy woodpecker, kinglets, willow flycatchers, and spotted towhee, along with predatory birds like belted kingfisher, kestrel, northern harrier, and red-tailed hawk. You can also expect to see some water-oriented birds like great blue heron, various types of ducks and in the winter, the occasional trumpeter swan.

Another wildlife watching area of note is found at 412-acre Spencer Island. Jointly owned by Snohomish County and the Department of Fish and Wildlife, the island is located in the Snohomish River Estuary near Everett. Dikes that cut across the island and go around its perimeter provide access for wildlife watchers and hunters. Not only will you see birds, but you'll also get the chance to see mammals as varied as river otters, coyote, and deer. Hunting is allowed from October to January for waterfowl on the northern portion of the island.

Getting There: The Snohomish River can be accessed at several places between Snohomish and Everett. The Skykomish runs close to US Highway 2 from Monroe past Skykomish with a number of launches and access points along the way. Finally, Snoqualmie Falls can be reached off of State Highway 202 near Snoqualmie. The river below the falls can be reached from several places off of State Highway 202 and 203 past Falls City, Carnation, and Duvall.

SCREAMIN' REELS GUIDE SERVICE

Derek Anderson
28507 NE 149th Place, Duvall, WA 98019 / 206-849-2574
www.screaminreels.net

Adventure Pricing: $$$ Lodging Prices: N/A

It's getting tougher and tougher to find a full-time guide who specializes in fishing the rivers around Seattle. These days, most guides go to southwestern Washington or the Olympic Peninsula for reliable salmon, sturgeon, and steelhead fishing. Fortunately, Derek Anderson, owner of Screamin' Reels Guide Service, is one guide who still fishes Seattle's suburban rivers on a regular basis.

If you ask Derek to tell you about himself, you'll soon figure out how passionate he is about his profession. Derek has wanted to be a fishing guide since he was a kid. He's been running a jet sled on the rivers since he was 13 and started rowing drift boats at 17. If you go out with him today on his roomy Alumaweld jet boat or Lavro drift boat you'll find he's an amiable guide who knows where the fish are and how to hook them. He employs a number of different techniques to get fish into the boat, ranging from flyfishing for chum salmon in the fall, hover fishing for chinook salmon in the spring, and drift fishing, trolling, or back trolling at other times of year.

While Anderson does spend a lot of time on the Skykomish, Snoqualmie, and Snohomish Rivers, he is more than willing to follow the fish to other waters. From December through February, he fishes the above three rivers for winter steelhead, but in March he'll head to the Cowlitz and Columbia Rivers to hunt for spring chinook averaging anywhere from 12 to 23 pounds. The fishing stays good there until the middle of May. That's about the time he heads to the Columbia River near Bonneville Dam to tangle with oversized sturgeon that commonly measure 7 to 9 feet long. From there, it's back to the Skykomish, Snohomish, and Snoqualmie Rivers for summer steelhead and chinook salmon. Around mid-July, Anderson goes back down to the Cowlitz for steelhead before heading to Buoy 10 at the mouth of the Columbia River in the latter part of August for trophy king salmon. In early September, he'll head back to the Cowlitz to catch some more of these salmon. By the middle of the month he is usually back on the Seattle-area rivers looking for silver salmon or pink salmon, which are abundant in odd-numbered years. By November, chum salmon are in the Skykomish, offering anglers hook-ups with hard-fighting fish and by the time December rolls around, the winter steelhead are running again.

Derek Anderson has a U.S. Coast Guard Master's License, is CPR certified and, as a former volunteer firefighter, can provide first aid if needed. He offers both half- and full-day fishing trips and if you want to spend a few dollars more, he'll be happy to provide you with a BBQ lunch as part of the package.

Getting There: Destinations vary.

SALISH LODGE & SPA

6501 Railroad Avenue, Snoqualmie, WA 98065 / 800-2SALISH (800-272-5474)
http://salishlodge.com

Lodging Prices: $$$ to $$$$ Adventure Pricing: $ to $$$

When you think of the Salish Lodge & Spa, you'll probably think of a luxurious resort perched at the top of a breathtaking 268-foot waterfall. You might also think of it as the perfect place to spend a honeymoon or anniversary. After all, this lodge along the Snoqualmie River has a four-diamond rating from AAA, which is as good as it gets. If that isn't enough, there are some wonderful spa services and a fantastic restaurant that serves what general manager Carl Meyer describes as "regional cuisine with a French inspiration".

As wonderful as the Salish Lodge is for all of these reasons, the opportunity to enjoy a variety of different outdoor activities is another reason to come. The most obvious one starts right outside the lodge where you can take in the view from the top of Snoqualmie Falls. If you're looking for a different perspective, hike the wide path a half mile to the base of the falls where you can really enjoy the sound of the crashing water and feel the cool mist on your skin. If you want, you can venture beyond the wooden boardwalk and lower observation deck towards the river itself for a photo opportunity, to cast for fish, or to simply dip your toes into the refreshing river water on a warm summer day.

If you are in the mood for more exercise, you can take off on a 0.75-mile nature trail from the upper Snoqualmie Falls visitor's lot and access the 31.5-mile Snoqualmie Valley Trail. Built on an old railroad grade, the trail stretches from Duvall to Rattlesnake Lake near North Bend and provides a great place to hike or bicycle year round.

The Salish Lodge offers an outdoor adventure program with a wide variety of activities designed to make your stay more memorable. The most inexpensive option is a guided hike. There are several destinations to choose from but many guests enjoy the easy 2.5-mile walk along the South Fork of the Snoqualmie River to Twin Falls. If you would rather pedal than walk, you can rent a bicycle from the lodge to explore the Snoqualmie Valley Trail on your own or go on a guided trip that will take you through a 2.3-mile tunnel passing through Snoqualmie Pass. Headlamps are provided for this unique 10-mile ride that runs on a gentle grade downhill along the old Milwaukee Railroad line. The area around Snoqualmie Pass is also a popular destination in the winter, when guided snowshoe trips are offered to Franklin Falls. The snowy walk is suitable for beginners and lasts half a day.

Another adventure involves fishing. The guides at Emerald Water Anglers (206-545-2197 – www.emeraldwateranglers.com) work with the lodge and will be happy to teach you the pleasurable art of angling with a fly rod on either the gravel

The Salish Lodge & Spa is perched at the edge of beautiful Snoqualmie Falls.

banks of the Snoqualmie River or on the beaches of Puget Sound within sight of the Emerald City for trout or salmon. No experience is required and everything you'll need is provided, except for a fishing license.

You can also get on the water with Seattle Raft and Kayak (800-625-7782 – www.seattleraftandkayak.com). If you are looking to paddle a kayak in calm waters, the Lakes to Lock Tour will take you from Lake Union, through the Ballard Locks, and into the saltwater of Puget Sound. Once you're in the saltwater you'll paddle past Westpoint Lighthouse before taking out at Golden Gardens Park. If you are craving more stimulation, try rafting the Skykomish River. You'll paddle through Class II and III whitewater rapids – thrilling and fun but not too technical for beginners. Advance reservations are required for these trips, some of which are seasonal in nature. Check with the lodge for further details.

After a day outdoors, come back to your room. There are 89 of them at the lodge, to include four suites. The 89 rooms are alike in that they share amenities meant to appeal to the senses. The two-person spa tubs are soothing to the body and the crackling fire from the wood-burning fireplaces keep you warm before you curl up in a goose down comforter for a good night's sleep on a soft featherbed.

Whether or not you stay at the lodge, a meal there should really be on your list of things to do. After all, the food has been a popular draw since 1916, when the original restaurant-fed travelers were halfway between Seattle and Snoqualmie Pass. Today, you can eat or get a drink in the casual Attic Bistro or get a reservation in The Dining Room at the Salish Lodge. You'll find the food to be superb in both settings. In fact, *Condé Nast* magazine recently listed the Salish Lodge & Spa as No. 2 in the category of Best Hotels in the United States for Food. Other recognitions include an Award of Excellence by the *Wine Spectator* and an Award of Distinction by the *Wine Enthusiast*. If you go to The Dining Room, Carl Meyer says you should not expect a dinner, but instead, "a culinary experience" that may well last three hours, allowing you to relax and enjoy each other's company. The food is well presented, imaginative, and tastes fantastic too. Start off your meal with a salad of regional greens or a cup of delicious salmon chowder. You might also want to try out the Snoqualmie River Hot Rocks, an offering of seafood and garnishes prepared on cut and polished rocks from the river. Beef, game, poultry, and various types of seafood are also available on the dinner menu.

Breakfast in The Dining Room is as popular as dinner. The lodge's country breakfast is a filling meal that traces its lineage to the restaurant's early days, and features a special touch known as "Honey from Heaven", where your server stands over your table and honey cascades onto your biscuits or oatmeal, much like the waterfall outside the lodge.

The Salish Lodge & Spa is open 365 days a year. Reservations for dinner or breakfast at The Dining Room and overnight stays are highly recommended.

Getting There: The Salish Lodge is a 30-minute drive from Seattle. Take Exit 25 off of Interstate 90 and follow the Snoqualmie Parkway north for 3.5 miles to the stoplight at Railroad Avenue. Turn left onto Railroad Avenue and travel 0.25 mile to the lodge.

The Skagit River

Washington Department of Fish and Wildlife
16018 Mill Creek Boulevard, Mill Creek, WA 98012 / 425-775-1311
www.wdfw.wa.gov

Lodging Prices

The Skagit River cuts a wide swath through northwestern Washington, and is known to many as an angler's stream. However, bird watching (especially for wintering bald eagles) and rafting are two other draws to this designated "Wild and Scenic River" that starts in Canada and flows into Puget Sound below Mt. Vernon.

The river starts in the mountains of southern British Columbia and flows south through the dammed reservoirs of Ross, Diablo, and Gorge Lakes that are part of the North Cascades National Park Complex. Below Gorge Lake the stream widens, following State Highway 20 past Newhalem, Marblemount, Rockport, Concrete, Sedro Woolley, and Mt. Vernon. Past Mt. Vernon, the river splits into two forks that flow on either side of Fir Island before entering Skagit Bay.

For years, the Skagit was known as one of the best salmon and steelhead rivers in Washington. Although diminished returns have tarnished the luster of its reputation, fishing is still productive for a number of different species. Big spring chinook salmon averaging 13 pounds have recently come back in large enough numbers that fishing is allowed for them again. During this same late-spring-early-summer time frame, sockeye salmon also fin their way up the Skagit to the Baker River near Concrete, and a small portion of the Skagit near the mouth of this stream is sometimes open for these fine eating fish. From early spring through early fall, smaller but still sizeable sea-run cutthroat and Dolly Varden trout can be caught in the lower stretch of the river. On odd numbered years, the Skagit becomes crowded with anglers who are after pink salmon. These 3- to 5-pound fish can flood the river in huge numbers in August and September. They are caught by both boat and bank anglers and several holes around Mt. Vernon are popular places to fish for them with pink-colored lures. With the cooler weather of fall come even more salmon. First into the river are the silvers, and they are followed in November and December by big chum salmon, known for their fighting as opposed to eating qualities.

December heralds the entry of hatchery steelhead into the Skagit – many of them bound for hatcheries near Rockport and Marblemount. You can catch these bright chrome fish well into January, and in February wild steelhead start showing up as well. You can't keep the wild steelhead in the Skagit, but you do have a legitimate shot at a big fish, with metal heads (as some call them) over 20 pounds being caught every year. The catch-and-release season for the wild fish often runs into mid-April, depending on the number of returning fish. Anglers can fish the Skagit in a variety of ways. Jet boats are a common sight on the lower stretches while drift boats are more

Guide Rob Endsley (left) and a happy client show off a nice salmon. Photo courtesy Rob Endsley.

common around Marblemount and Rockport. Bank anglers also get into the game, plunking bait off the bottom or drift fishing waters where steelhead are known to stack up.

As popular as the Skagit is for fishing, it has also become a popular destination in recent years for eagle watching. Every winter several hundred bald eagles winter along the Skagit, drawn by the fish that spawn and die here. The best place to see them is along the Skagit River Bald Eagle Natural Area, owned by the Nature Conservancy and several other conservation-minded partners. The 7,800-acre area is located along the Skagit between Marblemount and the mouth of the Sauk River at Rockport. You can see the birds from the highway and some of the public properties along the stream but the best way to see them up close and personal is by floating downstream. The prime time to see the eagles is between 7:00am and 11:00am, when the big birds (weighing 9 pounds with a wing span of 6 to 7 feet) can often be seen feeding on salmon carcasses on the gravel bars next to the water. If you have your own raft, kayak, or canoe you can launch at Marblemount above the mouth of the Cascade River and take out at Howard Miller Steelhead Park at Rockport. If you don't own a raft, there are a couple of companies that will be happy to take you downstream for a morning of wildlife watching (one of them, Blue Sky Outfitters, is found in this book).

The rafting companies don't just do nature floats on the Skagit. The upper section between Newhalem and Marblemount has several sections of Class II whitewater and one set of Class III rapids. The most popular float for rafters and whitewater kayakers takes off at the Goodell Creek Campground launch site and goes 8.5 miles downstream to the Copper Creek take out. Right after launching, you'll hit the Class II Goodell Rapids and then go through several other easy to handle whitewater sections before coming up to the S-Curve, a Class III section that can flip a raft if you're not careful and should not be attempted in a canoe. After traversing the S-Curve, you'll hit one more piece of Class II water known as Wavy Gravy before the take out.

If you want to stay overnight, there are a number of hotels in Mt. Vernon as well as a few resorts and small motels strung out along State Highway 20 to Marblemount. You can also camp at one of the national park campgrounds in Newhalem, Skagit County's Howard Miller Steelhead Park (54 RV sites, 10 tent sites and two Adirondack shelters – reservations accepted – 360-853-8808) near Rockport or Rasar State Park, a new 169-acre campground located 6 miles west of Concrete on the Skagit River. Rasar has 48 reservable camp sites (20 of them with water and electrical hook ups). This includes two Adirondack shelters and there are also plans to put in five cabins that should be built by the fall of 2009. Call 888-CAMPOUT to reserve your place at the park. Another place known for camping, Rockport State Park, has been converted into a day-use area open from May through October. The campground was closed due to concerns about old growth trees that are in danger of falling on the established camp sites.

Getting There: Interstate 5 crosses the Skagit River at Mt. Vernon. You can pick up State Highway 20 a short distance from there and follow the river east to Diablo Lake in the North Cascades National Park.

ROB ENDSLEY'S PACIFIC NORTHWEST SPORTFISHING

PO Box 1313 Bellingham, WA 98227 / 360-961-2116
www.pacific-northwest-sportfishing.com

Lodging Prices: N/A   Adventure Pricing: $$$

Rob Endsley is known as one of the finest steelhead and salmon guides in the Pacific Northwest. He started guiding in 1993 and built his reputation by getting clients into fish and making sure they had a good time in the process.

It helps that Endsley is personable, hard working, and extremely knowledgeable. He graduated with a B.S. in Environmental Science from Western Washington University and is now the chief instructor for Steelhead University as well as an instructor for Salmon University. Hundreds attend these one- to three-day fishing seminars every year to learn how to become better anglers. Rob hosted the Fisherman's Heaven television show for two years and has been featured as an expert in several regional and national fishing publications. He was also recently named as one of the top 25 salmon and steelhead guides by *Salmon & Steelhead Journal*.

Endsley spends most of his time in Washington fishing the Skagit and Sauk Rivers. The biggest river in northwestern Washington in terms of width and power, the Skagit flows from the Northern Cascades into Puget Sound west of Mount Vernon. Endsley targets acrobatic silver salmon, hard-fighting chum (also known as dog) salmon and, during odd numbered years, hordes of pink salmon from September through November. Around Thanksgiving, he'll switch to hatchery steelhead. Endsley typically spends the holiday season and first part of the year on the Skagit around Rockport and Marblemount, side-drifting egg clusters or sand shrimp from his jet boat for these chrome-colored fish.

From late January through April the focus shifts to big wild steelhead. How big? Well, Endsley and several clients have caught and released steelies weighing over 25 pounds from the Skagit as well as the Sauk River, a scenic stream that flows from the Cascades past pine forests, log jams, and gravel bars into the Skagit River at Rockport.

Another species of interest is the Dolly Varden trout. Dolly Varden and their resident freshwater cousins, bull trout, are protected in many streams. Fortunately, they are doing well enough on the Skagit, Sauk and a few other northwestern rivers like the Nooksack and Stillaguamish that you can actually fish for them. These trout, which are actually char, average 16 to 22 inches and sometimes weigh up to 10 pounds. A variety of offerings will draw strikes from them, though Endsley is partial to large rabbit-hair streamers. You are generally allowed to catch Dolly Varden on the Sauk and Skagit from June to March.

Rob Endsley can accommodate groups as small as two and as large as twelve thanks to a partnership he has with other area guides. Don't try booking trips with him in Washington during the summer. At this time of year you'll find Endsley fishing from his boat out of Craig, Alaska for salmon, halibut, and bottomfish. You can find more details about these Alaskan saltwater trips on his website.

Getting There: Destinations vary.

Guide Rob Endsley holds up a beautiful winter run steelhead. Photo courtesy Rob Endsley

BLUE SKY OUTFITTERS

9674 50th Avenue SW, Seattle, WA 98136 / 800-228-RAFT
www.blueskyoutfitters.com

Adventure Pricing: $$ Lodging Pricing: Included with some adventures

Blue Sky Outfitters has been taking people rafting on Washington's most popular whitewater rivers since 1982. Owned by Brad Sarver, the business offers not only whitewater adventures, but also some serious wildlife watching. This dual focus serves the company (and you as the guest) well, with trips occurring all year long.

The whitewater season starts in April with crews heading to the Wenatchee and Methow Rivers in eastern Washington. The Wenatchee below Leavenworth has lots of Class III whitewater that will get your adrenaline going and the smaller Methow River between Winthrop and Pateros has both Class III and IV whitewater to navigate through. You can raft the Wenatchee with Blue Sky Outfitters through July and the Methow in May and June. In fact, you have the option of doing a two-day trip to tackle both of these sunny eastern Washington rivers, camping overnight at an established RV park on the banks of the Methow.

As the whitewater season continues, guides from Blue Sky Outfitters head down to the White Salmon River in south central Washington. Billed as an intermediate skill level trip, you'll raft down a narrow canyon navigating Class III and IV rapids before you hit Husum Falls. Whether you choose to make the plunge over this waterfall is up to you, but if you do, it's an experience you'll never forget.

In September, Blue Sky hits the road again, following the whitewater to the Tieton River near Naches. This normally tame river gets rolling with non-stop rapids, thanks to a September water release from a dam that transforms the stream into a popular rafting destination.

You don't have to go to eastern Washington to raft with Blue Sky Outfitters. Their home water is the Skagit River in the northwestern part of the state. Whitewater rafting is possible all year on the upper river, departing from the Goodell Creek Campground at Newhalem. The four-hour float is a great introduction to whitewater rafting and suitable for kids who are five and older. In addition to floating past thick, old growth forests with good views of the North Cascades you'll also splash through several Class II rapids and one exhilarating Class III piece of whitewater called the S-Curve.

Another Skagit River trip takes off from Marblemount and ends in Rockport. This float doesn't have any whitewater, but it is rich in nature. You can take the trip year round, learning a lot about the trees and other flora that grow along the riverbank from your guide. However, most people come from December through March to see the bald eagles. Up to 300 of these big majestic birds can be seen on the 14 miles of river you'll float through. The eagles are drawn by the salmon and steelhead that spawn here at this time of year. In addition to eagles and salmon, you may also see osprey, mergansers, cormorants, and American dippers on the river as well as mammals like river otter, beaver, deer and, rarely, black bear.

After your wintery nature float you can warm up with hot chocolate, chili, and soup. The whitewater rafting trips all feature light snacks during the trip and a barbeque steak meal at the end, the perfect way to replace those calories you burned paddling.

Getting There: Destinations vary. Check the website for detailed information.

Whitewater fun on the Skagit River with Blue Sky Outfitters.

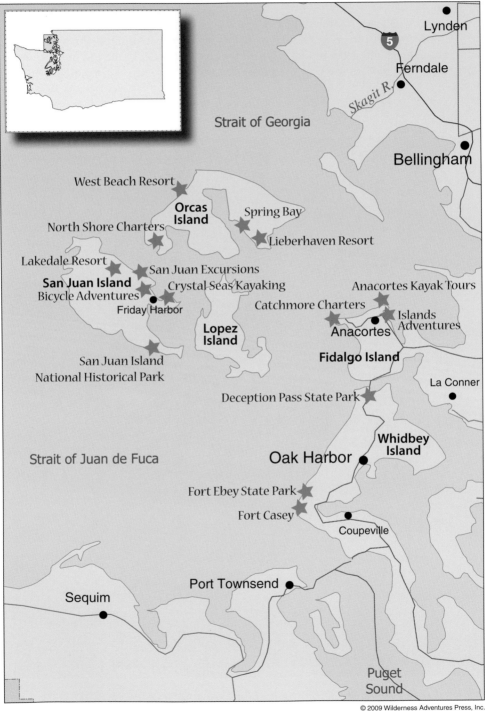

Lynden

Ferndale

Skagit R.

Strait of Georgia

Bellingham

West Beach Resort

Orcas Island

Spring Bay

North Shore Charters

Lieberhaven Resort

Lakedale Resort

San Juan Excursions

San Juan Island

Crystal Seas Kayaking

Bicycle Adventures

Anacortes Kayak Tours

Friday Harbor

Catchmore Charters

Islands Adventures

Anacortes

Lopez Island

Fidalgo Island

San Juan Island
National Historical Park

La Conner

Deception Pass State Park

Whidbey Island

Strait of Juan de Fuca

Oak Harbor

Fort Ebey State Park

Fort Casey

Coupeville

Port Townsend

Sequim

Puget Sound

© 2009 Wilderness Adventures Press, Inc.

San Juan Islands

San Juan Island

San Juan Islands Visitors Bureau
PO Box 1330, Friday Harbor, WA 92850 / 888-468-3701 ext. 1
www.visitsanjuans.com

Lime Kiln Point State Park
1567 Westside Road, Friday Harbor, WA 98250 / 360-378-2044
www.parks.wa.gov

San Juan County Park
50 San Juan Park Drive, Friday Harbor, WA 92850 / 360-378-8420
www.co.san-juan.wa.us/parks/sanjuan.html

Lodging Prices

More populated than its neighbors, San Juan Island is also the most popular destination for tourists. Many of them take tour boats, their own vessels, or ride a Washington State ferry into Friday Harbor. In addition to restaurants, stores, places to stay, and a large marina, Friday Harbor also hosts several whale-watching and kayak-touring companies.

The perimeter of the island covers some 74 miles of shoreline. Island roads that go over rolling hills through pastures and forests lead to a number of parks and bays. Orange poppies bloom in the early summer, distinctive madrona trees are visible near the sea, and wild roses are prolific. It all makes for a nice place to explore by car or bicycle. One thing to remember if you are staying longer than a day in the San Juans is to reserve accommodations in advance, especially in the summer when rooms at inns, B & Bs, and even campsite spaces are at a premium.

Anglers will find bottomfish and salmon offshore and a couple of lakes worth fishing inland. Sportsman's Lake at the northeast part of the island is a good place to explore in a small boat or canoe and the fishing for largemouth

bass is reportedly good. Little Egg Lake is close by and offers perch, bass, and trout fishing.

There is a lot of wildlife on and around the island. In addition to the deer (which are abundant on all of the islands), you can see raccoon, rabbit, and otters. You may even glimpse a fox or hear the gobbling of wild turkey. Seals, harbor porpoise, Dall's porpoise, and the occasional orca whale can all be seen offshore from land or sea.

One of the best places to see these marine mammals is at Lime Kiln Point State Park. A short trail from the parking lot on the west side of the island leads through fir and cedar trees to the rocky shore where you can gaze out beyond the kelp beds to look for wildlife. There are 1.6 miles of trails in the park, and a pretty red and white lighthouse built in 1919, which adds to the charm of the place. The day-use park is open all year long, but the best time to see whales is from late spring until early fall.

North of Lime Kiln is the one public park that offers camping on the island: San Juan County Park. It has 20 campsites within its 12-acre property that borders the water. The park's picnic tables, firepits, potable water, gravel beach, and boat ramp make it a good place to spend a few days. This is a popular spot though, and reservations are a 'must' during the summer months.

Other public lands on San Juan Island include Jackson Beach (south of Friday Harbor), where you can have a picnic or launch a kayak. English Camp to the north, and American Camp and Cattle Point towards the southern tip are also public areas of interest (see the San Juan National Historical Park entry for further details).

Getting There: Take State Highway 20 from Interstate 5 at Mt. Vernon/Burlington to Anacortes. Follow the signs to the Washington State Ferry Terminal. Sailing time to Friday Harbor varies from a little over an hour to almost two hours. Kenmore Air also offers daily service from Seattle to San Juan Island.

LAKEDALE RESORT

4313 Roche Harbor Road, Friday Harbor, WA 98250 / 360-378-2350
www.lakedale.com

Lodging Prices: $ to $$$$ Adventure Pricing: $

Known for years as a campground favored by bicyclists, San Juan Island's Lakedale Resort has expanded in a spectacular fashion. It now offers everything from basic to luxury camping, RV sites, lakefront cabins, and a beautiful lodge facility.

Sitting on 82 well-kept acres, the resort is spread out along three lakes that are good places for fishing, rowing, or paddling. The largest of them, Dream Lake and Neva Lake, are stocked with both native and Kamloops rainbow trout as well as bass that can weigh several pounds. Both lakes have swim areas and there is also a day-use area near the south end of Dream Lake. Fish Hook Lake is south of the main lodge. You'll find largemouth bass here and two of the resort's cabins sit along its shoreline.

The biggest building at the resort is the contemporary lodge on Neva Lake with ten luxurious guest rooms decorated in an earth-toned outdoor theme. Comfortable queen beds, gas fireplaces, slate tile bathrooms with Jacuzzi tubs, private balconies, Wi-Fi Internet access, and a satellite television (with limited channels) round out the amenities. Downstairs is a spacious lobby with a big fireplace, a large deck overlooking the lake, and a dining area where you can enjoy a pleasant continental breakfast.

On the other end of the spectrum are a hundred campsites found on the grass or under trees between Dream and Neva Lakes north of the lodge. Several of them are waterfront sites with great views, while others are walk-in, bike-in, or group sites. A centrally located wash house has restrooms and showers in a clean, modern facility. Four additional double-wide RV sites have water and new 50-amp electrical hook-ups (three camper sites also have electrical hook-ups).

If you are interested in a pampered camping experience, stay in one of the Canvas Cabins. Inside these big canvas tents you'll find wrought iron and wood furniture on a durable TREX floor. With a fully-made queen bed, dining table, and optional fold-out futon, these luxury tents sleep anywhere from two to four guests.

If you would rather have a solid roof over your head, you can opt for one of the six two-bedroom cabins or a three-bedroom lakehouse. Sleeping six to ten people, these lakefront and view cottages all have full kitchens, private baths, dining rooms, and fireplaces. A hot tub is available if you are staying at the lakehouse or cabins and a welcome basket has fixings for your first breakfast.

A general store at the resort stocks groceries, fishing tackle, firewood, and s'mores fixings for evenings around the campfire. You can also rent a rowboat, canoe, or paddleboat from here during the summer months to explore Neva Lake. Outside the resort, bicycling is popular along the island's road system while hiking and wildlife watching opportunities are possible at several parks and historical sites (see the San Juan Island entry for further details).

The Lakedale Resort is open all year. However, the store, camp, and RV sites are only open from the first of May through September. Pets are welcome at the resort but cannot be brought into the Canvas Cabins or the lodge. If you are staying at the lodge, children must be 16 or older.

Getting There: From the ferry landing in Friday Harbor follow traffic off the boat and turn right onto Tucker Avenue, which turns into Roche Harbor Road. The entrance to the resort is on Roche Harbor Road 4.5 miles from the ferry terminal.

The waterfront lodge at the Lakedale Resort.

BICYCLE ADVENTURES

P.O. Box 11219, Olympia, WA 98508 / 800-443-6060
www.bicycleadventures.com

Lodging Prices: Included in Adventure   Adventure Pricing: $$$ to $$$$

Way back in 1984 a biking enthusiast named Bob Clark decided to start a business dedicated to road bike touring in the Northwest. Today, Clark and a staff of 60 people run Bicycle Adventures from Olympia. The company offers vacations in Washington, Oregon, California, Utah, New Mexico, and Hawaii. Bicycle Adventures has even gone international, offering tours in Canada and New Zealand.

Despite their worldwide offerings, the company still has a significant focus in the Northwest, offering seven excursions in Washington alone. Five of these take place in the San Juan Islands. The most popular is a six-day tour with 20- to 45-mile daily rides on three islands to include bucolic Guemes Island, scenic San Juan Island, and pastoral Lopez Island. After a day on the road you can kick up your heels at a quality resort or inn. The vacation encompasses more than bicycling. You'll eat well and also get time off the bike for a guided kayak tour and to go on a wildlife cruise to look for orca whales.

Other San Juan bike tours include an abbreviated four-day outing (perfect for those on a time crunch) or an eight-day excursion that also includes bicycling in Olympic National Park to the south and Victoria, British Columbia to the north. This latter trip is geared for the more enthusiastic cyclist who doesn't mind climbing some hills and traveling 35 or more miles a day.

Two camping vacations are easier on the pocketbook but shouldn't be confused with "roughing it". The Family Camping trip is great for riders with limited experience. You'll cover anywhere from 8 to 28 miles a day before stopping at a campground where your guides will set up the tents and cook meals both you and the kids will enjoy. Sea kayaking off of Lopez Island, whale watching off of San Juan Island, and a hike up Mt. Constitution on Orcas Island are all part of the five-day tour. A five-day camping trip without the kids is also available and involves a little more cycling.

Experienced cyclists may want to check out the Volcanoes of Washington tour. This eight-day expedition starts off in central Washington and takes you to Mt. Rainier, Mt. St. Helens, and Mt. Hood before you are done. You'll average 50 miles a day (some of it challenging) and will also have the opportunity to do some hiking. Nights are spent at lodges or B & Bs and all meals are included except for one lunch and a dinner.

Believe it or not, Bicycle Adventures also offers a winter tour in Washington and cycling is not part of it. A trip to the Methow Valley will have you cross-country skiing and snowshoeing with guides in and around the Freestone Inn in Mazama and Sun

Mountain Lodge outside of Winthrop in north central Washington. Both experienced skiers and novices alike will enjoy this one, since you are divided into two groups based upon your skill level.

You don't need to be a hard-core cyclist to enjoy these vacations. In fact, you don't even have to own a road bike. You can rent a road bike or hybrid (a cross between a mountain and road bike) along with the gear you'll need to participate. Kids are welcome to come on the Family Camping tour, and if you get tired during the trip don't worry, there's a van with your gear just behind you to give you a lift for a few minutes (or for the rest of the day).

Bicycle Adventures makes it a point to employ local guides who are familiar with the local roads and landmarks. They offer tours for groups of 15 to 24 people from May through September. The Methow winter trips are available in January and February.

Getting There: Destinations vary. Pick up and drop off service is standard from several locations, to include the Seattle-Tacoma Airport.

Bicycle Adventures offer several vacations in the San Juan Islands (photo courtesy of Bicycle Adventures).

SAN JUAN EXCURSIONS

PO Box 2508, Friday Harbor, WA 92851 / 800-80-WHALE
www.watchwhales.com

Lodging Prices: N/A   Adventure Pricing: $ to $$

There are several whale watching companies operating out of the San Juan Islands, but in terms of comfort, convenience, and service, San Juan Excursions is one of the best. Their four-hour tours depart daily at 1:00pm from the Friday Harbor marina, giving you plenty of time to explore downtown Friday Harbor before you check in.

San Juan Excursions uses the 64-foot yacht "Odyssey" for its tours. Originally constructed during World War II to rescue downed aviators, the spacious boat seats up to 75 passengers. A large enclosed salon with lots of chairs and tables provides a good place to get out of the weather and read about the whales and wildlife around the San Juans. Or, you can take in the sights and feel the breeze on deck as you motor around San Juan Island. Once you are in sight of the whales you'll find plenty of open deck space both fore, aft, and along the sides of the vessel. You can try to photograph a breaching whale (easier said than done) or just watch them through a pair of binoculars (there are loaners on the boat).

There are about 90 orca whales that call the waters around the San Juans home from spring through fall. The largest member of the dolphin family, these black and white mammals have an average life span of 50 to 80 years and can reach lengths of over 27 feet. They travel in family groups called pods. The San Juan whales are designated the J, K, and L pods and each whale is scientifically assigned a number (i.e. J1). The whales are also known by more common names such as "Granny" or "Ruffles" among others. These whales are very demonstrative in their behavior. The sight of these whales breaching, spy-hopping, tail-slapping, or blowing mists of water and air as they surface has made them a favorite attraction.

Sometimes these animals get loved a little too much. San Juan Excursions abides by Whale Watch Operators guidelines. The boat stays least 100 meters away from the whales and parallels their course instead of cutting in on them. If a whale changes direction on its own and heads toward the boat, the captain will stop the engine so as not to disturb it.

Two "on-board" naturalists provide educational information and help you spot the whales. They also share their knowledge of other wildlife in the area. Dall's and harbor porpoise, seals, sea lions, and a variety of sea and shore birds are all commonly seen during these trips. For added family fun, a Junior Captain program allows kids to take the wheel of the boat while their parents photograph the real captain next to the young helmsman.

San Juan Excursions operates from May 1 through the end of September. Children under 12 pay a reduced fare. If you want to learn more about the orca whales, stop by the Whale Museum (800-946-7227 – www.whalemuseum.org) off of 1st Street in downtown Friday Harbor. The museum is "dedicated to the interpretation of whales living in the wild." Inside, you'll see interpretive exhibits as well as life-size whale models and skeletons. You can even pay a few dollars to "adopt a whale" and help preserve this unique species.

Getting There: San Juan Excursions and the Odyssey are both located a few steps north of the Washington State Ferry terminal in the Friday Harbor Marina.

A big stellar sea lion soaks up the sun near San Juan Island.

CRYSTAL SEAS KAYAKING

PO Box 3135, Friday Harbor, WA 98250 / 877-SEAS-877
www.crystalseas.com

Lodging Prices: N/A   Adventure Pricing: $$ to $$$$

Whether you want to paddle around the San Juan Islands for a few hours or a few days, Crystal Seas Kayaking has got something for you. The company is based out of popular San Juan Island, and their kayak tours are in high demand. Trips depart up to six times a day with one guide taking out groups of up to eight paddlers at a time in 19-foot tandem sea kayaks. No experience is necessary and basic instruction is provided.

Magnificent scenery and the opportunity to view the abundant sea life attract many people. Everything from colorful sea stars, swimming porpoises, curious seals, and the occasional killer whale can be seen up close from the cockpit of your kayak.

Many opt for the three hour "Taste of Kayaking" tour. You'll board your kayak from the dock at the Snug Harbor Marina without getting your feet wet. From there you may paddle north along the west side of the island or south to San Juan County Park before heading back to the marina. Longer day tours will have you on the water for about six hours. These trips start with a shuttle ride from Friday Harbor to Snug Harbor. From there you'll paddle to Lime Kiln State Park and have lunch before heading back to the harbor where a shuttle takes you back to town.

If you want a longer excursion, you'll love Crystal Seas' multi-day kayaking adventures. Available as two- to six-day tours for groups of eight people, you have the choice of camping each night or staying at different inns in the San Juan Islands. A typical trip might take your group and two guides to boat-only accessible state parks at Jones and Stuart Islands for overnight stays. "Gourmet camp cuisine" is the rule on these trips. Mango chutney and smoked salmon fettuccini are just two of the savory items you'll feast on during a multi-course dinner. Tents, mattress pads, and other items are provided so all you have to bring is a sleeping bag and clothing. You can expect to cover 8 to 10 miles a day in five to six hours of paddling.

If you want a little more luxury, book the multi-day "Inn to Inn" kayak expedition. One itinerary has you starting from Deer Harbor. From there you'll paddle to the Wasp Islands and have lunch before returning to Orcas Island for dinner and a stay at an inn in Eastsound. Day two has you on the ferry to San Juan Island. You'll travel to Snug Harbor, paddle to Lime Kiln State Park for lunch, and then head back to the marina so you can take a shuttle to the Friday Harbor where you'll spend the night. Day three involves more paddling along the west side of San Juan Island with a little hiking thrown in and the fourth day includes a morning on the water before heading back home. Breakfast and dinner are offered at the inns while lunch is prepared by your guide.

Crystal Seas also offers combination kayak and biking trips for the quintessential San Juans outdoor experience. These can be camping trips (for around $150 a day) or Inn-to-Inn tours (that run $350 to $400 daily). You can design the trip to fit your desires or take a standard trip where you spend half your time on the water and the other half riding a comfortable hybrid bicycle 20 to 30 miles a day. These kayak and bike tours often cover all three major islands (San Juan, Orcas and Lopez). If you want to take a little time out of the saddle (or cockpit), Crystal Seas can also arrange for you to spend half a day on a whale-watching trip.

Crystal Seas Kayaking offers their San Juans trips from May through early October. In the winter months they shift their operations south, offering tours and trips in sunny Florida and Costa Rica.

Getting There: You can drop by the office at 70 Spring Street, just up the hill from the ferry terminal in downtown Friday Harbor. You'll find the kayaks at the Snug Harbor Marina. Follow Beaverton Valley Road west from Friday Harbor to Mitchell Bay Road. Take a left and watch for the sign to Snug Harbor.

Washington's Marine State Parks are ideal destinations for kayakers.

San Juan Island
National Historical Park

PO Box 429, Friday Harbor, WA 98250 / 360-378-2902
www.nps.gov/sajh

It's hard to believe the peaceful San Juan Islands became a flashpoint for a near war in 1859. It's stranger still to know the spark that lit this fuse was the killing of a pig. The Pig War, as the near conflict is known today, originated as a dispute over whether America or Great Britain owned San Juan Island. In the 1850s, the island was uneasily shared by the Hudson's Bay Company and American settlers. In 1859 one of these Americans, Lyman Cutlar, shot a Hudson's Bay pig that was in his garden. The British company demanded restitution and threatened to arrest Cutlar when he did not pay.

Cutlar and the Americans asked for protection from the U.S. Government. In July, a company of US Army infantry under the command of George Pickett arrived to fulfill this request (this young captain gained fame four years later in the Civil War leading "Pickett's Charge" for the Confederate Army during the Battle of Gettysburg). The British Governor on Vancouver Island was incensed at the American military presence and dispatched three warships with instructions to dislodge Pickett's small force. As the summer progressed, the opposing forces on the island grew. By the end of August, the American garrison at the south end of the island had 461 soldiers and 14 cannons. They were significantly outnumbered by the British force of 2,140 troops who were supported by five warships that mounted 167 guns.

Fortunately, calmer heads prevailed and the incident did not escalate into a war. Diplomats on both sides agreed to a joint occupation of the island until a peaceful solution could be agreed upon. The US forces occupied American Camp on the southern tip of the island while the British made their home at English Camp on the northern portion of San Juan Island. In 1872, Kaiser Wilhelm I of Germany, acting as an arbitrator at the request of the American and British governments, ruled that San Juan Island would be an American possession. The troops were soon withdrawn and tranquility returned to the San Juans.

Today, American Camp and English Camp make up the San Juan Island National Historical Park. A visit to the two camps provides a glimpse into what life was like for the soldiers who lived here in the mid-19th century. Hiking and wildlife watching opportunities are added bonuses at these scenic locations.

At English Camp, you can visit four restored buildings and a formal flower garden next to Garrison Bay. The barracks building acts as a small visitor center during the summer. If you are in the mood for a walk, you can follow the 2-mile Bell Point Loop Trail towards Westcott Bay where shellfish harvesting is allowed at times (check state regulations beforehand). A more exerting hike takes you 1.25 miles past the camp cemetery to the top of 650-foot Young Hill.

Boaters and kayakers can have close up encounters with sea lions, gulls and other wildlife.

The tall trees that shelter English Camp give way to prairie grasslands at American Camp. A visitor center has exhibits and other information about American Camp and the Pig War. From there you can visit the earthen redoubt that housed artillery cannon or the two historical buildings that remain from that time period. A 1.25-mile interpretive trail starts and finishes at the visitor center. Other hikes lead to the beach at Grandma's Cove (0.25 miles) and along the grassy prairie (2.5 miles). A 3-mile loop trail will take you to little 250-foot Mt. Finlayson and a 2-mile walk along gravelly South Beach affords the opportunity to enjoy the longest public stretch of beach on San Juan Island. Further water access is possible at Fourth of July Beach and the 1.5-mile hike around Jakle's Lagoon is a charming walk among Douglas fir, cedar, and hemlock trees. Just west of the park boundary is the Cattle Point Interpretive Area, a Department of Natural Resources property where you can hike out to Cattle Point Lighthouse at the southernmost tip of the island.

The wildlife is varied and abundant within the 1,752-acre park. Birders can see over 200 species such as winter wrens, chestnut-backed chickadees, various swallows, and colorful American goldfinches. Raptors like great horned owls, peregrine falcons, and northern harriers hunt the prairies and bald eagles along with osprey nest in trees and snags close to the water. One species of note is the western bluebird. The Audubon Society and other conservation groups successfully reintroduced this species in the San Juan Valley and efforts are underway to release more of these birds. Columbian black-tailed deer and rabbits are abundant, river otters can be seen playing or feeding near the shore, and red fox (which come in several different colors) are also present. Marine mammals and birds can also be seen in or around the water (See the other San Juan Island entries for details). Finally, the park is a good place to look for butterflies. Thirty-two different species are found on San Juan Island, to include pale tiger swallowtails, silvery blues, brown elfins, and the rare marble butterfly.

The two camps are both day-use areas; open every day from dawn to 11:00pm except for Christmas and New Years Day. The visitor center at American Camp is open every day except for major holidays and during the last week of May. A small visitor center in the barracks at English Camp is open from May 31 through the first weekend of September. Pets are allowed in the park, but must be kept on leashes. National Park Service personnel offer a number of interpretive programs from June through August. Call ahead for specific schedules.

Getting There: Follow Roche Harbor Road from Friday Harbor to West Valley Road. Turn left and drive 1.5 miles to the entrance of English Camp. American Camp is 6 miles south of Friday Harbor. Follow Mullis Street and Cattle Point Road from town to get there.

Lopez Island

San Juan Islands Visitors Bureau
PO Box 1330, Friday Harbor, WA 98250 / 888-468-3701 x1
www.visitsanjuans.com
Spencer Spit State Park
521 A Bakerview Road, Lopez, WA 98261 / 360-468-2251
www.parks.wa.gov

Lodging Prices

Lopez Island is the first stop for most of the Washington State Ferries plying the San Juan Islands. Often described as a pastoral place with friendly people, the relatively flat 29.5 miles of island roads are well suited to bicycling. Lying in the rain shadow of the Olympic Mountains, Lopez and the other San Juan Islands typically receive less than 25 inches of rain a year. Throw in a fair amount of wildlife, several places to launch a small boat or kayak, and nice views of the countryside and sea and you have the makings for a relaxing island stay. For lodging, you can camp at a public park, book a room at a resort, or stay at one of the cottages or B & Bs on the island (see the San Juan Islands Visitors Bureau website for details).

Campers will find two public places of interest on the island. The first, Odlin County Park (360-378-1842 – www.co.san-juan.wa.us/parks/lopez.html), is on the north end of Lopez, only 1.3 miles from the ferry dock. The 80-acre park has low beach waterfront, places to put in a kayak, picnic sites, and 30 campsites. The park is also part of the 140-mile Cascadia Marine Trail (www.wwta.org/trails/CMT/index.asp) that stretches from British Columbia to the south end of Puget Sound.

On the northeast side of the island Spencer Spit State Park is another stop on the Cascadia Marine Trail and has 50 campsites within the 138-acre property. Thirty-seven of these sites can be used by tent campers or RVs (no hook ups), seven more are walk-in/bike-in tent sites, and the other six are

adjacent to the beach – handy for those who want to paddle to them or hike downhill from the main camping area. If you come by boat, mooring buoys provide a place to tie up for the night.

The main feature of the park is the sandy spit that extends out towards Frost Island. You can hike the half mile from the parking lot towards a rough log cabin near the end of the spit. Rabbits are abundant in the grassy area above the beach, and the sandy beach along the spit is an excellent place for clamming when the season is open. Crabbing is good just off shore and a salt chuck lagoon on one side of the spit is a good place for bird watching.

If you want to cast a line, you can try for bottomfish or salmon around the island or little Hummel Lake for trout. Public land around this lake has been made into a preserve, making it a good place to pause during a bike ride or to do a little bird watching for wren, heron, osprey, waterfowl, and hawks. Another place for wildlife watching and hiking is found at the south end of the island at Shark Reef Park, where a half-mile trail leads through old growth trees to the seashore where seals and sea lions often sun themselves on rocks.

You'll find provisions and eateries at Lopez Village, located at the mouth of Fisherman Bay. If you are looking for a sheltered place to kayak, this is a good place to paddle and nearby Otis Perkins Park is a day-use area that has almost a mile of beach to explore.

Getting There: Take Highway 20 from Interstate 5 near Burlington/Mt. Vernon to Anacortes. Follow the signs to the Washington State Ferry Terminal. The ferry ride to Lopez Island is about 45 minutes long.

A minke whale surfaces near the San Juan Islands.

Orcas Island

San Juan Islands Visitors Bureau
PO Box 1330, Friday Harbor, WA 98250 / 888-468-3701 x1
www.visitsanjuans.com

Moran State Park
Olga Road, Eastsound, WA 98245 / 360-376-2326
www.parks.wa.gov

Lodging Prices

Adventure Pricing

The largest of the San Juan Islands, Orcas Island's hills, forests, and beaches offer much to enjoy whether you are a bicyclist, kayaker, or hiker who just wants a laidback getaway in a natural setting. Like the other islands, Orcas offers travelers a variety of accommodations ranging from campgrounds to resorts, inns and B & Bs.

The first stop for most people is the Washington State Ferry landing at pretty little Orcas Village at the southwestern base of the horseshoe-shaped island. Orcas Road takes you by car or bike 13.6 miles from the landing to Eastsound, the largest community on the island. Side roads along the way take you to West Sound, Deer Harbor, and West Beach on the western side of the island.

Eastsound is a good place to go shopping, grab a bite out, or stock up on gas and groceries. The village sits at the head of the long bay it's named after, and a small waterfront park is a nice place to stop for a picnic. A short drive east from town will allow you to head south on Olga Road past historic Rosario Resort and into Moran State Park.

The 5,252-acre park is dominated by 2,409-foot Mt. Constitution while several lakes provide scenery and recreation. Cascade Lake is adjacent to the main road. A day-use area here has a playground and picnic area that is popular with the kids. A snack bar is open from Memorial Day weekend

through Labor Day and you can also rent a row boat or paddle boat to explore the lake during this time. If you want to wet a line, fishing for stocked trout can be good.

You'll find 151 campsites in the park, many of them spread out near Cascade Lake. While many of the sites can handle RVs and trailers, there are no hook-ups. A vacation house that accommodates eight can be rented well in advance and an Environmental Learning Center can handle up to 144 people. Traveling up the winding road towards Mt. Constitution you'll find Mountain Lake which has a nice campground. The lake is a pretty, tree-lined piece of water that also has decent trout fishing.

There are 30 miles of hiking trails in the park. Easy walks take you around Cascade (2.5 miles) and Mountain Lakes (4 miles). A 2.4-mile hike from the Mountain Lake campground will take you to the Twin Lakes and back while other hikes follow Cascade Creek to several waterfalls. If you want more of a challenge, you can hike or bicycle to the top of Mt. Constitution. However, for an easier go of it, just drive to the parking lot near the summit. From there you can walk to a stone observation tower constructed by the Civilian Conservation Corps in 1936. From the top of the tower you'll be able to take in panoramic views of the surrounding islands as well as the mainland United States and Canada.

Traveling south from Moran State Park, you soon reach the small hamlet of Olga, where a community dock stretches out into Eastsound. Not far from here, you can take Pt. Lawrence Road towards Doe Bay or continue further south along Obstruction Pass Road and turn right on Trailhead Road to reach Obstruction Pass State Park. You can hike a half mile through the forested 80-acre park to a campground that has ten tent sites. Just below the campground is a lovely agate-strewn beach with tide pools on each side worth exploring. Mooring buoys off shore provide a place to tie up a boat and the beach is a good place to come and go by kayak.

Continue south on Obstruction Pass Road to reach Obstruction Pass. Located next to Lieberhaven Resort (see their entry in this book for details), you can use the public launch and dock for a fishing, crabbing, or kayaking trip. Obstruction Pass represents the southeastern leg of the horseshoe on Orcas Island. While visiting Orcas (and the other San Juan Islands), make it a point to respect private property. Beach access is limited to just a few public sites on the populated islands.

Deer are quite abundant on Orcas Island. Raccoon and river otter are other common land animals, while seals and the occasional whale are seen off shore. Eagles, waterfowl, heron, oystercatchers, and various other avian species can be seen by birdwatchers near the water and further inland.

Getting There: Take Highway 20 from Interstate 5 near Burlington/Mt. Vernon to Anacortes. Follow the signs to the Washington State Ferry terminal where you can book passage to Orcas Island.

The gorgeous pastels highlight a stunning sunset at West Beach.

WEST BEACH RESORT

190 Waterfront Way, Eastsound, WA 98245 / 877-937-8224
www.westbeachresort.com

Lodging Prices: $ to $$$ Adventure Pricing: $ to $$

The sunsets alone make West Beach Resort a great place to stay. The resort sits on the northwest shore of Orcas Island, allowing you to watch the evening sun slowly dip across President's Channel behind Waldron Island. As it does, you are typically treated to a summer spectacle of soft pink, blue, scarlet, and lavender that slowly fades to darkness. Whether you enjoy the show sitting by a bonfire, sipping a glass of wine from the porch of your cabin, or soaking in the resort's hot tub, you are sure to feel a little more relaxed at the end of the day.

Known as a family vacation getaway, West Beach Resort has a little something for everybody when it comes to accommodations. The cheapest digs are found at the 20-plus tent sites or 22 RV sites (with water and electrical hook ups). A shower house offers restroom facilities and a laundry room comes in handy for those dirty clothes.

If you are willing to shell out more money you can stay in one of the 20 clean, well-furnished one- and two-bedroom cottages that sleep anywhere from two to seven people. Seventeen are ocean front or ocean view cabins and two garden cabins sit next to a small pond. Ducks frequent this pond and heron, mink, and even river otter have been known to visit. All of the cabins are heated and all but one has a kitchen, woodstove, and private bath. Every cottage also comes with a barbeque, covered deck, outdoor furniture, and a fire ring perfect for roasting marshmallows.

There's plenty to keep the kids busy. You'll see them bicycle around the resort, play on the beach or at the edge of the pond, swing at the small playground, or head to the store for ice cream and snacks. In the summer there is also a kid's program run out of the activities kiosk. Next to the kiosk is a store that has groceries, an espresso stand, and a lobby where you can register for your stay, sit and socialize, or catch up on your e-mail with the wireless Internet.

Fishing is a favorite pastime. You can catch greenling, perch, and the occasional dogfish shark from the resort's 400-foot pier. Kids also enjoy catch-and-release bass fishing at the freshwater pond. Fishing out of a boat will get you into some better saltwater fishing for rockfish, lingcod, and salmon. In fact, the resort owners say a record blackmouth (immature saltwater chinook) salmon weighing 42 pounds and a reputed 68-pound lingcod were both caught near the resort. If you still want more seafood, try dropping a crab pot and haul in some tasty Dungeness crab for dinner. You can launch your boat at the resort and moor it at a buoy or the floating dock next to the pier. A gas dock is also available for refueling.

If you didn't bring your own boat, you can rent a kayak, canoe, or seaworthy 14- to 16-foot boat with outboard motor. For that matter, you can also rent fishing gear and crab pots. If you prefer to have someone else take you fishing, you can book a charter during the summer months aboard the "Grayhawk", a 22-foot Boston whaler powered by a 225-horsepower Mercury outboard. You can catch bottomfish for dinner or if you are not in the mood for angling, just take in the sights and observe wildlife on a cruise where you'll likely see seals, Dall's porpoise, eagles, various sea and shore birds, and perhaps even a minke or orca whale. Back on land, bicycling is another popular pursuit. If you didn't bring your own bike, you can rent one at the resort.

If you want to get off the roads and back onto the water, Shearwater Adventures (360-376-4699 – www.shearwaterkayaks.com) offers guided kayak trips from the resort from June through September. Afternoon and sunset trips each last three hours and are suitable for novices. The first half hour is usually spent gearing up and getting instruction, leaving two and a half hours to explore the calm ocean waters near the resort. Routes vary depending upon the tides, but Point Doughty, the westernmost part of Orcas Island, is a popular destination with cliffs dropping into the sea and good views of Mt. Baker just around the point.

West Beach Resort is a very popular vacation destination; so much so there is a seven-night minimum (Saturday to Saturday) stay in July and August for both the cottages and ocean view RV sites. For the rest of the year there is a two night minimum stay (three nights during holiday weekends). This minimum stay requirement does not apply to camping and non-ocean view RV sites. Leashed pets are allowed at the resort and, by arrangement, in certain cottages for an additional fee.

Getting There: Travel 8 miles from the Orcas ferry landing to the outskirts of Eastsound. Instead of following the main road into Eastsound, stay left and travel a quarter mile to Enchanted Forest Road. Take a left and follow this road about 2.5 miles to the resort.

NORTH SHORE CHARTERS

P.O. Box 316, Eastsound, WA 98245 – 360-376-4855
www.sanjuancruises.net

Lodging Prices: N/A   Adventure Pricing: $$$ to $$$$

Marty Mead is a fishing guide and charter boat captain who cares deeply about the environment. His most obvious demonstration of this commitment is the Sally J, his new 30-foot Norstar boat. It's powered by twin 350-horsepower diesel engines that burn 100-percent biodiesel fuel. This green fuel is produced from canola or soy by American farmers and does not contribute to greenhouse gases in the way that traditional diesel fuel does.

From May through October, Mead offers bottomfishing trips from Deer Harbor on Orcas Island. If getting to Deer Harbor isn't convenient, Mead can pick you up on one of the other islands if you want to charter his boat. Anglers can expect to hook a variety of fish ranging from aggressive lingcod to colorful rockfish or tasty greenling, cod, cabezon, and flounder. If you book a full day trip, you can also go fishing for halibut. Seasons and bag limits vary for these fish, so be sure to check the regulations or call in advance.

Mead offers bottomfishing instead of salmon fishing because the action is generally fast paced with lots of hookups. It's something most beginning anglers and kids appreciate. These fish can get big. Forty-inch lingcod are not unheard of, and cabezon and rockfish tip the scales at 8 pounds or better on a regular basis. Mead encourages catch-and-release angling, especially since keeping a single rockfish or lingcod means you are done fishing for the day. However, Mead is not opposed to keeping fish to fry, bake, or barbeque during your stay on the islands, especially if you want to keep the more plentiful greenling, flounder, and cod found in these waters.

In addition to fishing, you may also be able to come home with some crab or shrimp. You'll generally drop the pot off on your way out to fish or explore and retrieve it as you return to the marina at the end of the trip. Dungeness crab and spot shrimp make for a delicious meal. Crab season traditionally runs from Memorial Day through Labor Day while the short spot shrimp season usually takes place in June.

Although Mead does not advertise wildlife watching, you will likely see your fair share of marine mammals and birds during a typical outing. Seals and porpoise are common sights, as are gulls, cormorants, and a variety of other shore and sea birds.

Marty Mead is more than a fishing guide. He also offers day-long family adventures full of activities that may include crabbing, fishing, exploring remote islands, and stopping at Friday Harbor or one of the island villages for a bite to eat and a bit of shopping. You can also charter a trip to the Canadian Gulf Islands. Visits to the Saturday farmer's markets on these islands are a popular booking. Other guests go to Sidney on Vancouver Island so they can spend the day visiting nearby Victoria. In the winter months, Mead can even take you from the San Juan Islands to mainland Canada if you want to spend the day skiing at Whistler, a popular British Columbia resort.

Mead has a second biodiesel-fueled boat that doesn't need a dock to beach at remote islands. Like his newer boat, the Rockhopper has an enclosed cabin, bathroom, and heater to keep the chill off during the cooler months. Unlike a fishing charter, Mead does not charge by the person. Instead, he charges by the hour for the use of his boats that can carry up to six people.

Getting There: From the ferry terminal at Orcas Island travel north on Orcas Road for 2.5 miles. Turn left and head west for 5 miles on Deer Harbor Road until you reach the marina.

Marty Mead holds up a healthy cabezon caught off of Orcas Island.

THE CABIN AT SPRING BAY

P.O. Box 97, Olga, WA 98279 / 360-376-553
www.springbayinn.com

Lodging Prices: $$$ Adventure Pricing: $

Looking for a quiet and secluded place to spend a couple of nights? Want to go hiking and kayaking too? Then a stay at The Cabin at Spring Bay ought to be on your short list of things to do.

Carl Burger and co-owner Sandy Playa retired as California State Park Rangers to open up the Spring Bay Inn. It was a leap of faith for the two that turned out well. The inn became a popular bed and breakfast that drew both a romantic and outdoor-oriented clientele. In 2009, Carl and Sandy decided to move into the inn and convert their cabin into a rental for guests to use.

Guests at the inn raved about the morning kayak tours. Fortunately, you can still go kayaking with Carl or Sandy, who are trained naturalists, as a visitor to the cabin, or as a member of the public if you make advance reservations. Tours generally depart at 8:30am and 4pm, though groups of three or more staying at the cabin can arrange for a different departure time if they wish. No experience is necessary and that is good, since the vast majority of guests are novices. You may paddle around Obstruction Island or to the nearby hamlet of Olga. Along the way you'll likely see harbor seals and lots of birds, which may include glaucous and Heerman's gulls, marbled murrelet, eagles, kingfishers, osprey and oystercatchers. Try looking into the water as you paddle to see orange or purple starfish and red rock crab that scurry along the rocky shell-strewn bottom amongst the eelgrass and kelp beds.

Exploring the 57-acre property around the cabin and inn is another fun activity. Wildlife such as deer, eagles, great blue herons and a variety of land-based birds can all be seen. If you are rusty on your wildlife identification borrow a field guide and a pair of binoculars while you wander the 2½ miles of signed trails on the property.

The Cabin at Spring Bay has a main room with a sleeping area (queen bed), a kitchenette (with a refrigerator and dishwasher) and living room with a table and chairs in front of the bay view windows and comfy furniture in front of a woodstove. In addition to a bathroom there is also a bedroom that has a twin bed and DVD player with monitor in case you want to watch a movie. Cell phone reception is spotty but you can keep up with what's going on in the outside world with a computer that has a fast Internet connection. The outside deck is just steps from the gravel beach and has a grill on it so you can BBQ your dinner. Finally, a hot tub is just steps away as well, perfect for resting your muscles after a hike, paddle, or long drive to the island from the mainland.

A maximum of three guests are allowed to stay in the cabin. Children are welcome but pets are not allowed. The cabin, as well as guided kayak tours, is available all year.

A morning kayak trip is included as part of your stay.

LIEBERHAVEN RESORT

1945 Obstruction Pass Rd. Olga, WA 98279 / 360-376-2472
www.lieberhavenresort.com

Lodging Prices: $$ to $$$ Adventure Pricing: $

If you are looking for a place to stay on Orcas Island that is open all year with no minimum night stay requirements, check out Lieberhaven Resort. Located at the southeastern tip of the island, this resort is a great place to unwind in a simple but beautiful oceanfront setting.

As far as accommodations go, you'll find eight basic waterfront cabins with kitchenettes that sleep anywhere from two to six people. There are also four nice inn-style rooms for rent that overlook Obstruction Pass. There are no telephones or televisions here; just peace and the rhythmic sound of lapping waves on the gravel beach, just steps from your door.

You can spend time watching eagles fly overhead or gaze seaward to look for seals, whose heads bob up for a look see. Playful river otters scamper along the docks and in the evening, deer and raccoon walk down the sidewalk that separates the cabins and gravel beach.

The marina has several interesting boats befitting the nautical background of the owners. One of them, the "Lieberschwan", is a two-masted schooner used in the Disney film "Pete's Dragon". Another vessel, the "Kitty B" is a reconditioned 1926 tugboat. Rowboats and kayaks are available for rent from Orcas Island Kayak Rentals at the resort. You can take out a single, tandem, or three-seat kayak or rowboat to explore the surrounding rocks and kelp beds where fishing is good and solitude is easy to come by. Exploring the beach or dropping a crab ring off the marina dock for tasty rock crab are additional options. Anglers also do well off the docks jigging for piling perch, kelp greenling, flounder, and the occasional lingcod. If you have your own boat, you can launch at the Obstruction Pass Launch adjacent to the resort to explore the surrounding islands or try your hand at salmon fishing.

If you are in the mood for a whale watching trip you'll be happy to know that San Juan Boat Tours (888-734-8180 – www.whales.com) offers the opportunity to do so every day from mid-May through Labor Day when its 50-foot boat stops at Lieberhaven's marina. This company also operates as a passenger ferry to Friday Harbor and other San Juan Island destinations from Bellingham on the mainland. Hiking is another recreational option, with several hikes available at nearby Obstruction Pass or Moran State Park (see the Orcas Island entry for details).

While you are at Lieberhaven, take some time to visit with the Baxter family. The amiable resort owners have some fascinating nautical and show business stories worth listening to. The Baxters operate a small store at the resort on an "as needed basis" (i.e. when customers wander in or kids staying at the resort get a hankering for ice cream). The rates for lodging are some of the most reasonable on the island and the no-minimum-night stay rule is a rarity among area resorts during the summer months. If you want to bring your dog or cat, you'll have to look elsewhere though since no pets are allowed.

Getting There: Take the main road around Orcas Island from the ferry landing through Eastsound and Moran State Park to Olga. Turn onto Point Lawrence Road and travel 0.75 mile to Obstruction Pass Road. Turn right and travel south on Obstruction Pass Road until you reach the resort.

River otters often make an appearance around the Lieberhaven Resort.

San Juan Islands National Wildlife Refuge and Marine State Parks

San Juan Islands National Wildlife Refuge – Care of Washington Maritime NWR
Complex / 33 S. Barr Road, Port Angeles, WA 98362 / 360-457-8451
www.fws.gov/pacific/refuges/field/wa_sanjuanis.htm
Washington State Parks
360-376-2073
www.parks.wa.gov

Lodging Pricing

Many think of the San Juan Islands as the four places where the Washington State Ferries stop (San Juan, Orcas, Lopez, and Shaw Islands). In reality, the islands include 700 islands and reefs; 176 of which are named. Some of them are exposed rock formations and reefs that appear and disappear with the changing tides. Others are islands of varying sizes with grassy or forested land.

Eighty-three of these are part of the San Juan Islands National Wildlife Refuge. However, only two of the refuge lands (Matia and Turn Islands) are open to public access. The others are closed to protect the birds, marine life, and mammals that call them home. Even though you can't go ashore, you can get close enough in a boat or kayak to see seals or sea lions that have hauled themselves out onto the rocks and look at birds as varied as tufted puffin, rhinoceros auklet, pigeon guillemot, black oystercatcher, and several species of gulls. Bald eagles nest in tall trees on some of these islands and off shore you may see common murre and marbled murrelet. When birds are nesting, kayakers and boaters are asked to stay 200 yards away from shore.

Matia and Turn Islands are not only part of a national wildlife refuge, but also have two of the twelve marine state parks within the San Juan Islands. All twelve of these parks are only accessible by boat and make great kayaking destinations. Beachcombing and tide pool exploration are also popular

activities. Off shore, crabbing, shrimping and fishing are options if you are hankering for a fresh seafood dinner.

Turn Island is a 35-acre marine park just 1.75 miles southeast of Friday Harbor and only a short distance from Jackson Beach on San Juan Island. There are three mooring buoys and a cove near them where kayakers can beach their boats.

Matia Island has a 5-acre camping area at Rolfs Cove and another 140 acres that are part of the refuge and San Juans Wilderness. A mile-long trail goes into the wilderness area, and within the camping area there is a 64-foot dock and two buoys for moorage purposes. There are six campsites on the island and a composting toilet. No water is available on either Turn or Matia Island.

Sucia Island, like Matia, is located north of Orcas Island in the Strait of Georgia. The Parks Commission considers Sucia to be the "crown jewel" of the marine state parks system. There are over 10 miles of hiking trails to explore on the 564-acre island and mooring buoys are found at several locations. There are also 60 campsites and day-use facilities in the form of picnic tables and covered picnic shelters. There are composting toilets on the island and, as of press time, drinking water is again available.

Clark and Patos Islands are also found north of Orcas Island. Both offer a few campsites and moorage. Patos also has a 1.5-mile loop trail to explore and a population of raccoons. Southwest of Orcas, Jones Island has 24 campsites, two of which are reserved for kayakers and wind-powered craft. You can anchor off north cove (where a dock is also available) or south cove, and a loop trail will take you down the center of the island and along the western shoreline of the 188-acre marine park.

Other marine state parks include Griffin Bay, a small strip of land bordered by private property on the south end of San Juan Island, and Posey Island, a small island near Roche Harbor on the north end of San Juan. Both parks are part of the Cascadia Marine Trail and have two camp sites for the exclusive use of boaters in human or wind-powered vessels. Blind Island is another state park on this trail that has four campsites for the use of paddlers and sailors. Located near Shaw Island, the crabbing around Blind Bay is reputed to be fabulous.

Yet another park that is part of this trail is at Stuart Island, 3.5 miles north of Roche Harbor. The 85-acre park has 18 primitive campsites and 3.5 miles of trails to explore. Clams and crabs are available in these waters and potable water is available from April through September.

Finally, James Island offers camping in three separate areas along with 1.5 miles of hiking trails. Located 3 miles west of Anacortes in Rosario Strait, it is the closest of this group to the mainland. All of the campsites on these islands are available on a first-come, first-served basis.

Getting There: The islands of this national wildlife refuge and these marine state parks are located at various places throughout the San Juan Archipelago.

Fidalgo and Whidbey Islands

Deception Pass State Park

41229 State Route 20, Oak Harbor, WA 98277 – 360-675-2417
www.parks.wa.gov

Lodging Prices   Adventure Pricing

Covering over 4,000 acres on the northern end of Whidbey and southern portion of Fidalgo Islands, Deception Pass is Washington's most popular state park. The dramatic view of the narrow pass between the rocky cliffs of the two islands is reason enough to visit. A high bridge that is part of State Route 20 spans the pass and several parking areas allow you to get out of your vehicle to take in the sight of the swirling saltwater below.

The pass was named by Captain George Vancouver who explored this part of Puget Sound in 1792. He named it Deception Pass because he mistakenly thought the strong currents passing through were from a river and not the sea. Whidbey Island was named after Master Joseph Whidbey, who commanded a small boat from Vancouver's ship and discovered the true nature of the geographic feature.

In the 1930s, the Civilian Conservation Corps developed the park with buildings, trails, and roads. Today, there are over 35 miles of trails within the forested park boundaries, 77,000 feet of saltwater shoreline, two lakes, day-use areas, campgrounds, and an environmental learning center.

Many of the park's 167 tent sites and 143 utility sites are found in the popular West Beach portion of the park on the northwest end of Whidbey Island. Entering this part of the park you'll find parking and a day-use area fronting Cranberry Lake – a 128-acre freshwater lake just a few yards away from the saltwater of Rosario Strait. There is a boat ramp and fishing pier here, and during the summer you can go swimming or rent a small boat. Only electric motors are allowed on this lake which has trout, bass, perch, and catfish for the taking.

Continue past Cranberry Lake and the campground to reach the ocean. Sunsets are beautiful here, and saltwater fishing from the beach for salmon and other species can be good at times. You can go for a walk along the gravelly beach or hike along the Sand Dune Interpretive Trail, enjoying views of both Cranberry Lake and Puget Sound along the way. A food concession is open during the summer near the parking lot and trailhead if you work up an appetite. There is also an amphitheatre in this part of the park where interpretive programs are presented.

Other camping areas are found at the Quarry Lake Campground (also known as the Sunrise Resort), Bowman Bay, and at three primitive group camps that can handle 20 to 50 people in the Cranberry Lake/West Beach portion of the park. Another group rental can be reserved in advance at the Cornet Bay Environmental Learning Center. The center has a lodge, cabins, dining hall, amphitheatre, and classrooms. Finally, a unique cabin is available on little Ben Ure Island near Cornet Bay. It's not part of the Learning Center and is available to kayakers and others who use human-powered vessels to reach the 12-by-24-foot dwelling that has a deck overlooking Puget Sound and Mt. Baker. Electric lights, heat, a bathroom, kitchen, and a hide-a-bed couch make up all the comforts of home you'll need during your small island stay.

A great blue heron forages for a snack (photo courtesy Edgar Reinfeld).

Ben Ure Island is only one of the islands that are part of Deception Pass State Park. Deception, Strawberry, Northwestern, Skagit, and Hope Islands are also part of the state park system. Camping is allowed on the latter two islands and the area outside of Hope Island's campground is a natural preserve. Several of these islands are good places to explore by kayak, but novice paddlers should steer clear of Deception Pass itself because of its strong currents.

One good place to launch a kayak is at Bowman Bay. Located at the southwest end of Fidalgo Island, this part of the park is much quieter than the more popular West Beach/Cranberry Lake area. In addition to 20 campsites, there is a boat launch, beach, and playground. Anacortes Kayak Tours (see their entry in this book) also offers tours for paddlers of all experience levels from Bowman Bay during the summer. Another concessionaire (Deception Pass Tours – 888-909-TOURS – www.deceptionpasstours. com) has also started offering sightseeing trips on a jet-powered catamaran from April to October. These tours depart from Cornet Bay, Thursday through Monday. Tickets can be purchased at the Deception Pass Bridge.

If you are in the mood for some land-based exercise, you can hike, ride a horse, or bike the 6.1-mile Hoypus Hill and Hoypus Loop trails through old growth forest on the southeast side of Deception Pass. Other hikes follow trails from Bowman Bay to Rosario Beach (0.6 mile), along North Beach on the south side of the pass (1 mile), or from Pass Lake to Ginnett Orchard. Pass Lake is worth mentioning in more detail. The 99-acre lake is next to State Route 20 north of the Deception Pass Bridge. It is open all year for catch-and-release flyfishing and has a reputation of being one of the best trophy trout lakes in the state. It's a good place to fish from a float, pontoon, or small boat (but motors are prohibited).

Other activities at the park or in the saltwater surrounding it include crabbing, clamming, and wildlife watching. Mammals within the park include muskrat, fox, skunk, deer, coyote, rabbit, chipmunk, and river otter. Harbor seals and porpoise are commonly seen by kayakers in the area. Birders can see up to 174 different species which includes everything from bald eagles, gulls, and great blue heron near the saltwater to woodpeckers, jays, owls, and hummingbirds inland.

Deception Pass State Park is open all year. Campsite reservations are suggested during the summer.

Getting There: The park is located off of State Route (Highway) 20, 9 miles north of Oak Harbor on Whidbey Island and 9 miles south of Anacortes on Fidalgo Island.

ISLAND ADVENTURES

1801 Commercial Avenue, Anacortes, WA 98221 / 800-465-4604
www.islandadventurecruises.com

Lodging Prices: N/A   Adventure Pricing: $$

There are a lot of good reasons to go whale watching with Island Adventures out of Anacortes. One is that you don't have to catch a ferry to the San Juan Islands to get to your tour boat. Another reason is that the Island Explorer 3 is one of the largest and most comfortable whale watching boats in the Pacific Northwest. The service-oriented and knowledgeable staff is another plus. Finally, Island Adventures offers (almost) year-round whale watching in Puget Sound, something the other companies simply don't do.

Shane and Jennifer Aggergaard started up Island Adventures in 1996. The company has grown quite a bit since then, culminating with the 2007 purchase of the 101-foot Island Explorer 3. All of their tours depart on this roomy vessel that can accommodate 150 passengers. You can completely walk around both the main and upper decks, and a long bow pulpit is perfect for getting that close-up whale shot. A protected area on the upper deck keeps you out of the wind and weather and a huge salon on the main deck is fully enclosed. Inside the salon are booths, bench seats, and tables to read the available whale and wildlife literature while enjoying a hot or cold snack from the galley. A big screen TV has a DVD player that shows pictures of whales photographed from the boat and kids may get the chance to see clips from one of their favorite marine movies. If you didn't bring your own binoculars, you can borrow a pair to help you spot wildlife and see it in detail.

There are two naturalists on board the boat, one of whom is usually speaking over a microphone, piping comments into speakers heard throughout the boat. A captain and engineer round out the crew. For most of the year, the boat departs from Anacortes and will travel up to 50 miles to find the whales.

From May to October, the focus is on orca whales. These beautiful black and white whales are the largest members of the dolphin family. The southern resident group of some 90 orcas calls the waters around the San Juans home for much of the year. They primarily feed on salmon, while the less often seen transient orca whales eat marine mammals like seals and sea lions. This is also a good time to see minke whales. These solitary whales can get up to 25 feet long and feed on bait fish.

From October into winter, the spotlight shifts to humpback whales. Reaching lengths of 50 feet, these whales have huge pectoral fins and can be seen migrating through the same general areas in which the orcas are found. In March and April, gray whale tours depart from the Port of Everett. These giants migrate from Mexico to Alaska every year, and many of them can be seen in the Puget Sound region.

Although whale watching is what most visitors come for, you'll likely see plenty of other wildlife. Both Dall's and harbor porpoise are common, as are sea lions and harbor seals. Also present are a variety of sea birds ranging from penguin-like common murre, fish-eating cormorant, and rare marbled murrelet. Great blue heron, oystercatchers, kingfishers, and bald eagles are frequently seen along the shoreline, as is the occasional black-tailed deer.

The Aggergaards are confident about their ability to find you whales. In fact, they boast a 96-percent success rate and offer a guarantee. If you don't see whales on your trip, you are welcome to come back as often as you would like until you do see one. Island Adventures is a member of the Whale Watch Operators Association Northwest and Shane Aggergaard is a past president of the organization. They make it a point to abide by guidelines to minimize disturbances to whales while providing the best possible opportunity to view them.

All bookings are made through the Island Adventures office on Commercial Avenue in Anacortes. During the peak season (mid-June through Labor Day) tours depart at 9:30am and 3:30pm. Tours depart at noon and return by 6:00pm the rest of the year.

Getting There: Take State Highway 20 from Interstate 5 at Mount Vernon/ Burlington. Drive west to Anacortes and turn north on Commercial Avenue. Island Adventures will be on your right prior to the turn for the Anacortes ferry terminal.

The Island Explorer 3 is a modern, well-designed whale watching boat.

CATCHMORE CHARTERS

4215 Mitchell Drive, Anacortes, WA 98221/ 360-293-7093
www.catchmorecharters.com

Lodging Prices: N/A   Adventure Pricing: $$$

Those in the know will tell you Captain Jim Aggergaard is a great guide for both salmon and bottomfish in the San Juan Islands. His 25 years of guiding experience, coupled with a career as an enforcement officer for the Washington Department of Fish and Wildlife, have given him a lot of insight when it comes to knowing where the fish are.

Although his enforcement days are behind him, Aggergaard doesn't plan on quitting anytime soon as the owner of Catchmore Charters. His trips depart from the Skyline Marina in Anacortes. This saves anglers the time and expense of catching a ferry to fish around the San Juan Islands and Aggergaard's new 27-foot fishing boat has a powerful engine that will get you to most of the hot spots in less than an hour. Up to six can fish out of the Shamrock brand boat and you'll appreciate the enclosed cabin, berth, and head with flushing toilet.

From January through March, Aggergaard trolls plug-cut herring for 6- to 14-pound blackmouth (chinook salmon) on either side of Rosario Strait using heavy duty Penn electric downriggers. The fishing can be fast and with a one-fish limit in effect, you are often back to the dock by noon with your catch.

With the arrival of April, Aggergaard starts looking for halibut in the Strait of Juan de Fuca. These great tasting bottomfish average 45 pounds. The limit is again one fish – but a catch this size makes for a lot of steaks and fillets.

Fishing for lingcod traditionally opens up on the first of May and you can keep one between 26 and 40 inches until June 15. These are also some great tasting fish. From April through June, you'll also get the chance to catch other species such as kelp greenling, cabezon, and rockfish.

Come July, it's time to go fishing for salmon again. Kings (chinook) and silvers (coho) usually fill out a two-fish limit, though sockeye are also caught at times. During odd-numbered years, the limit doubles thanks to large numbers of returning pink salmon. Summer salmon can weigh as little as a 3-pound pink or as large as 40-pound chinook.

Rates include your license fee and Aggergaard will clean and bag any fish you want to take home. In terms of refreshments, coffee is available on board but you'll want to bring any other drinks as well as lunch.

One note of caution is in order. The rules about these San Juan Islands fisheries are subject to change every year. While the above information is traditionally accurate, a check of the regulations or a call to Aggergaard in advance would be prudent to determine exactly what you can fish for – and how many fish you may be able to bring home at the end of the day.

Getting There: From Interstate 5 at Burlington travel west on State Highway 20 to Anacortes. Travel 4.3 miles through town along the Highway 20 spur. Stay straight and enter Sunset Avenue. Turn left on Skyline Way to reach the marina.

Jim Aggergaard has a reputation for knowing where the fish are between Anacortes and the San Juan Islands.

ANACORTES KAYAK TOURS

1801 Commercial Avenue, Anacortes, WA 98221 / 800-992-1801
www.anacorteskayaktours.com

Lodging Prices: Included in some adventures   Adventure Pricing: $ to $$$

Erik and Megan Schorr's Anacortes Kayak Tours provide fun and informative paddling around the northern islands of Puget Sound. Using single, tandem, and triple fiberglass sea kayaks, they specialize in trips for everyone from novices to experienced paddlers.

If you are short on time, there is one huge advantage to booking a trip with this company. They are based out of Anacortes, meaning you can drive to any of their launch sites without spending the time or money to take a ferry to the San Juan Islands.

Anacortes Kayak Tours' shortest and most budget-friendly tour departs from Bowman Bay just north of Deception Pass. For one and a half hours you'll explore calm waters around rocky outcroppings home to gulls, cormorants, and harbor seals. Great blue herons keep you company as you paddle, squawking as they lift off and fly ahead of you along shore. On the water, it's common to see harbor porpoise break the surface near your kayak.

Your naturalist guide will show you shallow caves where the incoming waves create a unique and unforgettable thumping sound against the rocks. You'll also get the chance to see purple sea stars and big goose neck barnacles up close and personal. In fact, you'll even have the chance to take a bite (if you dare) out of some of the big bull kelp that float along the surface near shore. This is truly a family friendly tour, geared for anyone from 3 to 83 years old.

A slightly longer experience can be had paddling around Burrows Island. This three-hour excursion departs from the easy-in/easy-out finger docks at Skyline Marina in Anacortes. The extended tour gives you more time to enjoy the wildlife and observe scenery that includes views of pretty madrona trees along shore and Mt. Baker in the distance.

The company's "Outer Islands" day trip begins with a ride aboard the MV Island Express to one of the San Juan's outer islands. The boat will stop to unload your kayaks at Cypress, Sucia, or Lopez Island. From there, you'll explore water off the chosen island for the day. Cypress Island is a favorite destination. Rising some 1,200 feet out of the sea and heavily wooded, you'll think you are truly far away from the world's cares.

So many guests enjoy paddling around Cypress Island that it has become a popular two- to three-day tour in its own right. It is the fourth largest island in the San Juans, but has little development since much of the island is a designated natural preserve. Other multi-day trips last up to five days and will have you paddling or staying at Sucia, Lopez, Clark, or the Wasp Islands. While you have to bring your own food and snacks on the day trips, everything is provided on the multi-day expeditions. Your guide will prepare three meals a day, and dinner may consist of spinach and pine nut pasta or Laotian red curry over rice. Tents and sleeping pads are provided so all you have to bring is your clothing and a sleeping bag.

Anacortes Kayak Tours offers the Burrows Island tour from March through mid-September. The Deception Pass tour, offered as a concession for Deception Pass State Park, takes place from May 1 through mid-September. The multi-day and outer island trips are available during the summer months.

Getting There: Take State Highway 20 from Interstate 5 at Mount Vernon/ Burlington. Drive west to Anacortes and turn north on Commercial Avenue. Anacortes Kayak Tours shares an office with Island Adventures, which will be on your right prior to the turn for the Anacortes ferry terminal.

Fort Casey and Fort Ebey State Park

Fort Casey State Park
1280 Engle Road, Coupeville, WA / 360-678-4519
www.parks.wa.gov
Fort Ebey State Park
400 Hill Valley Drive, Coupeville, WA 98239/ 360-678-4636
www.parks.wa.gov

Lodging Prices

Two military forts meant to protect Seattle and the shipyard in Bremerton have become state parks that are part of the Ebey's Landing National Historical Reserve. Together, Fort Casey and Fort Ebey provide magnificent oceanfront scenery and the opportunity to engage in a variety of outdoor activities.

Fort Casey was first garrisoned in 1890 and, by 1902, it boasted a complement of coastal artillery pieces and crews. The post's heavy guns were meant to interlock their fire with cannon from Fort Flagler and Fort Worden across Puget Sound, forming a "Triangle of Fire" that no enemy fleet could pass through. You can still see some of the old cannon at the fort, and an extensive system of batteries and casemates can be explored. Kids in particular will enjoy wandering through the dark concrete bunkers with a flashlight.

A lighthouse at the post was moved a short distance away from the gun emplacements and rebuilt as a brick and stucco structure in 1903. Today, Admiralty Head Lighthouse is an interpretive center operated by a non-profit group. The lighthouse is open daily during the summer and at selected times during the rest of the year (call 360-240-5584 for exact days and times).

If you want to stay awhile, there is a picnic and a camping area with great views of Admiralty Inlet. Both tent campers and RV enthusiasts can use the 35 campsites (no hook ups and a 40-foot maximum site length). A restroom

with a shower is available in this part of the park. The camping area is adjacent to the Keystone Ferry Terminal, and the comings and goings of the small ferries that operate between here and Port Townsend are always interesting.

Birders will enjoy wandering along Keystone Spit to enjoy views of the sound on one side and Crockett Lake on the other. Several species of waterfowl, owls, hawks, and in the spring, western sandpiper and dunlin can be seen in this area.

Other activities at the 467-acre park include fishing off the beach or in a boat for salmon and bottomfish. Divers will enjoy the underwater reserve just offshore and if you hit the tides right, you can actually hike 8 miles north to Fort Ebey.

Fort Ebey State Park's military history is more modern than Fort Casey's. The army came here in 1942 to defend Puget Sound from a possible Japanese sortie or invasion. Today, visitors to the 645-acre park can hike, bike, or ride horses on a trail system that covers over 25 miles. The most popular hike is along the 6-mile Bluff Trail where you can take in scenic views of the saltwater below and the Olympic Mountains. Quite often, you can also see paragliders soaring along the thermal air currents around here. If you enjoy fishing you can make a short trek to Lake Pondilla, a 3-acre pond with bass and other warmwater fish. Mountain bikers can pedal along the Kettles Trail, which runs past a series of indentations left by receding glaciers called kettleholes.

You can picnic near the concrete platforms that held the old gun batteries, near the beach, or at Point Partridge. There is also a campground with 40 standard campsites and 10 additional utility sites with electrical and water hook-ups. A group camp near Partridge Point will handle up to 60 overnight guests and there is also a single walk-in campsite open to kayakers and canoeists. Both Fort Ebey and Fort Casey State Park are open all year.

Getting There: Fort Casey and Fort Ebey are a short distance from Coupeville on Whidbey Island. Travel south from Oak Harbor on State Highway 20 or north on State Highway 525 from the Mukilteo-Clinton Ferry landing towards Coupeville and signs will direct you towards the parks. You can also take a ferry from Port Townsend to the Keystone Landing adjacent to Fort Casey State Park.

Admiralty Head Lighthouse at Fort Casey State Park houses an interpretive center for guests.

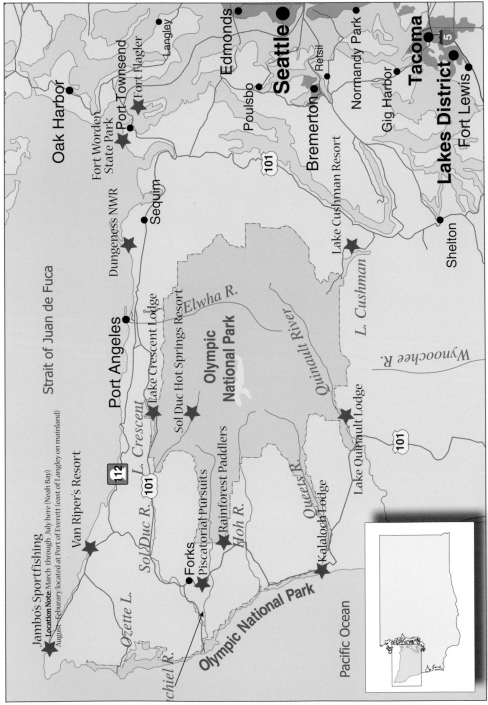

© 2009 Wilderness Adventures Press, Inc.

Olympic National Park

Olympic National Park

600 East Park Avenue, Port Angeles, WA 98362 / 360-565-3130
www.nps.gov/olym/

Lodging Prices

Adventure Pricing

When you think of Olympic National Park, a picture of lush forests full of giant old-growth trees under gray skies may come to mind. After all, the temperate rain forests within the park get up to 140 inches of rain a year. However, the 922,651-acre park is an incredibly diverse place that offers much more for visitors. There are 65 miles of unspoiled Pacific Ocean coastline to explore, a number of scenic streams, high ridges full of wildflowers, and snow-covered mountains dominated by 7,890-foot Mount Olympus.

There is a large and diverse variety of wildlife within Olympic National Park. In fact, it was nearly named Elk National Park because of the herds of Roosevelt elk found here. Other big mammals include black bear, mountain goat, cougar, bobcat, and black-tailed deer. Smaller mammals you may see include weasel, mink, marten, porcupine, skunk, raccoon, and fisher, a recently reintroduced species. Some animals are native to the Olympic Peninsula, like the Olympic marmot, snow mole, Olympic chipmunk, Mazama pocket gopher, and Olympic torrent salamander. If you visit the coastal portion of the park, you may spy sea or river otters, seals, sea lions as well as gray, minke, humpback, or orca whales.

Anglers will find trout in the upper reaches of the streams found in the park, and in several of the lakes as well. Summer is the best time to access most of these waters, but check with the Park Service before wetting a line since there are several special regulations in effect.

This isn't a place you can see in a day – and you'll just be scratching the surface in a week's time. Fortunately, there are a variety of different places to stay in the park during your visit. On one end are the lodges and resorts operated within the park. Along the coast is the Kalaloch Lodge and at Lake

Crescent at the north end of the park is the Lake Crescent Lodge, as well as the Log Cabin Resort. South of Lake Crescent along the banks of the Sol Duc River is the Sol Duc Hot Springs Resort. Finally, just outside the southwestern end of the park on Lake Quinault is the stately Lake Quinault Lodge. All of these places, except for the Log Cabin Resort, are covered in more detail elsewhere in this book. There are also 17 campgrounds scattered through the park. Rates are very reasonable, and several are open all year. RV enthusiasts are welcome at most, but there are no hook-ups at any of the sites. All of the campgrounds are open on a first-come, first-served basis except for Kalaloch, which takes reservations in the summer for the 170 sites available there.

To get a true taste of what the park has to offer, visit the different environments found here. Three different rain forests are found in the Quinault, Queets, and Hoh river valleys along the western interior. Towering western hemlock, Douglas fir, Sitka spruce, and western red cedar along with deciduous maple and cottonwood trees are found here, and toppled tree trunks provide a nursery for other trees as well as 130-plus species of mosses, lichens, and ferns. A walk through these woods is a wonderful way to experience them. The Cascading Terraces Trail (1-mile loop) takes off from the Graves Creek Campground upstream from Lake Quinault and the Sams River Loop Trail allows you to explore 2.9 miles of rainforest starting from the Queets Ranger Station. A stop at the Hoh Rain Forest Visitor Center offers additional educational opportunities. Once you've checked out the exhibits there, you can stroll along the 0.8-mile Hall of Mosses or the 1.2-mile Spruce Nature Loop Trail. If you want a backpacking adventure instead of a day hike, you can make the 18.2-mile trek from the Graves Creek Campground along the Quinault River to Anderson Pass. From there you can turn around and head back or push on to the Dosewallips Campground to the west. Be wary of bears if you take this hike; this area is known for having a healthy population of these big omnivores.

Other places to explore include the Staircase area at the southeast corner of the park and Lake Mills along the Elwha River to the north. Other recreational ideas can be found by reading the Lake Quinault and Lake Crescent Lodge entries as well as the one covering Sol Duc Hot Springs in this book.

While temperate rain forests make up much of the park, high vistas beckon as well. The Olympic Mountains are visible from much of northwest Washington, and a 17.5-mile trail from the Hoh Rain Forest Visitor Center will get you to Glacier Meadows on the north side of Mount Olympus – the highest peak within the mountain range. If you choose to climb the mountain you'll need crampons, an ice axe, and crevasse rescue skills to cross the glaciers along the flanks of the mountain. You'll also want to be on your toes for avalanches. Since the mountain receives over 100 feet of snow in an average winter, avalanches are a constant danger through the spring months. Because of these conditions, the National Park Service recommends bringing shovels, probes, and transceivers along.

If you aren't quite ready for a summit expedition, drive to the Hurricane Ridge Visitor Center south of Port Angeles. Named after the gusty winds that are prevalent here, the ridge offers expansive views of the Olympic Mountains, the Strait of Juan de

Fuca, summer wildflowers, and a number of hiking opportunities. Two-day hikes of note are the 2.8-mile (one way) Klahhane Ridge Trail that starts at the visitor center or the 3.2 mile (round-trip) hike to Hurricane Hill that starts at the end of Hurricane Ridge Road. There are also a couple of wheelchair accessible trails near the visitor center that cross open meadows and are less than a mile in length. In the winter, snowshoeing and cross-country skiing are options. If you want an easy time of it just wander the meadows above the visitor center. To get more of a workout, follow Hurricane Hill Road for 1.5 miles or explore up to 8 miles of the Wolf Creek Trail. Another test of endurance waits at the top of Hurricane Hill. If you choose to go, you'll gain 700 feet in 1.5 miles.

In additions to forests, mountains, streams, and ridgelines, the coastal portion of the park is worth investigating. Start at the southern strip of coastline near Kalaloch, a beautiful area to explore (see the Kalaloch Lodge entry for further information).

Heading north from Kalaloch are more beaches and tide pools to explore near La Push, a small town on the Quileute Indian Reservation. Second and Third Beaches are both south of town and accessed by short hikes (0.7 and 1.4 miles respectively) while Rialto Beach, north of La Push, is accessible by car. You can picnic here or hike north up to 20 miles, though you'll want to be cognizant of the tides if you do so. Many visitors will walk 1.5 miles to Hole in the Wall, a rock formation with several tide pools.

Finally, a unique experience awaits at Lake Ozette at the northern end of the coastal region. Start at the ranger station (open during summer months) and campground that sit near the head of Ozette Lake, a big freshwater lake that is a short distance from the ocean. A popular hiking route heads south 3 miles to Sand Point, north along the beach (or overland trail if the tide is high) past the Wedding Rocks to Cape Alava, and then back to the ranger station on the 3.1-mile Cape Alava Trail. Much of the 9.1-mile hike takes place in the woods on a wooden boardwalk, and this out of the way destination offers a memorable day hike or overnight camping trip.

If you do want to camp overnight here (and in many other places within the park) you'll need a Wilderness Permit. Reservations are required from May 1 through September 30 (360-565-3100). Other fees at the park include the entrance fee ($15 per vehicle for a single, seven-day visit and $5 for pedestrians, bicyclists and motorcyclists). This being a national park, you'll also have to keep your pets on a leash in the campgrounds and remember that they are not allowed on trails. Bicycling opportunities are limited to two trails within the park and the best one is near the Lake Crescent Lodge.

LAKE QUINAULT LODGE

PO Box 7 (345 South Shore Road), Quinault, WA 98575 / 360-288-2900
www.visitlakequinault.com

Lodging Prices: $$ to $$$$ Adventure Pricing: $

Situated on the shores of its 7-mile long namesake, you would think the Quinault Lake Lodge was the centerpiece of a national park. In terms of architecture, it looks a lot like some of the historic national park lodges. Like many of these buildings, it has a huge great room in the lodge with plush furniture and a massive stone fireplace where guests can socialize, read a book, play a game, or simply stare at the flames and relax after a day of hiking.

However, this lodge was constructed in 1926, before there was an Olympic National Forest or National Park. It was only after a visit here by President Franklin D. Roosevelt in 1937 that the park and forest gained national status. Today, there are 92 hotel rooms spread out among four buildings – all offering a comfortable place to spend the night. Many of the rooms offer lake views and several also have gas fireplaces. The lodge rooms are older but serviceable, while the Lakeside Lodge rooms are newer accommodations. The latter were built in 1991 and also have cable television available in case you can't make the complete break away from home.

The lodge's Roosevelt Room restaurant offers good views of the lake and specializes in quality Northwest cuisine with an emphasis on local seafood. A recommended specialty is the Cedar Plank Salmon for Two. After dinner, enjoy the indoor pool and two sauna rooms inside the lodge. If you really need to relax those muscles, make an appointment for a massage.

Outside is a huge, well-manicured lawn stretching towards the lake where you can rent a canoe, kayak, or sea cycle. Paddlers will enjoy the waters here. Often mist shrouded, the wide lake is surrounded by towering pine and cedar trees and bald eagles can often be seen soaring overhead. Other wildlife in the area includes Roosevelt elk, the infrequent black bear and occasionally, a bobcat that will inexplicably appear on the lawn outside the resort before returning to the dense forest.

Large Dolly Varden, cutthroat trout, and kokanee salmon are all found in this lightly fished lake. If you want to catch one, you'll need a Quinault tribal fishing permit that you can purchase from a nearby convenience store. The Quinault River below the lake gives up big steelhead between December and March but you have to hire a tribal guide to fish there.

The Quinault Rain Forest is what draws many here and it is truly unique. A temperate rain forest, it receives over 140 inches of rain a year. The wettest year in recent history occurred in 1999 when over 15 feet of rain fell in the Quinault Valley. All this rain makes for big timber. Thick stands of old-growth red and yellow cedar along with Douglas fir, Sitka spruce, mountain hemlock, and western hemlock can all be found in this vicinity. In fact, the largest examples of these species (in the United States and in some cases, the world) grow in the immediate vicinity. Even if you are short on time, make it a point to check out the largest Sitka spruce in the world. It can be reached by driving a short distance from the lodge towards the southeast end of the lake. Park here and walk a level path for less than five minutes to see it.

Hiking through the rain forest is very popular. One quick getaway can be found along the short half-mile Rain Forest Nature Trail. The loop trail is dotted with interpretive signs that explain the ecosystem of the rain forest that surrounds you. Other trails on the south shore of Lake Quinault include the 1.1-mile Lake Shore Trail, the 1.6-mile Falls Creek Trail where you can see both Falls Creek and Cascade Falls, or an extended loop that starts at the ranger station next to the lodge. This latter route encompasses all of these trails for a 4-mile walk. Other day hikes in the area include the 8.25-mile climb to the summit of Colonel Bob Mountain from Pete's Creek Trail. On a clear day you can view other mountain tops in the Olympic Mountain Range from this 4,492-foot peak and also take in Lake Quinault below.

The Lake Quinault Lodge is open throughout the year. During the summer there are free naturalist-led rainforest hikes. Saturday night campfire programs feature tribal storytellers and s'mores over the campfire for only $1 per adult (kids are free). From Thursday through Monday, up to ten people can pay $25 each to take a two-hour narrated cruise on a pontoon boat on Lake Quinault. These tours, as well as summer lodging at this historic inn, fill up fast and advance reservations are strongly recommended.

Getting There: Take US Highway 101 north from Aberdeen-Hoquiam for 40 miles. Turn right on South Shore Road and drive 2 more miles to the lodge.

This yellow lab is dwarfed by the world's largest spruce tree near Lake Quinault Lodge.

RAINFOREST PADDLERS

483 Upper Hoh Road, Forks, WA 98331 / 866-457-8398
www.rainforestpaddlers.com

Lodging Prices: $ to $$ Adventure Pricing: $ to $$

River rafting, kayaking, and estuary paddle trips are all offered by Rainforest Paddlers in and around the Olympic Peninsula's Hoh Rainforest. The company also offers bicycle rentals for those interested in exploring the roads of the rainforest outside of the car.

Christian and Anna Matsche own the company and live near the company headquarters. Anna may have come by her profession as an outdoors guide genetically. Her great grandmother, Minnie Peterson, was a well-known guide and outfitter on the Olympic Peninsula from 1927 until 1977, a time when women were rarely found doing such work. Anna grew up on a ranch just off the Hoh River where her parents still live.

The company's most popular offering is a half-day float through the rainforest. Book this and you'll spend nearly two hours on the water, floating 7 miles along the way. Your adventure starts at either 9:00am or 2:00pm. After a detailed safety briefing, you enter the water in a raft or inflatable kayak and drift down the green glacial waters of the Hoh River. Gravel bars and log jams are common, as are big pine, cedar, and spruce trees that are mixed in with white-barked alder on the banks of the river.

This trip is a great introduction to whitewater paddling and allows you to experience some unspoiled wilderness. For the first mile, you parallel a road but after that it's just you, the river, and the rainforest. Wildlife such as bald eagles, kingfishers, and waterfowl are common. Salmon and steelhead fin their way upstream, and the occasional deer, elk, or bear are sometimes seen along shore. A couple of Class II rapids present a bit of a challenge and will get you wet, with the most exciting whitewater waiting just before the take out. If you want a longer day on the water, you can also book a day-long trip on the Hoh where lunch is included in the price. The Hoh River trips are offered from February (when the water is clear and the weather crisp) until October.

Rainforest Paddlers also offers whitewater rafting from mid-February to June on two other Olympic Peninsula streams. The Elwha River has both Class II and III waters to navigate while the Sol Duc River offers the most exciting whitewater rafting west of Puget Sound with lots of Class III rapids.

A different paddling experience can be had from February to October where the Quillayute River meets the sea at La Push. The estuary kayaking tour starts at a tiny marina on the Quileute Tribal Reservation. From there you paddle a short distance up the river to explore the estuary. Wildlife is abundant. As you paddle, you may find yourself keeping pace with salmon heading upstream to spawn. Eagles and otter are frequently sighted, and Roosevelt elk also make an appearance at times. Towards the end of the half-day trip, you'll get a great view of the ocean sea stacks just offshore, which are large rocks that provide an important sanctuary for a number of ocean birds such as cormorant, common murre, and pigeon guillemot.

In addition to guided trips, Rainforest Paddlers also offers bike and kayak rentals by the hour or for the day. If you need a place to stay or eat, you can stop by the Hard Rain Café (360-374-9288 – www.hardraincafe.com) on the Upper Hoh River Road. In addition to basic food offerings, you can also purchase items at the small gift shop or stay in the campground there where hook-ups for RVs are available. If you prefer a roof over your head, they also have a cabin for rent.

One final thing worth noting is that some of your fellow paddlers may be speaking a different language. Anna's husband is of German descent and the couple is not only fluent in German, but speaks it at home. They cater to European travelers and up to ten percent of their clientele are German-speaking tourists.

Getting There: Follow US Highway 101 north to Kalaloch. Continue north for 21 miles and turn right on the Upper Hoh Road. Drive 4.9 miles east to the Peak 6 Adventure Store where most tours depart.

You can raft or kayak the Olympic Peninsula with Rainforest Paddlers.

KALALOCH LODGE

157151 US Highway 101, Forks, WA 98331 / 866-525-2562
www.visitkalaloch.com

Lodging Prices: $$ to $$$$ Adventure Pricing: N/A

If you like long walks along unspoiled ocean beaches you're bound to like Kalaloch. The tiny ocean front community along US Highway 101 is part of Olympic National Park. Stop here and you'll find a ranger station, campground, a well stocked convenience store that has unleaded gas, and the Kalaloch Lodge complex that is open all year.

The lodge sits on a small bluff above little Kalaloch Creek as it flows into the Pacific Ocean. Inside you'll find five rooms ranging from basic accommodations with a queen bed to the large Kalaloch Suite that has outstanding ocean views from the top floor of the lodge. A restaurant downstairs serves up three quality meals a day. Dinners are quite popular in the ocean view dining room and you'll want to make reservations during the summer months.

Running west and south from the lodge are 42 cabins, and almost all of them have a view of the ocean. At the end of the cabin area is the two-story Sea Crest building that offers hotel-room-style lodging. The cabins and the Sea Crest rooms sleep anywhere from four to six people. Most of the cabins have kitchens and many of the cabins and the nicer Sea Crest suites have fireplaces as well. Every room and cabin has a private bathroom and some have two bedrooms. By and large, the accommodations are "nice" though not "luxurious" and should serve a vacationing couple or family well. Pets are welcome and it's common to see playful dogs with their owners on the beach.

Almost 10 miles of beach can be explored from various trails around Kalaloch. The undeveloped shoreline gives the place a wild feel. Instead of beach homes, you see crashing waves, unspoiled sand, and large piles of driftwood that stack up against a thick forest of Sitka spruce. Ruby Beach lies 8 miles north of the Kalaloch Ranger Station. It is a rocky beach with spectacular views of large rocks in the ocean called sea stacks. Just off shore is Destruction Island, where a lighthouse warns mariners of the danger the island and rocky outcroppings pose to them. Beach Trail Four is south of Destruction Island and leads to an area full of tide pools. During low tides these small pools of seawater hold a variety of sea life. Small sculpin dart through the water among static barnacles, mussels, limpets, sea stars, urchins, and green anemones.

At certain times of the year, anglers come to Beach Trail Four to catch smelt in the surf with dip nets, while others fish the local beaches throughout the year for surf perch during high tides. Clamming, especially for tasty razor clams, is popular during low tides from fall through spring when the Department of Fish and Wildlife opens short seasons for them at Kalaloch's sandy beaches.

Beach Trails three and two are just north and south of the Lodge. These beaches, as well as the one directly in front of the lodge that is accessed by a short trail from the cabin area, offer lots of room to walk or sit on the driftwood and watch the crashing waves.

Beach Trail one lies 1.5 miles south of the ranger station. While it also leads to a sandy beach, it is of interest because of the burls – large bulbous growths – that appear on the Sitka spruce trees here between the highway and the beach. The sight of all of these burls gives the forest a strange, almost out-of-this-world appearance.

Not all of the trails lead to the beach. The Kalaloch Creek Nature Trail is a 1.2-mile loop trail that takes off from the campground just north of the lodge. It follows a well-maintained path through a thick coastal rainforest full of towering cedar trees. The silence of the forest, punctuated by bird songs, makes you feel like you are walking in a natural cathedral. Other visitors to Kalaloch drive north to explore the Hoh Rainforest or south to the Queets Rainforest, both of which lie within the boundaries of Olympic National Park.

From July through Labor Day, national park naturalists offer daily beach walks or tide pool interpretive sessions on the beach as well as guided hikes on the nature trail. During the winter months, the cabins and lodge at Kalaloch offer a great place for storm watching. Come March and April, visitors come in the hopes of seeing migrating gray whales in the distance. October through mid-May is considered the value season, when many of the cabins and rooms can be had for a comparative bargain.

Getting There: Follow US Highway 101 north from Aberdeen-Hoquiam for 76 miles to reach Kalaloch.

Perched just above the beach, the Kalaloch Lodge in Olympic National Park offers a memorable oceanfront experience.

SOL DUC HOT SPRINGS RESORT

P.O. Box 2169, Port Angeles, WA 98362 / 866-4-SOL-DUC
www.visitsolduc.com

Lodging Prices: $ to $$$$ Adventure Pricing: $

Olympic National Park offers myriad hiking, fishing, and wildlife watching options in a unique rainforest environment. One great place to stay while visiting is at the Sol Duc Hot Springs Resort. People have been coming to Sol Duc Hot Springs for over a century to soak in warm waters that some believed had "curative powers".

Today, guests can stay in modern cabins or an adjacent RV campground and make frequent visits to the relaxing hot springs. The water from the springs is piped into three shallow circular pools and the temperature stays between 100 and 104 degrees. Located next to the pools is a large heated freshwater swimming pool. The pool is well kept, and the hot spring pools are cleaned every day. If you need to unwind even more you can book a 30-minute or hour-long massage.

Hungry during the day? No worries, a deli on the pool deck offers a lunch menu. A day lodge next to the pools has a gift shop, very limited groceries, and a small sitting area. A restaurant inside provides the opportunity to eat breakfast, lunch, and dinner.

Guests can stay in one of the 32 small but clean cabins. Each is set up like a motel room with its own little building (two beds, a small sitting area, a bathroom, and small cabin porch). Some of the cabins have small kitchenettes and there is also a three-bedroom suite with a full kitchen available for rent. The cabins are set up in a grassy area south of the lodge. Some of the cabins are adjacent to the Sol Duc River, a small and scenic stream within the park boundaries. Picnic tables and large wooden swings dot the grounds and invite guests to linger outside. To further tempt people outside, there are no televisions, phones, or Internet access in any of the cabins.

The basic RV campground next to the lodge complex has room for 17 RVs with water and electric hook-ups. No tent camping is allowed here but a National Park Service campground is close by. Entrance into the hot springs and a hot breakfast are free for cabin guests. RV guests and the public can enjoy the hot springs and pool for a moderate fee.

There is a lot more to do outdoors than soak in the hot springs. Several trails provide good day hiking opportunities. Sol Duc Falls is a very popular destination that can be reached by hiking a 6-mile loop from the resort or by driving down Sol Duc Road to a trail head and walking just under a mile to the falls. Along the way you'll walk through a low elevation forest full of towering Douglas fir. Closer to the ground, sword, bracken, and other species of fern are found. The white flowers of bunchberry dogwood are a common and colorful sight in the forest from late spring through early summer.

Another short walk is found along the easy 0.6-mile Ancient Groves Nature Trail off of Sol Duc Road and the North Fork Sol Duc Trail will take you several miles along the part of the river it's named after. If you want to head towards alpine waters, Mink and Deer Lakes are in the area but require a bit of a climb through the forest to get to them. Mink Lake is a 2.6-mile one-way trip with a 1,500-foot elevation gain and Deer Lake is a longer 3.8-mile hike with 1,700 feet of terrain to climb. A longer day hike would take you 8 miles from the Sol Duc Falls Trailhead to Lunch Lake or Bogachiel Peak.

Both Mink and Deer Lakes offer trout fishing. Deer Lake can be particularly good for brook and rainbow trout. Fishing in the park is open from the last weekend of April until October 31. If you want to fish the streams in the park, feel free to do so from June 1 through the end of October. However, it is all catch-and-release fishing and you can't use bait. The one exception to the catch-and-release rule is if you hook into a steelhead. If it has a clipped adipose fin (meaning it's a hatchery fish), you are welcome to keep it and enjoy it baked, smoked, or barbequed. Check the National Park Service regulations for further details.

One place to see a lot of salmon and steelhead is at the Salmon Cascades. From late summer through early fall, these hefty fish work their way up these rapids and can be viewed from the riverbank just off the Sol Duc Road. Look, but don't get the urge to touch because no fishing is allowed here.

The Sol Duc Hot Springs Resort is open from late March until mid-October.

Getting There: Take US Highway 101 west from Port Angeles past Lake Crescent. Turn onto Sol Duc Road and travel 12 miles to the Hot Springs within Olympic National Park.

LAKE CRESCENT LODGE

416 Crescent Road, Port Angeles, WA 98363 / 360-928-3211
www.lakecrescentlodge.com

Lodging Prices: $$ to $$$ Adventure Pricing: $

One of the most talked about places to stay on the Olympic Peninsula, the charming Lake Crescent Lodge takes you back to another era. Originally known as Singer's Tavern, this sportsman's lodge was built in 1916 on the shores of 8.5-mile-long Lake Crescent. In 1937, President Franklin Roosevelt spent the night in one of Singer's cottages during a visit to what would soon be named Olympic National Park. Other notable guests over the years include Robert Kennedy, Supreme Court Justice William O. Douglas, and Laura Bush.

Today, Singer's Tavern is known as Lake Crescent Lodge in Olympic National Park. There are 52 overnight accommodations available for rent. The nicest are the four Roosevelt Cottages. Sleeping two to four people, these waterfront cabins have stone fireplaces and log furniture. Other amenities include a microwave, refrigerator, and a private bath. The Singer Tavern Cottages are close to the main lodge and can sleep anywhere from two to seven people. They also have private bathrooms and are tastefully decorated with alder wood furniture. Thirty motor lodge rooms provide basic motel-style accommodations and five clean, well-kept rooms with alder wood furniture are available on the second floor of the lodge itself, though you will be sharing a bathroom. In keeping with the national park experience, there are no televisions or telephones in any of the rooms, though wireless Internet access is available in the lodge itself if you have a laptop computer.

The lodge is a wonderful place to while away time. The main lobby is warm and inviting with dark hardwood floors and walls. A large sitting area is surrounded by northwestern Indian art ranging from colorful masks to small totem poles, all of which are for sale. Two large Roosevelt elk mounts stare out over the room and a big stone fireplace is lit upon request. A small bar in the big room is another reason to linger. Adjacent to the lobby is a covered sun porch. Full of windows, this bright room is filled with wicker furniture where guests sit and socialize or read while looking out at the lake. A nice restaurant serves three meals a day and offers a number of Northwest seafood dishes. Black-tailed deer often visit the resort grounds, as do raccoons that have been known to raid any food guests leave outside.

As nice as the lodge is, there is plenty of reason to explore beyond it. Surrounded by forest, 640-foot deep Lake Crescent is a good place to row a boat or paddle a kayak. Eagles are a common sight overhead, and you may see an otter sharing the water with you. Rowboats are available for rent at the lodge and kayaks can be rented from the Fairholme Store at the west end of the lake (the store is operated by the same company that runs the lodge). Anglers catch and release Beardslee rainbow trout and Crescenti cutthroat trout, strains unique to Lake Crescent that weigh up to 16 pounds. While motorboats are allowed on the lake, personal watercraft are not, making the lake less noisy than you would expect in the summer.

Around here, hiking and bicycling are just as popular as paddling and fishing. The Spruce Railroad Trail is a 4-mile (one way) path on the northwest side of the lake and is the only designated bike trail in the national park. Marymere Falls is a must-see destination for most lodge visitors. Cascading 90 feet down, the falls can be seen after an easy 0.75-mile walk through the forest. The short 0.67-mile Moments in Time Nature Trail gives those with limited time good views of the lake and the chance to visit old homestead sites near the lodge complex. If you want a workout, follow the Mount Storm King Trail 1.7 steep miles to a ridge overlooking Lake Crescent. The Pyramid Peak Trail can be found on the north shore of Lake Crescent. After climbing 2,600 feet in 3.5 miles you'll reach an old World War II aircraft spotter station at the top of the peak. From here, you can enjoy views of both Lake Crescent and the Strait of Juan de Fuca towards Vancouver Island in Canada.

Crescent Lake Lodge is open from mid-May to mid-October. The Roosevelt Cottages are also available for rent (without any other services) during the winter months for visitors who want an isolated getaway on the lake.

Getting There: The lodge is a 30-minute drive west of Port Angeles along US Highway 101.

The historic Lake Crescent Lodge is a great place to stay while visiting Olympic National Park.

Outside the National Park

Dungeness National Wildlife Refuge and Recreation Area

Dungeness National Wildlife Refuge
33 South Barr Road, Port Angeles, WA 98362 / 360-457-8451
http://pacific.fws.gov/refuges/dungeness

Dungeness Recreation Area – Contact Clallam County Parks
PO Box 863, Port Angeles, WA 98362 / 360-683-5847
www.clallam.net

Lodging Prices

Adventure Pricing

One of the longer spits in North America is found at the Dungeness National Wildlife Refuge. Hiking or kayaking to the lighthouse near the end of the 5-mile sandy spit are both popular activities, but are not the only attractions of this unique place on the north end of the Olympic Peninsula.

Most people traveling to the spit first go through the Dungeness Recreation Area. Adjacent to the refuge, this 216-acre property is one of the only places on the Olympic Peninsula where you can hunt pheasants on public land. Waterfowl hunting is also permitted here, as is horseback riding, hiking, and mountain biking along several trails that go along bluffs, upland meadows, and forest. To reduce conflicts between different user groups, hunting is only allowed on Saturdays, Sundays, and holidays between October and January. The Clallam County Parks Department also operates a campground here with 65 campsites (no-hookups) open from February 1 through September 30.

Continuing past the campground you'll soon come to a parking area for the Dungeness National Wildlife Refuge. The vast majority come here to hike to Dungeness Spit. The first half-mile of the hike goes through forested land before heading downhill to the sandy, 5.5-mile long spit. You are allowed to hike and fish year round along the north side of the spit for 5 miles until you reach the New Dungeness Light Station. Built in 1857, the 63-foot tall lighthouse is staffed by live-in volunteers who give daily tours from 9:00am to 5:00pm. Other portions of the refuge near the base of the spit are open seasonally for horseback riding (by reservation only – call 360-457-8451) along with fishing, hiking, and wildlife viewing.

If you don't want to hike to the lighthouse, you can kayak to it. Public day-use beaches and boat launches are available at Cline Spit and Dungeness Landing south of the spit. You can paddle to a designated boat landing zone near the light station throughout the year, but you'll need an advance reservation to do so (360-457-8451). Other places to paddle or explore by small boat are around Graveyard Spit, a southern attachment of Dungeness Spit. The water around it is a no-wake zone and it is closed to boat access from October 1 until May 14.

While hiking and paddling to the lighthouse are both popular draws, the wildlife at the refuge is the real reason this place is protected. Some 244 different bird species, 44 land mammals, and 11 marine mammal species frequent the refuge. The long sand spit serves as a boundary for a bay and tide flats used by a vast array of birds to include Pacific black brant, wigeon, common goldeneye, bald eagle, double-crested cormorant, gulls, Caspian tern, great blue heron, black oyster catcher, and lots of shore birds to include dunlin, sanderling, short-billed dowitcher, black-bellied plover, and western sandpiper. On the Strait of Juan de Fuca side of the spit, you may also see rhinoceros auklet and pigeon guillemot. Mammals on the refuge include black-tailed deer on land and harbor seals by sea, some of which haul themselves out at the end of the spit.

Pets are allowed in the recreation area, as are firearms during hunting season, but neither are allowed on the refuge. There is also a $3 user fee if you want to hike the trails of the refuge, unless you have a Federal duck stamp or other recognized pass.

Getting There: Take US Highway 101 west from Sequim. Turn north on Kitchen-Dick Road and travel 3 miles until it turns into Lotzgesell Road. The main gate to the Recreation Area and Refuge will be on your left.

JAMBO'S SPORTFISHING

PO Box 1537 Duvall, WA 98019 / 425-788-5955
www.jambossportfishing.com

Lodging Prices: N/A   Adventure Pricing: $$$

Whether you want halibut out of Neah Bay or salmon in the Sound, Jambo's Sportfishing is a good bet. Michael Jamboretz has been fishing the waters of the Pacific Northwest for over 30 years and has a 100-ton Masters License from the US Coast Guard.

If you ask what separates him from the other charter boat operators in the area, he'll tell you about his boat and his equipment. The Malia Kai (which means "calm ocean") is a 37-foot wide-bodied Delta charter boat. Built in the 1970s, these boats are able to stand up to the fierce waters of Alaska's Bering Sea. Jamboretz recently refitted the engines, and the boat is now powered by two turbo-charged 267-horsepower John Deere marine engines. Jamboretz takes pride in fishing with the best tackle he can get his hands on; an example of this is the expensive G Loomis rods he uses for bottom fish and halibut.

From May through August, you'll find Jamboretz fishing for halibut out of Neah Bay on the northwest part of the Olympic Peninsula. Jamboretz fishes both US and Canadian waters for these bottomfish. They get pretty big on the US side, ranging from 25 to 70 pounds. However, the limit on the U.S. side is one fish and the seasons have been short lived as of late. Because of this, Jamboretz spends a lot of time fishing on the Canadian side of the border for halibut. While the fish tend to be a bit smaller (averaging 20 to 30 pounds), you can keep two and the season is 10 months long. If all the anglers manage to get their limits, they'll fillet one and cook it for lunch during the two-plus-hour ride back to port. That's about the freshest seafood you'll ever get. Occasionally, if conditions are right, anglers on the Malia Kai will also get the chance for a few bonus lingcod, another very tasty fish that grows to a large size.

Come August, Jambo's Sportfishing moves from Neah Bay to the Everett Marina. From there, Jamboretz takes clients into Puget Sound for salmon. In the early fall, he targets silvers around Possession Bar and the south end of Whidbey Island. During odd-numbered years, pink salmon are also caught – usually in very good numbers. From November through February Jamboretz goes after blackmouth (chinook salmon). He finds these fish not only around Possession Bar but also in the Saratoga Passage. Generally, trolled spoons, plugs, or candle-fish-type hoochies will get salmon in the boat.

Jamboretz takes only six clients at a time on his charters, ensuring a more personalized experience for the angler. Current rates can be found on his website. Canadian fishing licenses can be purchased on the Internet via a link on his site.

Getting There: Take US Highway 101 west from Port Angeles to State Highway 112. Follow the State Highway to the marina in Neah Bay. The Port of Everett Marina can be reached from Interstate 5. Take Exit 193 and take Pacific Avenue towards the city center. Turn right on West Marine View Drive and take a left at 18th Street, which is the entrance into the marina.

Captain Michael Jamboretz (right) and his deckhand aboard the Malia Kai.

Van Riper's Resort

P.O. Box 246 (280 Front Street), Sekiu, WA 98381 / 360-963-2334
www.vanripersresort.com

Lodging Prices: $ to $$$ Adventure Pricing: $ to $$

Generations of saltwater salmon anglers have come to Sekiu for memorable fishing vacations; and while this waterfront town may not be a thriving metropolis today, it still hosts four different fishing resorts and a marina with plenty of moorage.

Van Riper's is the best place to stay in this small town on the north end of the Olympic Peninsula. The resort has a waterfront motel with 16 guest rooms, 46 full RV sites on the water and an additional mix of 35 tent and RV sites just up the hill. The rooms are clean and modern with private bathrooms and come equipped with kitchenettes (though you'll have to bring your own cookware).

Two of the motel's rentals are worth talking about in more detail. The first is a one-bedroom Penthouse Suite with three beds, lots of windows and a private deck that looks out over the marina and Clallam Bay. The second is the Water View Suite that sleeps up to eight people. This one features three bedrooms, five beds, an extra large kitchen with a dishwasher, an additional half bath, and a private deck above the marina.

There is a boat launch at the resort and dock space to moor your vessel. If you don't have your own boat, you can rent a 16-footer with or without a 15-horsepower outboard motor. Inside the main office, you'll also find a store with groceries, fishing tackle, and advice about where you can catch dinner.

Fishing starts in mid-April with anglers going west of the Sekiu River mouth for lingcod. On May 1, fishing opens in the waters off Sekiu for both lingcod and black rockfish. While these fish provide great table fare, the crowds don't really start showing up until halibut fishing opens. Anglers come in good numbers to catch 20- to 40-pound fish in 150 to 250 feet of water during a season that varies in length. As big as these fish are, the halibut around here can get much bigger. In June of 2005, one lucky angler landed a 246-pound brute off of Slip Point near the resort.

In July the salmon season opens and the crowds come in earnest. According to resort owner Chris Mohr, the kings (chinook) average 22 to 32 pounds while the silvers (coho) can run up to a respectable 19 pounds. Some weigh more than that. The state record coho salmon (weighing 25 pounds, 5 ounces) was caught off of Sekiu by a fisherman in a Van Riper's rental boat. Most people troll close to the bottom for the kings and work the upper 60 feet of the water for the silvers.

While fishing brings most people to Sekiu, there are also several hiking trails in the area. The closest is the One Mile Beach Trail. It starts out on an old railroad grade behind Olson's Resort in Sekiu. The level, forested trail runs a mile to One Mile Beach, and offers access along the way to caves, tide pools, and the beach where you can look north towards Vancouver Island and observe the occasional otter or sea lion. During low tide, you can walk an additional mile from One Mile Beach to Eagle Point.

A drive of about 20 miles from Sekiu west past the small fishing port of Neah Bay will bring you to Cape Flattery, the furthest point northwest in the lower 48 States. After a 0.75-mile walk along a trail built by the Makah tribe, you can view a wild, scenic coastal vista from several observation decks. Bring your binoculars because gray (and other) whales are sometimes spotted as well sea lions, sea otters, and sea birds such as puffin, pelagic cormorant, and pigeon guillemot. Several other hikes within Olympic National Park and Olympic National Forest (Lake Ozette, Marymere Falls, Sol Duc Falls) are less than an hour's drive away.

Van Riper's Resort is open all year. During fishing season there is a two-night minimum stay in the motel over the weekend (holiday weekends have a three-night minimum). Pets are welcome at the resort, but not in the motel.

Getting There: Drive west on US Highway 101 through Port Angeles. Turn onto State Highway 112 and follow it west 46 miles to Sekiu. Van Riper's Resort is on Front Street.

PISCATORIAL PURSUITS

Bob Ball – PO Box 919, Forks, WA 98331 / 866-347-4232
www.piscatorialpursuits.com

Lodging Prices: N/A   Adventure Pricing: $$$ to $$$$

In their listing of the top 25 west coast fishing guides, the *Salmon and Steelhead Journal* describes Bob Ball as "...one of the true nice guys in Washington guiding circles. Ball has the reputation of being able to catch fish in all types of situations." Ball is a busy man, getting clients into fish from November through April on the Olympic Peninsula near Forks and then heading up to Alaska to fish for salmon, rainbow trout, and halibut from the middle of May through August.

Ball has been a full-time fishing guide since 1994. Prior to that time he attended the University of Washington, graduating with a bachelor's degree with an emphasis in fisheries, business, and communications. In addition to being an ardent Huskies fan, Ball is also a husband and a father and maintains a website with a very active forum dedicated to salmon and steelhead fishing.

When guiding in Washington, Ball focuses on four rivers on the western side of the Olympic Peninsula: the Hoh, Bogachiel, Calawah, and Sol Duc. Book a trip with him and you'll get to spend the day in his 16-foot Wild Hair aluminum drift boat while he works the oars for a downstream float. Bring your foul-weather gear, because this part of the Washington is known for its abundance of cool rain. Fortunately, a propane heater in Ball's boat will help keep you warm. No matter how much it pours, at least one of the rivers Ball works is generally fishable for salmon or steelhead at any given time.

Serious stream fishing begins in October on the Peninsula with anglers going after chinook and coho salmon. The chinook come in first, averaging 20 pounds or better though there are a fair number of fish over 35 pounds and on rare occasion, a leviathan approaching 60. As October turns into November, coho (silver) salmon become more plentiful. These energetic fish average 10 to 11 pounds, but can top the 20-pound mark. Ball's favorite methods for catching the salmon involve back trolling sardine-wrapped Kwikfish, tossing spinners, or twitching jigs (a method that involves casting a salmon hoochie with a jig head and twitching it during the retrieve).

Steelhead season gets into full swing around Thanksgiving. The hatchery fish flood the river first. These bright silver-hued fish average 6 to 8 pounds with the occasional big fish getting into the low teens. By mid-January wild steelhead are in all four rivers. If you are looking for the steelhead of a lifetime, this is the place to come. The average wild fish averages 10 to 12 pounds and you have a legitimate chance at cracking the 20-pound mark fishing on the peninsula. The peak of the run usually arrives in mid-March, but trophy steelhead can be caught through the month of April.

If you go out with Ball, you'll likely catch your steelhead while drift or float fishing but if you prefer, you can swing a wet fly downstream for your fish.

Getting There: Destinations vary, but you'll probably meet Ball in the morning around Forks – a Clallam County town with a variety of overnight accommodations.

Bob Ball with a gigantic Olympic Peninsula steelhead.

Fort Flagler and Fort Worden State Parks

Fort Flagler
10541 Flagler Road, Nordland, WA 98358 / 360-385-1259
www.parks.wa.gov

Fort Worden
200 Battery Way, Port Townsend, WA 98368 / 360-344-4434
www.fortworden.org

Lodging Prices

Adventure Pricing

How about an outdoors vacation by the sea with some military history thrown in for good measure? That's what you'll get at Fort Flagler and Fort Worden at the northeastern end of the Olympic Peninsula. Both forts were built at the turn of the 19th century to defend the cities and shipyards of Puget Sound from enemy ships. Coastal artillery pieces that could fire up to 10 miles with deadly accuracy were mounted at both posts and the guns were sighted to interlock with the guns from Fort Casey across Admiralty Inlet.

Fort Worden was the headquarters of the Puget Sound Harbor Defenses. As such it was the largest coastal installation in Washington. Both Fort Worden and Fort Flagler were busiest during World War I, became quiet for two decades, and then had a revival of activity and troops during the Second World War. The last troops left these posts in the 1950s. Today, the State Parks Commission operates all three coastal forts with historical education, rest, and recreation being the orders of the day.

Fort Flagler

Removed from any major towns, 800-acre Fort Flagler is an inviting destination. History buffs will enjoy seeing the old buildings of the post on an expansive grassy bluff above Admiralty Inlet. Several of them are barracks

converted into retreat centers with names like Camp Wilson, Camp Richmond and Camp Hoskins. The largest (Hoskins) can accommodate 180 people. Families may be interested in renting the old Non-commissioned Officer's Quarters or Hospital Steward's House, both built between 1900 and 1903 and accommodating four people in a Victorian setting. Facilities include a kitchen, bathroom, living room, and bedrooms. The adjacent Waterway House, built in 1940, houses up to eight people in four bedrooms. Reservations are needed well in advance to stay at one of these vacation homes. The prices are low (considering what you are getting) and the kitchens are stocked with basic utensils, a stove, refrigerator, microwave, and coffee maker. You will, however, need to bring your own towels and linens.

Fort Flagler has plenty of room for camping, as well. Two group camps can handle 40 and 100 people respectively. Individuals can head to the upper camp with 47 tent sites in the woods or to the grassy lower camp area which has 68 sites (15 with full or partial hook-ups) for both tents and RVs next to the beach. Reservations are accepted in the summer but the campground is closed from November 1 through February.

Also in this lower section of the park is a canteen that stocks groceries and serves hot food and espresso from Memorial Day until early September. The picnic tables and fire pits near the canteen can be used during the day, and flying kites or

A coastal artillery gun at Fort Flagler stands watch over Admiralty Inlet.

kite-boarding in the waters of Kilisut Harbor are things you can try in this breezy place. Other amenities of interest in this part of the park include two boat launches, a moorage dock, and buoys. A fish- and shellfish-cleaning station is also located near the boat launch.

If you like beachcombing, you can wander along the spit that separates the bay and harbor near the camping area. It's also a good place to harvest clams in the spring and crabbing is good just offshore in the summer. Another beach walk is possible between the post's old pier and Marrowstone Point Lighthouse. The sandy beach is a great place to amble and if you're an angler, the waters off the point are a good place to cast for salmon in the summer.

A series of trails covering over 6 miles can be explored separately or together. Many of them lead to Fort Flagler's former gun emplacements. The bluff trail is the longest of these hiking-biking trails, going 1.5 miles along the bluffs above Port Townsend Bay past several gun and searchlight sites. While you are looking at the gun emplacements, be sure to take a look at the two 3-inch guns at Battery Wansboro and the big 120-millimeter anti-aircraft gun near the park office. A flashlight will come in handy if you want to explore the bunkers of Battery Bankhead, which used to house 12-inch mortars. More information about the military history of this post is available at the park museum, which also hosts interpretive programs during the summer.

Wildlife viewing is also good at both Fort Flagler and Fort Worden. Where soldiers once stood on parade grounds, deer now graze. The bluffs above the water once scanned by artillery spotters are now home to eagles looking towards the water below for their next meal. Other birds you may see include colorful American goldfinch, belted kingfishers and, at Fort Flagler, purple marten.

Fort Worden

Fort Worden was a large installation with lots of well-kept barracks and quarters for the soldiers that were stationed there. Today, this housing is the nucleus of a huge conference center. Quarters with anywhere from one to eleven bedrooms can be rented by groups, families, or individuals. All of them have kitchens with coffee makers, microwaves, and basic utensils. As you might imagine, these rentals are very popular and reserving them months in advance is prudent.

To learn more about the history of the coastal forts, check out the Puget Sound Coast Artillery Museum next to the parade grounds. The nearby Commanding Officer's Quarters are also open to the public and allow you to get a glimpse into the daily life of a senior officer and his family during the Victorian age. If it all looks somewhat familiar, there may be a reason for that. The popular movie, "An Officer and a Gentlemen" starring Richard Gere and Debra Winger was filmed here in 1981. Like Fort Flagler, there are a number of gun emplacements that can be explored, though none of the emplacements at this fort have any cannon in them.

Camping is also an option. Eighty spots are divided between a 30-site campground near the conference center and a 50-site camping area near the beach and Point Wilson. All of them have hook-ups for RVs and advance reservations are accepted.

The lower section of the park below the post housing is a great place to recreate. There is a beach to explore and it's possible to see both seals and sea lions just off shore from the Point Wilson Lighthouse. The current lighthouse was built here in 1913. It became automated (and closed to the public) in 1976. If you get hungry, the Cable House Canteen sells limited groceries and serves hot food during the summer months. If you are in the mood for kayaking you can rent one in the summer next to the canteen. A paddle from here to the Victorian seaport of Port Townsend and back is a great way to spend an hour or two and a boat launch across from the canteen allows you to get larger craft onto the water.

There is also a large pier here as well. You can fish for greenling, sculpin, rockfish, and dogfish sharks with some success or drop a crab ring into the water during the summer to catch a few crustaceans for dinner. Pigeon guillemots, a black and white seabird, nest in boxes built under the pier and sometimes river otters will bask on the floating dock below the pier, too.

The main attraction on this pier, though, is the Port Townsend Marine Science Center (360-385-5582 – www.ptmsc.org). For a small fee, you can come inside from April through October to see, and in many cases touch, marine life found in this area. The touch tanks are popular with kids and adults alike. You can reach into the cool seawater to touch sea stars, sea anemones, sea urchins, and shrimp. There are also several large aquariums with micro-habitats representing those found in this region. They include pilings, eelgrass, and kelp beds along with a representative sample of the fish, crustaceans, and shellfish that live in these environments.

Both Fort Worden and Fort Flagler are open all year. Camping closes at Fort Flagler from November through February.

Getting There: Fort Worden is just outside of Port Townsend on the northeastern tip of the Olympic Peninsula. Follow State Highway 20 to town and follow signs from there to the park. To reach Fort Flagler, follow State Highway 116 from Port Hadlock onto Marrowstone Island. Follow Flagler Road to the park.

The stately military quarters at Fort Worden are now part of a conference center.

The Eastern Peninsula

Olympic National Forest – Hood Canal Ranger District – Quilcene Office
295142 Highway 101 South, Quilcene, WA 98376 / 360-765-2200
www.fs.fed.us/r6/olympic

The natural wonders of Olympic National Park are known to many. However, there are other parts of the Olympic Peninsula worth exploring where wilderness areas and a national forest offer a multitude of experiences for hikers, climbers, anglers, and nature lovers. If you are wondering where to start, head towards Hoodsport, a good reference point for three general areas full of outdoor recreation.

The Olympic National Forest covers much of this area. Visitors here may see black-tailed deer, skunks, and black bear at lower elevations, while hikers going higher up might glimpse mountain goats or Olympic marmot. Bird watchers will find belted kingfishers along streams and hear the songs of wrens, Wilson's warblers, Pacific-slope flycatchers, or Swainson's thrushes around them. That rapid knocking noise among the maples may be northern flickers or red-breasted sapsuckers, and time spent watching the rivers will likely be rewarded by the sight of surfacing salmon, steelhead, or trout.

The Brothers Wilderness

The first general area to explore lies within the Brothers Wilderness. Here, you'll find two mountains of interest to climbers and hikers with a love for elevation. One of them is Mt. Jupiter, a 5,701-foot mountain between Hoodsport and Quilcene. You get there by taking Mt. Jupiter Road from US Highway 101 some 22 miles north of Hoodsport. After a 2.5-mile drive, you'll reach a gate. If it's open, drive another 2.5 miles to the trailhead. If not, get out and start hiking. Once you reach the trailhead, you'll follow a trail 7.2 miles to the summit. No technical gear is needed to get to the top, but you'll want to be in decent shape since you will gain 3,700 feet of elevation along the way. If you are interested in fishing, a scramble 900 feet down from the trail to the Jupiter Lakes will get you to some trout-filled waters.

If you are looking for a place to stay, follow Forest Service Road 2510 just south of Mt. Jupiter Road. It leads to Collins Campground (with 16 campsites along the Duckabush River) and to the historic Interrorem Cabin. Built in 1907 as the first administrative building for the Olympic National Forest, it is now available for rent as a primitive cabin. Two short trails starting from the cabin are less than a mile in length and offer a good opportunity to get out and stretch your legs.

Another mountain to climb is found at The Brothers, in the southern part of the wilderness area that bears its name. You can access the trail to the mountain on Forest Service Road 25 through the Hamma Hamma Recreation Area, 14 miles north of Brinnen

Pigeon guillemot can be viewed in the saltwater off the Olympic Peninsula.

Hoodsport. You'll follow the Forest Service Road 8 miles to the Lena Lake Trailhead. Lena Lake is a great destination in its own right, offering a good family hike to a place where you can fish for trout and enjoy the beauty of the 55-acre lake surrounded by second-growth and old-growth forest. You can camp at one of the 28 campsites here after a 3.2-mile jaunt or push on another 0.4 mile to reach the Brothers Trail at the north end of the lake. From here, you'll follow a 1.5-mile climbing route to the peak. If you intend to climb it, the Forest Service recommends having the appropriate climbing gear (helmet, ice axe, and climbing rope) to safely reach the 6,866-foot summit.

The Skokomish Wilderness

Other trips in the Hamma Hamma Recreation Area (and south of the Brothers Wilderness) include a 4.4-mile hike along a primitive trail to the Mildred Lakes or a strenuous 3-mile hike on the Putvin Trail towards the Lake of the Angels within the Olympic National Park. These trails lie within the Mount Skokomish Wilderness, which has over 12 miles of trails for hikers. The Lena Creek and Hamma Hamma River campgrounds offer nearby places to pitch a tent or park a small RV near the river. The Hamma Hamma Cabin, located by the latter campground, can be rented for a low price, sleeps six, and has two bedrooms along with a flush toilet (both the Hamma Hamma and Interrorem Cabin can be reserved online at www.reserveusa. com or 877-444-6777).

Mount Ellinor

One more mountain to climb on the eastern end of the Olympics is 5,944-foot Mt. Ellinor. To get there, take State Route 119 from Hoodsport past Lake Cushman and follow it to Forest Service Road 24. Turn right and go 1.6 miles to Big Creek Road. Take a left and drive north to the upper or lower trailhead. You'll have to travel 3.1 miles from the lower trailhead or 1.6 miles from the upper trailhead to reach the summit. In the summer, you can hike a steep trail to the top through meadows full of wildflowers like aster, buttercup, heather, and bluebell. However, during the winter you'll have to make your way up a chute where an ice axe, good boots, and climbing skills are necessary.

Camping and accommodations are available at Lake Cushman (See the Lake Cushman Resort entry for details) or at Big Creek, a Forest Service campground near the intersection of Forest Service Road 24 and State Route 119. There are 23 wooded sites available for campers and RVs up to 30 feet long at campground. There are also two loop trails here; one is an easy 1.1-mile route and the other is 4.3 miles long. Hike on either and you'll pass among maple, western hemlock, red alder, Douglas fir, and western red cedar trees while enjoying views of Big Creek.

LAKE CUSHMAN RESORT

**4621 N. Lake Cushman Road, Hoodsport, WA 98548 / 800-588-9630 or
360-877-9630
www.lakecushman.com**

Lodging Prices: $ to $$ Adventure Pricing: $ to $$

Hoodsport and Hood Canal are known mainly for saltwater fun, but the nearby Lake Cushman Resort is a great destination in its own right; offering a variety of prospects for paddling, fishing, and hiking.

The year-round resort sits on 1,400 feet of shoreline and encompasses 10 wooded acres. There is a good seasonal boat launch and a marina where you can dock your boat. If you didn't bring your own craft, you can rent a canoe, kayak, paddle boat, row boat, or 15-foot aluminum fishing boat with a 9.9-horsepower outboard motor. A large patio outside the resort's store is a good place to have a snack and look out over the lake or towards the swimming area, a popular hangout on warm summer days.

The resort has 52 tent sites and 20 RV sites (five of which are lakefront) with water and electrical hook-ups. There are also 11 cabins if you want a fixed roof over your head. All of them have bathrooms, refrigerators, and kitchenettes. Most are one-bedroom rentals sleeping up to four people, though there is a two-bedroom cabin and two of the cabins on the resort can be rented together as a three-bedroom accommodation. Some of the cabins have woodstoves and several are also on the water. You will need to bring your own cookware and if more than two people are staying in a cabin, you'll want to bring extra towels and bedding. You are welcome to bring your pet along for a small fee as long as you keep it on a leash.

While some visitors come to the 4,000-acre reservoir for motorized water sports, others are drawn here for canoeing and kayaking. With 22 miles of shoreline to explore, there are plenty of places to which one can paddle. Fishing, however, is what brings most people onto the water. The season never closes here and anglers have a shot at kokanee salmon (averaging 8 or 9 inches), rainbow trout (that commonly run up to 15 inches) and landlocked chinook salmon. Called Cushman kings, these salmon are usually caught by trollers using a downrigger to fish a cut-plug herring behind a flasher in the deep waters of the reservoir. The salmon get big, and 20-plus pounders have been caught in the last few years. The best time to fish for all of these species is from May through September.

Hiking opportunities abound nearby in the Olympic National Forest and at the southwestern end of Olympic National Park (see the Eastern Peninsula entry for further details). There's a good chance you'll see wildlife too. Deer, elk, and raccoon are all common sights in the area, and on rare occasions, you might even see a cougar or bobcat.

Getting There: Take Interstate 5 to Olympia. From there follow US Highway 101 northwest to Hoodsport. Take a left onto State Highway 119 and drive 4.7 miles uphill to the resort.

Korey and Rick Peele of Bremerton take one of the resort's canoes out on Lake Cushman.

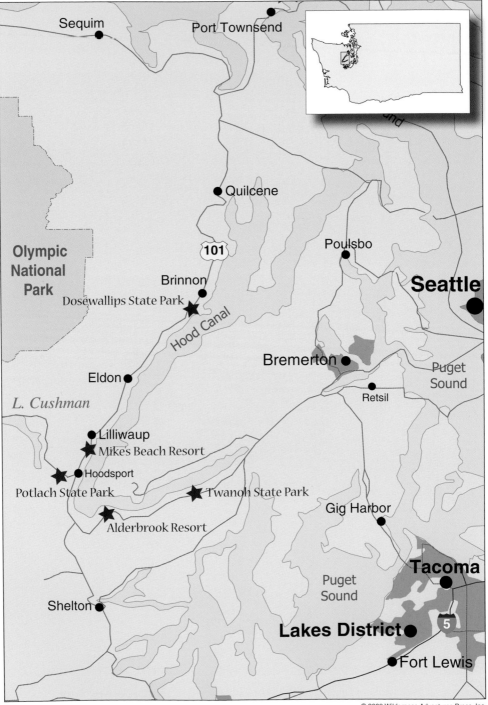

Sequim

Port Townsend

Quilcene

101

Poulsbo

Olympic
National
Park

Brinnon

Seattle

Dosewallips State Park

Hood Canal

Bremerton

Puget
Sound

Eldon

Retsil

L. Cushman

Lilliwaup

Mike's Beach Resort

Hoodsport

Potlach State Park

Twanoh State Park

Alderbrook Resort

Gig Harbor

Tacoma

Puget
Sound

5

Shelton

Lakes District

Fort Lewis

Hood Canal

Hood Canal State Parks

Twanoh State Park
12190 East State Route 106, Union, WA 98592 / 360-275-2222
www.parks.wa.gov
Potlatch State Park
21020 US Highway 101 (PO Box 1051), Hoodsport, WA 98548 / 360-877-5361
www.parks.wa.gov
Dosewallips State Park
PO Box 969 (or US Highway 101, Dosewallips River Bridge), Brinnon, WA 98320 /
360-796-4415
www.parks.wa.gov

Lodging Prices

Whether you enjoy shellfishing, hook-and-line angling, scuba diving, kayaking, wildlife watching, or hiking, the three state parks along Hood Canal offer a wonderful opportunity to enjoy them all. Twanah, Potlatch, and Dosewallips are not the only state parks along Hood Canal, but they are all very good ones that allow you to experience the best outdoors activities in this region.

Hood Canal is not a canal per se, but rather a saltwater fjord connected to Puget Sound between the Olympic and Kitsap Peninsulas. Over 60 miles long and 600 feet deep in places, the sheltered waters of Hood Canal are a favorite destination for divers who get to see a vast array of marine life. Kayakers and seafood lovers come for an abundant supply of clams and oysters. Dungeness and rock crab are two other shellfish you can catch, along with shrimp. The short shrimp season generally takes place in May and crabs can usually be retained between July 1 and Labor Day. Fishing can be good for some species – especially for chum salmon – around Dosewallips and Twanoh State Parks and near Hoodsport from October through November. There is also lots of hiking within the state parks and in the Olympic National Forest west of Hood Canal.

There is a variety of wildlife to be seen inside the parks. Raccoons and squirrels are common around the campgrounds and occasionally you'll see a black bear too. In the air, bald eagles can be seen flying over the water, and within the canal itself harbor seals are abundant.

Twanoh State Park is near the southeastern end of Hood Canal. The shallow waters here allow the water temperature to climb above 70 degrees during prolonged hot spells, making the swimming beach a very popular place. The day-use area at this park fronts 3,167 feet of pebble beach shoreline that is open for clamming in the late summer and generally open for oysters all year. If you want some of these latter shellfish, you'll be limited to 18 and you need to shuck them on the beach where you find them. There is a pier and dock where you can moor your boat for a reasonable fee or fish for pile perch for free. Other fishing is possible from shore in the saltwater near the mouth of Twanoh Creek. Chum salmon come into the freshwater creek to spawn, and anglers can have a good time hooking these tough-fighting fish from late October through early November. You can't fish in the small creek for these fish, but watching the salmon that have made their way into the tiny waterway is a fun treat.

A boat launch at the park is one of the few public launches in the southern end of Hood Canal. Also in the day-use area are log-hewn restrooms, kitchen shelters, and a picnic shelter, all constructed by the Civilian Conservation Corps between 1933 and 1942. Picnic tables sit on the grass and farther in among tall Douglas fir trees you'll find a tennis court and concession stand that is open in the summer.

On the other side of the highway is a campground with 47 separate sites in a wooded setting. Twenty-two of them are utility sites and all of them are available on a first-come, first-served basis. Two loop trails near the campground give you the chance to walk for 1.25 or 2 miles. The 187-acre park is open all year.

Heading up the canal you'll next come across Potlatch State Park. Only a short distance from Hoodsport, the park is named after the native-American tradition of having a gift giving festival. Several of these events took place at this site as late as the 1860s. Like Twanoh, the day-use area of this park is on the saltwater side of the highway and the camping area is on the other. The 37 non-reservable campsites include 18 utility sites, 17 standard sites, and 2 primitive sites. There are also two 1.5-mile-long single-track trails here that can be used by both hikers and mountain bicyclists.

The day-use area has expansive views of the saltwater that can be enjoyed from picnic tables on the grass. If it rains, there is one small picnic shelter that will squeeze in 25 people. Many people come here for the shellfish. The public beach is 9,570 feet long and seems to consist of oyster shells and river-rock-sized stones. The kids will enjoy turning over the rocks to find small crabs while the adults shuck oysters on the beach or dig up Manila, native littleneck, horse, butter, bent nose or eastern soft shell clams. The limit here is also 18 oysters per person, and you can harvest either 40 clams or 10 pounds of them, whichever comes first. The season for both oysters and clams at this state park runs from April 1 through August 31. There are emergency closures at times, so you may want to call 800-562-5632 or 360-236-3330 before you make the drive out to this region for shellfishing.

Finally, you'll find Dosewallips State Park north of the other parks at Brinnon. The Dosewallips River flows through the park property and is used by steelhead along with spawning chinook, coho, and chum salmon. Fishing is a possibility, but you have to use single barbless hooks, no bait, and where you fish in the park dictates whether or not you can keep the fish you may catch (check the regulations for further details).

On the west side of Highway 101 is a large campground with 130 campsites. Sixty of them have full or partial hook-ups for RVs. Many of these are found in a pleasant, grassy area with several shade trees. The rest of the campsites are used by tent campers and some of these are right along the river. If you want more comfortable camping try to rent one of the three canvas platform tents. Unlike the other two state parks, the sites here can be reserved in advance.

If you are in the mood for a walk, there are two hiking trails that take off from the campground. The Steam Donkey Loop Trail covers 3.5 miles west of the campground, while the shorter Maple Valley Trail loops around for 1.5 miles. The latter trail is named for a canopy of maple trees that can be seen from a particular viewpoint along the way.

To the east of the campground (on the other side of the highway) is a small day-use area that has a picnic area. There is also a separate saltwater access area that is a more popular destination. This latter access area is a parking lot just north of the Dosewallips River you can walk to from the campground or drive to from the highway. Once there, you can reach the saltwater by walking for five minutes along a level path. After a couple of minutes, you'll emerge from the trees and enter a grassy area that transitions to tidal flats full of clams and oysters. You can only harvest the clams from April 1 through September 30, but oysters can be had all year long.

Getting There: Twanoh State Park is located between Belfair and Union on State Highway 106. Potlatch State Park is 3 miles south of Hoodsport along US Highway 101 and Doswallips is also found on US Highway 101, at Brinnon.

MIKE'S BEACH RESORT

N. 38470 US Highway 101, Lilliwaup, WA 985555 / 360-877-5324
www.mikesbeachresort.com

Lodging Prices: $ to $$ Adventure Pricing: $

Well known among the diving community, Mike's Beach Resort is yet to be discovered by many other outdoors enthusiasts despite the fact that it's been around since 1951. You'll find the small, busy resort on the Olympic Peninsula side of Hood Canal off of US Highway 101.

For lodging, there are several small, older cabins that sleep three to four right on the water with kitchenettes, televisions, and tiny private baths. There is also a newer model large RV trailer on the water with its own hot tub, and another waterfront cabin with a Jacuzzi and fireplace. Budget-style motel rooms and dorm accommodations (often used by diving certification classes or for family reunions) are also on site as well as a three-bedroom cabin rental across the street from the resort. Also across the road from the resort is a campground with full and partial hook-ups to accommodate RV travelers and campers. Resort amenities include a nice pier, mooring buoys, boat launch, and air for divers. One unique draw is the small cinema at the resort. The owners open it up for guests who watch old 16-millimeter films on the theater's big screen. The shows may feature Laurel & Hardy, The Three Stooges, or episodes from old series like Flipper or Sea Hunt.

Divers come to see fish, octopi, and a variety of sea life at the bottom of Hood Canal. There is wildlife to be seen on the surface too: seal sightings are frequent and you may wake up to see some resting on the floating dock just off shore from the resort. In recent years, transient orca whales have been showing up in the summer, attracted by these same seals. In the air, bald eagles soar past the resort and on the beach, kids have fun looking at mussels, barnacles, and small crabs that scurry under the rocks.

Kayakers have discovered the calm waters of Hood Canal as a great place to paddle. Mike's rents both traditional open cockpit and sit-on-top kayak models along with row boats and a paddle boat.

During the summer and again in the fall, salmon fishing can be good between here and Hoodsport. However, a better bet if you want to bring home seafood involves putting away the rod and reel. Instead, drop a pot or ring a short row away from the pier to haul up some tasty shrimp or a combination of rock and Dungeness crab. Be sure to check the regulations before harvesting these shellfish because the seasons are subject to frequent changes.

One shellfishing opportunity that runs almost year round can be found on the private beach right in front of the resort. Every guest can dig up to 20 steamer clams and gather 15 oysters per day. To preserve the quality of the experience (and the population), guests are limited to a designated hour each day that occurs during the low tide.

If gathering sea food for dinner and exploring the water on a kayak isn't enough, there are several hiking opportunities a short drive away in Olympic National Forest's Hamma Hamma Recreation Area.

If you want to book a visit at the resort, there is a two-night minimum during the weekends and three-night minimum on holiday weekends. Maid service is available for an additional charge if you need it. The resort is open all year.

Getting There: Follow US Highway 101 northwest from Olympia through Shelton, Hoodsport, and Liliwaup. The resort is just off the highway 9 miles north of Liliwaup.

Hood Canal is one of the best places in the Northwest to find fresh oysters.

ALDERBROOK RESORT

10 East Alderbrook Drive, Union, WA 98592 / 800-672-9370
www.alderbrookresort.com

Lodging Prices: $$ to $$$$ Adventure Pricing: $ to $$$$

Alderbrook is a beautiful resort popular with Seattle-area residents who come to escape the hassle of urban living. Rebuilt and reopened in 2004, this spectacular place is located on the south shore of Hood Canal near the small village of Union. You'll notice the quality of the newly built property as soon as the smiling door person lets you inside the large, tastefully appointed lobby. It's full of windows that look out over green lawns, trees, and a great view of the saltwater. Comfy chairs around the lobby's fireplace make this a great place to socialize on a rainy day, while an outdoor fireplace near the spa is a place to gather in the evening.

The lodge offers 77 guest rooms in one wing and 16 two-bedroom cottages (with bathrooms and fully stocked kitchens) in another. There are TVs, phones, and DVD players in each room and complementary DVD movies are available at the front desk. In front of the lodging wings are ponds full of trout (you cannot fish for them), a small bubbling creek, trees, landscaped flower beds, and green lawns spilling down towards the beach.

There is an excellent restaurant on site specializing in Northwest seafood and locally grown produce. A patio bar next to the water also offers quality food, drink, and summertime musical entertainment in a casual atmosphere. Other amenities include a large stand-alone indoor pool building next to the beach with a well-equipped fitness room and full-service spa. Meeting rooms are available and the resort often hosts large events. A privately owned 18-hole golf course that shares the same name as the resort is located a short distance away.

At the beach you'll find room to walk during low tide. There is also a large dock with 1,500 feet of moorage space that includes electrical, telephone, and Internet hookups. Anglers have been known to catch and release sea-run cutthroat trout from the dock or in rental boats and you can catch tasty Dungeness crab right off the dock as well. In July, king salmon return to the Skokomish River and fishing for them can be good in this part of Hood Canal. There is also a very short shrimp season that generally runs for a few days in May.

Also on the resort dock you'll find Hood Canal Adventures (360-898-2628 – www.hoodcanaladventures.com). Owners David and Valerie Wagner operate their waterborne business from here and at the nearby Hood Canal Marina. You can rent a kayak, a stable Livingston boat with an outboard motor, or a 21-foot "green" electric-powered Duffy Boat by the hour or day. A larger motorized pontoon boat that holds up to 14 can also be rented, and if you want, you can rent a skipper to drive it for an additional fee. In case you didn't haul your crab ring or fishing pole to this luxury resort, you can rent one to catch your dinner and cook it in your cottage.

Kayak rentals include basic instruction. You're then free to paddle around the calm waters of Hood Canal. One recommended trip is a 20-minute paddle across the canal to the Tahuya River. Seals often congregate near the mouth and a short paddle upriver will put you within sight of various bird species.

If you want a guided tour, Hood Canal Adventures offers those too. One offering is a two-plus hour tour of the Skokomish River Delta. After launching at the edge of the estuary you'll paddle upstream, exploring different channels of the river to see birds ranging from great blue herons to eagles, osprey, kingfishers, grebe, and numerous species of waterfowl. After a short break you'll ride the river downstream back into Hood Canal. Entering the saltwater you glide past a rookery full of harbor seals and paddle back to the marina. No experience is necessary to participate, and children over five are welcome. If you want to do something besides kayak, Hood Canal Adventures also offers geo-caching (a GPS-related form of treasure hunt), and bicycle rentals from the resort.

More nature exploration and bird watching waits in nearby Belfair at the Sam B. Theler Wetland Trails (360-275-4898, www.thelercenter.org). There's almost 4 miles worth of trails to explore through tidal and freshwater wetlands as well as a lowland forested marsh. Stop by the exhibit building to pick up a loaner pair of binoculars and an electronic bird identifier that helps put together the songs you hear with the bird's you see. Common resident species include raptors like sharp-shinned, Cooper's, and red-tailed hawks, as well as eagles and owls. A wide variety of waterfowl can be found here, along with killdeer, belted kingfisher, pheasant, winter wren, spotted towhee, and red-winged blackbirds. Warblers, kinglets, hummingbirds, flycatchers, and many other birds visit the area on a seasonal basis.

The Theler Wetland Trails are open during daylight hours seven days a week. The Exhibit Building is open from Wednesday through Sunday from 10:00am to 4:00pm.

Hood Canal Adventures and Alderbrook Resort are both open on a year-round basis. Advance reservations are highly recommended.

Getting There: Take a Washington State Ferry to Bremerton from Seattle. From Bremerton go west on State Highway 304 to State Highway 3. Follow State Highway 3 south through Belfair, then take State Highway 106 and follow it along the south side of Hood Canal to the resort.

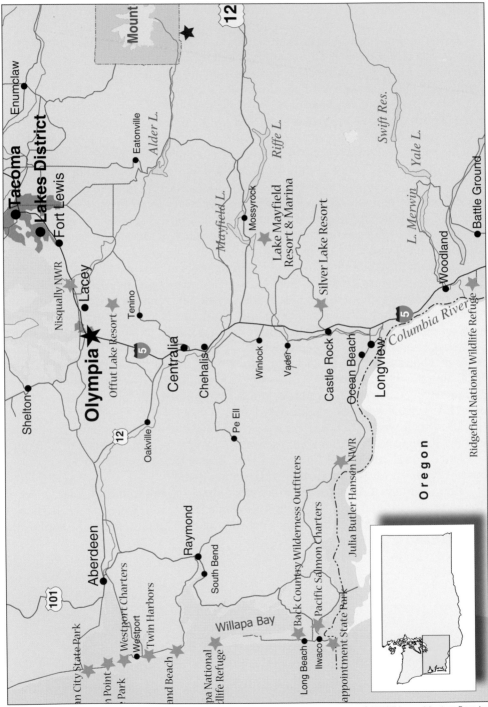

Columbia Gorge
National Scenic Area (West)

Western Columbia Gorge
(BONNEVILLE DAM – BEACON ROCK STATE PARK)

Bonneville Lock and Dam Visitor Center, Cascade Locks, OR 97014 /
541-374-8820 www.nwp.usace.army.mil/op/b/home.asp
Beacon Rock State Park, 3481 State Route 14, Skamania, WA 98648 /
509-427-8265 www.parks.wa.gov

Lodging Prices

Wildlife watching, excellent fishing, hiking, and rock climbing are all on tap in the small section of the Columbia River Gorge National Scenic Area located between Beacon Rock and Bonneville Dam.

Bonneville Dam, a huge hydropower facility spanning the Columbia, provides some unique wildlife watching opportunities on the Washington side of the river. Bird watchers spend time along the 1-mile handicapped accessible Strawberry Islands Loop Trail looking for swallows, warblers, downy woodpeckers, and raptors such as bald eagles, turkey vultures, and osprey. They are all found among 45-acres of woods and wetlands managed by the U.S. Army Corps of Engineers. Get there by turning onto the dam access road off of State Highway 14 at milepost 38.5 and drive 1.5 miles to the end of the Hamilton Island Recreation Area.

A different kind of wildlife watching is found at Bonneville Dam's fish ladder on the Washington side of the dam. Go inside the visitor center for an eye-to-eye view of salmon, steelhead, shad, and lamprey making their way up the watery ladder. Spring through early fall are especially good times to see lots of fish. The visitor center is open daily from 9:00am to 5:00pm.

After seeing all of these fish you may want to go out and catch some of them. Fishing is excellent below Bonneville Dam. This area is best known for trophy sturgeon that grow to a length of 11 feet. Catch-and-release angling for these prehistoric looking monsters is popular. You can also take home a sturgeon measuring between 38 and 54 inches from nose to tail fork, but you'll want to check the regulations before you keep any of these fish since

the "keeper" length and season varies from year to year. Boat anglers tend to do best, but bank anglers also catch their fair share.

From late May through June, several million shad pass over Bonneville Dam as they swim upstream to spawn. The rocks below Bonneville Dam are the best place on the river to cast for these 2- to 6-pound fish that look like overgrown herring on steroids. They are sporty fighters on light tackle and catching a couple dozen is commonplace. Steelhead and salmon are also caught on a regular basis by anglers below the dam. If you have a boat, you can get on and off the river from the Hamilton Island launch off of State Highway 14.

Hikers will find several alternatives around here. The first takes you north along the Pacific Crest Trail after it crosses the Columbia River at the Bridge of the Gods. If you aren't up for a month-long tramp to the Canadian border, you can opt for a shorter trek to the summit of 2,438-foot Hamilton Mountain. Start from the day-use area of Beacon Rock State Park and work your way to the summit to enjoy great views of Mt. Hood before continuing on a loop trail back to the park for a total of 9 miles. If you don't want to go that far, you can walk the first 1.4 miles of this trail to reach Hardy and Rodney Falls.

The most popular hike in this region is the steep walk to the top of 848-foot tall Beacon Rock. Touted as the second biggest monolith in the northern hemisphere, it is the site of a state park and serves as a prominent landmark along the banks of the Columbia. A trail follows a series of staircases and bridges that switchback a mile to the top of the rock.

You can also climb towards the top of Beacon Rock. The south and southeast faces of this volcanic core remnant are used by technical rock climbers who follow cracks up a 400-foot basalt rock face. This area is sometimes closed from February until mid-July to protect nesting peregrine falcons, so call ahead if you want to climb here during this time frame.

If you are looking for a place to stay, Beacon Rock State Park has 29 sites in a forested setting suitable for tents and smaller RVs. The 4,650-acre park also features a picnic area with kitchen shelters and a boat launch into the Columbia River. The park is open all year. However, all but a handful of camp sites are closed from late October until late March. Camp sites are available on a first-come, first-served basis.

Getting There: Bonneville Dam is located next to State Highway 14 at mile post 40. Beacon Rock State Park is found on both sides of the same highway at mile post 35.

STEVE'S GUIDED ADVENTURES

901 28th Street, Washougal, WA 98671 / 800-8872-6941
www.stevesguidedadventures.com

Lodging Prices: Included with some trips   Adventure Pricing: $$ to $$$$

Advertised as "Not just your average guide", long-time angler Steve Leonard is recognized by his peers as one of the best who works the Columbia River and its tributaries for salmon, sturgeon, steelhead, and walleye. Leonard has been a fishing guide for over 17 years and can accommodate anywhere from one to six guests in his new 24-foot Alumaweld boat that has a full top and heaters to keep the weather at bay.

Leonard spends 75 percent of his time with clients fishing the Columbia River from Bonneville Dam downstream to Multnomah Falls. He's looking for keeper sturgeon (38 to 54 inches long from nose to tail fork) and oversize sturgeon that can measure over 9 feet. He also fishes for summer and fall chinook salmon as well as steelhead in this stretch of the Columbia that separates Washington and Oregon.

Leonard doesn't just anchor up on the same piece of water every day. From mid-May through August you'll often find him fishing around the mouth of the Columbia and Buoy 10 for sturgeon and salmon and in the early spring he'll venture as far upstream as the John Day Dam for a shot at trophy walleye. Most guides on the Columbia tend to fish other than walleye in the summer, but Leonard is more than willing to go after these tasty fish in T-shirt weather.

When asked what separates him from the competition, Leonard says he likes to think he is "more diverse than other guides". Leonard's diversity is reflected by his willingness to fish several tributaries of the Columbia with up to two clients out of his ClackaCraft drift boat. You can drift with Leonard down the Klickitat, the Washougal, or the East Fork of the Lewis for chinook salmon and steelhead. Leonard also ventures onto the Cowlitz, Kalama, and the North Fork of the Lewis as well as several Oregon rivers for these fish.

In addition to day trips, Leonard offers several different multi-day fishing adventures. Three days of fishing for salmon, sturgeon, or both are accompanied by four nights of lodging in comfortable rooms at places like the Best Western Hotel at Cascade Locks or the Red Lion Hotel in Astoria. Sack lunches and full dinners are included with these packages.

Another bonus to fishing with Leonard is that he is a taxidermist. With Leonard, you can not only catch your trophy, but have it mounted too! If you choose to release your trophy after a photo opportunity, Leonard can make a fiberglass reproduction of the fish for you. Leonard provides fishing tackle and bait on all of his trips, as well as snacks and rain gear upon request. Any fish you keep will be bagged and put on ice for you to take home.

Getting There: Destinations vary.

DAN PONCIANO GUIDE SERVICE

3614 NW 129th Circle, Vancouver, WA 98685 / 360-573-7211
www.columbiariverfishing.com

Lodging Prices: N/A   Adventure Pricing: $$$

Ask industry experts for a short list of the best fishing guides on the lower Columbia River and Dan Ponciano invariably makes the cut. Salmon, sturgeon, and steelhead are the main focus for this man who has guided for over 15 years and has no plans of quitting anytime soon. Ponciano operates his business alone. He takes two to six clients at a time out on his 24-foot North River boat that has both a heater and covered top in case the weather turns nasty.

Ponciano's fishing calendar starts in January and heads into March with him hitting the Columbia River near Vancouver and Oregon's Willamette River for sturgeon that typically run 3 to 5 feet long. An Oregon license is required to fish the Willamette, and you'll want to check dates when you book your trip since retaining these tough-fighting fish is only allowed on certain days of the week. Ponciano continues to work these areas for sturgeon from April into May. However, he also targets chinook salmon that run 14 to 17 pounds and occasionally will venture into Washington's Wind River to find big spring chinook.

Ponciano spends the summer months fishing the Columbia and some of its tributaries all the way from its mouth at Buoy 10 to just below Bonneville Dam. Hooking sturgeon – at times big oversized ones as well as lots of smaller fish you can retain – makes up a typical summer outing. Other days on the water are spent catching salmon but fishing with Ponciano involves more than two species of fish. Summer steelhead is also a favorite quarry and angling can be quite good for them on both the Columbia and Lewis Rivers.

As fall arrives the focus shifts to fall chinook and silver salmon on the Columbia between Vancouver and Bonneville Dam. Good catches of these fine-tasting fish hold up through October. Come November, it's time to fish for bright winter steelhead. These fish often go into the teens in terms of poundage and Ponciano will fish for them through December on the Cowlitz and Lewis Rivers.

You may notice a few blank spaces in Ponciano's calendar, but it's not for vacation. From the end of August through fall, Ponciano also offers guided hunting trips for antelope, mule deer, and elk in eastern Oregon.

Ponciano provides quality fishing tackle for your use; an example being his G. Loomis rods and Shimano reels. He prides himself on keeping a clean boat and does his best to make sure you have a good time on the water. It must be working because customers keep coming back for more fishing trips, even after those rare days when limits are hard to come by.

Getting There: Destinations vary.

Dan Ponciano handles a hefty sturgeon (photo courtesy Dan Ponciano).

Central Gorge Recreation
(WIND RIVER – DOG MOUNTAIN – DRANO LAKE)

Columbia River Gorge National Scenic Area
902 Wasco Avenue, Suite 200, Hood River, OR 97031 / 503-386-2333
www.fs.fed.us/r6/columbia/forest/

A full spectrum of outdoor recreation is found in the Columbia Gorge between the Wind and Little White Salmon Rivers. Anglers, paddlers, windsurfers, kite boarders, hikers, and nature lovers will all find plenty to do throughout the year.

Salmonoid fisheries attract anglers from mid-March all the way to January. It starts off with the arrival of big chinook salmon in the spring. In mid-July summer steelhead start to show, and crowds soon arrive to fish the Columbia, Drano Lake, White Salmon, and Wind River mouths for both steelhead and fall chinook that are in thick by mid-August. Trolling plugs or fishing shrimp below a bobber are effective ways to catch summer steelhead through early fall. Silver salmon find their way into anglers' nets in September and by December winter steelhead arrive for hearty fishermen who brave cold and blustery weather for a shot at a big "metal head". Boat launches are available at both Drano Lake and at the mouth of the Wind River.

Extreme paddlers can tackle the Class IV and V waters of the Wind River every spring in both rafts and kayaks. Kayakers up to the ultimate challenge can also try their luck making it through the Class V whitewater found in the Little White Salmon. Put in at Lava Creek or at the Fish Hatchery. Only expert paddlers should tackle these rivers on their own. If you're not quite up to that level, there are a couple of commercial outfitters that offer trips on the Wind River.

A different type of water sport is very visible on the wind ruffled waters of the Columbia River Gorge. Wind surfing enthusiasts and kite boarders gather from spring through fall to ride the waves on boards decorated with bright sails or under small parachutes. Home Valley Park, operated by Skamania County, has a wind surfing beach to launch from (as well as 23 primitive campsites, playgrounds, ball fields and swim area). Other wind surfing beaches include Bob's Beach at Stevenson or the popular Spring Creek Hatchery east of White Salmon.

Hunters and hikers also have much to do around here. Big game hunters after Roosevelt elk and black-tailed deer look for their game in the southern portion of the Gifford Pinchot National Forest. Their weapons of choice vary from bow and arrow to muzzle loaders to modern firearms, depending on the hunting calendar that runs from September through November.

Hikers can summit 1,907-foot Wind Mountain next to the Wind Mountain Resort. A 45-minute to one-hour hike over rough trails will get you to the top of what is known as a guardian of the gorge in Native American lore. Great views of Mt. Adams, Mt. St. Helens, and the city lights of Vancouver and Portland are part of the reward from the top of the mountain.

Another steep hike in the Columbia Gorge is found at Dog Mountain. This 7.5-mile round-trip hike involves an elevation gain of 2,800 feet to reach the 2,948-foot summit. The pay off for your efforts is good. Not only do you get magnificent views of the Columbia Gorge, but you also get to see a variety of wildflowers and flowering trees from May into July. Early blooms include yellow-colored buttercup, glacier lily, and early blue violet. Later in the spring, chocolate and Columbia lily share the upper hillside with big flowering arrowleaf balsamroot. The crowded trailhead is found off State Highway 14 near milepost 53.

If you are looking for a less strenuous outing, try a 1.5-mile walk to Falls Creek Falls. The water drops 200 to 250 feet in three segments and offers stunning views. To get there drive up the Wind Mountain Highway north of Carson for 15 miles. Turn right on Forest Service Road 3062 for a mile and a half, turn right again on Road 57 and find the trailhead after 0.25 mile.

Getting There: You'll find the mouth of the Wind River between Carson and Home Valley along State Highway 14. Drano Lake is the mouth of the White Salmon River, some 7 miles east of Carson along the highway.

Wind Mountain Resort

50561 Highway 14 (Home Valley), Stevenson, WA 98648 / 509-427-5152
www.windmountainresort.com

Lodging Prices: $$ to $$$ Adventure Pricing: N/A

Rolf and Astrid Diek came from the Netherlands nine years ago to build their version of the "American Dream". In doing so, the couple constructed the Wind Mountain Resort from the ground up, establishing a great base camp for outdoor enthusiasts in the Columbia Gorge.

The resort has 13 large full hook-up RV sites built to accommodate not only RVs, but the boats that many guests bring with them to fish the Columbia River. There are also 10 other sites for tent campers and RV drivers who can get by with hook-ups providing only water and electricity.

A lodge has three clean, well-equipped motel rooms upstairs. The smallest, sleeping four, has a queen bed and hide-a-bed while the largest room can accommodate up to seven guests. The rooms have private baths, kitchenettes, cable television with VCRs, air conditioning, electric fireplaces, wireless Internet, and windows giving you filtered views of the Columbia River across the highway. The only complaint about the lodging is the sound of the trains that occasionally pass by on the far side of the road. If the trains bother you, the Dieks have thoughtfully placed ear plugs in the rooms to muffle the noise for a good night's sleep.

There is a café open to the public on the ground floor of the lodge. As of press time, it is serving hearty breakfasts and lunch meals five days a week from 7:00am to 3:00pm, though there are plans to expand the hours of the bright dining room decorated with fishing art and local nature photographs. Outside deck seating is also available.

The Dieks also operate the Home Valley Store a quarter mile down the road. The store sells not only groceries, but also a healthy supply of fishing tackle, bait, and ice. Advice on where to go fishing and what to use is free.

Anglers discovered the Wind Mountain Resort several years ago and make up much of the clientele. They come to fish the mouth of the Wind and White Salmon Rivers, nearby Drano Lake, and the Columbia River. Most of the anglers are after salmon and steelhead, fishing for one or the other throughout the year. Sturgeon, shad, and smallmouth bass fishing are also options for anglers staying here.

Although the Wind Mountain Resort is favored by anglers, it is also an ideal base for other outdoor enthusiasts. There is some serious whitewater paddling on the Wind River, though it is not for beginners. Hunters also come in the fall, lured by the prospect of taking a black-tailed deer or an elk in the Gifford Pinchot National Forest. Windsurfers can launch across the highway at Home Valley Park and hikers can summit adjacent Wind or nearby Dog Mountain for great views of the Columbia River Gorge.

The Wind Mountain Resort is open throughout the year for outdoor enthusiasts. Pets are welcome, though there is a small charge if they stay in one of the rooms at the lodge.

Getting There: Travel east on State Highway 14 from Vancouver or west from White Salmon. The resort is next to the highway at the small town of Home Valley, 5 miles east of Stevenson.

Inland Lakes and Refuges

Ridgefield National Wildlife Refuge

28908 NW Main Avenue, Ridgefield, Washington 98642 / 360-887-4106
www.fws.gov/ridgefieldrefuges

If you live in the greater Vancouver-Portland urban area and need a quick outdoors fix, the Ridgefield National Wildlife Refuge may do the trick. The 5,150-acre refuge's wetlands and woods border the Columbia River northwest of Vancouver. Wildlife watching is popular all year, as is waterfowl hunting from October through January. Hiking is also an option along two trails on the refuge.

The refuge headquarters are found on the outskirts of Ridgefield. Two of the five units on the refuge are open to the public. One of these is the Carty Unit. Highlights include the Lake River that flows into the nearby Columbia, Carty Lake, and several smaller waters. The 2-mile Oaks to Wetlands Trail is open all year during daylight hours and the name of the trail gives you a good idea of the terrain you'll be tromping through. A stop at the Cathlapotle Plankhouse along the trail will educate you about the Chinook tribe and other Native Americans who lived here before the arrival of white settlers. If you are up for more exploration, you can also hike cross country across the Carty Unit, observing plenty of wildlife along the way.

The River "S" Unit features a 4.2-mile auto loop that is perfect for casual nature viewing. There is an observation blind along the route where you can stop, stretch your legs, and try your hand at nature photography. Some of the mammals that live here are black-tailed deer, coyote, raccoon, skunk, rabbit, and river otter. Bird species range from diminutive white-throated sparrow, marsh wren, and nuthatches to big swans and herons. From fall through spring, thousands of ducks, Canada, and cackling geese congregate here as well. If you want to stretch those legs even more, the 1.2-mile Kiwa Loop Trail is handicap accessible and open for use from May 1 through September 30.

Waterfowl hunting takes place from 22 designated blinds at the River "S" Unit. You can reserve a spot in advance by applying for a permit prior to the hunting season or you can show up the day you want to hunt and try for any

untaken blinds that are doled out during an early morning lottery 1.75 hours before legal shooting time and again at 10:00am. Hunting is allowed on Tuesdays, Thursdays and Saturdays during hunting season, but don't bother showing up if a federal holiday happens to coincide with one of these days because the refuge will be closed to hunting. There is a $10-per-blind fee and you can only have 25 non-toxic shotgun shells in your possession while hunting here. Contact staff at the refuge or check out their website for further details.

The refuge is open throughout the year. There is a $3 entrance fee unless you have a federal duck stamp or annual pass. No bicycles, horses, or camping are permitted. Pets are also not allowed outside of automobiles unless they are dogs actively engaged in retrieving waterfowl during hunting season.

Getting There: Take Exit 14 off of Interstate 5 and travel west 3 miles to Ridgefield. Take a right on Main Avenue and travel north 1 mile to reach the refuge headquarters within the Carty Unit.

Julia Butler Hansen National Wildlife Refuge

46 Steamboat Slough Road, Cathlamet, WA 98612 / 360-795-3915
www.fws.gov/jbh/

If you want to see a unique subspecies of deer and lots of other wildlife, head to the Julia Butler Hansen Refuge for the Columbian white-tailed deer. The 6,000-plus acre national wildlife refuge sits along the lower Columbia River near Cathlamet and is named after a local legislator who was instrumental in establishing this protected area. Three islands within the refuge (Tenasillahe, Crims, and Wallace) are in Oregon while Hunting and Price Islands, along with a sizeable portion of the property on the north bank of the Columbia, are in Washington.

The habitat is a combination of forested swamp, sloughs, marsh, pasture, and brush that provide a home for the Columbian white-tailed deer, a subspecies found only in this part of the United States. Some 300 of these animals live on the refuge, with an equal number living on adjacent private lands. One way to tell the difference between the Columbian white-tailed deer and the more common black-tailed deer in the area is to look for the white eye ring visible on the face of the Columbian white-tail does.

In addition to rare deer, beaver and muskrat swim in the sloughs along with nutria, a non-native mammal. Both deer and elk are often observed in pastures from Steamboat Slough or Brooks Slough Roads. Waterfowl from Canada geese to mallard, wigeon, pintail, and tundra swan all flock to the refuge during the winter. In the summer, colorful cinnamon teal can be seen, as well as nongame birds like yellow warbler, American goldfinch, and purple martin. Swallows are prolific in the spring, and raptors such as osprey and bald eagles congregate near the river. Other raptors like northern harrier, sharp-shinned hawks, turkey vulture, and peregrine falcon can also be viewed at times.

While wildlife watching draws most visitors, hunting is also a prospect. Waterfowlers hunt the shoreline of Hunting and Wallace Islands from October into January. Meanwhile, muzzleloaders with special permits have

a chance to bag an elk on the mainland portion of the refuge when too many of these big animals are present.

Hiking and bicycling occur on the lightly traveled roads of the refuge or on the dike that surrounds Tenasillahe Island. As this book is being written, there are plans that may change the public trail access. Check in at the refuge headquarters to see what trails and roads are open for non-motorized use.

Whereas land-based exploration is limited, canoeists and kayakers have discovered the waterways and islands of the refuge are a great place to visit. This area is part of the Lower Columbia River Water Trail (www.columbiawatertrail.org). You can reach the upper end of the refuge by paddling from Cathlamet and the lower end from Skamokawa Vista Park. You can also get on the water from a public launch off of State Highway 4 between Cathlamet and Skamokawa. Some choose to paddle the waters of the Columbia, but changing tides, winds, and the big wakes from passing freighters can make this a challenging proposition. Safer passage and good wildlife viewing can be had by paddling the protected sloughs of the refuge.

Getting There: Travel on State Highway 4 west through Cathlamet. Two miles past of town turn onto Steamboat Slough Road to enter the refuge.

Killdeer are common sites around water in Washington.

SILVER LAKE RESORT

3201 Spirit Lake Highway, Silver Lake, WA 98645 / 360-274-614
www.silverlake-resort.com

Lodging Prices: $ to $$$ Adventure Pricing: $ to $$

Silver Lake Resort has a lot going for it. For starters, it's the closest motel to Mt. St. Helens, famous for blowing its top in a spectacular fashion in 1980. Today the mountain is not only an active volcano, but also a major tourist attraction. The Washington State Parks Visitor Center 1.5 miles away from the resort along the lake (Open daily – 360-274-0962 – www.parks.wa.gov) tells the story of the mountain and its famous eruption.

Another factor in the resort's favor is that it's situated on one of the best bass lakes in Washington. The biggest largemouth bass caught from this lake weighed in at 10 pounds, 2 ounces and bass over 8 pounds are caught every year.

The year-round resort offers 21 RV sites (some with full hook ups), 11 tent sites under pine trees, and five cabins. There is also a motel with seven rooms right on the water where you can catch fish from your own private balcony. You have a choice of studio, or one- or two-bedroom motel or cabin accommodations, all of which have kitchens, bathrooms, and cable television. While the exterior of the motel looks worn, the rooms inside both the motel and cabins are nicely decorated, well furnished, and have Wi-Fi Internet access. The nicest place to stay is the two-bedroom Silver Suite on the top floor of the motel. It has a fireplace, full kitchen, and Jacuzzi tub inside. Kids will like the small playground near the RV sites and feeding the tame ducks that waddle up from the boat launch to greet them. A fire pit near the water is great for evening relaxation and if you have your own boat, there is a boat launch and moorage space available at the dock.

The fishing is very good in this 3,000-acre lake. Docks, pilings, and lily pads all hold bass and anglers use soft plastics, spinnerbaits, or medium diving crankbaits to tempt them into biting. Crappie fishing can be excellent, though there is a ten-fish limit with a minimum size of 9 inches. Many are caught right from the dock, with worm-tipped jigs being a favorite offering. Trout are routinely stocked by the Department of Fish and Wildlife while bluegill, perch, catfish, bullhead, and carp are also pulled out of the water on a regular basis.

Wildlife is abundant around the lake, especially the feathered variety. Ospreys sometimes nest near the resort and woodpeckers, kinglets, western tanagers, and Hutton's vireos are some of the species that nest in the woods inland. Along the waterline it is common to see killdeer, Wilson's snipe, or Virginia rails, while pied-billed grebes and a variety of ducks swim along the surface of the lake.

If you need to rent a boat, there are several to choose from. Motorized pontoon boats, 14-foot boats with 6-horsepower motors, and a 15-foot pleasure boat can all rented by the hour or for the day. The resort also offers rowboats, paddleboats, and a canoe for those who want to go out under their own power. While kayaks are not available at the resort, they are a common sight on this lake. With lots of space to paddle on a lake surrounded by large portions of scenic, undeveloped woodlands in the shadow of a picturesque mountain, it's easy to understand why.

Getting There: Take Exit 49 (Castle Rock) off of Interstate 5. Travel east 6.5 miles along the Spirit Lake Highway to reach the resort.

You can fish from your room at the resort's waterfront motel.

LAKE MAYFIELD RESORT AND MARINA

350 Hadaller Road, Mossyrock, WA 98564 / 360-985-2357
www.lakemayfield.com

Lodging Prices: $ to $$$ Adventure Pricing: $ to $$$

Think about a large, clean, modern resort on a big tree-lined reservoir. Put that place anywhere and you'll be tempted to visit. Throw in the fact the fishing is good and you'll probably be hooked. When you also talk about this being a great place to canoe and kayak you'll make advance reservations. Finally, throw in some big tiger muskie (known as one of the toughest fighting game fish in North America) and you'll be hard pressed to resist a long stay.

The Lake Mayfield Resort & Marina offers all of this and more. The resort offers the only real marina on the 2,250-acre reservoir near the small town of Mossyrock. The spacious resort offers a variety of accommodations. Campers have 22 tent sites to choose from. Some of them are waterfront and others are on a small island linked by a moorage dock from the main resort. There are 49 RV sites (all but two have full hook ups) and several of these also are on the water. Finally, there are 27 guest rooms. Some of them are in a newly constructed motel while others are in cabins. The smallest is the "Itsy Bitsy Boathouse" that offers little more than a clean bed and chair in a tiny cabin. On the other end, the Aspen Lodge rooms have four queen beds, a full kitchen with a dishwasher, large bathrooms, satellite television, heat and air conditioning, and a covered deck with both barbeques and picnic tables. Additional units ranging from one to four bedrooms are also available.

The resort has a restaurant, a lounge, a store, and a large meeting hall that accommodates up to 250 people. Kids love to hang out at the two nice playgrounds and the swimming area. A small working lighthouse, reached by a short walk to an island from the resort, is also a favorite family destination that stands out on the resort property. Summer activities include Saturday night dances that kids flock to in droves where they do everything from the Chicken Dance to the Hokey Pokey to the Limbo Rock.

Kids and adults alike will enjoy the fishing dock. It is unique in that it offers padded chairs and loungers to relax on while you fish a worm under a bobber for trout or perch (try not to nod off between bites). Several other docks offer lots of moorage space and additional places for fishing.

There are lots of different fish to catch in Lake Mayfield. Shore and boat anglers alike catch rainbow and cutthroat trout between 12 and 18 inches. If you do catch a cutthroat trout, you need to release it. But feel free to keep any yellow perch you may catch. Largemouth bass up to 5 pounds are caught along with the occasional big coho salmon that are released into the lake.

Mayfield Lake's most interesting fish is the tiger muskie. Known as "the fish of a thousand casts", these fish fight hard when hooked and can get to an impressive size. The state record muskie was caught here in 2001, weighing over 31 pounds. The resort now hosts a muskie tournament every September and many anglers come to the lake specifically targeting these toothy trophies from late spring through early fall. Fishing is open all year at Lake Mayfield, though the best angling usually takes place between April and October.

Kayak clubs come here to paddle the 33 miles of shoreline, seeing the occasional eagle or river otter along the way. Paddling is best in the spring and fall, since powerboats and personal watercraft stir up the water during the summer months. If you do want to paddle in the summer, try going out early in the morning or around sunset for a little solitude.

If you didn't bring your own boat, the resort has kayaks, canoes, paddleboats, and aluminum boats with electric motors for rent. Groups may be interested in renting a pontoon boat that seats eight. The Lake Mayfield Resort is open all year. If you are looking for a bargain, visit from November 1 through April 30 when overnight rates drop significantly.

Getting There: From Interstate 5 take Exit 68 (south of Chehalis) and follow US Highway 12 east for 16 miles. Cross the Lake Mayfield Bridge and turn right at Winston Creek Road. Drive 1.5 miles to Hadaller Road. Turn right and stay to the right until you reach the resort.

The little lighthouse at the Mayfield Resort comes in handy for boaters returning after sunset.

Nisqually National Wildlife Refuge

100 Brown Farm Road, Olympia, WA 98516 / 360-753-9467
www.fws.gov/nisqually

Lodging Prices

The glacial waters of the Nisqually River flow from the flanks of Mt. Rainier into Puget Sound just north of Olympia – Washington's state capitol. The nutrient-rich delta and tide flats at the mouth of the Nisqually, along with the marsh, grassland, and riparian woodland habitat found around it has made this a magnet for wildlife and a bird-watching nirvana. The Nisqually National Wildlife Refuge was established in 1974 to protect the birds that flock here and the habitat that attracts them.

Waterfowl are especially abundant in the fall and winter. Colorful drake (male) wigeon, northern shoveler, mallard, pintail, and green-winged teal are all common residents. Brant, Canada, and cackling geese are also seen in the winter and spring. Long-legged birds such as great blue heron, killdeer, and greater yellowlegs are common, as are other shore birds like western sandpiper and dunlin. The woods and old farm pasture give a variety of swallows, wrens, warblers, red-breasted nuthatch, and other small birds a place to call home.

Seeing these birds and the habitat they live in is easy enough. Start by checking out the visitor center at the refuge. After you've looked over the interpretive exhibits explore some of the 7 miles of trails found here. The 1-mile Twin Barns Loop Trail is a good place to start. It is a handicapped accessible path that starts near the visitor center. Wander through woods and a forested marsh full of birds and other wildlife. Halfway through the hike you'll reach the barns that remain from a farm that used to be here. With several benches and interpretive signs, it's a good place to pause for a snack and to look out over the open grasslands of the refuge before heading back. If you prefer more open terrain, hike south from the parking lot and head

towards McAllister Creek. In the 0.75 mile it takes to get there, you'll pass through wetlands and ponds that are often full of waterfowl.

Both of these trails connect to the 5.5-mile Brown Farm Dike Trail loop. Encircling much of the refuge, the flat walk along this path allows you to walk close to the Nisqually River, McAllister Creek, and Puget Sound. The Brown Farm Dike Trail is closed from mid-October through most of January to avoid conflicts with waterfowl hunters.

While no hunting is allowed on the refuge itself, adjacent Washington Department of Fish and Wildlife land affords waterfowlers the opportunity to gun for birds during hunting season. Try setting up your decoys on the west side of McAllister Creek or along the tidal flats on the saltwater side of Brown Farm dike on a stormy day for your best chance at ducks and the occasional passing goose.

Fishing is also a possibility, though there is only one place you can actually do so within the refuge boundaries (that being along the banks of McAllister Creek). The marshy creek defines the western edge of the refuge and is accessible by foot paths. In the fall and early winter, chinook, coho, and chum salmon all migrate upstream in fair numbers. Better fishing for these fish is possible from boats on the Nisqually River or in the sound itself offshore from the Brown Farm Dike, where chinook start showing up in angler's nets as early as July. You can launch from a boat to fish and hunt Department of Fish and Wildlife lands from the Luhr Beach launch near the northwestern edge of the refuge.

Some activities are not allowed. Camping, jogging, and bicycle riding are among them. Pets are not allowed on this refuge, nor are firearms. The refuge is open all year from sunrise until sunset. The refuge office is open weekdays from 7:30am until 4:00pm and the visitor center is open Wednesday through Sunday between 9:00am and 4:00pm. There is a $3 fee per family to enter the refuge, unless you possess a federal duck stamp or other pass.

Getting There: Take Exit 114 off of Interstate 5 near Lacey. Go under the freeway and take a right onto the road that leads into the refuge and visitor center.

Offut Lake Resort

4005 120th Ave. SE, Tenino, WA 98589 / 360-264-2438
www.offutlakeresort.com

Lodging Prices: $ to $$ Adventure Pricing: $

If you need a quick getaway from the urban sprawl surrounding much of Puget Sound, a trip to the Offut Lake Resort may be just what the proverbial doctor ordered. Located southeast of Olympia, owner Becky Pogue has turned the small resort into a laid back, relaxing getaway destination.

Most people come here for the fishing. The 200-acre lake supports a solid trout fishery and the resort hosts several fishing derbies every year. While the average rainbow trout runs about 12 inches, they can get up to 7 pounds. Powerbait fished off the bottom is the ticket for dock anglers while boaters troll wedding ring spinners for rainbows and the occasional cutthroat trout. Largemouth and smallmouth bass are also found in the lake. Bass in the 2- to 4-pound range are common, and recently a huge 10-pounder was landed. Perch fishing is yet another pursuit for anglers though success rates fluctuate. However, during a good year it's easy enough to fill up a five-gallon bucket with perch, and a couple of them may tip the scales between 1 and 2 pounds. Other fish found in the lake include the occasional bluegill and bullhead (catfish) that sometimes end up on stringers.

If you want some contemplative time on the water, you'll find the lake is just the right size for a canoe, kayak, or row boat. One of the nice things about paddling here is that you don't have to compete with powerful boats and personal watercraft. There is a 5-mile-per-hour speed limit to ensure tranquil time on the water. The resort rents out canoes, rowboat, and paddleboats at low hourly prices. Anglers will also appreciate reasonable rental rates on newer model Lund aluminum boats with electric motors.

The resort offers some 20 tent sites. There are also 31 RV sites with full hook ups and some of these also have cable TV and Wi-Fi access. An unheated yurt by the water, a camping cabin, and four full-service cabins round out the list of available accommodations. The full-service cabins all have light wood interiors and kitchenettes along with cable televisions set up with DVD players or VCRs that come in handy on rainy days (the resort has an assortment of free loaner movies). The clean little cabins sleep two to four people, depending on which one you rent. All of them have private bathrooms.

Other features of the resort include a playground with an outdoor basketball court and a general store that sells tackle, snacks, and other essentials. From late April thru the end of September, the "Chuck Wagon" is open for business, serving up hot weekend breakfasts in the morning and burgers through the afternoon. On Saturday nights in the summer, families have fun singing karaoke with other guests in the campground.

If you are into wildlife, you'll want to visit Wolf Haven International (360-264-4695 – www.wolfhaven.org). Located just down Offut Lake Road from the resort, Wolf Haven is a sanctuary devoted to the conservation of wolves. At any given time, there may be more than 40 of these animals in half-acre fenced enclosures. Gray wolves along with endangered red wolves and Mexican gray wolves, as well as coyotes, can be seen on guided tours. You can also participate in a summer "howl-in" at the 80-acre property. Call in advance for more information about the tours and other programs.

If you prefer to see your wildlife outside of fences, drive 20 minutes north and take Exit 114 off of Interstate 5 to visit the Nisqually Wildlife Refuge. See the Nisqually National Wildlife Refuge entry for further details.

Bicycling on the Chehalis-Western Trail is another activity worth mentioning. The 14-mile paved bike and walking path runs north to south along Chambers Lake and the Deschutes River from an access point near the resort. The trail also links to the 14.5-mile-long Yelm to Tenino bike and walking trail south of the resort.

The Offut Lake Resort is open all year long, as is the lake for fishing. Reservations for cabins are recommended from spring through early fall, especially during weekends.

Getting There: Drive south from Olympia along Interstate 5 to Exit 99. Follow 93rd Street east to Old Highway 99. Travel south on Old Highway 99 approximately 4 miles to Offut Lake Road. Follow the signs east on Offut Lake Road until you reach the resort.

Renting a rowboat is an inexpensive way to explore Offut Lake.

Cape Disappointment State Park

P.O. Box 488 Ilwaco, WA 98624 (2 miles SW of Ilwaco on State Loop 100)
360-642-3078 / www.parks.wa.gov

Lodging Prices

Adventure Pricing

Cape Disappointment State Park has interesting geography, unique history, lots of wildlife, great scenery, fishing, hiking, biking, and sleeping accommodations to suit anyone's needs.

Formerly known as Fort Canby, the huge 1,882-acre park is located southwest of Ilwaco where the Columbia River meets the Pacific Ocean. Two unique features here are the working lighthouses. The Cape Disappointment Lighthouse sits at the southern edge of the park. Built in 1856, it is the oldest operating lighthouse on the West Coast. A 0.75-mile trail takes you to the black and white structure and the cape for spectacular river and ocean views. At the opposite end of the park is the North Head Lighthouse. No stay at this park is complete without a trip to the scenic bluff where it is located. A wide, level 0.25-mile path takes you to this working sentinel that has been keeping seafarers safe since 1898. Tours of this lighthouse are generally available on weekends in the off-season and daily during the summer. Even if you can't get in the lighthouse for a tour, the view towards the jetties at the mouth of the Columbia and the wide ocean expanse is fantastic. As an added bonus, sea lions and the occasional school of porpoise can sometimes be seen swimming in the surf below.

In between the lighthouses are miles of sandy beach and a long rock jetty that offers some saltwater fishing opportunities for shore anglers. However, park rangers emphasize the jetty is not designed for fishing and can be hazardous. Casting for surfperch from the beach or trying for freshwater bass at little Lake O'Neil might be safer choices.

Perched on a bluff just north of the Cape Disappointment Lighthouse is the Lewis and Clark Interpretive Center. Exhibits inside tell the story of the early 19th century expedition headed by Captains Meriwether Lewis and William Clark that started in Missouri and reached its westernmost point near here in the fall of 1805. Other features at the park include a day-use area called Waikiki Beach, a small camp store near the park entrance and a large boat launch at Baker Bay near the mouth of the Columbia River.

If you're in the mood for a walk, explore 7 miles of maintained trails in the park and saunter along Benson Beach between the North Jetty and the North Head Lighthouse. One popular hike starts near a campsite occupied by Captain Clark on November 18, 1805. It follows the footsteps of his party as they wandered through a forest of Sitka spruce towards the area where the North Head Lighthouse was eventually built. From here you can pick up the Westwind Trail, which continues to follow Clark's approximate route towards the beach. The total distance of this walk from Clark's campsite is about 2.6 miles. Another option for hikers is found along the 8-mile long Discovery Trail. The part-paved, part-gravel, part-boardwalk path connects Ilwaco, Beards Hollow, and Long Beach. The paved portion of the Discovery Trail at Long Beach extends for 2 miles and is perfect for an easy stroll or bike ride.

There is a lot of wildlife to be seen within the boundaries of the park. Black-tailed deer are abundant, as are squirrels and raccoon. River otters can also be seen frolicking in the saltwater near the jetties or by the Columbia River boat launch. The park is part of the Audubon Birding Trail in southwestern Washington. A variety of birds from marsh wrens to warbling vireos to Wilson's snipe can often be seen at scenic Beard's Hollow. Along the coast, pelicans, brant, cormorants, and Caspian terns are observed on a regular basis. Plovers and sandpipers can be spied on the beaches and if you are lucky you may also catch sight of the increasingly rare western snowy plover.

There are a variety of lodging options at this popular park. To start with, there are 231 camp and RV sites, 60 of which offer water, sewer, and electrical service. There are also three rustic cabins along the shore of Lake O'Neil and 14 yurts dispersed through the camping area. The yurts are round-walled canvas structures with hardwood floors that sleep up to six people. They all have electric light and heat, something you'll appreciate after a day of storm watching on the beach. While they are only 16 square feet in diameter, they feel light and spacious with a domed skylight on top and windows on the sides.

A very unique overnight experience can be had at three residences near the North Head Lighthouse. The Head Lighthouse Keeper used one of the homes and the other is a duplex that was used by his two assistants. Each of these beautiful white and red Victorian era residences has three bedrooms, a full kitchen, and bathroom as well as living and dining rooms. Modern amenities like microwave ovens, dishwashers, and televisions are provided. These rentals can be expensive for a single couple but are more cost effective for groups or extended families. If you want to save money, book an Assistant Lighthouse Keeper's residence during the off-season between November and early May. Stays at these beautiful homes in an unforgettable setting are in high demand, with bookings often made nine months in advance.

The park is open all year. Day-use of the facility is free. Tours of the North Head Lighthouse and Lewis & Clark Interpretive Center have a modest fee.

Getting There: From Vancouver, take Interstate 5 north to Longview. Turn west onto State Highway 4 and follow it to US Highway 101. From Olympia, drive west on State Route 8 to Montesano and then take US Highway 107 south to US Highway 101. Follow Highway 101 south to Long Beach and Ilwaco. Follow the signs from Ilwaco for 2 miles to reach the park.

You may see a raccoon or two while visiting the park.

BACK COUNTRY WILDERNESS OUTFITTERS

P.O. Box 327, Seaview, WA 98644 / 360-642-2576
www.backcountryoutfit.com

Lodging Prices: Included in some adventures   Adventure Pricing: $ to $$$$

You would think a company with a name like Back Country Wilderness Outfitters would be all about ferrying hunters by horseback to and from backwoods camps. In reality, you would only be half right.

Rick Haug, with help from his guides and wranglers, does a fair bit of hunting for Roosevelt elk, a subspecies of the big ungulate found west of the Cascade Mountains. Elk season runs from the first of November through the 9th in the forests southwest of Mount Adams. One option is to ride in on horseback with your gear to a drop camp near the Indian Heaven Wilderness. From there you hunt for three-point bulls or better during the short season until you get your elk or run out of time. At that point pack animals take you, your gear (and in most cases your game) out.

You can also opt to hunt for your bull out of a "Super Camp" around Lone Butte in the Cascades of southern Washington. You ride into camp but once there, a wrangler sets up a canvas wall tent for you to stay in and a cook serves up three meals a day. This allows you to focus on hunting (and relaxing after the hunt). Haug says these trips are great for groups. He'll generally have a horse-drawn wagon take several hunters from camp after a dawn breakfast; dropping them off with a rifle, binoculars, and a thermos of coffee every half mile so they can glass meadowlands for elk in the early morning light.

Back Country Wilderness Outfitters also takes hunters to private land along the Snake River in southeast Washington for big mule deer. These hunts take place in mid-October under open skies and involve lots of riding along the big ridgelines that rise above the river. These expeditions are also done in the "Super Camp" mode, a popular choice for many who come to Washington from other states. If you need some extra help getting deer or elk in range, guided hunts are available. Once you get your animal, you can leave it with the outfitter who will butcher and process it for you.

While hunting is an important part of Haug's business, his company spends much of its time at a corral at Long Beach. From May through September tourists, horse enthusiasts and novices alike, go for horseback rides on the beach. With the Pacific Ocean for a backdrop, a steady breeze blowing, and Cape Disappointment State Park ahead, there is lots to soak up as you walk or trot along the ocean shore. A two-hour beach ride departs daily from the corral at 9:00am. Shorter one-hour trips leave several times daily starting at 10:30am. Even though there are lots of horses on hand, reservations are recommended in the summer since over 100 people a day may come out to ride during a typical weekend. Children are welcome to ride by themselves if they are over five and those under that age can ride in front of their parent at no additional cost.

Another very popular activity put on by Back Country Wilderness Outfitters is their "Cream Can Dinners". These generally take place during low tides on Wednesday and Friday evenings over the summer. You start off the four-hour excursion with an hour-long horse ride on the beach to scenic Beard's Hollow below a working lighthouse. If you don't ride, you can hitch a ride in a horse-drawn wagon.

Once there a bonfire is lit and dinner is prepared. The meal consists of sausages, potatoes, corn on the cob, cabbage, onions, and carrots all layered inside a large stainless steel cream can. After steaming in a mixture of beer and water for an hour, the contents are dumped into a clean washtub where you can pick and choose what to put on your plate for a unique and delicious seaside buffet.

After dinner, you ride back in the dark to the corral with the beacon from North Head Lighthouse shining behind you and the glow of the luminescent surf next to you. Space for this trip fills up fast so call early, find out what nights are available, and make a reservation.

Getting There: Take US Highway 101 into Long Beach and head north on State Highway 103. Turn left onto Sid Snyder Drive and drive towards the beach. The corral for Back Country Outfitters will be on your left.

Heading down the beach for the popular Cream Can Dinner (photo courtesy Long Beach Peninsula Visitors Bureau).

PACIFIC SALMON CHARTERS

P.O. Box 519, Ilwaco, WA 98624 / 800-831-2695
www.pacificsalmoncharters.com

Lodging Prices: N/A   Adventure Pricing: $$ to $$$$

The charming fishing village of Ilwaco sits at the mouth of the Columbia River, providing anglers a smorgasbord of fish to catch ranging from sturgeon and salmon to halibut, bottomfish, and even tuna. There are several fishing charters here, but few have been around as long as Pacific Salmon Charters. Milt and Sarah Gudgell have owned the company since 1985, though it has actually been in existence since the 1950s. Today, eight different fishing boats operate under the company's umbrella. Milt's personal boat is the 36-foot Sarah Kay. Built to handle the sometimes-rough waters of the Columbia Bar, it will accommodate 10 guests. Several other boats are 40 to 43 feet long and have names like the Northern, Alika, Kingfish, Westward, Sea Venture, Star Dust, and Katie Marie. Many of these comfortably fish 15 anglers at a time.

The fishing season generally kicks off on the first of May with a halibut fishery that stays open for about a month (depending on yearly harvest allocations). Charter boats head west into the Pacific where you drop your hooks with anywhere from 2 to 4 pounds of weight into water that is 600 feet deep. This is where halibut averaging 25 to 35 pounds are taken, and sometimes they go as big as 80 pounds.

The second week of May heralds the opening of the "keeper sturgeon season". One sturgeon measuring between 41 and 54 inches from nose to tail fork may be retained per day through June. This may not sound like much, but the typical boat will catch and release several fish under the 41-inch mark and a couple over 5 feet long before everyone manages to land a keeper. Smoked sturgeon is a tasty delicacy prepared at local canneries in Ilwaco.

Salmon fishing starts as early as June and by July is usually very good. Anglers target both king and coho salmon, with the acrobatic cohos being the most numerous catch taken. Early in the season, the salmon only average 3 to 6 pounds, but by August the silvers (coho) run from 19 to 25 pounds while the big king salmon go over 30 pounds.

Bottom fishing charters set out from May through September to catch up to ten tasty rockfish and two lingcod per person and sometimes salmon-bottomfish combo trips are available. From the end of July through September albacore tuna come close enough to shore that charters will run 22 to 50 miles onto the ocean to intercept them. You are allowed to catch up to ten of these fast running, line smoking fish each. Averaging 15 and getting up to 25 pounds in size, you'll be ready for a long break after catching this many fish that will provide all the fillets you'll ever want.

Pacific Salmon Charters is open from May 1 through the end of September. Most trips depart between 5:00 and 6:00am. Expect to be on the water for eight hours or until limits of fish are in the boat. The tuna trips are 16 hours long, departing very early in the morning and coming back in the evening. There is coffee on board, but you will want to bring your own lunch and refreshments.

Getting There: Take US Highway 101 north from Astoria, Oregon or south from Aberdeen, Washington to Ilwaco. Pacific Salmon Charters is located at the marina.

You'll find Pacific Salmon Charters in Ilwaco's charming Marina (photo courtesy Long Beach Peninsula Visitor's Bureau).

Willapa National Wildlife Refuge

3888 US Highway 101, Ilwaco, WA 98624 / 360-484-3482
www.fws.gov

Lodging Prices

Willapa Bay is a large estuary on the east side of the Long Beach peninsula fed by the Naselle, Willapa, and North Rivers. The shallow bay is unique in that half of the water inside of it leaves with every tide. A plethora of birds, mammals, and marine life frequent the waters, exposed tidal flats, islands, marshes, beaches, and woods of the refuge established here.

The Willapa Bay National Wildlife Refuge consists of five different sections covering over 15,000 acres. The headquarters and a boat launch are located at the southeastern end of Willapa Bay. There is a small fee to launch or park here. The launch is a short boat ride or kayak paddle away from 5,640-acre Long Island. This rain-soaked land mass supports a 274-acre old growth forest that features a 900-year-old red cedar grove along with younger hemlock and Sitka spruce trees. Hikers can explore the island on a 10-mile-long trail system. The most popular walk is found at the Trail of the Ancient Cedars. It starts at the landing across the inlet from the main boat launch and takes you into the heart of the old growth forest. Other trails lead to five campgrounds on the island that have a total of 24 tent sites available on a first-come, first-served basis. The one exception to this rule takes place the week before the archery hunting season in September when camping reservations are required.

Hunting on Long Island is a unique experience for bowhunters. Deer, elk, black bear, and grouse are all fair game in the fall for archers, though you need to know that neither firearms nor dogs are permitted on the island. A special permit from the refuge headquarters is also required to hunt here.

On the other hand, no special permits (outside of normally issued state ones) are needed to hunt on the mainland. Waterfowlers visit the Lewis and

Leadbetter Units for walk-in hunting while others try to draw a good blind at the Riekkola Unit in hopes of bagging an Aleutian, dusky, cackling, or Canada goose. The Lewis and Riekkola Units are located on the south end of Willapa Bay. If you have never hunted here, make it a point to check with the staff at the refuge before heading afield as shooting is prohibited in some areas.

Leadbetter Point is at the north end of the Long Beach Peninsula. Visitors have the opportunity to see both the bay and the Pacific Ocean by hiking 1.3 miles along the Blue or 1.8-mile Yellow Trail. Other paths include the 2.1-mile Loop Trail and the half-mile Green Trail. Forests, salt marsh, sand dunes, ocean beaches, and tidal flats around the point are great for bird watching. Over 100 species have been observed here, including shorebirds like sandpipers, sanderlings, and short-billed dowitchers. The snowy plover, a rare species, nests on a section of beach closed to public access from March through September.

In other portions of the refuge you'll spy not only waterfowl, but also egret, common loon, and several different types of grebe. Great blue heron abound on Long Island with a rookery on the northern tip. Peregrine and Merlin falcon hunt small birds and bald eagles are seen year round. In the late summer, large brown pelicans are commonly seen just offshore. Black bear are frequently seen (especially around Leadbetter Point and Long Island), as are beaver, muskrat, and on occasion, river otter and bobcat.

The fertile waters of this estuary also support a huge shellfish population. The bay is known for its oysters, harvested primarily by private and commercial interests. However, there are some public areas in the bay where you can gather oysters, manila clams, and cockles. Another shellfish of note is the razor clam. You'll find these on the Pacific Ocean beaches near Leadbetter Point. Short seasons for these tasty clams open on an infrequent basis over the course of the year. Crabbing is also an option with both Dungeness and red rock crab found in the bay.

The Willapa National Wildlife Refuge is open all year. A check of the tide charts is essential before venturing into the bay. Fluctuating tides have left more than one kayaker and flats walker stranded. Pet owners should also be aware that dogs are not allowed anywhere on the refuge unless they are service animals or actively being used for waterfowl hunting.

Getting There: Take US Highway 101 north from Ilwaco or south from Raymond. You'll find the refuge headquarters and boat ramp near mile post 24.

Beach Camping
(GRAYLAND BEACH – TWIN HARBORS – OCEAN CITY STATE PARKS)

Grayland Beach State Park
925 Cranberry Beach Road, Grayland, WA 98547 / 360-267-4301
www.parks.wa.gov
Twin Harbors State Park
420 State Route 105, Westport, WA 98595
360-268-9565
www.parks.wa.gov
Ocean City State Park
148 State Route 115, Hoquiam, WA 98850 / 360-289-3553
www.parks.wa.gov

Lodging Prices

When it comes to outdoor getaways, a weekend at the beach is always a great choice. Three state parks along the Washington coast offer plenty of beach access and places to stay. Summer visitors generally enjoy sunny days and breezy conditions perfect for kite flying. In the off season, storm watching is a draw. Listen to the fury of the crashing waves and then walk the beach after they have subsided to see what has washed ashore.

Razor clamming is popular, but seasons open and close on short notice so you'll want to check with the Department of Fish and Wildlife before you break out that clam shovel. Fishing for surf perch is a possibility along this stretch of the coast and bird watching is yet another reason to come. The raucous call of sea gulls is heard year round over the rolling surf, and in the summer brown pelicans fly low over the cresting waves. Various shorebirds like plover stay just ahead of beach walkers and curious dogs. Common tern, cormorants, scoters, loons, and grebes all show up on the ocean waters and bays in the spring and stay through fall. If you venture out to sea in a boat you'll likely see murre, marbled murrelet, and pigeon guillemot.

Grayland Beach State Park is a 418-acre park in an area known not only for its ocean side location, but also for its cranberries. RV enthusiasts choose among 60 full hook-up sites and an additional 42 sites have electricity and water. Tent campers can stay in seven standard or primitive camp sites. You can also stay in one of the 14 heated yurts that sleep up to five people. There is no picnic area in the park, but there is a short 0.25-mile interpretive trail that leads to the beach.

Twin Harbors State Park is a small 172-acre park 3 miles south of Westport. A lot of camp sites are jammed into this park (250 tent spaces and 49 utility spaces for RVs). A group camp site accommodates up to 10 cars and 60 people. There is also a small day-use area consisting of a kitchen shelter and a few picnic tables. A walk along the Shifting Sands Nature Trail after a meal is a pleasant diversion. The 0.75-mile trail takes you through pine trees, sand dunes, and beach grass. You can exit the trail at the halfway point and walk onto the beach or stay on the path and loop back to the trailhead.

Ocean City State Park is the third place to pitch a tent or park an RV near the ocean beaches. This park is located north of Grays Harbor near the resort town of Ocean Shores. You'll find 149 tent sites and 29 utility sites, some of which have full hook-ups. There are also two group sites that can each handle 20 to 30 tent campers and the day-use area has a small number of covered and open picnic tables. If you go, be sure to bring your foul weather gear since this part of Washington can get up to 100 inches of rain a year.

Getting There: You can reach Grayland Beach State Park by following State Highway 105 for 22 miles from Aberdeen to Grayland. Signs in the small town will direct you to the park. Twin Harbors State Park is 3 miles south of Westport on both sides of Highway 105. Ocean City State Park is north of Ocean Shores. Drive west 16 miles from Hoquiam along State Highway 109. Turn onto State Highway 115 and travel south 1.2 miles to the park.

WESTPORT CHARTERS

P.O. Box 466, Wesport, WA 98595 / 800-562-0157
www.westportcharters.com

Lodging Prices: N/A   Adventure Pricing: $ to $$$

The fleet at Westport is smaller than it used to be. A combination of fewer fish, mandated harvest allocations, higher fuel costs, and not as many oceangoing anglers all contribute to this reality. Despite that, there is still a lot of good fishing around here. In recent years, anywhere from 15,000 to 30,000 salmon were taken each season by anglers, making this one of your best bets if you want to hook into a saltwater salmon during the summer months.

Several charter businesses operate out of this well-established fishing port. The largest of them with a fleet of ten boats is Westport Charters. Owned by Steve and Kelly Westrick, their office doubles as a gift shop and is located across the street from their boats at the marina. The Westport Charter fleet consists of boats ranging from the 14-passenger, 40-foot Tornado to the big 56-foot Swifty. Other boats include the Discovery, Freedom, Gold Rush, Pescatore, Playboy Too, Sea Angel, Tally Ho, and Steve Westrick's Hula Girl.

One of the younger captains in the Westport fleet is Brian Miramonte, skipper of the Sea Angel. He explains Westport Charter boats are popular because the crews have a reputation of being very professional. In his words, "We don't just go out for a bottomfishing trip and head back the minute we get a limit of rockfish. We'll put in some extra effort and try to get our guests into some lingcod too." Kelly Westrick is proud of the fact that their boats are clean, their crews personable, and that 80 percent of their business consists of repeat customers, many of whom go out with the same boat year after year.

Bottomfishing trips for black sea bass and lingcod start in March and go all the way to October. Miramonte says the rockfish average 2 to 3 pounds each and there is currently a 10-fish limit. You can also get up to two lingcod a day. These delicious fish average 10 pounds but can get much larger.

Later in the spring, a halibut season brings out a crowd to catch the flat-bottomed fish averaging 26 pounds. In recent years, this has been a short-lived fishery. Harvest allocations in 2007 only allowed a six-day season for these big bottom dwellers.

Salmon fishing charters are the most popular trips booked at Westport. The season kicks off in early July. Depending upon the fishing and regulations it can last into mid-September. According to Miramonte, coho from 5 to 10 pounds make up the majority of the catch in July but as the fish grow in the ocean the average size increases towards 15 pounds. Chinook salmon are also caught on a regular basis, and they can get big. Last year an angler on Steve Westrick's boat pulled in a 47-pound monster. If you want to catch both bottom fish and salmon, combination fishing trips are available.

Another Westport fishery has created an avid following in recent years. Albacore tuna can be caught anywhere from 30 to 65 miles from port in August and September. Boats will head out for short one-day or standard two-day trips. Miramonte says it's common to catch 10 to 12 line-peeling albacore ranging from 12 to 15 pounds each during a two-day excursion. Because these are overnight trips, the boats take fewer clients, so advance reservations are a good idea.

If you want to do something else, whale watching is an option from March through April. Wildly popular in the 1990s, the whale-watching craze at Westport has cooled some in recent years. This is despite the fact this same activity remains a strong draw in the San Juan Islands of Puget Sound. Kelly Westrick may have the best explanation for it: "Everyone wants to see Free Willy, but nobody wants to come and see Barnacle Bill anymore." While San Juan orcas may be more elegant, the big gray whales that pass by here are quite impressive and well worth the trip. Weighing up to 40 tons, they are known to be curious, often swimming right up to the boat. Better still; rates for these trips are very cheap – running well under $50 a person.

Rates for salmon and bottomfishing trips are also affordable, often half of what you would pay to go fishing with a river guide. This is because the boats are taking out a lot more passengers. You may find yourself fishing with a couple of dozen other anglers on a typical charter excursion out of Westport. Fun and camaraderie are the norm and fast friendships often develop among customers on these outings. The fishing boats typically depart early in the morning and return by early afternoon.

Getting There: Westport Charters is located at the Westport Marina. Westport is located off of State Route 105 at the southern tip of Grays Harbor.

Damon Point State Park and Oyhut Wildlife Area

Damon Point State Park
Discovery Avenue SW, Ocean Shores, WA 98569 / 360-902-8844
www.parks.wa.gov
Oyhut Wildlife Area – Washington Department of Fish and Wildlife, Montesano
360-249-4628 – www.wdfw.wa.gov

Two seldom-visited public lands south of Ocean Shores are worth a visit if you are in the mood for a walk and some bird watching. Damon Point State Park and the nearly adjacent 640-acre Oyhut Wildlife Area are located at the north end of Grays Harbor where it meets the open Pacific Ocean. Damon Point is a good place for a hike and the wildlife area offers fair waterfowl hunting in the fall and winter. Both places boast good wildlife viewing, especially for birds, throughout the year.

Damon Point is a 61-acre day-use site that juts out into Grays Harbor. It wasn't long ago that you could drive out along a spit towards the end of the point. However, the road washed out and the picnic tables and interpretive signs placed at the park are now overgrown with brush. Today, you hike over a mile from the mainland at low tide to reach Damon Point on Protection Island. On one side of the point are the crashing waves of the Pacific Ocean, barely tamed at the mouth of the big harbor. On the other side the waters of the bay are calmer, and birds are abundant. A walk around the perimeter of the island and point back to the parking lot covers over 3.5 miles.

Expect to see plenty of shore birds. Several species of plover and sandpiper are found near the waters edge, and rare snowy plover and streaked horned lark nest here in the spring (please stay away from their nesting sites). Offshore, you'll often spy red-throated loon or scoters. Raptors are also numerous. Bald eagles, red-tailed hawks, peregrine falcons, and northern harriers can be seen year round at both Damon Point and the Oyhut Wildlife Area. Marine mammals are also around. The head of a harbor seal bobbing just above the waterline is a common sight and in the spring you might just glimpse a gray whale.

The nearby Oyhut Wildlife Area doesn't have any trails per se, and isn't even marked with much signage to let you know it's there. However, a short walk through tall grass will bring you to a salt marsh area of channels and intertidal flats. Bufflehead and mallard are two frequently seen waterfowl species and deer are common on land.

If you are looking for solitude this is the place. The Oyhut Wildlife area gets little use and even during hunting season you aren't likely to have much company.

There are no facilities at the Oyhut Wildlife Area or at Damon Point State Park. Both are open all year for day-use activities.

Getting There: Follow Point Brown Avenue south from the entrance of Ocean Shores at State Highway 115 until it ends at Marine View Drive. Turn right onto Marine View Drive and you'll soon see the sign and parking turnout for Damon Point State Park. Continue south on Marine View Drive 0.8 miles to Tonquin Avenue. Turn left and travel a short distance to a dirt parking lot to enter the unsigned wildlife area.

Good numbers of juvenile and adult bald eagles winter around Ocean Shores.

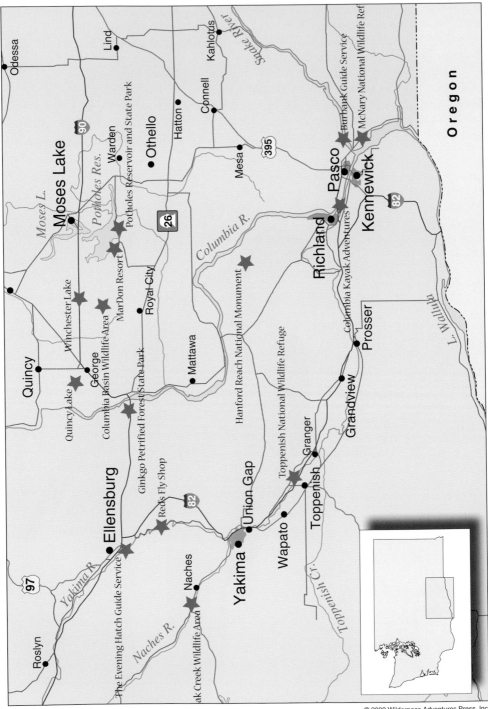

Odessa

Lind

Kahlotus

Snake River

Burbank Guide Service

McNary National Wildlife Ref

Oregon

90

Warden

Potholes Reservoir and State Park

Othello

Hatton

Connell

395

Mesa

Moses L.

Potholes Res.

Moses Lake

26

Columbia R.

Pasco

Kennewick

82

MarDon Resort

Royal City

Richland

Columbia Kayak Adventures

Winchester Lake

Quincy Lake

George

Columbia Basin Wildlife Area

Mattawa

Hanford Reach National Monument

Prosser

L. Wallula

Quincy

Ginkgo Petrified Forest/State Park

Toppenish National Wildlife Refuge

Grandview

Ellensburg

Red's Fly Shop

82

Union Gap

Granger

The Evening Hatch Guide Service

Yakima

Wapato

Toppenish

97

Naches

Yakima R.

ak Creek Wildlife Area

Naches R.

Toppenish Cr.

Roslyn

© 2009 Wilderness Adventures Press, Inc.

Yakima River Country

The Yakima River and Toppenish National Wildlife Refuge

Washington Department of Fish and Wildlife - Sunnyside/Snake River Wildlife Area: I-82 and Sunnyside Headquarter Units
2030 Holaday Road, Mabton, WA 98935 – 509-837-7644
http://wdfw.wa.gov/lands/r3sunny.htm
and http://wdfw.wa.gov/lands/r3i82.htm

Flowing over 200 miles from Keechelus Dam in the Cascades to the Columbia River at the Tri-Cities, the Yakima River is managed by the Bureau of Reclamation to irrigate agricultural fields, orchards, and vineyards southeast of the Cascade Mountains. Despite that focus, this stream boasts great fishing along with good paddling and wildlife watching.

The river's first 75 miles from Keechelus Dam to Roza Dam is the state's only designated "Blue Ribbon" trout fishery. A 2003 survey by the Washington Department of Fish and Wildlife demonstrates how good the fishing in this stream can be. There are an estimated 39,000 rainbow and cutthroat trout in the upper river and most of them (about 1,129 per river mile) are concentrated in the Yakima River Canyon from Ellensburg downstream to Roza Dam. Whitefish are also common and brook trout occasionally show up at the end of your line in the upper reaches of the river.

One reason for the excellent fishing is the restrictive regulations that apply here. While the upper Yakima (above Roza Dam) is open all year to trout fishing, it is strictly a catch-and-release affair. No bait is allowed and you must use lures or flies with single barbless hooks. Because of this the river is a favorite of flyfishers, though you can also use spinners and spoons to catch your fair share of trout.

There are numerous public access sites to the river from Easton all the way to Roza Dam. Bank anglers can access several places from Cle Elum to Ellensburg, but the favorite place for many anglers, hikers, paddlers, and wildlife watchers is in the Yakima River Canyon. State Highway 821 (the Canyon Road) runs south from Ellensburg towards Yakima through a scenic canyon frequented by mule deer, bighorn sheep, upland birds, and wintering bald eagles. The Wenas State Wildlife Area borders the west side of the canyon.

One way to explore it is by taking a hike along Umtanum Creek. The trailhead starts at a BLM access point 12 miles down the Canyon Road. Cross a suspension bridge over the Yakima and follow the trail along Umtanum Creek and several beaver ponds for about 2 miles. Enjoy the desert landscape and keep your eyes open to see a variety of different birds, mammals, and reptiles (watch for rattlesnakes in the summer).

Paddlers in rafts and canoes float 18 miles of the calm and scenic Yakima within the canyon, with several put in and take out points available. There is also paddling further upstream. You can put in near Cle Elum and float 13 miles towards a diversion dam near Thorp. This float has a few Class II rapids in case you are craving a little excitement to go with the ample sunshine, cool waters, and pleasing country scenery that accompany most of these trips.

Below Roza Dam the river flows past Yakima. A paved 10-mile trail called the Yakima Greenway parallels the river part of the way and provides outdoors recreation in an urban environment for hikers, bird watchers, and bicyclists. Below Yakima, access to the river is possible between Union Gap and Zillah at the 980-acre I-82 Unit of the Sunnyside/Snake River Wildlife Area. Fishing in the river and several nearby ponds is popular for trout, bass, and panfish. In the fall, there is decent waterfowl hunting here along with fair shooting for quail and the occasional pheasant.

Continuing east towards Sunnyside you can access the Yakima through the Satus Wildlife Area, managed by the Yakama Indian Nation. With some 20 miles of river frontage, sloughs, ponds, and wetlands, this is a popular place for duck hunting. A tribal permit is required to hunt here.

Just downstream from the Satus Wildlife Area is the 2,786-acre Headquarters Unit of the Sunnyside/Snake River Wildlife Area. Also bordering the Yakima River, the stream and surrounding ponds offer good duck hunting in the fall and winter. Excellent bird-watching opportunities occur in the spring for migratory waterfowl, several species of heron and hawks, long-billed curlew, western grebe, and loggerhead shrike. Managed by the Washington Department of Fish and Wildlife, some access has been restricted due to vandalism and littering.

Another public land in this area is the Toppenish National Wildlife Refuge (509-865-2405 – www.fws.gov). While a portion of the 1,978-acre refuge encompasses wetlands and tributaries near the Yakima River, the main portion of the property is located a few miles south of Toppenish off of US Highway 97. A small part of the refuge near the headquarters is open for wildlife viewing all year. Another area off of Pumphouse Road (west of the refuge headquarters) is open for hunting in the fall and winter. Hunters can only have 25 non-toxic shot shells in their possession while gunning for waterfowl, quail, and pheasant here. If you are hunting ducks or geese you also have to stay within 50 feet of the established hunting sites that are available on a first-come, first-serve basis. Non-game birds you may see in this area include night herons and other birds common to marshy areas like black-necked stilt, sandpipers, and American avocet.

The Yakima flows at a more gentle pace as it continues through the Lower Yakima Valley towards the Tri-Cities, providing good smallmouth bass fishing and the opportunity to catch channel catfish in some places. Finally, the Yakima reaches the Columbia River between Richland and Kennewick. Kayakers and canoeists can explore the delta at the mouth of the Yakima to see great blue heron, shorebirds, waterfowl, beaver, deer, and coyote. If you don't care to paddle you can hike around 160-acre Bateman Island from the Columbia Park Trail near Kennewick to observe wildlife.

Getting There: See above.

A yellow-bellied marmot making sure all is well.

The Evening Hatch Guide Service

2308 Canyon Road, Ellensburg, WA 98826 / 1-866-482-4480 or 509-962-5959
www.theeveninghatch.com

Adventure Pricing

Lodging Prices

No discussion of flyfishing in Washington is complete without mentioning the Yakima River. Managed as the state's only "Blue Ribbon" trout stream, the 70 miles of river from Easton to Roza Dam in the Yakima River Canyon boasts year-around fishing for rainbow and cutthroat trout that average 10 to 13 inches in length and sometimes get up to 2 feet long.

Several guides call the Yakima River their "home water". One of them is Jack Mitchell, owner of the Evening Hatch Guide Service. Mitchell started his business in 1988. Today, he employs five to ten experienced guides at any given time and expects to offer 750 trips a year. A typical day starts by meeting your guide at the fly shop around 9:00am before heading to the river. One or two of you will then share a raft or drift boat with your guide for eight to nine hours. During that time, you'll cover anywhere from 3 to 20 miles of water depending on the river flow.

The fishing is done with fly rods, but there is no need to be intimidated. Mitchell says, "We are service oriented and take care of our guests. We understand this is their adventure. Thirty percent of our guests are novices and it's our intent to make their day enjoyable. We have great instructors when it comes to teaching you how to get the fish to bite and how to gain skill in flyfishing." Included with your trip are snacks and a BBQ shore lunch. A fly rod, reel, tippet, and flies are also provided if needed.

The Yakima is not the only piece of water the Evening Hatch fishes. They also offer anglers day trips and overnight flyfishing expeditions on several streams to include:

The Klickitat River

Jack Mitchell and his guides help you catch summer steelhead from drift boats and rafts in a 35-mile stretch of this south central Washington river from September through November. They also have a three-bedroom guest ranch on 40 acres if you are booking an overnight trip. In addition to hard-fighting steelies, you can also catch some nice resident rainbow trout.

The Upper Columbia River

Head up towards the Canadian border and fish the Columbia near Northport, Washington from March through June. You'll fish dry flies, streamers, and nymphs in 10 to 20 feet of water for big, wild rainbow trout. How big? Well, in 2006 they landed a 13-pound rainbow and the average fish runs over 3 pounds. You'll spend the night in an A-frame lodge near Northport after a full day on the water.

The Kettle River

Clients fishing the Upper Columbia may also get the chance to explore the Kettle River in northeastern Washington. Lightly fished, this pristine river flows through rural country and holds rainbow trout that average 13 inches.

The Methow River

This beautiful fishing stream has an abundance of fishy pools, riffles, and tail outs that provide good catch-and-release fishing from July through September for rainbow and cutthroat trout. When enough summer steelhead return to the river, the stream stays open for fishing and offers excellent flyfishing from October through the winter.

The Naches River

You can fish this technically difficult river by request from a raft with a guide during the summer months for cutthroat and rainbows. Even though the average fish run around 9 inches, there are enough big fish in this steep, fast flowing stream to make things interesting.

The Evening Hatch Guide Service is open all year. You can also arrange for shuttles and rent drift boats or fishing rafts from the fly shop in Ellensburg.

Getting There: Take Exit 109 off Interstate 90 in Ellensburg. Travel south about 200 yards to reach the fly shop on the left side of Canyon Road.

RED'S FLY SHOP & GUIDE SERVICE

Milepost 15, Canyon Road (or PO Box 186), Ellensburg, WA 98826 / 509-929-1802
www.redsflyshop.com

Lodging Prices: $ to Price to be determined   Adventure Pricing: $$ to $$$$

When it comes to fishing the Yakima River, Red's Fly Shop and Guide Service has got something going for it the competition doesn't. Real estate pros call it "Location! Location! Location!" Luckily for Red's, their fly shop and guide service is located right on the banks of the Yakima River in a scenic canyon south of Ellensburg.

You can stock up on gear at the fly shop or launch your drift boat or raft from the property. You can also arrange for a shuttle (so your vehicle is picked up where you put your boat in and waiting at the take out point downstream). If you don't have a boat, you can rent a drift boat or fishing raft with the shuttle operation included in the price. Recreational rafts can also be rented and the Yakima River Canyon's Class I rated waters make for a pleasant float in a raft or canoe.

Another thing that separates Red's from their competitors is their lodging. The brand new Canyon River Ranch featuring a ten-room lodge with outdoor pool and nine cabins is scheduled to open in 2009. Although the lodge and cabins are privately owned, rooms at the lodge will be available to rent from the owners through the fly shop. Those wanting a more rustic experience for less money can rent one of the existing 12-by-16-foot canvas tents next to the river. Featuring two cots, carpeted wooden floors and a wood stove, these accommodations meet the needs of many visitors just fine.

Red's co-owner Steve Joyce keeps eight guides busy by offering clients daylong flyfishing trips for trout on the Yakima River, as well as smallmouth bass fishing trips on the lower Yakima, steelhead trips on the Klickitat or Methow Rivers, trout fishing trips on the Naches River, and upland bird hunting trips on leased land in the Yakima Canyon and Columbia Basin.

One of Red's long time guides is Rod Griffin. He'll typically take two anglers at a time for a full day of flyfishing on the upper Yakima. A gourmet barbeque lunch along with snacks, soft drinks, flies and accessories are included in the price.

You can get a similar float trip on the lower Yakima River from spring through summer and target smallmouth bass. Griffin says they flyfish for these bass from the boat using streamers and surface poppers. Most anglers catch lots of bass. While many are small, fish from 2 to 4 pounds are common and Griffin has seen smallmouth up to 8 pounds in this part of the river.

On the Naches River, you'll spend as much time wading as you do floating while you fish for cutthroat and rainbow trout. If you go with Red's to the Klickitat River, you can drift for steelhead in the summer and fall. When enough fish make it up the

Columbia River, summer steelhead can also be pursued from fall into the winter on the scenic Methow River in north central Washington. You can book these as day or overnight trips that feature stays in wall tents with the promise of good food and full days of fishing.

When it comes to hunting, Red's offers the opportunity to work with their Labrador retrievers or English setters to hunt quail and chukar. Griffin says this "is not for the faint of heart." A typical hunt will have you scrambling up basalt rock and dry grassy ridges to pursue these wild birds, but the reward of hunting behind good dogs and getting shots at up to a half dozen coveys a day makes it worthwhile. Most of the hunting takes place on the Mt. Baldy Ranch – 15,000 acres of leased land just a few minutes from Red's Fly Shop. The length of the hunt depends on the level of the client's fitness and how well he or she shoots. Trained dogs, transportation to and from the fly shop, field dressing of the birds, as well as a nice lunch and snacks are all provided. The upland bird season generally runs from early October through mid-January.

Red's Fly Shop is open all year. Call in advance to reserve a guided trip or a place to stay.

Getting There: Take Exit 109 off of Interstate 90 in Ellensburg. Follow Canyon Road south 13 miles to reach Red's Fly Shop.

A beautiful Yakima River rainbow (photo courtesy Joe Rotter, Red's Fly Shop).

Oak Creek Wildlife Area

16601 U.S. Highway 12, Naches, WA 98937 / 509-653-2390
www.wdfw.wa.gov/lands/r3oakcrk.htm

One of the best places to view wildlife in Washington is at the Oak Creek Wildlife Area northwest of Yakima. During the winter, you can see elk and bighorn sheep up close as they congregate near feeding stations. Venturing farther into the wildlife area, you may also see mule deer, upland birds, raptors, and songbirds.

Rocky Mountain elk were brought to the foothills of the eastern Cascades from Yellowstone National Park in 1913. The introduction was successful; so much so that damage to area crops and orchards from the big ungulates became a significant problem. In response, the Oak Creek Wildlife Area was established and during the 1940s, fencing was put up around the state property to keep the animals on public land. In 1967, California bighorn sheep were brought to the wildlife area. This Cleman Mountain herd of sheep now numbers some 150 animals. Another introduction of bighorn sheep in the Tieton River Canyon has produced a separate herd of some 120 rams and ewes that also live within the wildlife area boundaries.

With the fencing of the wildlife area, came the responsibility to take care of the animals. Daily feedings occur at designated sites for the elk and sheep during the winter. Up to 2,500 elk at a time show up near the headquarters site after food is put out at 1:30pm. Meanwhile, bighorns from the Cleman Mountain herd make their way down to a nearby sheep feeding station. Feeding generally occurs from mid-December until early March, depending on weather conditions.

The wildlife area is popular, receiving close to 100,000 visitors a year. Most of the visitors are content to watch the wildlife from the viewing area near the wildlife area headquarters. A volunteer staffed visitor center is open daily from 9:00am to 4:00pm in the winter. There is no charge to view the wildlife but donations are gladly accepted to help pay for the feeding program.

There is more to see besides elk and sheep. The wildlife area is intersected by the Tieton and Naches Rivers, along with several seasonal streams. Shrub-steppe habitat in the lower elevations supports sagebrush, bitterbrush, bluebunch wheatgrass, and rabbit brush. Oregon white oak is found near the stream beds while a combination of ponderosa pine, fir trees, and Engelmann spruce can be found at higher elevations.

Golden eagle, raven, and prairie falcon nest on rocky cliffs while Merriam's turkey, chukar, blue, spruce, and ruffed grouse are a few of the game birds that inhabit the area. Mule deer are common, and birders will be interested to know both loggerhead shrike and Lewis's woodpecker are found here.

Climbers also come to the Oak Creek Wildlife Area. Cliffs up to 500 feet high rise out of the ground near the Tieton River, attracting rock-climbing devotees. The most popular spot is called the Royal Columns, though the Bend and the Moon Rocks also have their share of visitors who work their way up cracks between the rock columns. The Royal Columns are located across the Tieton River from the wildlife area headquarters. The Bend is close by and the Moon Rocks are 3 miles west off of US Highway 12. Climbing on all three of these crags can be done year round, depending on the weather. You do need to watch out for rattlesnakes from spring through fall. You should also know that some of the cliffs, trails, and range area near the feeding stations are closed at certain times of year to minimize disturbances to nesting raptors and other wildlife.

Getting There: The wildlife area is located at the junction of US Highway 12 and State Highway 410 some 20 miles northwest of Yakima near Naches. The headquarters and visitor center are located 2 miles off of US Highway 12 west of the junction. The bighorn sheep feeding station is located off of State Highway 410 near the junction on the Old Naches Highway.

The Royal Columns above the Tieton River.

Potholes Reservoir and State Park

Potholes State Park
6762 Highway 262 East, Othello, WA 99344/ 509-346-2759
www.parks.wa.gov
Columbia Basin Wildlife Area (Potholes Unit)
6653 Road K NE, Moses Lake, WA 98837 / 509-765-6641
http://wdfw.wa.gov/lands/wildlife_areas/columbia_basin/

Lodging Prices

A 28,000-acre lake, state park, and unique wildlife area are all found at Potholes Reservoir. Formed in the early 1950s after the construction of O'Sullivan Dam, the reservoir provides irrigation for farms in this dry part of central Washington that averages less than 9 inches of rain a year.

The reservoir and public lands that border it are a great destination for anglers, hunters, pleasure boaters, and wildlife viewers. There is some unique topography here. For those that consider Washington to be a wet and soggy state, the presence of sagebrush, sand dunes, willow trees, and thick stands of cattails will come as a surprise. The reservoir is primarily fed by Crab Creek to the north and also receives water from Winchester and Frenchman Hills Wasteways to the west. The level of the reservoir drops when water is released from the spillway at O'Sullivan Dam, which forms the southern edge of the reservoir. While the south end of the reservoir is a deep lake, the northern end becomes a series of isolated potholes, channels, and shallow ponds that form as the reservoir level rises in the fall and drops again in summer.

Wildlife is abundant. Deer and coyote populate the sand dunes while beaver and muskrat swim in the shallow waters around them. The number and variety of birds to be seen here is staggering. White pelicans cruise silently over the dunes in the early fall and sandhill crane can also be heard and seen flying overhead. Great blue heron, night heron, gulls, western grebe, and snowy egret are all common, as are northern harrier (marsh hawk), owls, red-headed blackbird, meadowlark, magpie, pheasant, and quail.

The shallow waters and ponds are an important breeding place for waterfowl and a popular stopover destination for ducks and geese as they migrate to and from Canada. Commonly seen species include Canada geese, mallard, green-winged teal, wigeon, gadwall, coot, and shoveler. The northwest end of the reservoir is defined by the Job Corps Dike. North of here is the Potholes Game Reserve, a good bird-watching destination from June through September. Be aware that this reserve is closed to all public access from March 15 through May 30 and again from October 1 through February 1.

Fishing can be outstanding on the reservoir. Largemouth and smallmouth bass, walleye, rainbow trout, channel catfish, bullhead, carp, perch, crappie, and bluegill all end up at the end of an angler's line. The fish also get big. Crappie and rainbow trout weighing well over a pound are common. Bass can top 7 pounds, and every year there are several walleye caught that go 12 pounds or better.

As you might imagine, all of this fish and wildlife makes the Potholes Reservoir a veritable Mecca for sportsmen. Pleasure boaters also enjoy the big waters of the lake and those in canoes and kayaks can spend several days paddling around the sand dunes in the north, camping on their own private islands at the end of the day. Wildlife-viewing enthusiasts who hike, paddle, or boat around the potholes and channels at the north end of the reservoir will also have an enjoyable outing, especially in the spring and early fall before hunting season gets underway.

Access to the reservoir is easy enough. In the north, you get there via gravel roads that pass through the Potholes Unit of the Columbia Basin Wildlife Area and end at Crab Creek or the Job Corps Dike. Both places have rough, unimproved launch sites to launch small boats. At the south end of the reservoir, you can launch larger craft from Potholes State Park, Mar Don Resort, and paved boat launches on either side of O'Sullivan Dam. To the east of O'Sullivan Dam, there are gravel roads that provide public access to Lind Coulee, an eastern arm of the reservoir often sheltered from the wind that offers good fishing.

If you are looking for a place to stay, there are two private resorts on the south end of the reservoir along with Potholes State Park. The 640-acre park borders the reservoir and the mouth of Frenchman Hills Wasteway. In addition to having a nice boat launch, there is also a large shaded, grassy day-use area with playground equipment and four picnic shelters. You can stay overnight at one of the 61 campsites or 60 hook-up sites for RVs. Hikers and wildlife watchers can take a quick walk on a short loop trail at the southern end of the park or strike out to the west to explore Frenchman Hills Wasteway. Potholes State Park is open all year.

Getting There: The south end of Potholes Reservoir can easily be reached from State Highway 262 north of Othello. Several gravel roads heading south from the frontage road between Hiawatha Road (Exit 69) and Mae Valley Road (Exit 74) off of Interstate 90 will get you to the north end of the reservoir.

MARDON RESORT – MESEBERG DUCK TAXI – CAST AWAY FISHING & TOURS

8198 Hwy 262 SE Othello, WA 99344 / 800-416-2736
www.mardonresort.com – www.ducktaxi.com

Lodging Prices: $ to $$$ Adventure Pricing: $ to $$$

Located at the south end of 28,000-acre Potholes Reservoir, MarDon Resort has a legitimate claim as the hunting and fishing capitol of eastern Washington. The Meseberg family has owned the resort since 1972 and they have plenty of adventures for the outdoor enthusiast to enjoy.

The large resort offers accommodations ranging from campsites to RV spaces to simply furnished motel rooms that sleep two to four people. They also have more deluxe accommodations with their new park cottages that sleep up to six people in a bedroom and loft area. Each cottage has a full kitchen as well as a gas fireplace and satellite television in a small living room. Outside the cottages are covered decks and lots of open space for grilling up dinner or looking out over the lake. A store provides groceries, gifts, and lots of fishing and hunting gear. A café and lounge offer decent food, ice cream for the kids, or a cold drink after a full day playing outside.

There is a swimming beach at the resort and water sports are popular in the summer. A huge 500-foot dock provides lots of fishing opportunities for guests from spring through fall. Rainbow trout, walleye, panfish, catfish, bullhead, carp, along with largemouth and smallmouth bass are all found in the reservoir. In fact, Potholes is a popular destination for both walleye and bass tournaments, a testimony to the quality and quantity of fish found here. You can rent a fishing boat or bring your own to launch from the resort. A gas dock allows you to top off before heading out onto the water to fish, play, or just explore the secluded sand dunes in the north end of the lake.

Just across the road from the resort is the northern boundary of the Columbia National Wildlife Refuge. Featuring 23,000 acres of channeled scablands full of lakes, ponds, streams, and wetlands, the refuge is an ideal place for wildlife watching, hunting, fishing, hiking, and canoeing. See the Columbia NWR entry for further details.

West of the resort is the Desert Unit of the Columbia Basin Wildlife Area, managed by the Washington Department of Fish and Wildlife. Frenchman Hills and Winchester Wasteways flow through a landscape of sagebrush, sand dunes, cattails, and Russian olive trees to Potholes Reservoir. Wildlife watching, waterfowl hunting, paddling, and fishing are all good choices here. The entry for the Columbia Basin Wildlife Area has additional information.

With all of this water and wetlands, it's no wonder Mar Don Resort draws hunters, anglers, and birdwatchers too. Anglers may want to contact Levi Meseberg who operates Cast Away Fishing and Tours. His Everglades-style airboat offers a thrilling ride back into the shallow waters found among the sand dunes where snowy egrets, western grebe, and herons are abundant. Anglers enjoy fishing with Meseberg for bass, panfish, and walleye in this area from spring until early October.

Come fall, the focus shifts to bird hunting. The Meseberg Duck Taxi has been operating out of the resort since 1972. The Mesebergs and other longtime guides will take you on a thrilling boat ride to a blind in the sand dunes in the pre-dawn darkness. The blinds generally come alive with gunfire shortly after shooting time as ducks and geese try to land amongst the decoys. If you go with a guide you'll watch their dogs do great retrieves and get the opportunity to enjoy freshly cooked duck kabobs in the blind. After a full morning of hunting, it's a meal fit for a king. Unguided hunts are also available. They run a little cheaper – but you don't get the kabobs, dogs, or professional calling from the guides. As the reservoir freezes, hunting shifts to agricultural fields for Canada geese. Upland bird hunting for quail and pheasant is also available in the area.

Summer is the busiest time of year at the resort, and calling ahead is a good idea if you want to book one of the comfortable park cottages. Reservations are also recommended for the guided fishing and hunting trips.

Getting There: MarDon Resort is located along State Highway 262 on the south end of Potholes Reservoir. Most people access Highway 262 from State Highway 17 between Othello and Moses Lake.

Guide Levi Meseberg's airboat provides an ideal way to get into some late summer fishing and early season waterfowl hunting at Potholes Reservoir.

Columbia National Wildlife Refuge

Refuge Manager
735 East Main Street, Othello, Washington 99344 / 509-488-2668
www.fws.gov/columbiarefuge

Lodging Prices

The 29,596-acres of channeled scabland, mesas, and basalt cliffs of the Columbia National Wildlife Refuge (NWR) were formed by massive floods from the last ice age. Today, the refuge is an ideal place to go for wildlife viewing, bird watching, hunting, fishing, hiking ,and paddling. The principal portion of the refuge is located between Potholes Reservoir and Othello and has been managed by the U.S. Fish and Wildlife Service since 1944. Water from Potholes Reservoir and delivery canals has created seepage and filled up a series of lakes, ponds, and creeks in this rocky desert, providing important habitat for a variety of birds and mammals in the process.

There are a number of waters to fish within the refuge. In the north, Corral, Blythe, and Chukar Lakes all have rainbow trout, while nearby Soda Lake provides angling for rainbows, walleye, bass, panfish, and whitefish. Soda Lake also offers the only place you can camp at the refuge. Several campsites and pit toilets are available on a bluff above the lake and boat launch. In the middle of the refuge, Upper and Lower Hampton Lakes kick out good numbers of rainbow trout every spring and if you are looking for a hike-in trout fishing expedition, consider walking to Pillar, Poacher, and Widgeon Lakes. Hutchinson and Shiner Lakes offer not only fishing, but a scenic 3-mile paddling route for canoeists and kayakers. Small boat launches are available at Hutchinson, Lower Hampton, North and South Teal, Blythe, and Soda Lakes. Many of these lakes are open from April 1 through September 1. Check the fishing regulations for details. Other lakes just outside the refuge are on state-owned land and offer additional fishing and primitive camping opportunities.

Wildlife viewing is excellent. The refuge is part of the Coulee Corridor Scenic Byway which includes the Audubon Society's "Great Washington State Birding Trail". Nearly 250 different bird species have been observed in this specific area. Waterfowl are abundant from fall through the spring and one place to view them is from the overlook at Royal Lake. You'll also see waterfowl at the other lakes at the refuge, and in the marsh units. Other birds you'll see cover the gamut from turkey vultures to raptors, shorebirds, gulls, woodpeckers, flycatchers, vireos, thrushes, larks, swallows, warblers, tanagers, finches, sparrows, waxwings, blackbirds, and more.

One bird of particular note is the sandhill crane. There are about 25,000 cranes in the Pacific Flyway and the majority of them migrate through here in early spring (mid-February to early April) and early fall (mid-September to early October). The big gray birds have long necks and legs and a 6-foot wingspan that allows them to soar far above land in flocks as they ride thermal currents and sing their own distinctive song. Waste grain is a favorite food source for the cranes and there is generally plenty of it to be found in the irrigated fields of the Columbia Basin that lie close to the refuge. The refuge is such an important staging area for these birds that the Othello Sandhill Crane Festival takes place for three days at the end of March to celebrate their return. Tours to view cranes and other wildlife are available as are lectures regarding the geology of the area and the birds that call it home. A website (www.othellosandhillcranefestival. org) gives further details.

Other wildlife commonly seen at the refuge includes coyote, mule deer, muskrat, beaver, and yellow-bellied marmot. Reptiles like western skink also scurry across rocks while six different species of snakes slither along the ground, including the western rattlesnake.

Hiking through the refuge is great fun, particularly in the spring when the landscape is green and flowers like pink phlox and yellow arrowleaf balsamroot are blooming. Three hiking trails are found in Marsh Unit II. The Frog Lake Trail provides a 1-mile hike to Frog Lake and around the top of a small nearby butte. The 1-mile Marsh Loop starts at the same trail head, while the Crab Creek Trail starts off at the north end of Morgan Lake Road. Another great thing about desert hiking is that you can head cross country. With plenty of small waters, canyons, cliffs, and hills to ramble around, a walkabout on a sunny early spring day makes for a great adventure.

In the fall, hunters also walk the refuge for waterfowl, deer, and upland birds such as pheasant, quail, and chukar. Only certain portions of the refuge are open to hunting. The northern part of the refuge below O'Sullivan Dam, along with designated areas near Crab Creek and Canal Lake, are open every day for hunting during regular seasons. Hunters can only use shotguns or archery gear to pursue game and all scatter gunners must use non-toxic shells. Marsh Unit I is managed as a quality duck hunting area and Farm Unit 226-227 offers special permit hunting blinds for ducks and geese. These areas are only open for hunting on Wednesdays, Saturdays, Sundays, and federal holidays.

The Columbia National Wildlife Refuge is open all year, though some areas are closed at certain times to protect wildlife. Bicycle and horseback riding is limited to the gravel roads open for vehicle use. Spring and fall are the most popular times to visit. Many of the lakes ice up in the winter and the summer sun can be brutally hot. The refuge headquarters in Othello is open weekdays from 7:00am to 4:30pm.

Getting There: The refuge is located near Othello. The northern part of the refuge is best reached from State Route 262. The center of the refuge can be accessed off of McManamon Road while the southern portion can be found on either side of State Highway 26.

The Columbia National Wildlife Refuge is rich in scenic beauty.

Desert and Winchester Lake Units
COLUMBIA BASIN WILDLIFE AREA

Department of Fish and Wildlife, Region 2 Office
1550 Alder Street NW, Ephrata, WA 98823 / 509-754-4624
www.wdfw.wa.gov/lands/wildlife_areas/columbia_basin/

A wasteway is a peculiar name for water that provides so much for both wildlife and outdoors enthusiasts. Winchester and Frenchman Hills Wasteways came into existence in the mid-20th century as part of the Columbia Basin Irrigation Project that provided much needed water for this parched part of central Washington.

The 1,950-acre Winchester Lake Unit is visible to motorists traveling along Interstate 90 between the small town of George and Moses Lake. Located immediately north of the Dodson Rest Area, this wide spot of Winchester Wasteway is a 3-mile long lake. There is state land on both sides of the lake and two public access points along the eastern shore accessible off of Road 2 and Road 3. Another access point is found just north of the lake where the wasteway narrows into a canal at Road 5. In the past, pheasant hunters walked the edge of the lake to flush pheasants released here every year. However, the Department of Fish and Wildlife recently discontinued these releases due to conflicts with waterfowlers who gun for ducks on the lake in the fall and into the winter.

Anglers can expect to catch carp and perch in the shallow lake, but in the winter, the perch migrate up the wasteway and stack up on either side of Road 5. This makes for a good late-season opportunity to catch plenty of spiny rays that run anywhere from 5 to 10 inches long.

The 35,100-acre Desert Unit generally follows Winchester Wasteway south of Interstate 90 and Frenchman's Wasteway from Adams Road all the way to Potholes Reservoir. The two waterways are bordered by sandy hills, sagebrush, willows, Russian olives, and cattails along with innumerable lakes and ponds. Each wasteway has a reserve area closed to shooting where waterfowl quickly learn to congregate after hunting season begins. Wigeon, gadwall, green-winged teal, and shovelers are common in the fall while mallards, goldeneye, and Canada geese are the predominant birds during

the winter. Upland bird hunters beat the cattails and brush to flush wild pheasants and quail, while big game hunters lucky enough to draw a permit come looking for mule deer.

The Desert Unit offers reliable hunting all season long and is also a wildlife watching destination. You can hike, boat, or paddle along Winches Wasteway and access Frenchman Hills Wasteway at various points off of Frenchman Hills Road, Road C, or from Potholes State Park. In addition to game birds, great blue heron, sand hill crane, killdeer, meadowlark, red-winged and yellow-headed blackbird are all commonly seen and heard. Also vocal are the coyotes that frequent the area and sing their own tune once the sun goes down.

Boating access comes in bits and pieces along Frenchman's Wasteway due to culverts and fences that cross the water in places. Until recently, a unique adventure was possible on Winchester Wasteway for canoeists and kayakers. You could launch from Dodson Road and paddle along the slowly flowing stream as it wound through this strange combination of desert and marsh all the way to Potholes Reservoir. Unfortunately, proliferating reeds have obscured the path of the waterway, making this 25-mile through trip all but impossible. You can still paddle portions of Winchester Wasteway from Road C or Dodson Road, but you'll be fighting the upstream current either going or coming back.

Waterfowl hunters flock to the Columbia Basin Wildlife Area every autumn. Bill Gebhardt and Russell Johnston show off a mixed bag of ducks.

While you're on the water, you may want to make a few casts with a fishing pole. Big largemouth bass, decent smallmouth bass, rainbow trout, carp, and perch are all found in the wasteways and ponds of this wildlife area. One angling location of note is Beda Lake. Located just south of Winchester Wasteway off of Dodson Road, the Department of Fish and Wildlife manages this as a trophy trout fishery. Most anglers use float tubes and fly rods in the spring and fall to catch and release big rainbow and tiger trout.

Getting There: Winchester Lake can be reached from Road 2, Road 3, and Road 5 by traveling west from Dodson Road north of Interstate 90. The Desert Unit is accessed at various points off of Dodson Road, Frenchman Hills Road, and Road C SE south of Interstate 90. Dodson Road is signed as Exit 164 on Interstate 90 between George and Moses Lake.

Frenchman Hills Wasteway is an ideal place for birding.

Quincy Lakes Unit
COLUMBIA BASIN WILDLIFE AREA

Washington Department of Fish and Wildlife
1550 Alder Street NW, Ephrata, WA 98823 / 509-754-4624
www.wdfw.wa.gov/lands/wildlife_areas/columbia_basin/

The 15,226-acre Quincy Lakes Unit is a popular early spring destination for sun seeking anglers, horseback riders, and hikers. It's also a good place to hunt birds and catch fish in the fall. Lakes, ponds, and creeks are found amongst coulees full of sagebrush and bunchgrass. Basalt rock formations up to 800 feet tall form coulee walls that tower towards the sky and spring waterfalls add an oasis-like quality to a mixed environment of desert and wetlands.

The lakes here are managed for different fisheries. Evergreen Reservoir is the largest body of water. It contains bass, walleye, panfish, and a few tiger muskie. Just north of Evergreen are Burke and Quincy Lakes. Both are heavily fished for stocked rainbow trout in the wake of the traditional March 1st early opener. North of these is Stan Coffin Lake. This is a small catch-and-release largemouth bass lake that provides very good fishing. If you want to keep a few fish, target the bluegill, pumpkinseed, crappie, or channel catfish that are also found here.

All of the above lakes are accessible by a gravel road that runs north-south through the wildlife area from White Trail Road southeast of Quincy. This road (along with launches on the western end of Evergreen Reservoir, Quincy and Burke Lakes) is closed during hunting season. However, boat launches on the eastern end of Evergreen Reservoir and Burke Lake can be used year round from Road Three off of State Highway 281.

Several other lakes are accessible by foot, bicycle, or on horseback. The most popular is Dusty Lake. It is managed as a trophy trout lake with a limit of one fish per day and rules mandate the use of single, barbless hooks with no bait. You can hike to Dusty Lake along a short but steep half-mile trail down (and back up), or you can opt for a longer 3.5-mile hike, bike, or horseback ride along the Columbia River breaks and into the basalt rock coulee where the lake is located.

Four small bodies of water called the Ancient Lakes can also be reached from the Columbia River breaks. To get there; follow Road 9 west until it terminates at Ancient Lakes Road. Follow this road south until it ends. A 1.5-mile hike or ride from the trailhead will take you to the lakes within a wide coulee just north of the coulee where Dusty Lake is located. You can also hike into the Ancient Lakes from the top, walking past the scenic Judith Pools and a pretty waterfall that flows into the first of these lakes. Three of the lakes hold panfish and the other one is sporadically stocked with trout.

Several other smaller lakes are also found in the wildlife area. Several are hike-in waters stocked with a few rainbow trout for spring anglers. Two lakes, (Cree and H Lakes) are both accessible by car, but offer only mediocre angling for warmwater species. There are no formal campgrounds on this state land, but primitive camping by several of the lakes and near the main gravel road is popular in the spring.

Fall is a good time to return to the Quincy Lakes. While some of the waters here close at the end of July, Dusty and Stan Coffin Lake, as well as Evergreen Reservoir, provide excellent late summer angling as the weather begins to cool. Dove hunting can be decent in September, and walk-in hunters find a mixed bag of quail, pheasant and migrating waterfowl throughout the area from October into January.

Getting There: Located 4.6 miles south of Quincy. The easiest access is off of White Trail Road from State Highway 28 or 281.

Hanford Reach National Monument

3250 Port of Benton Blvd., Richland, WA 99354 / 509-371-1801
www.fws.gov/hanfordreach/

You would be forgiven if you think this presidentially proclaimed 195,000-acre monument is a whole lot of nothing. Much of the terrain, especially from summer through winter, is colored a dreary brown and dull green by native grasses, dirt, and sagebrush. The reasoning is reinforced as you pass through thousands of acres scorched by recent fires that left little but dirt and charred sage brush branches in its wake.

First impressions are deceiving though. The area, bisected by the last free-flowing stretch of the Columbia River, is full of life if you are willing to slow down and look. The Columbia flows south past sand bars, small islands, and scenic white bluffs with riffles and minor rapids. On shore, you'll find shrub-steppe habitat that supports 725 different plant species, most noticeably the big sagebrush, gray rabbit brush, and bunchgrasses that dominate much of the landscape.

Hanford became important during World War II, when scientists and engineers built a nuclear reactor that produced plutonium for the first atomic test and for the atom bomb dropped on Nagasaki that led to the end of the war against Japan in 1945. The reactor remained online until 1968. Today, workers labor to clean up the radioactive byproducts produced by this piece of 20th century history. The reactor, along with other nuclear facilities, lie on the Hanford Site operated by the Department of Energy (DOE) between State Highway 240 and the west banks of the Columbia. Public access is not allowed except through prearranged tours.

The Hanford National Monument surrounding the DOE's Hanford Site is managed for wildlife and habitat protection. The Fitzner/Eberhardt Arid Lands Ecology Reserve's 77,000 acres are found on the west side of State Highway 240. Established to preserve one of the largest remaining shrub-steppe habitats left in Washington, the reserve is home for a herd of Rocky Mountain elk and other species to include 46 different species of

butterflies and rare plants like the Rattlesnake Mountain mild-vetch and Piper's daisy. This reserve is closed to public access, as is the Saddle Mountain Refuge north of the Columbia River next to State Highway 24.

Public access is available to the monument just north of the Vernita Bridge where State Highway 24 crosses the Columbia River. A boat launch here provides a great jump off point for kayakers wishing to paddle downstream through the heart of the monument, taking out at the White Bluffs launch or at Ringold Springs. This stretch of river also provides excellent fishing for salmon in the summer, steelhead in the fall, and smallmouth bass in all but the coldest months of the year. Bird watchers will enjoy the sight of ducks and geese on the water and herons near shore throughout the year. Killdeer are common in the spring, as are white pelican in the summer and eagles in the winter.

The Wahluke Unit on either side of State Highway 24 is home to mammals ranging from coyotes and porcupine to a healthy population of mule deer that muzzleloaders and archers hunt in the fall. Upland bird gunners work the brush for chukar and quail, while waterfowl enthusiasts jump ducks from the Wahluke ponds or set up decoys along the shores of the Columbia.

If you are up for a hike, you can travel cross country on top of the White Bluffs that tower above the eastern edge of the Columbia River. You can start your walk above the White Bluffs boat launch and wander north or south, enjoying views of the river as you go. Hikers also follow an old jeep trail for 2 miles to the Wahluke lakes. Spring is an excellent time to visit when you'll see desert wildflowers and non-game birds like sage sparrows, blackbirds, horned lark, and meadowlark. Reptiles such as gopher snakes, lizards, and the Great Basin spadefoot toad also call the monument home. All of these reptiles and small birds attract raptors. Northern harrier, red-tailed hawk, and prairie falcon are some of the hunting birds you'll likely see.

The Hanford Reach National Monument is a day-use area, and solar powered gates at the Wahluke entrance close after dusk and don't open again until early morning. While hiking is allowed in some areas, bicycling is only allowed along the roads of the refuge open to motorized vehicles.

Getting There: You can reach the Vernita Bridge by traveling south on State Highway 243 from the Vantage Bridge at Interstate 90 to the intersection of State Highway 24. You can also get there from the Tri-Cities by traveling north on State Highway 240 to Highway 24. Travel north five miles on Highway 24 to the Vernita Bridge.

COLUMBIA KAYAK ADVENTURES

710-D George Washington Way, Richland, WA 99354 / 509-947-5901
www.columbiakayakadventures.com

Lodging Prices: N/A   Adventure Pricing: $ to $$

There is organized kayaking in Washington outside of Puget Sound! That's good news for those wanting to visit the sunny side of the state. Based in the Tri-Cities, Columbia Kayak Adventures offers scheduled half and full day tours from April through October on the Columbia, Yakima, and Palouse Rivers.

Owner and guide Pat Welle has a lifelong love for paddling. She grew up canoeing the lakes of northern Minnesota and has been seriously kayaking since 2001. She is a certified American Canoe Association kayak instructor and also has a wilderness first responder (first aid) certification. Today, Welle operates a shop steps away from waterfront Howard Amon Park in Richland where she offers kayak rentals, sales, instruction, and tours.

A great introduction to flat water kayaking can be found on the three-hour Yakima Delta tour. No prior experience is necessary. Novice paddlers are given basic instruction before exploring the Yakima River just upstream from where it enters the Columbia. Expect to see lots of wildlife. Osprey, terns, herons, beaver, and deer are all commonly seen on this popular trip scheduled on a regular basis throughout the year.

A seldom offered, but unique, six-hour tour allows you to paddle up the Palouse River. In the spring and fall you launch at the mouth of the river and head upstream 4 miles before turning around. Navigating through the narrow canyon with basalt rock walls on either side is a unique southeastern Washington experience.

Finally, Welle offers full day trips on the Hanford Reach. The tour starts at Vernita Bridge. From there, you'll spend five hours on the water paddling downstream to gain a historical and natural perspective of this unique region that President Clinton designated as a National Monument. Along the way, you'll likely see pelicans, heron, long-billed curlew, and a variety of raptors, waterfowl, and songbirds. Salmon and steelhead may jump beside your kayak and you may get a chance to observe coyote, deer, elk, rabbit, and beaver along shore.

Most of the kayaking takes place in calm water, though there is one mild set of rapids to navigate. Your total trip time from pick up to drop off is about eight hours. Experience is helpful, but not an absolute necessity, for this tour.

Columbia Kayak Adventures posts their scheduled tour dates on their website. Classes are also available if you are interested in learning more about kayaking. Their store by the park (and Columbia River) is open from Tuesday through Sunday.

Getting There: Take the George Washington Way Exit off Interstate 182 in Richland. Drive north on George Washington Way to Lee Boulevard. Take a right towards Howard Amon Park. Columbia River Kayak Adventures is located near the park entrance.

McNary National Wildlife Refuge

P.O. Box 544 (311 Lake Road), Burbank, WA 99323 / 509-547-4942
http://midcolumbiariver.fws.gov or www.nwr.McNary.wa.us

Whether you are a waterfowl hunter or avid bird watcher, you'll find plenty to like at the McNary National Wildlife Refuge (NWR) located near the confluence of the Snake and Columbia Rivers. The 15,000-plus-acre refuge consists of two major units. The Burbank Slough Unit is the more popular of the two and is located just outside of Pasco. The Wallulla Unit is found farther south where the Walla Walla River flows into the Columbia.

Both areas are a magnet for waterfowl with over 50 percent of the mallard ducks within the Pacific Flyway spending the winter here. They are joined by several other duck species to include American wigeon, northern shoveler, canvasback, and redhead along with Canada geese. The waterfowl are drawn here by the availability of grain in and around the refuge, water in two big rivers and adjacent wetlands, and the mild winter climate found in this part of Washington.

The huge number of wintering ducks makes this a popular hunting destination. Shooting is allowed along a portion of the Burbank Slough unit south of Humorist Road. You can apply for a permit prior to hunting season or show up an hour and a half before shooting time the day you want to hunt to draw a blind during a lottery process for any of the 29 blinds not spoken for. Most of the time, you can get a blind on a standby basis, and if you don't get one in the morning you can come back at 11:30am to get a blind for the afternoon shoot. There is a $10 daily blind fee and you must hunt within 100 feet of the blind site. Most of the blinds are located on the edge of Burbank Slough, so having a good dog comes in handy for the deep-water retrieves you'll likely encounter. Other hunters shoot from field blinds for ducks and geese as they come in to feed. Pheasant and quail hunters also come here and are not tied to any blinds, but they are only allowed to hunt after noon. No entry is allowed in this hunting area except on hunting days (Wednesdays, Saturdays, Sundays, Thanksgiving, and New Years) from 5:00am until one

and a half hours after sunset. You are also limited to 25 non-toxic shells per day no matter what you are hunting.

Those wanting fewer restrictions may want to head to the Wallula Unit, where hunting is allowed seven days a week. If you need a place to stay, the Madame Dorian Park is a 45-acre property with 15 primitive tent or RV sites located on US Highway 12 just north of the junction with Highway 730.

Back at the Burbank Slough Unit, camping can be found along the banks of the Snake River next to the US Highway 12 Bridge at Hood Park. This US Army Corps of Engineers park has 69 tent or RV sites with electrical hook ups, a sizeable day-use area, and nice boat launch. The launch comes in handy if you want to fish the Snake for steelhead in the fall and winter months. In spring and summer you can fish around the Strawberry Islands that are near the park and part of the McNary NWR. You are not allowed to physically walk on the islands, but smallmouth bass angling can be very good just offshore.

Wildlife viewing is popular all year but is limited to a small portion of the Burbank Slough Unit next to the refuge headquarters. Walking a wide, flat path for 1.9 miles around a small lake is a great way to see a representative sample of the refuge. The nature trail starts at the Environmental Education Center next to the headquarters on Lake Road. A short paved path leads to an enclosed blind at the water's edge where you can observe and photograph swimming birds. In addition to the waterfowl already mentioned, you may also see trumpeter swan, double-crested cormorant, and American white pelican. Continuing around the lake, you'll pass through brushy habitat with Russian olives, willows, and other deciduous trees that provide habitat for birds as varied as Bullock's oriole to short-eared owls, goldfinch, magpie, and quail. At the end of the lake, you'll reach a bridge where you just might spook a great blue or black-crowned night heron. Yellow-headed and red-winged blackbirds sing loudly from the bulrushes, especially in the spring. Skunk, coyote, and raccoon are also attracted to nesting waterfowl and you might stumble into a close encounter with a mule deer before the animal bounds back into the brush.

Birding is also an option at the 1,900-acre Wallula Unit. Summer is a good time to see several different types of migrating shorebirds at the Walla Walla River delta while winter is a good time to see a variety of gulls and raptors. In the spring, terns, waterfowl, and pelicans are present in good numbers.

The McNary National Wildlife Refuge is open all year, though several areas are closed to public access to better protect the birds and animals. Dogs are allowed, but have to be kept on a leash unless you are hunting.

Getting There: To get to the refuge headquarters, drive south from Pasco on US Highway 12 over the Snake River Bridge. Turn east at the second light (a short mile from the bridge) onto Humorist Road. Travel 100 yards and take a left onto Lake Road. You'll find the headquarters at the south end of the lake. To reach the hunting area, continue east on Humorist Road until you reach a dead end. You'll see the turnoff into the hunter's check station on your left. The Wallula Unit can be reached by driving 12 miles south on US Highway 12 from the Snake River Bridge.

BURBANK GUIDE SERVICE

370 McNary Ridge Road, Burbank, WA 99323 / 509-545-8000
www.burbankgoose.com

Lodging Prices: Included with some adventures   Adventure Pricing: $$$ to $$$$

You'll hear some people with a country bent talk about "living the dream", a statement meant to show they are doing exactly what they always hoped to do in life. Paul Sullivan, a duck and goose hunting fanatic, is a man who is "living the dream" as a waterfowler.

Sullivan is the owner and chief guide of the Burbank Guide Service near Washington's Tri-Cities. He started guiding over 30 years ago as a way to pay for the hunting land he was leasing. Today, Sullivan and five experienced guides gun for Canada geese and ducks (primarily drake mallards). Most of the hunting is done on Sullivan's farm that is planted with crops that waterfowl love to eat. Sullivan also has three ponds on his farm and up to 20,000 ducks at a time have been known to congregate on them in the fall and winter. In the rare event birds are not flocking to Sullivan's property, he has lease arrangements with nearby farmers who allow him to place both decoys and well-camouflaged goose pits on their land. All of these properties are located between the McNary National Wildlife Refuge and the Snake River, an area Sullivan calls, "The most consistent place in the state to find geese".

Sullivan bucks conventional wisdom when it comes to hunting. He generally uses less than three dozen decoys for ducks or geese whereas many believe the more decoys you have, the better. While he is out in the fields before first light for goose hunting, his clients don't even arrive at the blind for ducks until 8:00am, an unheard of luxury for waterfowlers used to hunting at legal shooting time when it's just light enough to make out the birds in front of them. Because of the prime location he has available, Sullivan is also able to hunt the same locations day in and out, and you'll be hard pressed to hear his guides yell "take em!" until the birds are within 25 yards and firmly committed to landing in the decoy spread. In spite of these unconventional tactics, limits are the norm for duck and goose hunters alike.

Sullivan works hard so the "casual hunter can experience a hunt with us they wouldn't be able to otherwise." He is able to make this happen year after year by having a prime location (where the birds want to be), using quality decoys, and building better blinds. Sullivan is such a big believer in these factors that he started his own company, Aero Outdoors (www.aerooutdoors.com). Aero Outdoors manufactures a variety of high end goose and duck decoys as well as portable duck and goose blinds made out of metal and EZ-FAB, a patented all-weather poly mesh blind material.

The Burbank Goose Club has lots of repeat customers, so it's best to book your trip well in advance. Anywhere from one to five hunters can go out at a time for a guided outing. If you book a goose hunt you'll start your day before dawn (around 90 minutes before legal shooting time). Unless you limit early, you can expect to field hunt for geese until noon. Even though duck hunters get to sleep in, they often finish their hunting day with limits from Paul Sullivan's ponds by 11:00am. Duck and goose combination hunts can also be booked at times; call for details. The guide service does not have their own lodging, but they work with business class hotels in the Tri-Cities to put together one-, three-, or five-day packages that include daily hunting, lodging, licenses, lunches, and more.

Waterfowl hunting typically occurs from mid-October until late January. Goose hunting is limited to certain days of the week. A youth hunt takes place in September, along with an early goose hunting season. Check the state bird hunting regulations for more information.

Getting There: Hunters hook up with their guides at the Jackpot gas station located at the intersection of Humorist Road and US Highway 12. To get there, drive south on US 12 from Pasco over the Snake River Bridge. The intersection is 1 mile south of this bridge.

Mallards make up most of the limits when duck hunting with the Burbank Goose Club.

GINKGO PETRIFIED FOREST STATE PARK AND WANAPUM RECREATION AREA

Ginkgo Petrified Forest State Park – P.O. Box 1203, Vantage, WA 98950
509-856-2700 – www.parks.wa.gov

Lodging Prices: $ Adventure Pricing: N/A

Millions of years ago, during the Miocene period, the dry shrub-steppe around Vantage was a swampy area where many species of trees grew, including ginkgo and cypress trees. About 15.5 million years ago lava flows from erupting volcanoes covered the area and, over time, many of the trees from this era became petrified. The petrified wood here, looking every bit like wood but feeling like stone, was discovered in the late 1920s and excavated in the 1930s. Soon after, the Ginkgo Petrified Forest State Park was created as part of a national historic preserve to protect this bit of geologic history.

Most visitors content themselves with a stop at the park's interpretive center near Interstate 90. Perched on a high basalt cliff above the Columbia River, you'll find examples of petrified wood inside and outside of a building open from 10:00am to 6:00pm daily during the summer and generally on weekends at other times of the year. Also at the center are the Vantage Petroglyphs. Originally discovered a mile north of this tiny community, they reside today outside the center and provide a glimpse into how art and history were recorded long before white settlers came to this region.

If you are interested in seeing more, drive to the Trees of Stone Interpretive Trail 2 miles north of the interpretive center. Two loop trails cover 2.5 miles. The lower loop, covering 1.5 miles, allows you to see petrified maple, fir, spruce, walnut, elm, and ginkgo. The upper trail has the remains of horse chestnut and redwood trees. Along the way you may hear the charming song of meadowlarks and perhaps glimpse a coyote among the rock and sagebrush. This being the desert, you should carry water and also keep an eye out for rattlesnakes.

A short drive south from the interpretive center brings you to the Wanapum Recreational Area, a camping and day-use area that is part of the Ginkgo Petrified Forest State Park. There are 50 RV sites with full hook ups at this riverfront park. Tent campers are welcome to use the sites, but have to pay the full RV price to do so. The park has an improved boat launch with ample parking and a day-use area with lots of unsheltered picnic tables and a nice swimming beach.

Wanapum Dam is visible just downstream from the park. This stretch of the Columbia receives little pressure from anglers, though walleye, smallmouth bass, salmon, and steelhead are all found between here and the recreational community of Crescent Bar to the north. Waterfowl hunting, especially for diving ducks, can also be good during the winter and chukar are known to run along the ridges and bluffs above the river.

The Wanapum Recreational Area is open daily except from November 1 through March 21, when it is only open on weekends and holidays. The campground does get crowded at times, especially when concerts occur at the nearby Gorge Amphitheatre.

Getting There: The park's facilities are both easily accessible from the Vantage Exit (136) off Interstate 90. Travel north from the exit a mile to the interpretive center or travel south from the exit on Huntzinger Road for three miles to reach the campground.

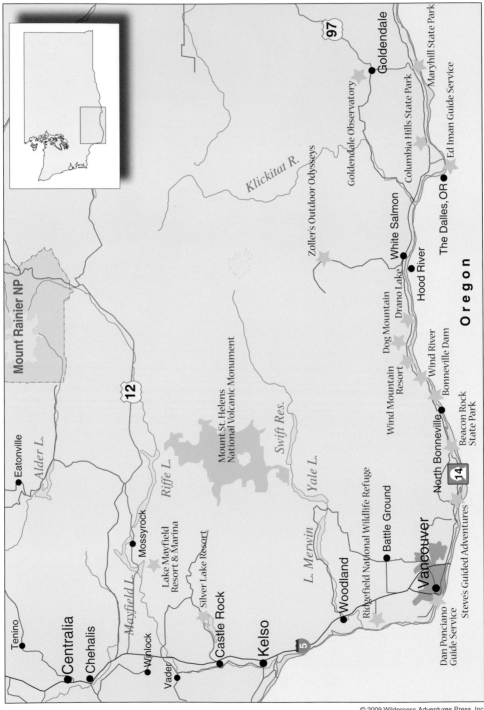

Columbia Gorge
National Scenic Area (East)

From the White Salmon to the Klickitat

Columbia River Gorge National Scenic Area (U. S. Forest Service)
902 Wasco Ave. Suite 200, Hood River, OR 97031 / 541-308-1700
www.fs.fed.us/r6/columbia

Drive east past White Salmon along the Washington side of the 80-mile long Columbia River Gorge National Scenic Area and you'll notice the landscape and weather begin to change. Thick stands of pine and gray skies give way to sunshine and oak savannah. The White Salmon River acts as an informal dividing line between western and eastern Washington. Fed by a combination of springs and melting snow from Mount Adams, the river runs 47 miles from the Mount Adams Wilderness until it pours into the Columbia River. Twenty-nine miles of the river are nationally designated as "Wild and Scenic", ensuring protection of this unique waterway that flows much of its length through a narrow, lava rock canyon.

For whitewater enthusiasts looking for a place to go when rivers reach mid-summer lows, the White Salmon River offers a consistently reliable destination. The coldwater springs that flow into this stream provide enough water for year-round whitewater fun. If you want to raft, the small hamlet of BZ Corner is a good place to start. There is a large public access area here used by freelancers and several commercial outfitters.

Below BZ Corner are a series of Class III and IV rapids with names like Shark's Tooth, Grasshopper, Corkscrew, Waterspout, and Stair Step Falls. As exciting as these are, they pale in comparison to Class V rated Husum Falls near the small village of Husum. This 14-foot waterfall features a 9-foot vertical drop guaranteed to get everybody on board wet from head to toe. If you view whitewater rafting as more of a spectator sport than a participative one, you can watch the rafters go over the falls from the bridge at Husum.

If you raft or paddle the White Salmon, you'll not only need the right gear, but also a good working knowledge of this small, fast-moving stream. Wet suits are a good idea all year long; the springs that feed the river keep it on the chilly side even in the heat of summer. If you haven't been down the

river before, you should go at least once with one of the commercial outfitters found in BZ Corner and Husum.

Anglers will find good fishing for decent-sized rainbow trout along the White Salmon above Condit Dam. However, most stream anglers drive east 13 miles along State Highway 14 to the Klickitat River near Lyle. Fishing near the mouth of the Klickitat is good from August through September for chinook and silver salmon, and angling for summer steelhead can be a very productive pursuit throughout the river from July into the fall. Rainbow trout can get up to 16 inches and whitefish will also bite flies or lures cast their way.

There is plenty of public access to the Klickitat off State Route 142. The road follows the river north about 21 miles upstream to its confluence with the Little Klickitat River. Whitewater rafters come here from April through June to surf lots of Class III and a few Class IV rapids; often covering 20 miles in a few hours time. After the water drops in the summer, anglers float the river in rafts and drift boats to fish the river at a more leisurely pace.

Bicyclists and hikers can also take in views of the river along the Klickitat Rail Trail that follows the river upstream from the mouth for 17 miles before continuing another 14 miles into Swale Creek Canyon. The former rail line is paved in some places but gravel in most. There are a number of different places to access the trail off SR 142.

If you enjoy watching wildlife, you'll like the Klickitat. The Balfour-Klickitat Day-use Area is located on the east side of the river near State Highway 14 where it enters the Columbia. A paved half-mile trail leads to great views of the two rivers. Birds such as swallows, lesser goldfinch, and Lewis's woodpeckers are often seen here. In the winter months, majestic bald eagles congregate near the mouth of the river. Further upstream, you'll see mergansers and kingfishers along with Bullock's oriole, red-eyed vireo, yellow warblers, and other songbirds.

Another prime wildlife watching spot is found at Catherine Creek. It's located east of Lyle near Rowland Lake. Part of the National Scenic Area, Catherine Creek features a paved mile-long trail with great views of the Columbia Gorge and lots of interpretive signs. The trail passes through groves of oak, basalt rock formations, and grasslands peppered with the occasional ponderosa pine. You can expect to see not only song birds and swallows but also raptors, hawks, falcon, and osprey all soar in the sky. California ground squirrels are abundant, as you might expect in an environment of oak trees and acorns. Summer visits are pleasant in the morning and evening, as are fall outings. However, spring time is the perhaps the best time to come. Wildflowers bloom along the hillside with Columbia Gorge lupine, arrowleaf balsamroot, camas, yellow bell, and lilies among the colorful flora you'll find here. Catherine Creek is open all year as a day-use area.

Getting There: You can access this part of the Columbia River Gorge from State Highway 14 between the towns of Lyle and White Salmon.

ZOLLER'S OUTDOOR ODYSSEYS

1248 State Highway 141, (BZ Corner) White Salmon, WA 98672 / 800-366-2004
www.zooraft.com

Lodging Prices: $$$$ Adventure Pricing: $$ to $$$$

You can have a rafting adventure any time of year on south central Washington's White Salmon River. There are several reputable outfitters that float this stream, but the best may be Zoller's Outdoor Odysseys. Located in BZ Corner, they were recognized in 2005 as the Washington State Family Business of the Year. Their large building houses a gift shop, deli, and registration desk. Outside is a large picnic and barbeque area that guests are welcome to use before or after their trip. It is also in this picnic area that your guides will outfit you with the neoprene wet suits, booties, life jackets, and helmets you'll need for your whitewater excursion.

After a safety briefing and orientation you launch onto the river. You'll generally share a raft with five other paddlers and a guide. You hit the first rapids right away and keep working them as you paddle down the tightly constricted lava canyon, formed thousands of years ago after multiple eruptions from Mt. Adams. Cedar, pine, and deciduous trees grow along the rocky shore. Wildlife from deer to water ouzels to mergansers and colorful harlequin ducks are frequently observed. As scenic as the river is, it's the whitewater that draws rafters here. You'll spend a little over two hours on the water covering 8 miles and nine different Class III or higher rapids before you reach the take out point. One of the rapids is Husum Falls, a Class V piece of water featuring a 9-foot vertical drop. Going over the falls is optional but if you decide to take the plunge, it is an unforgettable experience.

Zoller's prides itself on hiring and keeping experienced river guides (they average 10 years professional experience). The guides are friendly, knowledgeable, fun loving, and safety conscious all at the same time. Most live in the area and are happy to share the history of the river with you as you travel downstream. At the end of the trip you'll be shuttled back to BZ Corner. After you strip off your wet gear you can look at pictures taken by staff during the trip and purchase some as mementos.

Zoller's also rafts the nearby Klickitat River from April until the middle of June. Mark Zoller, owner of Zoller's Outdoor Odysseys, describes the Klickitat as "a fast river" with "lots of long Class III rapids and continuous whitewater". If you choose to raft the Klickitat with Zoller's, you'll meet up with their crew at BZ Corner and get shuttled there and back for a full day expedition.

Finally, Zoller's is one of the few outfitters permitted to raft the Snake River through Hells Canyon. They offer three- and five-day trips that start in northeastern Oregon. On the shorter excursion, you'll cover 33 miles. The longer trip takes you 79 miles through this deep scenic canyon before you take out in Washington near the Grande Ronde River.

Group sizes are small on these multi-day expeditions. Generally there is a maximum of 18 guests accompanied by six guides for an excellent client-to-guide ratio. Even though you are camping overnight, you'll feel decidedly pampered as you drink a pina colada from a pineapple husk, eat upside-down cake baked in a Dutch oven, and take a hot shower with solar heated water at the end of a day on the river. Meals vary from a steak and lobster dinner to Dutch oven chicken or barbequed salmon. You'll start off the morning with a mocha or latte before tackling the Snake River again. Mark Zoller says there is "lots of big water" with "plenty of roller coaster ride rapids" in the canyon. Animal sightings are common; deer, coyote, bighorn sheep, bear, and mountain goat all frequent this national recreation area. You can raft Hells Canyon in an inflatable kayak, small raft, or regular 8-person raft depending on how much adrenaline and adventure you're seeking.

Adventurous kids as young as 7 and adults as old as 90 have rafted with Zoller's. Give them a call to find out about specific trip dates and times.

Getting There: Take State Highway 14 to White Salmon. Turn north on State Highway 141 (Alternate) and drive 10 miles to BZ Corner. Zoller's Outdoor Odysseys will be on your right.

The optional drop over Husum Falls is the exciting highlight of a White Salmon rafting excursion (photo courtesy Zoller's Outdoors Odysseys).

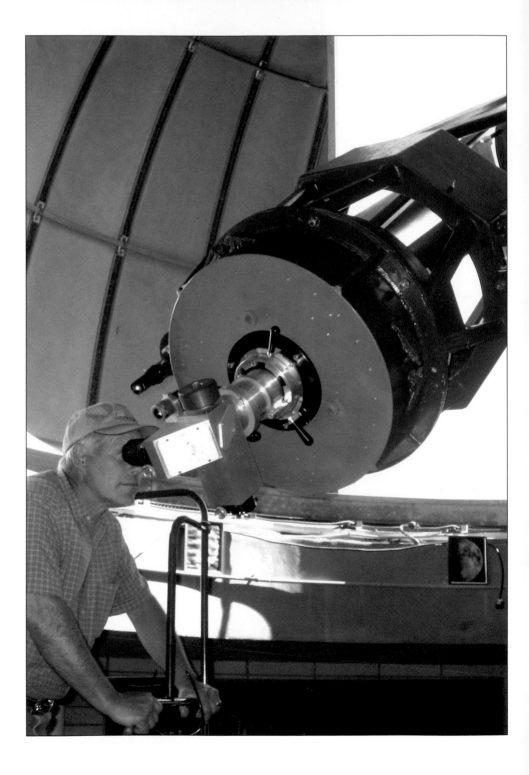

State Parks of the Eastern Gorge: Columbia Hills
MARYHILL – GOLDENDALE OBSERVATORY

Columbia Hills State Park
P.O. Box 426, Dallesport, WA 98617 (physical location – State Highway 14, Milepost 85) / 509-767-1159
www.parks.wa.gov

Maryhill State Park
50 U.S. Highway 97, Goldendale, WA 98620 / 509-773-5007
www.parks.wa.gov

Goldendale Observatory State Park
1602 Observatory Drive, Goldendale, WA 98620 / 509-773-3141
www.parks.wa.gov or www.perr.com/gosp.html

Lodging Prices

Three state parks along the blustery eastern portion of the Columbia River Gorge offer very different experiences. The most unique of these is found at the Goldendale Observatory located above the small town of Goldendale. Amateur astronomers and novices alike gaze into the heavens through a 24.5-inch telescope. The telescope is inside the observatory building perched on top of a hill that sits at an elevation of 2,100 feet. Park staff gives interpretive programs throughout the year between 2:00 and 5:00pm where you can learn more about the facility, the telescope, and engage in solar (sun) viewing. The real fun starts at nightfall. From 8:00pm until midnight staff members allow you to look at the moon, planets, stars, nebulas, and galaxies through the large telescope in the observatory, and also at times with portable telescopes set up outside. From April through September, the observatory is open from Wednesday through Saturday. For the rest of the year, it is open Friday through Sunday.

Drive south from Goldendale along U.S. Highway 97 to the Columbia River and you'll find Maryhill State Park next to the bridge that crosses the river into Oregon. Open all year, the 99-acre park has 20 tent sites and 50 utility sites suitable for RVs. Restrooms with showers, covered picnic shelters, a swimming area, and a good paved boat launch are also available at the park that has 4,700 feet of frontage on the Columbia.

Many people come here to see the replica of Stonehenge or the Maryhill Art Museum, both a short distance away. However, there are lots of outdoor opportunities in this part of the gorge. For starters, the fishing is very good, especially for smallmouth bass. If you have a boat, you can fish downriver from the U.S. Highway 97 Bridge towards Miller Island to catch lots of bass from spring through fall that can weigh up to 6 pounds. Across from Miller Island in Oregon, the Deschutes River flows into the Columbia. Trolling in front of the river mouth for chinook and silver salmon as well as steelhead is a good bet in September and October. Boating is best in the morning, because stiff winds are notorious along this section of the gorge in the afternoon.

One group that doesn't complain about the breeze is the windsurfing crew who launch from Maryhill to ride the Columbia's whitecaps. Windsurfing is very popular in the Columbia Gorge, and several parks and sites within the national scenic area cater to several thousand enthusiasts who come to enjoy the wind and water in the spring and summer months.

Maryhill State Park is open all year. If it's full, the adjacent Peach Beach RV Park is a tidy, well-kept waterfront park that is also a good place to stay.

Columbia Hills State Park is reached by driving west along State Highway 14 from U.S. Highway 97. Formerly known separately as Horsethief Lake State Park and Dalles Mountain Ranch, this 3,338 acre park offers camping along the Columbia River, fishing, rock climbing, hiking among wildflowers, bird watching, and the opportunity to see Native American rock art.

The camping area is located by Horsethief Lake, a 90-acre impoundment of the Columbia River that is stocked every spring with trout. Open for fishing from the last Saturday in April through October 31, you'll find bass, perch, and the occasional walleye here. If you want to stay overnight there are 8 RV sites and 10 tent sites to choose from. A restroom, dump station, picnic area, and boat launch round out the amenities. Worth seeing are the ancient Indian petroglyphs (carved into rocks) and pictographs (painted onto rocks) at the park. The petroglyphs are found at an interpretive display in the park while the "She Who Watches" pictograph can be seen during a short half-mile guided hike with park rangers on Fridays and Saturday mornings from April to October. Reservations are required to participate in this hike.

Overlooking the lake with scenic views of the gorge, Horsethief Butte is a large rock formation popular with climbers. To get there, drive east for a half mile from the entrance of the camping park. Climbers do need to watch out for poison oak that grows in places along the rock walls and be cautious for the rare rattlesnake that might be sunning itself on the basalt. There are multiple routes that get you to the top of the butte. You are asked to respect the two areas that are closed to climbing and limit the use of chalk while scaling the rocks.

Hiking is popular at the former Dalles Mountain Ranch area, now part of the park. You can get there by driving north along Dalles Mountain Road from State Route 14 just west of Horsethief Lake. Park near the buildings left from the old ranch and walk up the dirt road or go cross country along the grassy windblown hills that come to life every spring with yellow balsamroot, purple lupine, desert parsley, and Dalles Mountain buttercup. There's more to see than flowers. Various raptors to include turkey vultures, northern harrier, Swainson's hawk, and several types of owl hunt here while several different types of wren, magpie, Townsend's solitaire, and yellow-breasted chat can also be observed. After 2 miles you'll reach the fenced and gated boundary of the Columbia Hills Natural Area Preserve, managed by the Washington Department of Natural Resources. From here you can hike along the road (cross-country travel not allowed) to the top of Stacker Butte, gaining close to 2,000 feet from start to finish. If you want to cut down on the hiking, you can drive the rough ranch road up to the gated entrance of the preserve.

The Horsethief Lake portion of the state park is open from the first of April through the last weekend of October. The Dalles Mountain Ranch area and Natural Area Preserve is open as a day-use area all year.

Getting There: Maryhill and Columbia Hills State Park: See above. Goldendale Observatory: Drive down Broadway in Goldendale (off of U.S. Highway 97) until you get to a four-way stop. Turn north and travel 0.75 mile to a fork on the road. Bear right and travel another 0.75 mile to get to the observatory.

ED IMAN GUIDE SERVICE

3480 Browns Creek Rd., The Dalles, OR 97058 / 541-298-3753

Lodging Prices: N/A   Adventure Pricing: $$$

If you want to go fishing with a legend, give Ed Iman a call. Iman was a pioneer in putting walleye fishing on the map in the Pacific Northwest at a time when most area anglers didn't know what one of these toothy fish looked like. Ed Iman was one of those fishermen around 1978 when he and a friend fished plugs for steelhead on the Columbia River near Biggs Junction. The two of them started catching strange looking fish and eventually figured out they were walleye. During his early fishing for these popular midwestern (but completely unknown northwestern) fish, Iman landed several walleye from 5 to 8 pounds. Iman began fishing for them with a passion and attempted to learn all he could about them. He soon contacted Randy Amenrud; a fishing professional with a well-known midwestern tackle company called Lindy-Little Joe, Inc. that specialized in walleye fishing tackle. Iman told Amenrud about the walleye in the Columbia and sent him a couple of pictures along with enough money for a small order of lures. Iman soon received a huge shipment of tackle at his home valued at several hundred dollars with a note that simply said, "Send more pictures".

It wasn't long before Iman joined a select group of anglers as part of the Lindy-Little Joe Pro-Staff. By 1980, he was giving seminars and people started paying him to take them fishing. Not long after this the one-time construction worker made the leap of faith to become a full-time fishing guide with an emphasis on walleye.

Since then anglers all over the United States have come to recognize the Columbia River as one of the premier fisheries in the nation for trophy walleye. Iman has not only co-authored a book on the subject, Walleye Fishing Simplified, but continues to give seminars throughout the Northwest. How big do walleye get on the Columbia? Well, both the Oregon and Washington records were caught on this big river and weigh in around 20 pounds. In fact, Iman himself may have caught, and inadvertently released, a new world record walleye weighing close to 23 pounds in the spring of 2007.

Today, Iman guides walleye anglers four months out of the year on the Columbia River between The Dalles Dam and McNary Dam near Boardman. In March and April he is targeting both the big trophy females and smaller male walleye below the John Day Dam in The Dalles Pool with jigs and blade baits. Iman hits the water again during the months of June and July to troll crawlers in harnesses with bottom bouncers or deep-diving plugs around Boardman for fish that commonly weigh 4 to 8 pounds.

Iman can take anywhere from two to five anglers for full day trips in his 22-foot Alumaweld boat powered by a 200-horsepower Yamaha outboard engine. His guests will appreciate not only the quality tackle and electronics that Iman uses while fishing, but also the opportunity to learn from a master of the sport.

Getting There: There are several departure points between The Dalles and Boardman, Oregon.

Ed Iman is the Northwest's best-known Columbia River walleye guide.

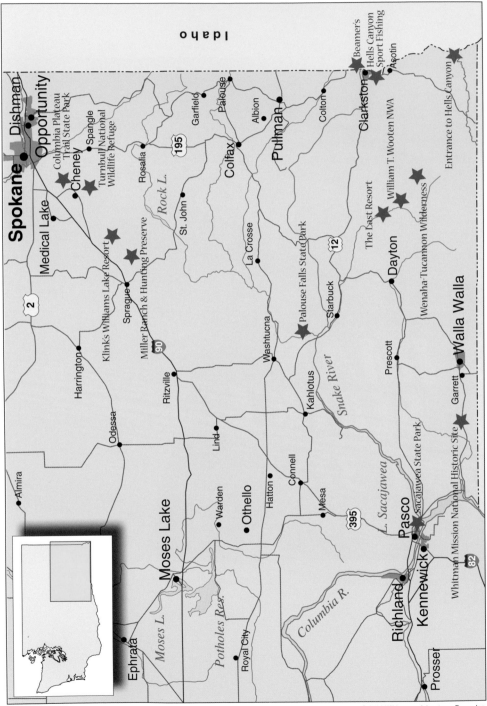

© 2009 Wilderness Adventures Press, Inc.

Channeled Scablands

Turnbull National Wildlife Refuge

26010 South Smith Road, Cheney, WA 99004 / 509-235-4723
www.fws.gov/turnbull

Adventure Prices

If you want to view wildlife in a pleasant setting not far from Spokane, head to Turnbull National Wildlife Refuge. Established in 1937, the 27-square-mile refuge is named after early settler Cyrus Turnbull. The landscape is picturesque. Open forests of ponderosa pine and stands of aspen transition to grasslands and rock scoured thousands of years ago by water that flooded through here. Today, small rolling hills rise above numerous wetlands and small lakes. Wet meadows and dry grassy terrain produce a bounty of flora. Camas, an important food source for early Native Americans, is common at the refuge, as are flowers like arrowleaf balsamroot, bitterroot, and elkhorns clarkia. Varieties of buttercups, roses, figworts, mustard, aster, and other plants are all common.

The bird life is as varied as the flora. One-hundred-and-ninety-nine different birds call the refuge home depending on the season and at least 24 other species have also been seen at times. The wetlands and waters of the refuge provide important habitat for a number of birds to include waterfowl, yellow-headed blackbird, red-tailed hawk, killdeer, black tern, mourning dove, northern flicker, willow flycatcher, eastern kingbird, magpie, pygmy nuthatch, marsh wren, robin, western meadowlark, and a variety of sparrows and swallows.

A large number of other wildlife species are also found within the refuge boundaries. Big animals like Rocky Mountain elk, mule and white-tailed deer, and moose can all be seen, as can smaller mammals such as river otter, coyote, badger, beaver, muskrat, porcupine, squirrels, and bats.

You can take a quick (and easy) tour of the refuge by following the 5-mile Pine Creek Auto Tour Route. You can stop to stretch your legs at

three very short loop trails found at designated environmental education sites near Blackhorse and Kepple Lakes. One of these is actually an American Disabilities Act (ADA) accessible wooden boardwalk. Other trails emanate from the area of the refuge headquarters. The Pine Lake Loop Trail is a short stroll that takes you around its namesake and Winslow Pool. Longer outings are available by hiking the Headquarters or Bluebird Trails, both of which are about 1.5 miles long (one way). Finally, bicyclists and hikers alike can use 4.75 miles of the Columbia Plateau Trail that passes through the west side of the refuge.

There is no hunting or fishing on the refuge. About 2,300 acres of the 16,000-acre refuge is open to the public all year. The rest of the refuge is closed to minimize disturbances to wildlife.

Getting There: Drive 4 miles south from Cheney along the Cheney-Plaza Road. Turn left on South Smith Road and travel 2 miles to reach the refuge headquarters, auto tour route, and hiking trails.

A western tiger swallowtail butterfly displays its stunning color.

Columbia Plateau Trail State Park

North Office – 15 Union Street, Cheney, WA 99004 – 509-235-4696
South Office – 100 SW Main Street, Washtucna, WA 99371 – 509-646-9218
www.parks.wa.gov

The Columbia Plateau Trail is not a state park in the traditional sense. Instead, it is a 130-mile long trail along the old Spokane, Portland, and Seattle Railway Line that runs from Cheney southwest towards Pasco. Used by Burlington Northern for freight travel until 1987, Washington State Parks acquired the rail corridor in 1991. In 1995, the Parks Commission negotiated an agreement with the U.S. Fish and Wildlife Service at Turnbull National Wildlife Refuge and the trail was born.

Today, 23 miles of the trail from Fish Lake near Cheney to Martin Road east of Sprague have been developed and are used by hikers, bicyclists, and equestrians for much of the year. In the winter, snowshoeing and cross-country skiing are popular activities.

The Columbia Plateau Trail can be reached from several places. The northernmost access point is at the Fish Lake Trailhead. The 3.75-mile trail from here to the next trailhead at Cheney is paved. You may want to bring your fishing pole. Fish Lake is just off the trail and land owned by Spokane County allows access to the shoreline and a boat launch. Spring and fall fishing for brook trout can be very good at this 47-acre lake.

At the Cheney trailhead the path transitions from asphalt to gravel and continues that way for 19 miles to Martin Road. Horses are allowed on this stretch, which continues south and passes through 4.75 miles of the Turnbull National Wildlife Refuge before reaching the Amber Lake Trailhead. From Amber Lake it is another 7.5 miles to the Martin Road Trailhead, located a few miles from the small farming community of Sprague.

The trail between Cheney and Martin Road is rife with wildlife viewing opportunities. Some 200 bird species have been recorded around the Turnbull National Wildlife Refuge, and deer, elk, and even moose roam the area. Other mammals seen from the trail include the occasional bear, bobcat, or badger. Rabbit, coyote, squirrel, chipmunk, and marmot are frequently seen during

the day and towards evening skunk and raccoon may make an appearance. The trail cuts through volcanic fields eroded by great floods from the last ice age and the views can be quite scenic. Interpretive signs along the trail tell the story of both the human and natural history of the trail and land that surrounds it.

South of Martin Road, the remainder of the Columbia Plateau Trail remains undeveloped and much of it is not available for public use. Heading south to Washtucna and on to the Snake River, there are five tunnels that are up to a half mile long. There are also six railroad trestles along this stretch of the trail, some of which are 0.33 miles long and up to 200 feet high. These trestles are located along the Snake River and are gated to prevent access. There are plans to open up an additional 14.5 miles of this trail in this southern portion of Washington between Ice Harbor Dam and the junction of the Snake River; check with the office in Washtucna for updates.

There is no camping at this park which is open daily from 6:30am until dusk. Spring and fall are the best times to be on the trail if you are looking for wildlife. Summertime temperatures can be extreme, reaching over 100 degrees. There are restrooms and parking at the developed trailheads but very little in between. If you venture forth on this trail do so with plenty of water, sunscreen, and layered sets of clothing.

Getting There: Take Exit 270 (Cheney/ Four Lakes) off of Interstate 90. Drive 6.5 miles to Cheney on State Highway 904 and turn south on the Cheney – Spangle Road. Drive one more mile and turn left to reach the Cheney trailhead.

Yellow-bellied marmot and other animals are frequently seen from the Columbia Plateau Trail.

KLINK'S WILLIAMS LAKE RESORT

**18617 W. Williams Lake Road, Cheney, WA 99004 / 800-274-5420 or
509-235-2391 www.klinksresort.com**

Lodging Prices: $ to $$ Adventure Pricing: $

For a place that's off the beaten path, Klink's Williams Lake Resort has a lot to offer. Anglers, paddlers, hikers, bicyclists, and nature lovers all have plenty to do around this place located 45 minutes southwest of Spokane. The resort sits along a 380-acre rock-bottomed lake that tends to run deep. The shoreline is bordered by basalt rock cliffs, pine trees, and grasslands, making it a scenic place to paddle a canoe or kayak as you watch osprey scout the lake for fish and listen to colorful red-winged and yellow-headed blackbirds trill from the cattails.

If you like to fish you'll enjoy this 3-mile-long lake. Opening day, anglers generally catch limits of rainbow and cutthroat trout that average a solid 12 inches. The good size might have to do with the fact that Williams Lake is one of a handful of managed trout lakes in eastern Washington. Resort owner Jerry Klinkenberg supplements Department of Fish and Wildlife stockings with fast growing Kamloops rainbow trout that can reach 12 pounds by the time a lucky angler reels one in.

The resort has 165 RV sites with hook ups, though quite a few are leased out on a seasonal basis. There are three affordable studio cabins for rent on a two-night or weekly basis. These dry cabins sleep up to four people and don't have kitchens or baths (though there are plans to add cabins with these amenities in the near future). If you stay at a cabin, your pet will have to stay outside and you'll also need to bring your own bedding. There are also several places to pitch a tent for a low price.

Kids enjoy the swings at the playground, though most quickly wander to the sandy beach and swim area at the lake. There is very good fishing off the docks, with most anglers using worms, PowerBait, salmon eggs, or a combination of these to catch trout. If you want to rent a boat the resort has a dozen aluminum boats with motors along with several paddleboats and kayaks. There is also a boat launch and moorage if you have your own boat. A store serves as the registration/rental office and sells fishing tackle, groceries, and gifts. If you need to catch up on your e-mail or the news, Wi-Fi Internet service is available.

Near the docks is a stage used for music concerts in the summer. If you are lucky, you'll get a chance to listen to the owner's son, Dusty Klink. He is a professional country western musician with a couple of CDs full of catchy tunes to his credit.

Of special note is "Klink's On the Lake Restaurant". To find such a restaurant so far outside an urban setting is akin to finding an oasis in the desert. Quality breakfast, lunch, and dinner meals are served for guests who can eat on the deck or inside the tastefully decorated dining room. The owners describe the experience as "casual dining with upscale food". Sandy Klinkenberg (Jerry's wife) is a talented pastry chef who works with a trained culinary arts chef and an attentive staff to prepare a variety of delicious offerings. The wine list at Klink's Restaurant is impressive with over a hundred different bottles to choose from and morning guests appreciate a shot of espresso with breakfast. This is a popular place despite its remote location, so dinner reservations are recommended.

There is plenty to do beyond Williams Lake. Mountain bikers, hikers, and equestrians will appreciate the proximity of the Columbia Plateau Trail. The Martin Road Trailhead is located just a short drive west from the resort. Meanwhile, the Turnbull National Wildlife Refuge is located a few miles north of the resort. You can enjoy exceptional wildlife viewing opportunities on foot or in a car for a variety of mammals and up to 200 different kinds of birds on the 27-square-mile refuge.

Klink's Resort (and Restaurant) is open from April 1 to October 31. Fishing season runs from the last weekend of April through September 30. The resort stays open through October to accommodate deer hunters and for those just seeking a pleasant outdoor experience before winter sets in.

Getting There: From Spokane, drive west on Interstate 90 to Exit 270. Take State Highway 904 to Cheney. In Cheney, take a left and travel south on the Cheney-Plaza Road 12 miles to Williams Lake Road. Turn right and travel 3 miles to the resort.

Caleb and Dillon Rhoades of Malden caught this nice stringer of trout off the dock at Klink's Resort.

MILLER RANCH AND HUNTING PRESERVE

PO Box 249 (Williams Lake Road), Sprague, WA 99032 / 509-370-5535
www.millerranch.com

Lodging Prices: $$$ Adventure Pricing: $ to $$$$

To call the Miller Ranch a shooting preserve is a true understatement. Homesteaded in 1886, the Miller family ranch is a massive 20-mile by 2.5-mile landholding between Sprague and Cheney in eastern Washington. The topography is made up of channeled basalt scabland and rolling farm fields. The vegetation transitions here from sagebrush and grasslands to a wooded landscape of pine and birch. Creeks, ponds, and lakes dot the area and 15 lakes are found within 20 miles of the ranch. Three of these lakes, a creek, and flooded fields are located on the ranch proper.

All of this makes for a great hunting destination – which explains the Miller Ranch tag line of "Birds, Bucks and Ducks". Scott Miller has run a shooting preserve here since 1997 where you can book hunts for birds, big game, and predators.

Most people come to shoot upland birds. During a typical year Miller will release 12,000 pheasants and 1,500 chukar. He takes great care to raise and release quality birds. In fact, more than one visitor has complained the birds are "too wild". Miller simply replies, "We try to make it the most realistic adventure you can get." With a variety of different terrain to hunt, Miller does a very good job of this.

Guided and unguided upland bird hunting is not the only game in town. Guided waterfowl hunts are also popular and in the spring you can hunt the ranch for wild Merriam's or Rio Grande turkey. Big game hunters come in the fall for big mule deer. There is a three-point-minimum regulation, but guides have had very good success finding three- and four-point bucks on this property over the years. Varmint hunters are also discovering Miller Ranch as a place to target coyotes and ground hogs.

Two lodge buildings at the ranch provide overnight accommodations. Both are tastefully furnished in an outdoors motif and can handle up to ten guests each. A kitchen gives you a place to cook meals and a hot tub is a great place to soak weary bones. If you need a bird dog, they've got them. You can also bring your own dogs and house them in a heated kennel. Before you go afield you can warm up at the sporting clays course with a round of shooting. A clubhouse features several big buck mounts, stuffed pheasants, and a pool table. It is a comfortable place to relax and talk over the day's hunt while watching the latest ball game on satellite television.

There's more to do here than shoot. From April through August, the ranch is a great destination for wildlife watchers and nature enthusiasts. In addition to the species already mentioned, you might get the chance to see the occasional badger, elk, or stray moose and a wide variety of birds. In the spring, green hills are accented by yellow arrow-leaf balsamroot and purple iris for a colorful floral display.

Anglers can use the ranch as a base camp to explore the myriad of lakes in the area. On the ranch itself, Downs Lake offers bass and panfish angling, Williams Lake gives up plentiful trout, and a small 12-acre lake on the ranch fed by Negro Creek offers opportunities for all three.

Mountain bikers will enjoy exploring miles of rough roads and jeep trails on the ranch while both hikers and equestrians can explore miles of this scenic environment cross country. Just off the ranch property is a trailhead for the Columbia Plateau State Park, a converted railroad grade offering miles of trail for hikers, bicyclists, and horseback riders to enjoy.

Bird hunting is available at the shooting preserve from September to April. No hunting license is required. Other hunting opportunities follow state guidelines and seasons. Lodging at the ranch is quite cost effective for groups of four to ten. You can also pay a moderate fee to access the ranch as a day visitor if you are not hunting or staying here. If you decide to bring your horse, corral facilities are available.

Getting There: From Spokane drive west on Interstate 90 and take exit 245 at Fishtrap. If you are coming from the west take exit 254 at Sprague. Follow a road designated as the Old State Highway to Williams Lake Road. Turn south and drive 8.5 miles to the Miller Ranch clubhouse.

Shooting birds only scratches the surface of what you can do at the huge 15,000-acre Miller Ranch.

Palouse Country
and the Blue Mountains

Palouse Falls State Park

P.O. Box 157 (Palouse Falls Road), Starbuck, WA 99359 / 509-646-3252
www.parks.wa.gov

Lodging Pricing

The Missoula Floods that occurred some 15,000 years ago cut a geological swath through eastern Washington. It's seen today in the form of channeled scablands consisting of basalt rock formations, cliffs, and creek beds. Some of these creek beds are dry, while others hold water in the form of small streams, ponds, wetlands, and lakes. The most spectacular example of water flowing through these ancient channels is found in rural southeastern Washington at Palouse Falls State Park.

Palouse Falls cascades 198 feet into a basalt rock bowl. Particularly impressive from spring through early summer, the waterfall seems decidedly out of place in an arid landscape that receives only 8 inches of rain a year.

Getting here takes some effort and animals far outnumber humans in this part of Washington. Expect to see grazing cattle on the way to the park, along with watchful coyotes and soaring red-tailed hawks. In and around the park is a surprising amount of wildlife to include rabbit, deer, groundhog (yellow-bellied marmot), mourning dove, meadowlark, and red-winged blackbird. The birdsong is pleasant, but gets drowned out as you near the edge of the cliff where you can view the waterfall in all of its glory.

There are no stores or amenities close to the 105-acre park. If you want to spend the night, there are ten sites suitable for tents or RVs (no hook-ups) to choose from. Each campsite has a picnic table and fire ring. There are two communal water spigots in the grassy camp area that has a number of deciduous shade trees to ward off the heat of the summer sun. A couple of vault toilets round out the basics found at the cozy campground.

There is some hiking here, though the trails are not maintained by state park personnel. If you wander north from the park, you'll reach the Palouse

River above the falls. The trail covers some 2 miles and is a particularly pleasant walk in the spring when the sagebrush and native grasses are lush green. Balsamroot, lupine, and camas are just a few of the colorful plants that bloom at this time of year and this walk is not overly strenuous. A hike to the base of the falls can be tricky. You walk south from the camping area along a working rail line before cutting down a steep, rough trail to the Palouse River. Watch for snakes, though you can take some comfort knowing most of the ones you see will probably be bull snakes instead of rattlers. Once you reach the river you can get a bottom-up view of the falls or cast out a line with some bait to hook some of the catfish that school here.

Palouse Falls State Park is open all year, though the water at the camping area is shut off between September and April.

Getting There: Drive to the tiny farming community of Washtucna off of State Highway 26. From there head 6 miles south to State Route 261, turn left at a grain elevator, and drive some 9 miles southeast to Palouse Falls Road. Follow this gravel road about 2.5 miles to the park.

Palouse Falls is a magnificent sight in an isolated setting.

William T. Wooten Wildlife Area & Wenaha-Tucannon Wilderness

Wooten Wildlife Area
2134 Tucannon Road, Pomeroy, WA 99347 / 509-843-1530
www.wdfw.wa.gov/lands/r1woot.htm
Pomeroy Ranger District (Umatilla National Forest and Wenaha-Tucannon Wilderness)
71 West Main, Pomeroy, WA 99341 / 509-843-1891
www.fs.fed.us/r6/uma/pomeroy/index.shtml

Lodging Prices

Located at the northern end of the Blue Mountains, the William T. Wooten State Wildlife Area and Wenaha-Tucannon Wilderness offer a lot to the outdoor enthusiast. The wildlife area has nearly 16,000 acres of land managed by the Washington Department of Fish and Wildlife while the Wenaha-Tucannon consists of over 177,000 acres within the greater Umatilla National Forest.

The region is well liked by southeast Washington anglers. The Tucannon River runs through the area and is open for rainbow trout fishing from June through October. Spinners and flies are the main way to catch fish where selective regulations prohibit the use of bait in many places. Steelhead fishing can also be decent on this small stream from November through April 15.

In the W.T. Wooten Wildlife Area, you'll find eight small man-made lakes. All of them are just off of Tucannon Road and all are stocked with rainbow trout. The majority open on March 1, and give trout anglers an early dose of lake fishing before the general opener the last weekend of April. Most of the trout are on the small side, ranging from 6 to 10 inches. However, there are a few triploid rainbow trout weighing a pound and a half or more. One of the lakes, Big Four, is a fly-fishing only water and generally has bigger trout in it than the other impoundments. The best lake fishing is in the spring, though it tends to pick up again in the fall after the heat of the summer passes.

Hunting attracts many to this region. A big wildfire in the summer of 2005 scarred several square miles of wilderness but it may have been a boon for wildlife, as new seedlings grew and provide easy forage for big game.

Deer hunting is popular in autumn. White-tailed deer are found in the agricultural areas while mule deer are found deeper in the wilderness. Some elk hunters come here for a spike-only bull elk season and bird hunters also roam the area for grouse, pheasant, and quail. A spring turkey season brings out hunters looking for Rio Grande gobblers, the most abundant species in the Blue Mountains. Hunting can be good. According to the Department of Fish and Wildlife, this part of Washington is actually the second best place to bag one of these big birds (northeast Washington is your best bet for a spring turkey).

Camping is available at several primitive campgrounds in the W.T. Wooten Wildlife Area that offer little more than a dirt parking lot and a nearby toilet. Better camping can be found at the U.S. Forest Service's Tucannon Campground. This campground has 18 sites for campers or RVs, restrooms, and a designated picnic area. Camp Wooten is a Washington State Parks Environmental Learning Center just south of the Tucannon Campground, but it is only available to groups who register in advance.

There's more to this region than fishing, hunting, and camping. The wildlife and wilderness areas provide lots of wildlife and bird watching opportunities. In addition to the birds and mammals, you may also observe bighorn sheep, black bear, pine marten, coyote, and cougar or feathered species such as ducks, woodpeckers, and various songbirds.

If you are a hiker the Wenaha-Tucannon Wilderness has 276 miles of managed trails to traipse through. One of them is the Tucannon River Trail, a 9-mile round-trip trek located at the end of Forest Service Road 4712. A family friendly half-mile hike takes you on an easy 15-minute walk along Sheep Creek to Sheep Creek Falls where you can stand under a cold, natural waterfall to beat the summer heat. The trailhead for this excursion is a few hundred yards before the end of this same road. Other hikes up to 17 miles long on the Panjab and Turkey Creek Trails can also be found off of Forest Service Road 4713. Both of these Forest Service Roads can be reached by traveling south to the end of the Tucannon River Road from Camp Wooten.

Getting There: Drive east on US Highway 12 from Dayton or west from Pomeroy. Turn south on the Tucannon River Road and drive 22 miles south to reach the W.T. Wooten Wildlife Area.

THE LAST RESORT

2005 Tucannon Rd., Pomeroy, WA 99347 / 509-843-1556
www.thelastresortrv.com

Lodging Prices: $ to $$ Adventure Pricing: N/A

You don't have to be a big resort to be a good one, but being a clean, well-run place on the edge of the wilderness sure helps. The Last Resort is a tidy place with 36 RV sites, several tent sites next to a small creek, a park model trailer for rent, and two new cabins. The cabins each sleep up to five guests. They have surprisingly nice interiors with kitchenettes, bathrooms, and a living room area with satellite TV. The RV sites have full or partial hook ups. Tent campers can use a building with restrooms, showers, and laundry machines or have lunch in a covered picnic shelter. A store provides groceries, gas, fishing tackle, and espresso. Wi-Fi Internet is available if you need to catch up on your e-mail and there is also a small meeting hall seating up to 30 with some impressive big game mounts on the walls that can be rented for banquets, reunions, or retreats.

What the resort doesn't have in size it makes up for in location and amenities. Just south of the resort is the entrance to the Tucannon – Wenaha Wilderness Area as well as the W.T. Wooten Wildlife Area (see the entry in this book for further details). There is a basic US Forest Service Campground as well as several very primitive campgrounds managed by the Department of Fish and Wildlife here, but they generally offer little more than a place to park, camp, and sleep.

Recreational opportunities abound in the immediate area. The Tucannon River and several manmade lakes are popular destinations for trout anglers. Big game hunters look for deer, elk, and bear while bird gunners go after pheasant, quail, grouse, and turkey. When it's not hunting season these same birds and animals, as well as non-game species, can be viewed by wildlife watchers. Miles of hiking trails within the Tucannon-Wenaha Wilderness Area and Umatilla National Forest offer even more to do outdoors.

The Last Resort is open all year. If you are looking for a bargain you'll find the rates for cabin rentals drop in the winter months.

Getting There: Drive east on US Highway 12 from Dayton or west from Pomeroy. Turn south on Tucannon Road and drive 19 miles to the resort.

Whitman Mission National Historic Site

Whitman Mission National Historic Site
328 Whitman Mission Road, Walla Walla, WA 99362 / 509-522-6360
www.nps.gov/whmi

Adventure Prices

The life and death of Marcus and Narcissa Whitman, two missionaries who came to the Oregon Country in 1836 to bring the gospel to the Cayuse Indians, had considerable impact upon our young nation. Marcus was a country doctor by trade, and an energetic, industrious man by character. Narcissa was his new wife who became (along with another missionary woman) the first females to cross the country overland to present day Washington State.

The Whitman's established their mission near Walla Walla, at a place called Waiilatpu (which translates to "place of the people of the rye grass"). Over the next 11 years, the two attempted to minister to the Cayuse. This venture met with little success but their mission provided a sanctuary for early travelers on the Oregon Trail. Tensions between the missionaries and the Cayuse built over the years. One problem had to do with the cultural misunderstandings between the well-meaning Whitmans and the tribe. The sight of an increasing number of settlers passing through the area was another cause for strain between the whites and Native Americans. Tensions reached a boiling point in 1847. That was the year whites passing through the mission introduced a measles epidemic. Marcus Whitman was able to treat many of the white victims with some success but could do little for the Cayuse, who had no hereditary immunity to the disease. Within a few months, half of the tribe died of illness.

Rumors spread among the regional tribes that Whitman was poisoning the Cayuse. On November 29th, Cayuse Indians attacked the mission, killing 13 (a 14th victim vanished during the attack and was also presumed dead). Among the dead were Marcus and Narcissa Whitman. The other victims

were male adults and teen boys. Fifty women and children were taken captive. Three died of disease but the rest were ransomed to representatives of the Hudson's Bay Company, which brought them to safety.

The reaction among whites to the event, known for years as the "Whitman Massacre", was immediate. Settlers formed militias that pursued the 200-plus members of the Cayuse tribe for the next two years. Others in the region lobbied for federal protection. This led to the designation of present day Washington, Oregon, Idaho, and part of Montana as the Oregon Territory in August of 1848.

The ultimate price the Cayuse paid was high indeed. In 1850, the Cayuse surrendered five men who supposedly took part in the attack. They were tried and hanged by authorities in Oregon City. In 1855, the Cayuse, Umatilla, and neighboring Walla Walla tribes were put on the same reservation. Meanwhile, a monument (and later, a national historic site) was established at the mission. The Whitmans are remembered in other ways, as well. Whitman College, a private school, has provided educational opportunities for students in nearby Walla Walla since 1882.

Today, visitors to the 98-acre Whitman Mission Historical Site today find a pleasant and peaceful place to wander. The visitor center's exhibits do a good job of telling the story of the Whitmans and of the Cayuse. Paved trails, covering a mile in all, lead to a mass grave where the victims of the attack were buried and to the top of a small hill where a 27-foot tall monument was erected on the 50th anniversary of the attack. South of the visitor center, you can see the remnants of the Oregon Trail that passed by the mission in 1844 along with the sites where buildings from the old mission once stood. While there are places along the Oregon Trail where the original wagon ruts are still visible, that is not the case here, where the ruts have been reconstructed.

Creeks, irrigation ditches, and a millpond on the grounds provide sanctuary for waterfowl. The sounds of pheasant and quail are common, as are the sight of mammals like deer and rabbit. Other mammals you may spy include coyote, skunk, and on rare occasion, otter, weasel, or badger. Red-tailed hawk and northern harrier are some of the more common raptors you'll see, and red-winged blackbirds as well as great blue heron are often found near the water.

The Whitman Mission is open daily except for Thanksgiving, Christmas, and New Years Day. The historic site can be visited from 8:00am to 6:00pm during the summer and until 4:30pm the rest of the year. Leashed pets are permitted and there is also a picnic area at the site. Overnight accommodations are available in Walla Walla.

Getting There: Located off US Highway 12, 7 miles west of downtown Walla Walla. Turn at the sign and follow Whitman Mission Road a short distance to the visitor center.

Lewis and Clark in Washington

Washington State Parks and Recreation Commission
www.parks.wa.gov/lewisandclark

Lewis and Clark Trail State Park
36149 Highway 12, Dayton, WA 99328/ 509-337-6457

The Sacajawea Interpretive Center – Sacajawea State Park
2503 Sacajawea Park Road, Pasco, WA 99301 / 509-545-2361

Lewis and Clark Interpretive Center – Cape Disappointment State Park
P.O. Box 488, Ilwaco, WA 98624 / 360-642-3029

Lodging Prices   Adventure Pricing

The journey of Lewis and Clark through the frontier of a newly born nation was an incredible achievement. The Corps of Discovery began their journey west from St. Louis, Missouri on May 14, 1804. The leaders of the expedition, Captains Meriwether Lewis and William Clark, were under orders from President Thomas Jefferson to find a water route to the Pacific Ocean. The expedition that reached the ocean consisted of 31 men, a young Shoshone mother named Sacajawea, and her infant son. The single woman of the group proved critical to the success of the endeavor that took the group over 4,100 miles up the Missouri River, across Montana, through the northern portion of Idaho, and across Washington to the sea.

The expedition entered Washington on October 10, 1805 and made good time down the Snake and Columbia Rivers, reaching the mouth of the Columbia and the Pacific Ocean on November 15. After enduring a wet and miserable winter near the Oregon coast at Fort Clatsop, the group turned around and headed back east, completing their journey in September of 1806. Remarkably, the group only lost one man (to illness) during the entire journey.

During their travels the explorers mapped critical routes across the American West, catalogued a large number of new animal, plant, and tree species, established friendly relations with numerous Native American tribes, and blazed a path for fellow frontiersmen, pioneers, and settlers to follow into the west as the century progressed.

A series of state parks in Washington lie along the path blazed by the Lewis and Clark Expedition. From east to west, they include Lewis and Clark Trail, Sacajawea, Maryhill and Columbia Hills, two windsurfing destinations (Doug's Beach and Spring Creek Hatchery), Beacon Rock, Station Camp (under development), Fort Columbia, and finally, Cape Disappointment State Park.

Three parks in particular tell the story of the expedition. Lewis and Clark Trail State Park is located between the small southeast Washington towns of Dayton and Waitsburg. On the south side of US Highway 12, a day-use area has several outdoor displays detailing the expedition's trip through this region on their way back from the Pacific Ocean in the spring of 1806. Across the highway is a campground in a heavily wooded setting. Interpretive programs are offered on Saturdays between Memorial Day weekend and Labor Day. Several address the Lewis and Clark Expedition and cover topics like the weapons the members carried or the medical knowledge and techniques used to keep the group healthy at the beginning of the 19th century. Be sure to call ahead since the times and topics of these programs are subject to change.

Traveling east towards Pasco, Sacajawea State Park sits at the confluence of the Snake and Columbia Rivers. This day-use park is not only a great place to picnic or launch a boat, but also a wonderful place to learn about a young Shoshone woman's important role as interpreter and diplomat for the expedition. From October 16th through the 18th of 1805, the Corps of Discovery camped here with several different tribes that came to fish for salmon at the confluence of the two mighty rivers. Today, the Sacajawea Interpretive Center has a number of modern exhibits and displays that tell the story of both the expedition and her remarkable life. The center is open daily from March 28 to November 1 from 10:00am to 5:00pm.

Finally, the Lewis and Clark Interpretive Center at the mouth of the Columbia River marks the westernmost point of Washington visited by the Corps of Discovery. Maps, murals, artifacts, and interactive exhibits cover the expedition's travels, focusing in particular on the time they spent in this area. The center is located within Cape Disappointment State Park (see entry in this book for further details) and is open daily, all year long, from 10:00am to 5:00pm.

Getting There: See above.

The Sacajawea Interpretive Center near Pasco has a number of exhibits and displays that tell the story of Sacajawea.

ENTRANCE TO HELLS CANYON:
Snake River – Grande Ronde River – Chief Joseph Wildlife Area

Hells Canyon National Recreation Area – Snake River Office
P.O. Box 699, Clarkston, WA 99403 / 509-758-0616
www.hellscanyonvisitor.com

Tucked into the combined borders of Washington, Oregon, and Idaho, Hells Canyon is an incredible, must-see destination that is known as the deepest gorge in North America. The distance from the east rim of the canyon at He Devil Peak to the Snake River below is 8,043 feet. The Grand Canyon, in comparison, is only about 6,000 feet deep.

Traveling the river through the canyon is an exciting adventure. It's tackled by whitewater rafters who float a series of long rapids downstream and jet boats that push their way upriver before powering back through the whitewater. The Snake drops an impressive 8.7 feet per mile from Hells Canyon Dam to the Washington border, with the river running anywhere from 2 to 105 feet deep along the way. A jet boat can make it from Clarkston to Hells Canyon Dam (117 miles) and back in a day, while rafters who float the river and hikers working their way along the Snake River National Recreation Trail are in for a multi-day expedition.

Much of this impressive region is encompassed within the 652,000-acre Hells Canyon National Recreation Area (HCNRA). The river receives additional protection from development due to its Wild and Scenic designation. Managed by the U.S. Forest Service, the HCNRA actually starts just below the Washington border with the official entrance into Hells Canyon at Cache Creek. Accessible only by boat, you can stop here to get river permits and visitor information. Between here and the Hells Canyon Dam lies a vast array of human history found at places like the Nez Perce Crossing (where Chief Joseph's Nez Perce Tribe crossed the Snake in their flight from U.S. soldiers) and the Kirkwood Historical Ranch, where interpretive and historical exhibits are found at an early 20th century sheep station.

While the Snake River north of the Washington border is not part of the HCNRA, it does share many of its characteristics. Steep hillsides on either side of the river are colored green, yellow, and pink in the spring from blooming grass and flowers that slowly fade to a uniform brown as the heat of summer takes hold. Wildlife is plentiful. Bighorn sheep and mule deer are frequently seen near shore, and within the 9,735-acre Chief Joseph Wildlife Area (located between the Snake River, Grand Ronde River, and Oregon border), elk, wild turkey, and upland game birds also present. Other birds seen in this area on a regular basis include goldeneye and merganser ducks, Bullocks oriole, pine siskin, Lazuli bunting, western kingbird, wrens, and nighthawks.

Flowing into the Snake River at the northern edge of the Chief Joseph State Wildlife Area, the Grande Ronde River is known for its healthy run of summer steelhead that anglers cast for from fall through early spring. From late spring through the summer you can catch rainbow trout and smallmouth bass here as well. Be sure to check the regulations for specific openings, closures, and lure restrictions. You can access the river at Boggan's Oasis by following a steep winding road from Anatone. If you launch a boat or raft from here, you can fish 8 miles to Schumaker Grade or float 26 miles of the Grande Ronde to the mouth. The river is not known for wild water, but you will encounter a few Class II and one set of Class III rapids as you float towards the Snake River near Heller Bar.

The fishing is also excellent in the Snake River for steelhead, bass, and very big sturgeon. Check the Hells Canyon Sport Fishing entry for further details.

Bird hunting is something else you can do on the Washington side of the Snake River near Hells Canyon. Chukar hunting is the most popular (and strenuous) pursuit, though quail, gray partridge, blue and ruffed grouse also provide opportunities in the fall. In the spring, you can go after Rio Grande turkey, though they are not as abundant here as they are elsewhere in the state.

Getting There: The easiest way to access this southeastern-most portion of Washington is to drive south on the Snake River Road from Asotin 23 miles to Heller Bar. There is a boat launch on the Snake River here near the mouth of the Grande Ronde River. You can follow the road another 4 miles from the launch to reach several access points on the lower Grande Ronde. If you launch from Heller Bar its only 7 miles up the Snake River to the Oregon border and official boundary of the Hells Canyon National Recreation Area.

A jet boat travels along the Snake River in Hells Canyon.

BEAMERS HELLS CANYON TOURS

1451 Bridge Street, Clarkston, WA 99403 – 800-522-6966
www.hellscanyontours.com

Lodging Prices: $$ to $$$$ Adventure Pricing: $$ to $$$$

You can find a soft adventure or a hardcore fishing experience in this part of the world where Oregon, Idaho, and Washington all meet around Hells Canyon. Beamer's Hells Canyon Tours is arguably the most popular tour company that ventures into this region of the Snake River. They have been taking people on guided jet boat excursions and fishing trips for 30 years. In addition to fishing boats and a designated mail boat, the company also has six jet boats ranging from 34 to 58 feet in size, the largest seating up to 66 passengers.

Most customers book a daylong excursion on the Snake River. Leaving at 8:00am from Clarkston, Washington you travel 100 miles to the "End of Navigation" point within the Hells Canyon National Recreation Area. Along the way you'll see ancient Indian petroglyphs, the remains of a turn of the century mining town, and hear about the human history of this remote and rugged part of the American West. You'll also get a chance to stretch your legs at two lodges owned by Beamers and at the Kirkwood Historic Ranch, which is a Depression-era sheep-herding station maintained by the U.S. Forest Service.

The real star of the show is Mother Nature. As you punch through the rapids of the Snake River you are surrounded by miles of towering cliffs and rock formations. Spring visitors enjoy a canvas of green hillsides splashed with yellow arrowleaf balsamroot and patches of pink phlox. Wildlife is plentiful. Bighorn sheep have taken the place of domestic sheep and are a common sight along shore, as are mule deer. Above the river, osprey and eagles both perch on rocks and trees or fly overhead looking for an easy meal.

You won't spend the whole ten hours sitting in the boat. A continental breakfast is served at Heller Bar Lodge, located 30 miles upstream (south) from Clarkston near the mouth of the Grande Ronde River. You stop again for lunch at the Kirkwood Historic Ranch. On the way back from the "End of Navigation", you also stop at Copper Creek Lodge, located 70 miles upriver. If you book a multi-day package, you'll be interested to know this lodge offers accommodations in 23 shaded (but not air-conditioned) cabins. Meals are taken in the main lodge and you can socialize in the game room, swim in the river, or cast a line for a catfish off the dock in the evening to round out your day. For day trippers, a final stop back at the Heller Bar Lodge in the late afternoon offers another chance for refreshments.

If you are short on time, Beamers also offers half-day tours to the Cache Creek Ranch – known as the official entrance to the Hells Canyon Recreation Area. Evening dinner cruises and Sunday brunch tours take you on the boat from Clarkston to Heller

Bar for a nice meal at the lodge. Beamers also offer one- or multi-day guided fishing trips on the Snake River for steelhead, big sturgeon, and aggressive smallmouth bass. Salmon fishing takes place on Idaho's nearby Clearwater River. If you choose to fish for more than one day you'll spend your nights at either the Heller Bar or Cabin Creek Lodge.

One unique and affordable trip that encompasses the best of nature touring and fishing is the Historic U.S. Mail Boat Tour. This boat departs every Wednesday morning and returns Thursday afternoon. The main purpose of this trip is to deliver mail to the ranchers and residents who live within Hells Canyon. Along the way you'll get to take in the natural surroundings, check out the wildlife, and do some fishing. Steelhead angling is very popular during this tour from October through February. Wednesday night is spent at the Copper Creek Lodge. On Thursday, you'll boat to the "End of Navigation" which signifies the last stop on the mail run before heading back to Clarkston.

Getting There: The Beamers Office is located in Clarkston at 1451 Bridge Street (US Highway 12). To reach their marina, turn north on 13th Street towards the Snake River. Pass Port Drive and turn right onto Port Way. You'll find a parking area just above the marina.

Beamer's jet boats take you into Hells Canyon to explore North America's Deepest Gorge.

HELLS CANYON SPORT FISHING

Jason Schultz – 1922 13th Street, Lewiston, ID 83501 / 208-305-4549
www.hellscanyonsportfishing.com

Lodging Prices: $$$$ Adventure Pricing: $$$ to $$$$

Certain individuals are called to a place or profession in life and Jason Schultz seems to be one of those people. He caught the angling bug in a big way while growing up in a small western Washington town. One day he was watching a television show about fishing the Snake River in Hells Canyon for sturgeon. By the time the program ended, the teenager decided he was going to go fish with that guide. He saved his money and took off that summer to Lewiston, Idaho. Schultz caught his sturgeon and impressed his host in the process. Shortly after graduating high school, Schultz moved to Lewiston, went to work for the guide service and never looked back.

Within a few years, Jason Schultz started guiding on his own. Now in his mid-30s, he has owned his own guide service, Hells Canyon Sport Fishing, for over ten years. Two other guides assist Schultz. The three of them fish year round in four different jet boats, the largest being a spacious 29-foot Hells Canyon Marine Jet Boat. Schultz also has a riverfront lodge available for guests at certain times of the year.

Schultz's home water is the Snake River in and around the scenic and rugged Hells Canyon National Recreation Area. He is one of a handful of outfitters licensed by the U.S. Forest Service to operate in this special place bordering the states of Oregon, Idaho, and Washington.

From mid-September through March, Schultz targets two runs of steelhead on the Snake River and the Clearwater River, a tributary that flows into the Snake at Lewiston. The smaller "A Run" steelhead average 4 to 7 pounds, while the big "B Run" fish go 7 to 12 and can run over 16 pounds.

In March, Schultz takes his show on the road, targeting trophy walleye on the middle-Columbia River below McNary Dam. Schultz has caught 18 pounders in this stretch of the Columbia, and the fish are so big, some midwestern anglers travel here every year to catch the biggest walleye of their lives. Depending on the salmon runs, Schultz may stay on the road into April, fishing for spring chinook on the Columbia River between Kalama and the mouth of the Cowlitz near Kelso.

By the end of the April, Hells Canyon Sport Fishing is back on the Snake River. From April until mid-September, the fishing is hot for smallmouth and solid for sturgeon. Most of the smallmouth measure 8 to 10 inches but are fun to catch on light tackle. The fun multiplies as four people in a boat often catch a hundred of them in a day of summer fishing. If you are looking for bigger bass, try fishing for them in the spring. It is not uncommon to take 2- to 3-pound bass and occasionally you can hook into a 5-pound trophy.

Sturgeon fishing on the Snake is all catch and release, but if you want to hook into a true monster, there are few better places. Schultz fishes deep eddies for these fish that run anywhere from 2 to 10 feet long. Once you hook a fish, be ready for a battle. Even with the heavy gear Schultz uses, the average fight lasts 20 to 40 minutes before you can get a sturgeon to shallow water for a quick photo opportunity.

When September arrives it's "cast and blast" time. These popular packages can be booked as a one- or multi-day package in the early fall. Either way, you'll spend time chasing chukar along the rocky slopes that run on either side of the Snake River. These birds have an affinity for running and climbing before flying, so being in shape helps for this kind of upland bird hunting. Back in the boat, you can cast for steelhead or wait for a sturgeon to bite.

Schultz also has a lodge available on the banks of the Snake River for groups of six to twelve from September through February. By booking a three-day/two-night package, you'll get good meals, a comfortable bed, and the opportunity to relax between full days of fishing and hunting in some ruggedly beautiful country.

Getting There: Departure points vary depending upon the destination.

Jason Schultz with an 8-foot Snake River sturgeon.

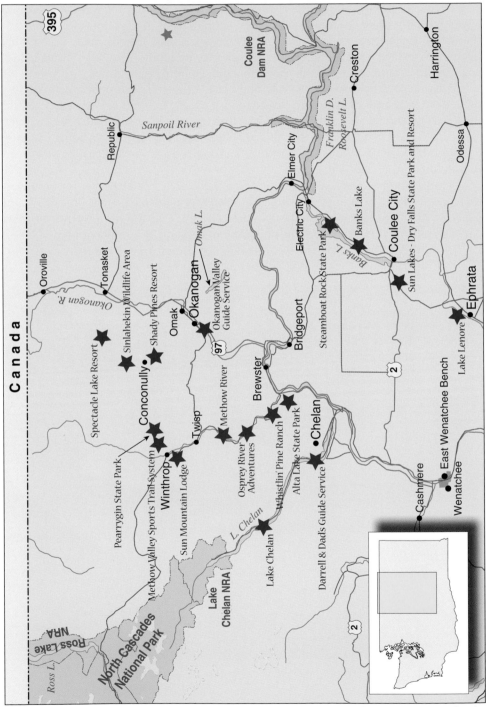

The Okanogan, Lake Chelan, and the Sun Lakes

Conconully

Conconully Chamber of Commerce / 877-826-9050 - www.conconully.com
Conconully State Park
PO Box 95, Conconully, WA 98819 / 509-826-7408 – www.parks.wa.gov

Lodging Prices

Few towns roll out the welcome mat for the outdoor recreationist like little Conconully. The town is ideally situated between two lakes, adjacent to forest service land, and close to two state wildlife areas. Festivals like the Opening Weekend Fishing Derby, January Outhouse Races, and Snow Dog Super Mush keep the town's taverns, restaurants, shops, and gas station doing a brisk business throughout the year.

Three waterfront resorts and a state park are options if you are looking for a place to stay. Conconully State Park is located just off of Main Street on the east end of town. You can camp at one of 82 sites in the grassy park that's dotted with a few trees. There are no hook-ups available, though there are plans to put some in soon. There are two boat ramps and a dock along with lots of waterfront along Conconully Reservoir. Restrooms with showers along with a day-use area offering picnic tables and a covered kitchen shelter are also at the park.

Conconully is an unpretentious place. Many of the streets are unpaved and ATVs and snowmobiles share the roads with automobiles. Deer freely wander the town and adjacent state park, and the small community quickly turns back into a forested environment beyond city limits. In short, leave your big city attitudes at the door. They won't impress anybody around here.

On the other hand, a big fish or trophy buck will raise a few eyebrows and garner nods of approval. Most of the waters in the area open to fishing the last weekend of April. Both Conconully Reservoir on the southeast edge of town and Conconully Lake to the north kick out limits of stocked rainbow trout from spring through fall and some of them are very big. Smallmouth bass are

also present in both lakes. At 415 and 313 acres respectively, both have plenty of room for fishing, rowing, or paddling if you have a canoe or kayak. In the summer, these two lakes also attract their share of power boats and personal watercraft. Additional trout fishing is possible at Fish Lake (6 miles north of town) or at several lakes within the Sinlahekin Wildlife Area (about 15 miles north of Conconully).

Generations of deer hunters have used Conconully as a fall base camp, but mule and white-tailed deer are not the only game around. Wildlife areas and public lands also provide bird hunters the opportunity to bag dove, grouse, and quail in the early fall. Bear and cougar are also taken on occasion. If you are interested in wildlife watching, sharp-tailed grouse, a rare game bird for the area, can sometimes be seen at the 8,700-acre Scotch Creek Wildlife Area between Conconully and Okanogan. Eagles, osprey, gulls, heron, and waterfowl are commonly seen at Conconully Lake and Reservoir.

Bicycling is popular on the dirt and gravel roads that surround Conconully. One loop ride from town covers 18 miles and takes you around Mineral Mountain. Other rides on a road network covering up to 50 miles emanate from Salmon Creek Meadows or Kerr, a state sno-park popular with snowmobilers 3 miles west of town.

Hikers can access several trails within the immediate area. The hike up the Angel Pass Trail is a 3.5-mile day hike that starts from the Salmon Meadows Campground northwest of Conconully. A short walk suitable for families also takes off from Salmon Meadows and follows little Mutton Creek for a mile.

Those wanting more of a challenge can tackle the 6.2-mile Granite Mountain Trail that takes you on a steep hike towards the summit of 7,366-foot Granite Mountain southeast of Conconully Reservoir. Another mountain-top experience can be had by walking the 6-mile Golden Stairway Trail to the top of Starvation Mountain where a fire lookout was once located.

Getting There: State Highway 20 and US Highway 97 both lead to Okanogan. From Okanogan follow the Conconully Road 18 miles northwest to Conconully.

SHADY PINES RESORT

125 West Fork Salmon Creek Rd (PO Box 44), Conconully, WA 98819 / 800-552-2287
www.shadypinesresort.com

Lodging Prices: $ to $$ Adventure Pricing: $

Shady Pines is the best of several decent resorts around the small but lively town of Conconully – where deer freely graze and both ATVs and snowmobiles are welcome on city streets. The resort sits on the shore of 450-acre Conconully Reservoir, a long time favorite for opening day anglers who come at the end of April to catch rainbow trout that commonly weigh up to 1.5 pounds. The fishing holds up well through June, picks up again in September and lasts until the lake closes for fishing at the end of October. If the fishing is slow at the reservoir, nearby Conconully Lake or Fish Lake are other places to wet a line.

Shady Pines has 21 full hook-up RV sites on their 3.5-acre property along with two tent sites and six cabins that each sleeps four to six people. The largest cabins are in a duplex unit. Decorated in an outdoor motif, they are surprisingly spacious. Each has a kitchen, refrigerator, and private bathroom. Linens and towels are included with all of the cabin rentals. Other amenities include snacks that can be bought at the office, massages by appointment, and Wi-Fi Internet access. Leashed pets are welcome at this quiet resort.

Summer days can be hot here, but spending the day on the water or in the nearby forest is a good way to beat the heat of the day. Because the waterfront resort sits at an elevation of 2,300 feet, the temperature cools to a comfortable level by early evening.

Fall is another great time to visit. Bird hunters come to hit the woods for spruce, ruffed, and blue grouse in September. In October, the resort is filled with deer hunters looking for three point or better bucks. Many opt for a "cast and blast" getaway, hunting in the morning, fishing in the afternoon, and then hunting again around sunset.

There are plenty of other things to do besides shooting or casting. The resort has rowboats and paddle boats for rent, along with one 12-foot aluminum boat with a 6-horsepower outboard motor. Those who enjoy kayaking and canoeing can launch from the beach in front of the resort or head to one of the nearby lakes.

Wildlife watching provides an added value to a vacation here. In addition to the deer that wander onto the grounds of the resort, birds such as osprey, heron, eagles, and even the occasional loon can be seen on or above the lake. Additional wildlife watching opportunities are available at the Scotch Creek and Sinlahekin Wildlife Areas (see the Sinlahekin Wildlife Area entry for more information).

Other outdoor activities in the immediate area include hiking, bicycling, ATV riding, and in the winter, snowmobiling (the Conconully entry has further details). The Shady Pines Resort is closed from November through December.

Getting There: State Highway 20 and US Highway 97 both lead to Okanogan. From Okanogan follow the Conconully Road 18 miles northwest to Conconully. Take a left at the state park and follow the road along the west side of the reservoir to the resort.

Shady Pines Resort has RV sites with spectacular views.

Sinlahekin Wildlife Area

Washington Department of Fish and Wildlife
P.O. Box C, Loomis, WA 98827 / 509-223-3358
www.wdfw.wa.gov

Established in 1938 to protect mule deer habitat, the 14,000-acre Sinlahekin Wildlife Area can lay claim to being the oldest state wildlife area in Washington. Located in the Okanogan Highlands a short distance from the Canadian border, this swath of public land offers a place to hunt and fish, watch wildlife, and more.

Much of the Sinlahekin Wildlife Area sits in a 16-mile-long valley. The terrain is a mixture of shrub-steppe habitat, wetlands, and forest consisting of both ponderosa pine and Douglas fir trees. Wheatgrass, bitterbrush, and serviceberry provide forage for wildlife.

The animals who call the valley home include mule and white-tailed deer, black bear, and California bighorn sheep. Cougar and moose are seen on occasion, and game birds such as grouse and quail are abundant. Hunting takes place during designated seasons for all of these species, and viewing them outside of hunting season is a popular activity from vehicles along the Sinlahekin Road, or by visitors who roam the state land on foot or horseback. Other animals you may see are of the cold-blooded variety. Western painted turtles and Pacific tree frogs are both abundant, as are rattlesnakes. Other wildlife here includes snowshoe hare, red squirrel, and yellow-bellied marmot as well as pheasant, gray partridge, and a variety of butterflies. On the waterways you may see loons, red-necked grebe, great blue heron, tundra swan, and several other waterfowl species. Hawks and eagles are frequently seen, as are mourning dove, downy woodpecker, northern flicker, and great horned owls.

Several lakes within the Sinlahekin Wildlife Area provide places to fish, row, and paddle. All of them are open for angling from the last weekend of April through October 31. Blue Lake is the largest. Ten miles north of Conconully, the 186-acre lake has both rainbow and brown trout that average

12 to 18 inches. Selective regulations are in effect and although there is a gravel boat launch, only electric motors are allowed on boats. Forde Lake is farther north, some 6 miles south of Loomis. This 24-acre lake is known for big brook trout and has also been stocked with tiger trout. Both Forde and Blue Lakes have primitive camp sites. Across the road from Forde Lake is little Reflection Pond, which also has some nice-sized brook trout in it. Finally, Sinlahekin Creek has brook and rainbow trout in it as well as some whitefish.

Getting There: Follow Sinlahekin Lake Road 16 miles from Conconully to the wildlife area or drive the same road south from Loomis.

California bighorn sheep are frequently seen in the Sinlahekin Wildlife Area.

SPECTACLE LAKE RESORT

10 McCammon Road, Tonasket, WA 98855 / 509-223-3433
www.spectaclelakeresort.com

Lodging Prices: $ to $$ Adventure Prices: $

The Spectacle Lake Resort is an ideal base camp for exploring the Okanogan Highlands. The resort is west of Tonasket on the southeastern end of Spectacle Lake. Several other lakes good for fishing and paddling, a large wildlife area, and miles of quiet country roads for bicycling are all nearby.

The resort has 38 grassy RV sites (all but three have full hook ups), two tent sites, two travel trailers for rent, and 14 motel rooms in two buildings. The motel rooms are set up in a strip configuration, but once inside you'll find rustic, cabin-style accommodations with private bathrooms, kitchenettes, and refrigerators. Linens, towels, and kitchen utensils are all provided. Most rooms have air conditioning and are equipped with two double beds set up as bunk beds. The largest units (sporting two and three bedrooms) also have fireplaces and televisions. If you didn't get a room with a TV, you can rent one along with a DVD player and movies at the resort. Leashed pets are allowed on this property.

The resort is popular with kids. There is a beach, a dock where you can fish, a swimming pool, a sandbox for smaller children, and areas for volleyball and horseshoes. On the off chance it rains, there is a game room with a pool table and several arcade games. A store sells candy, groceries, gifts, and fishing tackle.

Sagebrush, grass, and the occasional ponderosa pine grace the shores of 314-acre Spectacle Lake. It's a pleasant place to fish or paddle with sunny skies and light breezes being the norm. Row boats, canoes, and aluminum boats with 6-horsepower outboards are available for rent, and there is also a launch if you bring your own craft.

Owner Bryce Leep says, "Spectacle Lake has a reputation as being one of the best trout lakes in Washington." The season opens on the first of April and closes at the end of September. May and April are the best months to hook into rainbow trout measuring 10 to 14 inches. Larger fish lurk within the lake. A 10-pound rainbow was once caught here and every year brown trout over 7 pounds seem to find the hook of some lucky angler. Smallmouth bass are also present, though they are not very big. Crayfish, a tasty freshwater crustacean, can also be caught. Kids catch them by turning over rocks, and if you want to boil some bigger ones up for dinner, drop a baited trap to the bottom of the lake.

A bevy of other lakes within a short drive of the resort beckon to anglers, kayakers, canoeists, and other small boat owners. Wannacutt Lake to the north is a cool, deep lake with solid rainbow trout fishing throughout the summer. Blue Lake lies just beyond Wannacutt and is one of the few waters in the state with Lahontan cutthroat trout. A short distance east of the resort is Whitestone Lake, which holds both largemouth bass and channel catfish. Palmer Lake north of Loomis has a reputation of being one of the best big smallmouth bass waters in the state and also boasts a nice kokanee fishery with fish running 14 inches long. Chopaka Lake is a flyfishing-only lake that has picky, but big, rainbow trout. The nearby Sinlahekin Wildlife Area also has several trout lakes.

Hunting is just as popular as fishing in this part of Washington. Deer hunters hit this region in force in October for both mule and white-tailed deer. There is also good hunting for grouse in September as well as quail, pheasant, ducks, and geese in the fall. In the spring turkey hunters also bag their share of gobblers. If you don't have permission to hunt on private land, the 14,000 acre Sinlahekin Wildlife Area offers an exciting alternative (See the Sinlahekin Wildlife Area entry for more information).

Wildlife sightings are a given in the Okanogan. Besides the game animals mentioned above, you may also get a chance to see bighorn sheep that like to graze between Spectacle Lake and Loomis. Bird watchers will get a chance to see a variety of raptors as well as kingfishers, yellow-headed and red-winged blackbirds. Orioles and bluebirds are also seen at times near the resort.

If you want some exercise bring your bicycle. Miles of lightly traveled paved, gravel, and dirt roads wind over rolling hills and through scenic valleys. The same lakes that attract anglers, kayakers, and canoeists also make nice places for a shoreline lunch during a bike ride.

Spectacle Lake Resort is open from April 1 through mid-December. The resort is open on a limited basis the rest of the year, so be sure to call in advance if you plan on visiting.

Getting There: Turn west onto 4th Street from US Highway 97 in Tonasket. Cross the Okanogan River and turn north onto Tonasket Airport Road. Travel some 10 miles north along this road as it changes into Holmes Road. Take a left on McCammon Road near the east end of Spectacle Lake and follow the signs a short distance to the resort.

OKANOGAN VALLEY GUIDE SERVICE

Jerrod Gibbons – 8 Norway Pines Road, Tonasket, WA 98855 / 509-429-1714
www.okanoganvalleyguideservice.com

Lodging Prices: Included with some adventures   Adventure Pricing: $$$ to $$$$

Jerrod Gibbons has a lot of outdoors experience under his belt for a man who is under 30 years old. Fortunately for the rest of us, he decided to put it to good use by becoming a guide who specializes in deer and turkey hunts as well as salmon and steelhead fishing in north central Washington.

Gibbons has a healthy base of clients, and one of his memorable hunts took place when he got the chance to guide well-known outdoors writer Jim Zumbo. Gibbons has enough business on his hands that he uses the assistance of up to 16 seasonal guides. Most come to hunt deer near Tonasket or Curlew on ranches (covering 30,000 acres) that Gibbons has access to. Archery, muzzleloader, and modern firearms hunts can all be scheduled between October and mid-December. Mule deer make up the vast majority of game harvested, though there are also some impressive white-tailed deer in the area. Multi-day black bear hunts are another option. Gibbons promises a one on one guide-to-client ratio during all of his three- to five-day hunts. After a day in the field, you'll head to a ranch for one of your three daily meals before getting some sleep on a cot inside a canvas tent.

If you prefer birds to big game, Gibbons provides one-day spring turkey hunts between April 15 and May 15. Canada goose hunts are popular in the fall and winter. The goose hunting typically takes place out of portable blinds in wheat or barley fields around Brewster or Omak. Hot coffee and snacks are on hand while you wait for the birds to fly. Once they arrive, your guide's hard-charging Labrador retrievers will pick up any birds you drop.

Gibbons is also a fishing guide who takes up to three clients at a time onto the Upper Columbia River between Pateros and Bridgeport in his 20-foot Alumaweld Super Vee boat. From July into September, he targets big chinook salmon weighing up to 40 pounds. In October, he'll shift his focus toward steelhead when enough of them migrate upstream (and more than enough usually do) for a season to open. These summer-run fish average 6 pounds but can get up to 17 pounds. Working jigs under slip bobbers and trolling plugs are two of his favorite methods to hook into these hard-fighting fish well into winter.

Gibbons and his guides can also take you fishing for smallmouth bass, hunting for coyotes, or wingshooting for ducks, quail, and dove in season. If you can't decide whether to fish or hunt, cast and blast trips are available with goose hunting in the morning and steelhead fishing in the afternoon.

Getting There: Destinations vary.

Methow River

Washington Department of Fish and Wildlife, Region 2 Office
1550 Alder Street NW, Ephrata, WA 98823 / 509-654-4624
www.wdfw.wa.gov

Lodging Prices

If you like to fish for trout and summer steelhead, you'll think you've gone to heaven when you reach the banks of Methow River. Flowing from the North Cascades into the Columbia River at Pateros, this scenic stream is so full of good-looking pools, runs, and riffles that you'll have a hard time deciding where to start casting. Access is plentiful off of State Highway 20 from Mazama to Twisp and then along State Highway 153 to Pateros. There are several Forest Service campgrounds along the upper reaches of the river above Mazama and a number of public access sites downstream of Winthrop. The 847-acre Big Valley Unit of the Methow Wildlife Area (located 3.5 miles northwest of Winthrop) offers not only another place to reach the river, but also a place to hunt, hike, and watch wildlife.

The Methow is a particularly scenic stream. The river runs clear most of the year, and along shore are gravel bars, basalt rock formations, and vegetation ranging from bitterbrush and sagebrush to stands of Douglas fir, ponderosa pine, aspen, and cottonwood. Civilization is making inroads as the river flows by summer homes, several small towns, and a number of fruit orchards. By and large though, time on the Methow is time away from the worries of the world.

One way to leave those worries is by catching a few trout, and there are plenty of them here. Wild rainbow and cutthroat trout are the predominant species. Ten- to twelve-inch trout are common, and it's reasonable to expect you'll tie into a trout measuring between 16 and 20 inches in a day of fishing. On rare occasion, you might even hook a trout up to 25 inches long. At certain times of year, these big trout are a lot more common. That's because summer

steelhead, an ocean-going strain of rainbow trout that average 6 pounds, make their way back to the Methow in September and stay in the system all the way through March. The steelhead are joined by a spawning population of chinook salmon in September and October.

Catch-and-release trout fishing is open in certain portions of the river from June 1 through September 30. Steelhead fishing has been open from mid-October through the winter in recent years, and you are encouraged to keep hatchery (adipose-fin-clipped) fish. Salmon fishing has not been open on the Methow but a winter fishery for whitefish provides an additional opportunity to wet a line. Check the state fishing regulations for further information since there are several additional restrictions.

While fishing is what draws most people to the Methow, whitewater rafting and kayaking is also an option from Carlton all the way downstream to a state-owned boat launch near the mouth of the river. The most exciting whitewater paddling occurs from April through June when flows are at their highest, and some segments can be floated all the way into early August.

Whether you are spending a day on the water rafting or fishing, the wildlife in the area will provide a pleasant addition to the experience. Mule deer are very abundant and on occasion you may also see a black bear, coyote, or the rare cougar. Birds along the river include eagles and osprey hunting for food, blue grouse along shore, and several species of woodpeckers are often heard drumming on trees. In the Big Valley unit alone, the Washington State Audubon Society reports 137 different bird species are present at different times of the year. During hunting season, the abundance of public lands in the region is very popular with those seeking deer and grouse.

Getting There: In eastern Washington take US Highway 97 from Omak or Wenatchee to reach the mouth of the river at Pateros. Follow the river upstream along State Highway 153 and then State Highway 20 to Mazama. Many visitors from western Washington travel to Mazama along State Highway 20 during the summer from Interstate 5 at Burlington.

Osprey River Adventures

P.O. Box 1305, Twisp, WA 98856 / 800-997-4116
www.ospreyriveradventures.com

Lodging Prices: N/A   Adventure Pricing: $$

Not to be confused with Osprey Rafting in Leavenworth, Osprey River Adventures floats the Methow and Skagit Rivers of northern Washington. David Dunn owns the company and he and his staff are the only rafting outfit to call the Methow River home. They are also the preferred outfitter for guests staying at the Sun Mountain Resort near Winthrop.

The Methow is a gorgeous stream that flows past a series of small towns (Mazama, Winthrop, Twisp, Carlton, and Methow) to the Columbia River at Pateros. Raptors and waterfowl are frequently seen and mule deer are abundant along shore. Sunny skies are the norm during the four-month rafting season, making summertime dips into the cool water an inviting option.

Osprey River Adventures offers three different excursions on the Methow. The first is the Black Canyon trip that features both Class III and more challenging Class IV whitewater rapids. The second is the Gold Creek run that starts a little further upstream. You'll raft through fun Class II rapids along with several slower stretches where you can soak up the scenery or go for a short swim. If you've ever wanted to try river kayaking, use one of the company's inflatable kayaks during the Gold Creek run. You'll paddle alongside the rafting group and get advice from the guides along the way. Both trips are about four hours long. You'll beach midway to stretch your legs and enjoy a flavorful deli lunch featuring fruits, pastas, and sandwiches. Soda and water are provided, as are wetsuits, booties, and a courtesy shuttle.

A third offering focuses not on whitewater, but relaxation. You can rent an inner tube and float the placid waters and riffles of the Methow past the Western-frontier-themed town of Winthrop. The hour-long float is a great way to cool down on a hot summer day and includes both drop off and pick up service.

The Black Canyon trips are offered from May through July while the dependable Gold Creek rafting adventure takes place all the way from the end of April into early August. The inner tube floats are available from mid-July until Labor Day.

While the Methow is the bread-and-butter river for Osprey River Adventures, the company also offers rafting on the Skagit River from July through October. Starting off in the North Cascades National Park, this excursion features floating calm sections of river interspersed with a several Class II to III whitewater rapids. It's all set among a backdrop of dark green forests and snow capped peaks. This is also a four-hour trip, staring near Newhalem and ending by Marblemount off of State Highway 20.

Most of the guides are local residents and all are safety conscious. Each guide has basic first aid and CPR certifications and many return to work year after year. You can reserve a trip in advance or call the night before (most trips meet at 9:30am) to see if space is available for a rafting expedition. No reservations are required for the inner tube float trips.

Getting There: Destinations vary – see the company website for details.

A clear, cool river under sunny skies equals a great day on the water!

Pearrygin and Alta Lake State Parks

Pearrygin State Park
561 Bear Creek Road, Winthrop, WA 98862 / 509-996-2370
www.parks.wa.gov

Alta Lake State Park
191-A Alta Lake Road, Pateros, WA 98846 / 509-923-4723
www.parks.wa.gov

Lodging Prices

Two nice state parks in the Methow Valley offer lakefront base camps from which to explore the Methow River, hike the trails of the valley, and investigate public land for deer and grouse hunting.

Alta Lake State Park is located 4 miles from Pateros, a small town that sits at the mouth of the Methow River. The park is located on 2-mile-long Alta Lake, a scenic destination with lots of pine trees, rock fields, and cliffs that spill down towards the lake. The state park covers much of the northwestern portion of the lake and a private ranch (see the entry for Whistlin' Pine Ranch) offers additional lodging at the southwest end.

Two boat ramps at the north end of the lake are popular with water skiers and personal watercraft enthusiasts who are allowed on the lake from 9:00am to 6:00pm. Anglers also use these ramps to launch boats and fish for stocked 8- to 14-inch rainbow trout from the last Saturday in April through September. Windsurfers can be seen at times on the water and if you are a paddling enthusiast you'll be able to enjoy some quiet time in the morning and evening when the pleasure boats are off the water.

The park has 32 sites with hook-ups for RVs and another 168 tent sites. A group camp accommodates an additional 20 to 64 people but has no hook-ups for RVs. The day-use area has grassy lawns, a swimming area, and a concession store that sells snacks and firewood. Several picnic tables (some of them sheltered) are also available in this portion of the park.

In addition to fishing there is also some good bird watching around the lake. In the spring, flycatchers, kingbirds, and hummingbirds are all frequently observed. Scaup, ruddy ducks, and ring-necks are some of the diving ducks you'll see on the water along with the more common mallard and several types of gulls.

Farther up the Methow Valley near Winthrop, Pearrygin Lake State Park sits along 11,000 feet of the lake it is named after. Like Alta Lake, Pearrygin offers good rainbow trout fishing from boats and from a fishing pier at the park. Watersport enthusiasts also like this 212-acre lake. Like Alta Lake, the use of personal watercraft and water-skiing is restricted to certain hours to keep mornings and evenings pleasant for those who want a little peace and quiet in the outdoors.

The large 696-acre park has 71 sites for campers or RVs with hook-ups and another 92 with no utilities. Two group camps can accommodate 48 and 80 people respectively, and if you don't have a tent or an RV you may be able to rent one of the two cabins in the park. Each one sleeps up to four people and can be rented from the end of April until mid-September. Reservations are highly recommended.

Willows and ash trees in the park provide shade on hot days, and summertime park ranger interpretive programs are offered several evenings a week from Memorial Day through Labor Day. Two park stores serve up hot food and drinks, sell groceries and fire wood, and also rent boats so you can explore the lake. The day-use area includes a boat launch with two ramps, a swimming beach, picnic sites, and a place to play volleyball or toss a Frisbee. Raptors like hawks, eagles, osprey, and owls are common in the air, and mule deer, squirrels, and chipmunks are abundant on the ground. Sometimes you may catch sight of a marmot, bear, or cougar. Several avian species frequent the park, making it a good place for bird watching. Both Pearrygin and Alta Lake State Park are open from late March until late October.

Getting There: Alta Lake State Park – Drive to Pateros on US Highway 97. Turn west onto State Highway 153 and travel two miles to Alta Lake Road. Turn onto Alta Lake Road and go another two miles to the State Park. Pearrygin Lake State Park – From State Highway 20 in Winthrop drive north just over 1.5 miles as the road turns into East Chewuch Road. Turn right onto Bear Creek road and follow the signs to the park.

SAWTOOTH OUTFITTERS AND WHISTLIN' PINE RANCH

P.O. Box 284 (321 Alta Lake Road), Pateros, WA 98846 / 509-923-2548
www.altalake.com

Lodging Prices: $ to $$ Adventure Pricing: $ to $$$$

Located on Alta Lake where sagebrush mixes with pine, the Whistlin' Pine Ranch and Sawtooth Outfitters offer hunting and fishing vacations with an equestrian theme.

The Varrelman family established Whistlin' Pine Ranch in 1945. Today, Brian Varrelman runs both the ranch and outfitting business. Spend just a little time with Brian and you'll see he is passionate about hunting, horses, and the wilderness he roams. He is a past president and current member of the Washington Outfitters and Guides Association and has a bounty of stories to share about his life outdoors.

While Sawtooth Outfitters offers some summer pack trips into the eastern slopes of the Cascade Mountains, much of their business is geared toward big game hunters. Between September and early November hunters on horseback venture into the Pasayten Wilderness northwest of Winthrop and the Sawtooth Wilderness between Alta Lake and Lake Chelan. The most popular quarry is migratory mule deer. Most hunters glass for quality three-point bucks, but some hunt for black bear weighing several hundred pounds. Sawtooth Outfitters also accommodates bighorn sheep and mountain goat hunters if you are lucky enough to draw a once in a lifetime tag for one of these unique animals.

You have three options when booking a trip with Sawtooth Outfitters. You can book a drop camp: You and your gear are packed into a campsite and then left until you are packed out on a later specified date. A canvas wall tent and woodstove are provided to keep you warm.

The second option is to establish a deluxe camp. This is a six- to eight-day expedition where a wrangler takes care of the camp chores and cooking. Typical evening meals include roast beef, baked salmon, or lasagna. A hot breakfast in the morning will be served by 5:00am so you can be hunting during that first hour of daylight when you'll have the best chance of bagging your trophy.

The last and most expensive option is to hire a guide to work with you during your deluxe camp stay. The guide will work with no more than two hunters at a time for up to five days. If your main goal is to bag a nice animal, this is a smart way to go since the guides are familiar with where the animals are located. If you hunt on your own you may spend valuable hunting time in non-productive areas.

Meanwhile back at the ranch (cliché intended), there is also plenty to do. It starts with a place to stay. There are 32 tent sites and ten RV sites with hookups (power and water) as well as nine cabins. All but one of the cabins are primitive, offering nothing more than a roof, four walls, and a place to unroll your sleeping bag. On the other hand, the one deluxe cabin is pretty nice. Built by Varrelman, it features a pine interior and includes a knotty pine full-size bed. A small kitchenette has a microwave, sink, and refrigerator and there is a private bathroom as well.

Most ranch visitors spend time at pretty 187-acre Alta Lake. Cliffs that end at the top of Arbuckle Ridge tower over the water on one side while pine, sagebrush, a few summer homes and a pleasant state park surround the rest of the lake. Stocked with rainbow trout, the fishing generally starts strong the last weekend of April and holds up until the lake closes at the end of September. A typical stringer of trout features fish measuring 8 to 14 inches long. The biggest one Varrelman has ever seen was caught in 1988 and weighed 18 pounds. The water in front of the ranch property is pretty shallow, but you can rent a rowboat to get to deeper water where most of the fish are found.

The clean deep water also gives the lake a blue hue that is pleasing to the eye. Kayakers and canoeists haven't discovered this lake in great numbers, but with eagles and osprey flying overhead, lots of sunshine, and plenty of scenery, this is a good place for paddling. Check out the Alta Lake State Park entry for more details about this Okanogan County lake.

While fishing and water play are popular, others come for the horseback riding. One-, two- and four-hour trips all depart from the ranch that 70 horses and mules call home. The shorter trips venture into Alta Lake Coulee, a scenic area with rocky walls, dispersed ponderosa, blue skies, and generally flat trails that riders of all experience levels and ages will enjoy. The more challenging four-hour ride winds all the way around Alta Lake. The ride covers over 10 miles and takes you onto the 10,000-acre Arbuckle Ranch. In addition to seeing cattle on the ranch you'll be able to look from a high ridge down on to Alta Lake. Sitting in the saddle with sweeping views of the Columbia River and surrounding country will make you feel more like the Marlboro Man than the casual cowboy you probably are.

The 400-acre Whistlin' Pine Ranch is open from mid-April through Labor Day. Dogs are not allowed. Additional lodging as well as food, gas, and limited groceries are available in nearby Pateros.

Getting There: Drive to Pateros on US Highway 97. Turn west onto State Highway 153 and travel two miles to Alta Lake Road. Turn onto Alta Lake Road and go another 2 miles to the State Park. Continue past the State Park to the Whistlin' Pine Ranch.

Colton Thompson is ready to ride!

Methow Valley Sports Trail System

Methow Valley Sport Trails Association (MVSTA)
209 Castle Avenue (PO Box 147), Winthrop, WA 98862
Trail Report Line: 800-682-5787 – www.mvsta.com

Adventure Pricing

If the folks at the Methow Valley Sports Trail Association (MVSTA) took a break from trail maintenance long enough to pat themselves on their backs, most of us would be okay with that. The reason why is simple: The non-profit organization has developed a 124-mile trail system on the eastern slopes of the North Cascades that has been given great media reviews by the *Los Angeles Times*, *Sunset Magazine*, *The New York Times* and even the Weather Channel; which named the Methow Valley their "Top Winter Family Getaway" in 2008.

Volunteers came together in 1977 to build the Methow Community Trail, the heart of the system. The 32-kilometer trail links the small towns of Mazama and Winthrop, following the Methow River much of the way. Since that time the organization has helped to create and maintain a number of other trails that traverse both public and private land. In the winter they are used by scores of cross-country skiing enthusiasts who stay in Mazama, Winthrop, or at some of the nice resorts outside of these communities like the Sun Mountain Lodge. The trails are groomed on a regular basis and even after a week of skiing you'll still have plenty of new trails to explore.

Trails are rated as easy, more difficult, and difficult. There are several rated as favorites on the MVSTA website. The toughest one takes you 2,000 feet up to Rendezvous Pass from the Cub Creek Trail. You can catch your breath at a warming hut before skiing downhill on the Rendezvous Trail to Mazama, covering 11 miles in the process. On the other end of the spectrum, you can ski easier trails like the 6-mile Cassal Loop from the North Cascades Base Camp near Mazama, the 3.5-mile Beaver Pond Loop from the

Chickadee Trailhead at Sun Mountain Lodge, or just cover some of level terrain on the Community Trail near Winthrop. If you don't know how to ski don't worry; daily ski lessons and rentals are available from the Methow Valley Ski School (509-996-4735) at several different locations. If you enjoy snowshoeing the MVSTA also has several trails for this purpose ranging from less than a mile to over 5 miles. A pass is required on the trail system for both snowshoers and skiers. They can be purchased at various locations in Winthrop, Twisp, and Mazama.

From spring through fall, the trail system is used by mountain bicyclists, trail runners, hikers, and in some areas, by equestrians. April and May are good times to be on the trail system, since yellow and purple wildflowers add beautiful splashes of color to a green landscape that is, more often than not, topped by a canopy of blue skies.

In addition to panoramic scenery, you'll also see a lot of wildlife. The Audubon Society has several locations in this region listed on the Cascade Loop of the Great Washington State Birding Trail. One of them is found around a suspension bridge along the Community Trail that crosses the Methow River between Mazama and Winthrop. Bird watchers may be treated to the sight of mergansers and colorful harlequin ducks along the river while crossbills, grosbeaks, juncos, chickadees, and nuthatches flit among the branches of trees along shore. In addition to birds, you'll probably also see mule deer, which are very common throughout the Methow Valley.

Getting There: Winthrop is located on State Highway 20 in North Central Washington. You can drive State Highway 20 from Interstate 5 in Burlington during the summer if you are coming from western Washington. In eastern Washington, you can get to Winthrop by taking State Highway 20 from US Highway 97 at Okanogan.

SUN MOUNTAIN LODGE

PO Box 1000 (604 Patterson Lake Road), Winthrop, WA 98862 / 800-572-0493 –
www.sunmountainlodge.com

Lodging Prices: $$$ to $$$$ Adventure Pricing: $ to $$$

Sun Mountain Lodge is Washington's most luxurious lodge east of the Cascades and the only resort that boasts AAA 4-Diamond ratings for both its lodging and restaurant. With excellent accommodations, fine dining, great service, and a host of outdoor options to choose from, it's no wonder this place is popular far beyond the Pacific Northwest.

The 3,500-acre resort lies west of Winthrop, a small western-themed town on the eastern slopes of the North Cascades. Highlights include a lodge that sits on top of 2,900-foot Sun Mountain, the cabins below at Patterson Lake, and 40 miles of trails used by hikers, bicyclists, horseback riders, cross-country skiers, and snow shoeing enthusiasts. These trails, maintained by the Methow Valley Sport Trails Association (see separate entry) are part of a linked, regional 124-mile trail system open to the public.

The lodge building's decorative theme can best be described as "western outdoors" with several magnificent big game and bird mounts gracing the log and stone interior walls. Outside the main lobby are sitting rooms, a game room, and a gift shop. There is also an activities center with a full service fly shop where you can book an outdoor adventure, purchase fishing gear or outdoors apparel, rent a mountain bike, and get tips on what to do outside during your stay. In the winter, the activities shop becomes a ski shop, offering cross-country ski and snowshoe rentals along with a place to sign up for skiing lessons if you are new to the sport.

The dining room has garnered a number of awards. Rob Thorlakson is the Director of Sales and Marketing at Sun Mountain Lodge. He describes the food as "Northwest regional cuisine". The chefs use a lot of fresh, organically-grown produce to accent a seasonal menu. A glass of wine nicely complements these meals and a 5,000-bottle wine cellar with 450 different labels gives you plenty of varieties to choose from. Another restaurant in the lodge, the Wolf Creek Bar and Grill, offers dining and drinks in a more casual setting with fantastic views of Mount Robinson and Mount Gardner.

There are 97 different rooms to choose from at the lodge. Forty-five of them, each with great views, are found in the main lodge building. The two-story Gardner building has 26 spacious rooms and two suites that are a step above the standard offerings. Each features large tile-floor bathrooms, gas fireplaces set in stone, private decks, a wet bar, and sitting area. The Mount Robinson building's 24 luxury rooms and suites are the nicest at the resort. Primarily used by couples, they feature king beds in large rooms with sitting areas, gas fireplaces, jetted whirlpool tubs, and private decks. All of the rooms at the lodge are accented with locally crafted furniture and art. Additional amenities include terrycloth robes you can slip into during your stay, Wi-Fi Internet access, and stereos in each room. One thing you won't find in your room is a television and with so much to do outdoors, this is a blessing. Two outdoor pools and hot tubs, along with tennis courts, an exercise room, and full-service spa are also present at the lodge. Parents staying at Sun Mountain will also appreciate the fact there are children's programs and babysitting available. Make arrangements for your pets because they are not allowed in the guest rooms.

Down the hill from the lodge are 16 cabins at the head of 1.7-mile Patterson Lake. All of them are roomy (sleeping anywhere from five to twelve), comfortable and well furnished. Gas fireplaces, air conditioning, and ceiling fans keep things comfortable throughout the year. A large kitchen with a refrigerator, range, and dishwasher makes it easy to do your own cooking and covered verandas facing the lake provide a good place to relax. Don't worry about making the bed or exchanging towels because housekeeping is included. Summertime swimming and sunbathing on the grass above the beach are a few steps away from your front door.

While hiking, biking, cross-country skiing, and snowshoeing are all popular, additional activities wait beyond the trails. Paddlesport enthusiasts can book a Methow River rafting or kayaking trip with Osprey River Adventures (see their entry for details) through the activity shop. Patterson Lake is also a good place for small boats. You can launch at the public access site or rent a rowboat, canoe, kayak, paddle boat, or small sailboat at the Patterson Lake Cabins to explore the 143-acre lake.

Anglers tend to be happy here. Kevin VanBueren is the owner of North Cascades Fly Fishing (www.fishandfloat.com) and works out of the Lodge's activity shop. In the summer you can book a guided trip on the Methow, Twisp, or Chewuch Rivers to catch and release cutthroat and rainbow trout. Guided steelhead fishing on the Methow is also a possibility from fall through winter when this fishery is open. Flyfishing lessons are also available.

One special place to fish through the guide service is at the private Moccasin Lake Ranch. Only flyfishing is allowed at the 35-acre lake and only six rods are allowed on the water at a time. The fishing season runs four days a week between May to mid-June and again from mid-September through mid-October. This is true trophy catch-and-release trout angling. The average size rainbow or brown trout is anywhere from 1.5 to 3 pounds. Fish up to 7 pounds are common, and if you are lucky, you might hook into a monster that weighs over 12 pounds. Trips to Moccasin Lake can only be booked through Sun Mountain. If you want to go, reserve early because the waiting list to fish this lake is often a year long.

There is plenty of fishing to be had without a guide as well. The Methow River is full of fishy-looking pools and Patterson Lake has stocked rainbow trout, perch, and some good-sized bass for the taking. In recent years, an ice fishery has developed at the lake for perch up to 11 inches long.

Wildlife watching is another worthwhile pursuit. Deer are prolific, often grazing around the main lodge. Squirrels and chipmunks scamper across trails and coyotes can sometimes be heard at night. A variety of birds are found around the lodge complex including both bald and golden eagles, osprey, kingfisher, grouse, woodpeckers, and western tanager. If you have time, take a half-hour stroll around the beaver pond on the lodge property from the Chickadee Trailhead. You'll get a chance to see several if not all of these species as you wander around the marshy pond that is part of the Audubon Society's Great Washington State Birding Trail.

Finally, 1.5-hour and half-day horseback rides are available at Sun Mountain. From mid-May through mid-October, you can also take part in a Cowboy Camp Dinner or Buckaroo Breakfast. Take your horse, or ride in a horse-drawn wagon, to an old homestead for some good grub eatin' to the accompaniment of a crooning cowboy. If you want to bring your own horse, boarding facilities are available.

Sun Mountain Resort is open all year. If you are looking for a bargain, rates drop slightly from mid-October until June.

Getting There: From eastern Washington – Take State Highway 20 to Twisp. Continue 6 miles and turn left onto Twin Lakes Road. Drive 1.6 miles and turn left onto Patterson Lake Road. Drive 6.4 miles to the lodge. From western Washington: Take the North Cascades Highway (State Highway 20) to Winthrop. Drive through Winthrop approximately a mile and cross the Methow River. At the Y Intersection, turn right onto Twin Lakes Road. Drive 3.2 miles to Patterson Lake road. Turn right and drive 6.4 miles to the lodge.

The lodge sits on top of Sun Mountain, providing panoramic views of the Cascade Mountains and Methow Valley.

Lake Chelan

Lake Chelan State Park
7544 South Lakeshore Drive, Chelan, WA 98816 / 888-226-7688
www.parks.wa.gov

US Forest Service – Chelan Ranger District
428 W. Woodin Avenue, Chelan, WA 98816 / 509-682-2576
www.fs.fed.us/r6/wenatchee/about/chelan

Lodging Prices   Adventure Pricing

Sunny Lake Chelan is a getaway for legions of western Washington vacationers who enjoy swimming, boating, and buzzing about the lower portion of the lake on personal watercraft in warm weather months. The cool, clean waters of the lake also offer good fishing, paddling, and lots of camping, hiking, hunting, and wildlife viewing.

The huge glacially-carved lake is 50.5 miles long and 1.5 miles wide. The resort town of Chelan sits at the southeastern outlet of the lake. Resorts, condominiums, and expensive summer homes line the shoreline up to Manson and Wapato Point on the north shore of the lake, and all the way up to Twenty-Five Mile Creek on the south shore. Beyond here it is essentially roadless. Public land borders the shore of the narrow and deep (almost 1,500 feet deep in places) lake all the way to Stehekin, a small, remote community within the Lake Chelan National Recreation Area. The recreation area borders North Cascades National Park and some of their facilities are located in the small hamlet. You'll need a boat to explore this part of the lake. If you don't have one, you can charter a plane from Chelan to drop you off or take one of the Lake Chelan Boat Company's passenger ferries (509-682-4584 – www.ladyofthelake.com) from Chelan or Fields Point (on the south shore of the lake) to Lucerne and Stehekin.

If you want to go camping there are a number of places to choose from. The City of Chelan's Lakeshore RV Park has 165 full hook-up sites and is popular with both the RV and tenting crowd (509-682-8023 – www.cityofchelan.us/ parks). The campground is adjacent to a day-use park, several restaurants, and a marina.

On the south shore of the lake are two separate state parks. Lake Chelan State Park is 9 miles from Chelan and is open year round. The 127-acre park is laid out nicely and advance reservations are essential for overnight summer stays at this popular place. There is a boat ramp, two dock areas, and a large day-use area at the park along with grassy lawns for summer sports, lots of picnic tables, a kitchen shelter, a store, and a swimming area. Just outside the park entrance is a small restaurant operated as a park concession. Camping is available at 109 tent spaces and 35 utility spaces suitable for small RVs (less than 30 feet in length).

If Lake Chelan State Park is full, try driving 6 more miles along the south shore to Twenty-Five Mile Creek State Park. Situated along the banks of the creek it is named after, the park has a lakefront marina and is a good launching point to explore the upper lake by boat. There is a small day-use area, a park store, a swimming beach, and plenty of room for fishing off the marina. Twenty-Five Mile Creek State Park is closed from October 7 through March 31.

Between Twenty-Five Mile Creek and Stehekin are 12 boat-in campgrounds. Most are small with only a few tent sites, tables, fire rings, docks, and toilets. However, they do offer a remote setting for a wilderness getaway full of boating, fishing, and wildlife watching. Paddling a canoe or kayak from campground to campground is another adventurous vacation option. A boat permit, obtained from the forest service, is needed to use these facilities.

One boat-in site of note is found at Lucerne. Passenger ferry boats stop here to drop off people heading towards Holden, an abandoned mining camp turned Lutheran retreat center that is reached by bike or shuttle 11 miles away (509-687-3644 – www.holdenvillage.org). Holden is open to the public and, while many people are happy to hang around the retreat center, you can also use Holden as a jumping off point to hike into the Glacier Peak Wilderness. Other hikers skip the ride to Holden and instead hike 2.5 miles from Lucerne to Domke Lake. The 1.5-mile long lake has a rustic resort and two campgrounds if you decide to stay awhile. Trout fishing and wildlife watching are both popular at this unique hiking destination. If you decide to camp, take precautions against big four-legged visitors of the furry persuasion (bears).

At the far end of the lake is the remote community of Stehekin; a fantastic destination for the outdoor enthusiast. Lodging is available throughout the year and camping is possible after the snow melts. (Read the Stehekin and Stehekin Valley Ranch entries for details).

A lot of wildlife is visible along the shores of Lake Chelan. If you are lucky you may see black bear, bighorn sheep, mule deer, and mountain goats as you travel up or down the lake. Hunting for these bear, deer and, on a very limited basis, bighorn sheep is possible during designated seasons. The area around Mitchell Creek is one well-known bear hunting destination. Fishing for lake trout, chinook and kokanee salmon, and rainbow trout is popular in the lower end of the lake, while anglers in the upper end sometimes find cutthroat trout on the end of their lines.

Getting There: From Wenatchee, take US Highway 97 Alternate north 37 miles to the resort town of Chelan which sits at the southeastern end of the lake. You can reach Lucerne, Holden, and Stehekin from Chelan or from locations along the south shore of the lake by boat, passenger ferry or chartered float plane.

Bernie Miller and Jaqui Brown Miller of Olympia decide where to bike next on one of trail systems available around Lake Chelan.

DARRELL AND DAD'S GUIDE SERVICE

Anton Jones – 231 Division, Manson, WA 98831 / 866-360-1523 or 509-687-0709
www.darrellanddads.com

Lodging Price: $$ to $$$ Adventure Pricing: $$ to $$$

If you want to catch a big trout in north central Washington, give Darrell and Dad's Guide Service a call. Named after the owner's son, Anton Jones's guide service specializes in catching coldwater fish out of Lake Chelan and Rufus Woods Reservoir on the Upper Columbia River. Anton is a short man with a big heart and a bountiful amount of fishing knowledge. He is assisted by long-time guide Al Brooks and a couple of promising up-and-coming prospects.

Much of the fishing takes place in the lower half of 55-mile Lake Chelan, catching lake trout, kokanee, and the occasional landlocked chinook salmon. The lake trout, also known as mackinaw, can reach gigantic proportions. The state record fish, weighing 35.44 pounds, was caught here on New Year's Eve in 2001. While fish over 20 pounds are uncommon, limits of 3- to 6-pound lakers are routine if you know what you are doing. "Knowing what you are doing" is the catchphrase for many. The mackinaw fishery is a technical one. Anton and his guides generally troll lures at slow speeds and constantly adjust downriggers to keep the lure just off the bottom at depths of 120 to 240 feet or more. Good electronics, the right trolling speed, and knowing where the fish congregate are all essential ingredients to a successful outing. Day in and day out, Anton and his guides solve the riddle and put fish in the boat.

While lake trout and chinook salmon come out of the deep water, tasty kokanee salmon are caught trolling shallower depths in the summer. A half dozen of these pan-sized fish taste excellent off the barbeque. You can book either a full or half-day fishing trip on Lake Chelan.

While Lake Chelan is a year-round fishery, the waters of Rufus Woods between Bridgeport and the Nespelem net pens draw a lot of attention during the winter. Anglers are after big triploid rainbows that run anywhere from 3 to 20-plus pounds. These football-shaped trout can be caught using bait, casting lures, fishing flies, or trolling. Despite the emphasis on big winter rainbows, there is also good fishing to be had during the rest of the year for nice-sized kokanee salmon as well as walleye. Boats with enclosed cabins and propane heaters keep the chill off so you can enjoy the fishing.

Darrell and Dad's recently began offering half-day trips to Roses Lake near Manson. This 131-acre lake has good numbers of stocked rainbow trout and occasionally you'll see a brown trout come out of here as well. Largemouth bass, crappie, and channel catfish are also present. If you are looking for a low pressure fishing experience with lots of action, or want to get a child hooked on fishing, going out in a boat on this lake with one of Anton's guides is a good choice.

If you need a place to stay, the basement of Anton's home is a separate residence known as The Fisherman's Hideaway. This place is big enough for the whole family with three bedrooms, a kitchen, full bath, and a fireplace. Cable television and wireless Internet service are two great features. Several rooms have lake views and the small town of Manson is just down the hill. Combination lodging and fishing packages are available.

Finally, if you want to fish on your own at Roses Lake or Lake Chelan you can rent a 14-foot boat with an electric motor for the day. If you don't barbeque your catch right away, Darrell and Dad's will get it brined, smoked, and vacuum packaged for a reasonable price.

Getting There: Destinations vary.

Anton Jones and Michelle Kruse show off a nice Lake Chelan mackinaw trout.

Sun Lakes – Dry Falls State Park

34875 Park Lake Road NE, Coulee City, WA 99115 / 509-632-5583
www.parks.wa.gov

If you are looking for a well-rounded outdoors vacation experience, you can pretty much do it all at Sun Lakes – Dry Falls State Park. Located in a part of Washington State known for lots of warmth and very little rain, the 4,027-acre park offers activities to include boating, swimming, water sports, fishing, hiking, bicycling, golf, wildlife watching, and the chance to see a geological wonder.

The main feature of the park is Dry Falls, formed millions of years ago when lava flows engulfed the area. These flows hardened and were then sculpted in a dramatic fashion by catastrophic floods that flowed through here some 16,000 years ago during the last ice age. That's when a huge ice dam repeatedly formed and broke near present day Missoula, Montana. The huge lake behind the dam rushed through the breach and into eastern Washington at speeds of up to 65 miles per hour, forming deep coulees and the geologically unique portion of the state known as the Grand Coulee and the channeled scablands.

One place these glacial floods flowed through was Dry Falls. At the time, it was one of the largest waterfalls on the planet; ten times the size of today's Niagara Falls. Today, the falls are dry but still offer a breathtaking view with towering 400-foot basalt cliffs that stretch 3.5 miles. A small visitor's center sits at the top of the cliffs, offering great views and interpretive exhibits. It is open from mid-May through September and there is a small admission fee.

The lowlands below the falls compromise the state park and offer much for the outdoor lover. Within its boundaries are several lakes surrounded by sagebrush, grasslands, and basalt rock. The weather is generally sunny and warm – hence the name of the state park and the informal name for the lakes in this region.

There are ten lakes within the park (Park, Dry Falls, Deep, Perch, Vic Meyers, Castle, Mirror, Meadow, Green, and Red Alkali). Green and Red

Alkali Lakes do not have fish, but angling can be first rate at some of the other lakes. Park Lake as well as Perch and Vic Meyers all provide good trout angling in the spring and less visited Deep Lake also has kokanee salmon. These lakes all open for fishing the last weekend of April and close at the end of September.

Dry Falls Lake is your best bet for consistent trout fishing. Specially managed to ensure a quality angling experience, this is a favorite for float tubers and fly anglers. Shore access is limited due to cattails that grow along much of the shoreline. Once on the water though you can expect to catch rainbow, brown, and tiger trout, most of which will be between 12 and 16 inches long. This is a selective-gear fishery (no bait, no outboard motors, single barbless hooks only and a one-fish limit) that is open from April 1 through November 30.

Bicyclists will enjoy the closed road along the east end of Park Lake that has become a 5-mile "there-and-back" bike path. They can also share a paved and gravel road inside the park with automobile traffic and cycle to Deep Lake (2.5 miles from the campground) or Dry Falls Lake (about 3 miles). Hikers can explore a variety of trails within the park that cover 15 miles or just wander cross country and explore this land of sagebrush, lakes, and tall basalt walls and cliffs.

If you bring a motorized boat or personal watercraft, you can launch at the north end of Park Lake. Moorage is available at the Sun Lakes Resort near the launch. Smaller craft like rowboats, canoes, kayaks, or pontoon boats can be launched at Deep, Dry Falls, Park, Vic Meyers, or Perch Lake.

There is quite a bit of wildlife to be seen within the park. Upland game birds such as chukar, quail, and pheasant are found along with migratory waterfowl and mourning dove. Hawks, osprey, and owls as well as the occasional eagle are also present. Deer, coyote, marmot, rabbit, raccoon, and the rare bobcat round out the list of mammals you may see here.

The main camping area is located on the north end of Park Lake. There are 152 campsites and 39 utility sites for RVs. There is also a grassy, treed day-use area with lots of picnic tables. Groups can make arrangements to stay at Camp Delaney, an environmental learning center within the park that has a conference center, dining facility, and guest cabins that can accommodate 76 people.

A unique amenity at the park is the nine-hole Vic Meyers Golf Course and Sun Lakes Resort, which offer additional RV sites and guest cabins for individual or family use. A store, snack bar, mini-golf course, and water fun round out the amenities offered through the resort (see the Sun Lakes Resort entry for additional information).

Sun Lakes State Park is open all year. Late spring and summer tend to be crowded at the park and reservations are recommended.

SUN LAKES PARK RESORT

34228 Park Lake Rd. NE, Coulee City, WA 99115 / 509-632-5291
www.sunlakesparkresort.com

Lodging Prices: $ to $$$ Adventure Pricing: $

The Sun Lakes Park Resort is a unique spring and summer outdoor destination operated as a concession for the 4,000-acre Sun Lakes–Dry Falls State Park. Within the park are several good lakes for trout fishing, kayaking, canoeing or rowing, desert hiking, wildlife watching, and bicycling. The centerpiece of the park is the Dry Falls Interpretive Center where you can view the skeleton of massive ice age waterfall (for more information, check out the Dry Falls-Sun Lakes State Park entry).

Back at the resort are 129 sites with full hook-ups for camping. Those wanting a roof and four walls can choose from 59 cabins. They range from rustic lakeview cabins to 60s-style poolside duplexes, two-bedroom singlewide mobile homes installed in the mid-80s, or the brand new duplex cabins on the lake. You won't find any televisions or phones in these cabins, but with so much to do outside, it's really not an issue. There is also a gift shop and a grocery store to buy essentials and fishing supplies.

The resort and state park share a marina and boat launch that juts out into the north end of Park Lake. It's a popular place for the pleasure boat crowd that comes and goes on jet skis and power boats in the summer months. Row boats, paddle boats, and canoes are available for rent from the resort for those wanting to paddle, row, or fish awhile. A swimming area with a beach and outdoor pool are both crowded on hot summer days.

The resort also has other diversions like a newly remodeled putt-putt golf course, a water wars game where you can shoot water balloons at each other for summer fun, and a snack shop where ice cream in the evening is particularly popular. In case that's not enough, the resort also manages the nine-hole Vic Meyer's Golf Course. Located just above the resort in the state park, the course has a shop offering cart and club rentals.

Outside of the park boundaries are several lakes to the south that are part of the Sun Lakes Wildlife Area (Blue, Alkali, and Lenore). All of them offer fishing, and Lake Lenore is known for its big Lahontan cutthroat trout. A side trip to the Lake Lenore Caves is an interesting option, as is the chance to canoe or kayak these sun-drenched lakes. In the fall, you can chase after chukar around here, a bird with a special affinity for running uphill before flying away.

A short drive north towards Coulee City brings you to Banks Lake. This 27-mile-long impoundment offers very good fishing, hiking, rock climbing, horseback riding, and good wildlife viewing (see the Banks Lake entry for details).

Sun Lakes Park Resort rents RV spaces and cabins from March 30 through October 15. The resort is fully operational (with all of the above amenities) from Memorial Day weekend through Labor Day.

Getting There: The resort is located within the boundaries of Sun Lakes–Dry Falls State Park off of State Highway 17 between Soap Lake and Coulee City.

Trout fishing below the Dry Falls Intepretive Center can reap rewards.

A yellow-headed blackbird clings tightly in the gusty winds.

Lake Lenore
(COLUMBIA BASIN WILDLIFE AREA–SUN LAKES UNIT)

Washington Department of Fish and Wildlife
1550 Alder Street NW, Ephrata, WA 98823 / 509-754-4624
www.wdfw.wa.gov/lands/r2sunlks.htm

Well known by trout anglers, Lake Lenore is also a great destination for paddlers, bird watchers, upland bird hunters, and those interested in natural history. The narrow 4.5-mile-long lake sits next to State Highway 17 north of the small town of Soap Lake.

Surrounded by sagebrush, hills, and basalt cliffs, the 9,140-acre Sun Lakes Unit of the Columbia Basin Wildlife Area is a popular place in the spring. The centerpiece of the unit is Lake Lenore. Late March brings crowds of fly anglers to the north and south ends of the lake to catch and release the big Lahontan cutthroat trout that congregate in these areas. These fish average 2.5 pounds and can reach up to 7 pounds in weight. Black chironomid patterns under strike indicators are a favorite offering for anglers who fish from shore, float tubes, and pontoon boats in the hopes of hooking a dozen or more of these leviathans in a day of fishing.

The lake is also a good place for kayaking and canoeing. There are rough launches at three locations along the east side of the lake off of the highway and an additional access site (with no launch) at the north end of the shallow lake. You can either paddle from the north end of the lake to the southernmost take out or from one end to the other and back for a 9-mile round trip. The skies tend towards blue and along the way you'll probably see several types of diving ducks and Canada geese on the water. Chattering chukar are often heard from the cliffs above the lake, and occasionally you'll spy a mule deer along shore or on one of the islands that rise out of the water. The best time to be in a boat (where no outboard motors are allowed) is in the morning. Winds often kick up to make the water choppy as the day progresses.

Fishing tapers off in the heat of the summer but kicks into high gear again in September as the trout fatten up for the winter. Both nymph flies and spoons with single barbless hooks work well for catching fish from boats or

from shore. You are allowed to keep one fish per day from June 1 until angling closes at the end of November. The lake opens again for catch-and-release fishing on the first of March, though the lake is sometimes still frozen on this date.

Chukar hunting is another fall activity worth mentioning. Chukars are imported birds that love to run uphill and fly downhill, just the ticket for an extreme exercise program. They are found in the hills surrounding the lake, along with the occasional California (valley) quail and gray (Hungarian) partridge.

If you enjoy watching wildlife, you're in luck. Waterfowl species include ringnecks, goldeneyes, ruddy ducks, redheads, canvasback, and mallards. Besides deer you may see mammals like coyote, jackrabbit, and marmot in the area. You can also see the Lahontan cutthroat up close at times without a hook and line. In April and May, thousands of the trout cram into a small stream along the east shore of Lake Lenore. A small hatchery enclosure near a parking lot off the highway has been built to accommodate them. Biologists come there to take eggs and sperm from a number of these fish to replenish not only the fish in this lake, but also to stock Lahontan cutthroat lakes throughout the northwestern United States. As you might imagine, fishing is not allowed in this stream.

If you enjoy hiking and a little bit of history you may want to check out the Lake Lenore Caves east of Highway 17. Accessible from a gravel road near the north end of Lake Lenore, the shallow depressions are actually more rock shelters than caves. Petroglyphs are visible in some of the shelters, used for thousands of years by Native Americans as places to store food or get out of the weather. Getting to them is easy enough along a maintained trail that runs some 1.5 miles. Snakes, to include rattlesnakes, can be an issue at times, but by keeping your eyes open you should have few problems. If you go in the spring you'll get a chance to enjoy the blooming landscape that turns the hills and coulee floor green with grasses and sagebrush. Wildflowers like desert shooting stars and different varieties of parsley are also common.

The best times to visit Lake Lenore are from March through May and again from September through October. Summer and winter temperatures tend to be extreme in this country.

Getting There: Drive north on State Highway 17 from Soap Lake for 9 miles to reach the north end of the lake and the turn off to the Lake Lenore Caves. You can also get there by traveling south on Highway 17 from US Highway 2 just west of Coulee City.

Banks Lake and Steamboat Rock State Park

Steamboat Rock State Park
P.O. Box 370, Electric City, WA 99123 / 509-633-1304
www.parks.wa.gov

Lodging Prices

Dammed (in the physical sense) on both ends, Banks Lake is a 27-mile-long reservoir with a plethora of activities for the outdoor enthusiast. Camping is possible at a large state park, a nice city park, and at several private resorts. Fishing, pleasure boating, and bird hunting are all popular. There is also hiking, bicycling, horseback riding, bird watching, and even some rock climbing available. Add to the equation that you can do this in an area known for sunny skies and little rain and you've got a great outdoor getaway.

Access to the lake is easy since public land surrounds much of the 91 miles of shoreline. The small town of Coulee City sits on the southern edge of Banks Lake, next to US Highway 2 and the Dry Falls Dam. The city maintains a nice park with 55 RV or campsites, restrooms, a boat launch, and marina. There are several obvious access points on the east side of the lake as you drive north along State Highway 155, but you won't find too many amenities until you get close to Electric City. Across the lake from there you can access the northwest part of the lake from Barker Canyon Road. Back on the east side of the lake you'll find two private resorts close to Electric City.

South of Electric City is Steamboat Rock State Park. The big 3,500-acre park's most prominent feature is Steamboat Rock, an 800-foot basalt butte that, to some, looks like an old sternwheeler. In addition to biking, hiking, and horseback trails within park-managed property, there are 100 utility sites with full hookups for RVs and an additional 26 tent sites available in an expansive lawn area protected from the wind by big poplar trees. Restrooms with showers are available in the main camping area. Additional primitive camp sites can be found at Osborn and Jones Bay (no water available) along

with 12 boat-in/hike-in campsites. A day-use area in the park offers a playground, swimming beach, picnic tables, and a boat launch.

Hiking and wildlife watching are two popular activities at the park, which is located on a peninsula with 50,000 feet of waterfront. Many hikers climb to the top of Steamboat Rock. Trails lead from the main camping areas and day-use portion of the park. In the spring you'll be rewarded with the sight of yellow balsamroot and buttercup on this 2-mile round trip hike that gains 650 feet in elevation before you reach the top of the butte. When you reach the high point, you can explore another 600 acres of land with panoramic views in every direction.

Steamboat Rock at Banks Lake provides a beautiful backdrop for a day of fishing.

In addition to hiking and bicycling within the main park, you can also strike out on foot, on a bike, or in the saddle into nearby Northrup Canyon, a natural area managed by the state park. There is an equestrian area near the entrance of the canyon that offers basic facilities for horseback riders along with primitive camping, though no fires are permitted. A 6-mile trek through the pine and aspen will get you to Northrup Lake and back. Touted as Grant County's only "alpine lake", little Northrup Lake sits at an elevation of 2,137 feet and offers good fishing for 12- to 18-inch rainbow trout. A shorter 1.5-mile hike or ride will take you along an old wagon road, aptly named the Wagon Road Trail that follows the south side of the canyon.

If you enjoy soaring raptors, the state park and Northrup Canyon are good places to visit. Bald and golden eagles, red-tailed, rough-legged, sharp-shinned, marsh, and Cooper's hawks share the skies with prairie, peregrine, and Merlin falcon. American kestrel (sparrow hawks), great horned and long eared owls round out the birds of prey you may see. Fall and winter are the best times for raptor viewing.

One unique geological feature found in this basalt rock landscape is the existence of several granite rock formations, especially towards the north end of Banks Lake. This granite draws rock climbers who are often seen making their way up cliffs along the east side of the lake or next to the equestrian area at Northrup Canyon.

Hunting is another option. Upland bird gunners walk the state-owned grasslands near Steamboat Rock State Park for pheasant and hunt the hills and draws that surround the reservoir for quail, Hungarian (gray) partridge, and the occasional chukar. Goose hunting takes place in the wheat fields around the reservoir, and duck hunting is possible on the lake itself.

Finally, Banks Lake has earned a reputation as one of the best fishing destinations in the state. The Washington state record for largemouth bass was caught here in 1977. While healthy largemouth are still found in the big reservoir, smallmouth bass are the predominant species now. Walleye are also abundant and, in the winter, perch can be caught in good numbers whether or not the water freezes up. An often overlooked trout fishery can get you into respectable 2-pound-or-better rainbows from late fall into early spring.

There are a few minor nuisances to deal with around Banks Lake. Ticks can be a problem for pets in the spring and mosquitoes can be a pest at times in the summer. If you are hiking you may want to watch your step since rattlesnakes are found in this country. However, the pros of a Banks Lake visit far outweigh the cons.

Steamboat Rock State Park is open all year. You can reserve a camping spot through the Washington State Parks website (recommended in the summer) or just drop in. The Wagon Road Trail is closed from late fall through the winter to minimize disturbances to the bald eagles that nest in this portion of Northrup Canyon.

Getting There: Take US Highway 2 to Coulee City. Travel north on State Highway 155 along the east side of Banks Lake. Steamboat Rock State Park is located towards the north end of the lake, 12 miles south of Electric City.

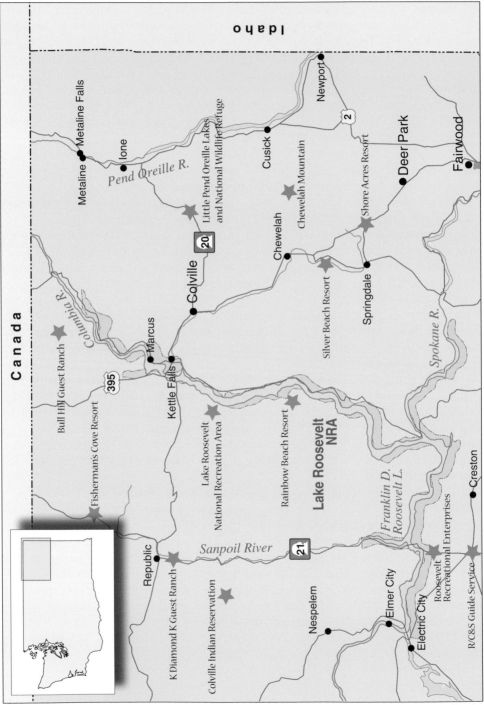

© 2009 Wilderness Adventures Press, Inc.

Colville Country

Republic Area Recreation

Curlew State Park
62 State Park Road, Republic, WA 99166 / 509-775-3592
www.parks.wa.gov

Colville National Forest
765 South Main Street, Colville, WA 99114 / 509-684-7000
www.fs.fed.us/r6/colville/

Rural Ferry County has a lot to offer to the outdoor recreationist. Water-based fun, alpine trail excursions, gold panning, and even fossil discoveries are all possible in this sparsely populated part of the state.

Curlew Lake is the most popular vacation destination in the county. You'll find the 870-acre lake 8 miles north of Republic off of State Highway 21. There are three privately-owned resorts around the lake offering cabins along with sites for RVs and tent campers. Curlew State Park is another good place for a camping vacation. The 123-acre park is open from late March until the end of October. There are 25 utility sites for RV enthusiasts and 57 tent spaces in two camping areas near the lake. It's a pleasant place and if you own a small plane, you can land it on the small airstrip adjacent to the park for a different sort of camping experience. Restrooms with showers and a day-use area that offers boat ramps, picnic tables, and swimming round out the amenities.

The 5.5 mile-long lake is perfect for paddling, and stops at the different resorts and park give you a good excuse to stretch your legs. Anglers catch rainbow trout that commonly measure between 14 and 22 inches, largemouth bass to 4 pounds and tiger muskie. The muskie were introduced in 1998 and the minimum size limit for these toothy fish is 36 inches. They are not as easy to catch as the bass or trout, but some informed sources believe the next state record muskie will come out of Curlew Lake.

If you are interested in mountain biking, horseback riding, backcountry skiing or hiking, the Kettle Crest National Recreation Trail and its various feeder trails are worth exploring. The best place to access the 43- mile trail is off US Highway 20 at Sherman Pass some 25 miles east of Republic. You can

hike, bike, or ride north for 30 miles. You can do the same activities heading south from the pass past the Barnaby Buttes and White Mountain before reaching the White Mountain Trailhead at the 13.5-mile mark where a road leads back to the highway.

Other recreational opportunities can be found south of Republic. The San Poil River follows State Highway 21 from Republic until it empties into Lake Roosevelt. The small river supports populations of rainbow and brook trout as well as whitefish (a Colville Tribal fishing permit is required to cast a line into the stream from tribal lands). The Ten-Mile Campground is next to the highway some 10 miles south of Republic. You'll find nine campsites there if you want to pitch your tent next to the river.

Just north of the campground, Scatter Creek Road (Forest Service Road 53) takes you to three Forest Service campgrounds; each located next to an alpine lake. The most popular is Swan Lake, a 7-mile drive from the highway. The 52-acre lake sits at 3,641 feet and is stocked with rainbow trout. Twenty-five campsites are popular with both tent and trailer campers. There is a boat ramp, swim area, and fresh water at the campground. A 1.5-mile trail loops around the lake and a short side trip will take you to the top of Swan Butte for nice views of the lake and surrounding countryside.

Nearby Ferry Lake is smaller, at 19 acres, and is also stocked with rainbows. If you want to get away from the crowds, the nine tent sites here are seldom full. Finally, Long Lake is another place worth visiting. This is a flyfishing-only lake where you can catch cutthroat trout up to 17 inches long. Camp at one of the 12 tent/trailer sites available here, all of which have access to the lake. There is also a short 0.4-mile trail that takes off from the campground if you are looking for a short walk after dinner. Chipmunks and deer are common and the throaty sound of loons can sometimes be heard echoing from the lakes. Bear-proof garbage containers help to keep these big animals away from the campgrounds.

Fall hunting is popular throughout this region for white-tailed and mule deer as well as turkey and black bear. Turkey hunting is also possible in the spring and in September scatter gunners walk the woods for grouse.

Looking for something else? Try panning for gold! Republic started out as a mining town and there is still gold to be found in area creeks. Lambert or Trout Creek as well as the San Poil River are all worth a try. Who knows, you may strike it rich enough to pay for your vacation!

Finally, the frontier-themed town of Republic is also worth a visit. The Stonerose Fossil Site sits at the northern edge of the small town. A shale hillside holds impressions of fish, insects, and plants that lived here some 50 million of years ago in what was then an ancient lake. Today, you can visit the Stonerose Interpretive Center a couple blocks away to learn more and register for your own fossil dig. After paying a small fee for a permit and for rental tools, the staff will show you how to dig for your very own bit of pre-history to take home with you.

Getting There: You can reach Republic by traveling east from US Highway 97 at Tonasket for 40 miles along State Highway 20, traveling north on State Highway 21 for 67 miles from US Highway 2 at Wilbur, or traveling west on State Highway 20 for 43 miles from US Highway 395 at Kettle Falls.

FISHERMAN'S COVE RESORT

15 Fisherman's Cove Road, Republic, WA 99166 / 888-567-2955
http://fishermanscove.us

Lodging Prices: $ to $$$ Adventure Pricing: $ to $$

People come to Curlew Lake for fishing, hunting, and all sorts of other outdoor fun. This place north of Republic is so popular that three different resorts and a state park all operate along the 5.5-mile lake. While all of them offer a quality vacation experience, Fisherman's Cove Resort gets the nod as the best of the bunch.

You'll notice the quiet and welcoming atmosphere soon after arriving at the 31-acre resort. Owners Jack and Sandy Beck have been running Fisherman's Cove for over 15 years and their sociable nature contributes to the resort's ambience. Jack is a smiling handyman who is always working on projects while Sandy is the sort of person who will cook up your breakfast and ask to join you for a visit once she cooks her own meal.

The resort has nine RV sites as well as 16 recently renovated waterfront cabins that sleep anywhere from two to eight guests. One of them – the Couples Cabin – is a new hand-built log dwelling that is gorgeous inside and out. As you can tell from the name, the well-furnished cabin is primarily meant for adults. All of the cabins have bathrooms, kitchens, modern appliances, electric heat, and linens (though you do need to bring your own towels). The Couples Cabin also has cable television.

If you get hungry, the Snack Shack is a small, outside diner that is the only restaurant on the lake. Sandy Beck serves up hot breakfasts, espresso, lattes, and burgers for lunch. Every other week you can come and enjoy "Friday Night Fine Dining". It's a popular event for resort guests and locals who come to feast on Thai food, steak, and shrimp or salmon and crab combos for less than $25.

A small store stocks fishing tackle, gifts, soda, snacks, and limited groceries. A deck outside has tables where you can take advantage of the free WI-FI and keep up on your e-mails. Flowering plants from Sandy's greenhouse line the deck and entice colorful hummingbirds to visit feeders put out for them. It all makes for a relaxing place to sip a latte or soda pop, whether or not you have a laptop computer.

Water sports are popular in the summer and you can rent a personal watercraft from the resort if you want to join the fun. You can also rent row boats, paddle boats, and 12-foot fishing boats with outboard motors. If you have a kayak or canoe you can launch it from the resort and paddle around the lake. In addition to soaking up some sunshine, you'll probably get the opportunity to get close to swimming muskrats or turtles sunning themselves on logs.

Four docks give you room to moor a boat and a place to fish. You can also remain on shore by the swim area or in the gazebo at the edge of a beach kept in great shape for sunbathers and swimmers, thanks to fresh sand that is trucked in every year.

While many come to play on (or in) the water, hunting and fishing are also popular activities. Rainbow trout, largemouth bass, and big, ferocious-looking tiger muskie can all be caught out of Curlew Lake. Hunters target grouse, turkey, and bear in the early fall, and in mid-October gun sights shift towards white-tailed and mule deer. A refrigerated meat locker is available to keep game cool and makes the resort a good base camp for those who want to hunt in the morning and fish in the afternoon. The resort is also a good place to stay if you want to bike, hike, or ride horses on nearby trails. Fisherman's Cove is open for full operations from mid-April until late October. During the off season you can rent a cabin (two-night minimum) and explore the area on snow shoes or cross-country skis.

Getting There: From Republic follow State Highway 21 north for 8 miles until you reach Curlew Lake. Take a left off the highway and follow the signs to the resort.

The clean, comfortable cabins at Fisherman's Cove are just steps away from Curlew Lake.

K DIAMOND K GUEST RANCH

15661 Highway 21 South, Republic, WA 99166 / 888-345-5355
www.kdiamondk.com

Lodging Prices: $$$ Adventure Pricing: Included with lodging

Putting a dude ranch close to a former mining town with an "old west" motif is a good idea if you want to get your guests into the spirit of things. The 1,600-acre K Diamond K Guest Ranch is only 3 miles south of Republic, the seat of rural Ferry County. Established in 1961 by June and Steve Konz, the scenic property is a mixture of pasture, pine trees, hills, and valleys. The small, pretty San Poil River flows for a mile through the ranch.

There is a lot of wildlife here. Deer seem to be everywhere, turkeys are frequent visitors, coyote can be heard singing at night, and during the day you'll enjoy the melody of meadowlarks and bluebirds. In fact, a wide variety of bird species are found at the ranch and it is becoming a popular destination for birdwatchers.

Most people come in the summer for three- to five-night stays, though there is no minimum night requirement and the ranch is open all year. For about $150 a night you get an all-inclusive stay that includes lodging, three meals a day, and activities. Children between 3 and 5 can stay for about half that price. The vast majority of guests come for the horseback riding. Because of that, most mornings start out after breakfast with a guided trail ride on one of the 30 horses the ranch has on hand. During the afternoon you can ride some more, explore the old 100-foot-long mine that is on the ranch property, float the little San Poil River through the ranch on an inner tube, or go for a swim in nearby Swan Lake. If you want to pitch in and help out with the day-to-day activities that take place on a working ranch, you are welcome to do so. After dinner you can hitch a ride on the hay trailer, sitting on a bale as the tractor takes hay around the ranch. As sunset turns to dusk the fire pit becomes a popular place to enjoy a campfire and sing-a-long with one of the guitar-strumming ranch hosts. After that you can sit and enjoy an unspoiled night sky or retire to your bed in the brand new 16-room log lodge. Featuring a kitchen, dining area, and two wings of rooms covering two stories, the building was built with timber logs from the ranch itself. Thoroughly modern and decorated with nice touches like saddles over log beams and wagon wheel chandeliers, you'll enjoy your time here.

This should be enough for most families on vacation, but you can do a few more things at the K Diamond K. The San Poil River actually has some pretty good trout fishing, so walking and wading for trout with spinners and flies is worthwhile for rainbow trout that average 9 inches, but can get up to 19 inches long. Hikers (and in the winter, snowshoeing enthusiasts) can wander the open fields of the ranch cross country or take trails leading to overlooks like the top of Camelback Ridge. If you don't have your own snowshoes, you can borrow some at the ranch.

Getting There: Drive 3 miles south of Republic on State Highway 21 to reach the ranch.

The picturesque San Poil River runs through the K Diamond K Ranch near Republic.

Colville Indian Reservation

Colville Tribal Enterprise Corporation
Box 5, Birch Street, Suite A, Coulee Dam, WA 99116 / 509-634-3200
www.colvilletribes.com/fishing.htm

Lodging Prices

Adventure Pricing

The recreational possibilities on the 1.4 million acre Colville Indian Reservation remain largely undiscovered. Bordered in the south and east by the Columbia River and to the west by US Highway 97, this large swath of land has the characteristics of both high desert and mid-elevation forest. There are several lakes on the reservation. These, along with the Columbia River, provide good angling, uncrowded paddling, and the chance to see wildlife in a region that remains largely undeveloped.

In recent years anglers have been coming to the southwestern part of the reservation to catch fat triploid rainbow trout near the net pens at Rufus Woods Reservoir. The pens are used to raise trout sold commercially. You obviously can't fish in the pens, but you can catch the escaped refugees close by, along with the occasional kokanee and walleye. At the height of the chilly winter season, dozens of anglers will bundle up and cast spinners or bait from shore while boaters troll for trout that average 3 to 4 pounds and go much larger. In fact, the state record rainbow, weighing 29.6 pounds, was caught from Rufus Woods Reservoir in 2002. Trout are found not only by the net pens southwest of Nespelem but also above Chief Joseph Dam by Bridgeport State Park. Boat launches are available on the 51-mile reservoir near both locations. If you choose to fish with bait, remember the daily limit will be the first two trout you catch.

Omak Lake is another excellent fishing destination. Located 9 miles southeast of Omak, this lake is primarily known for its large Lahontan cutthroat trout. The state record for this species, weighing in at 18.6 pounds, was caught here in 1993. Casting spinners and spoons from shore, fishing

flies from float tubes, or trolling lures from small boats are all good ways to catch trout in this lake that is 300 feet deep in places. A boat launch at the north end of the lake provides a place to get on the water for anglers as well as paddlers interested in exploring the inlets and beaches of this 12-mile long, 3,200-acre lake.

The Twin Lakes west of Inchelium are a great place to go if you are a bird watcher, since they are one of the few places in Washington where loons nest every year. There are two resorts (one on each forest-lined lake) that provide boat rentals, food, cabins, RV sites, and places to camp. Respectable largemouth bass, along with rainbow and brook trout, are caught in both of these lakes that cover over 1,700-acres (see the Rainbow Beach Resort entry for further details).

Finally, Buffalo Lake is a place to go that is far from the masses. You get there by taking Buffalo Lake Road southeast from the Colville Indian Agency south of Nespelem. Once there you'll find a 542-acre lake at 2,000 feet that is fun to explore in a canoe or row boat. Anglers enjoy fishing for rainbow trout, kokanee salmon, and largemouth bass. Crawdads, known in some circles as a poor-man's lobster, offer an additional treat if you can trap a few and boil them up. There is a resort with tent and RV spaces along with several rustic cabins. You can also rent a boat (with or without a motor) from there as well.

Tribal permits are required to fish on the Colville Indian Reservation. They can be purchased for a modest price at several stores near the reservation or at resorts on the reservation.

Getting There: See above.

Eighty-five year old Robert Hamman of Spokane caught these big rainbow trout at the Rainbow Beach Resort.

RAINBOW BEACH RESORT

18 N. Twin Lakes Road, Inchelium, WA 99138 / 509-722-5901 or 888-862-0978
www.ctecorp.org/recreation

Lodging Prices : $ to $$$ Adventure Pricing: $

If you are looking for a Canadian fishing resort experience south of the border, visit the Rainbow Beach Resort at North Twin Lake. The resort sits on the eastern end of a forest-lined lake connected by a small channel to South Twin Lake. Being on the Colville Tribal Reservation, both lakes remain largely undeveloped. The resort is in many ways undiscovered, though there is a dedicated base of vacationers who return here every year to enjoy good fishing on a quiet lake with unspoiled scenery.

Accommodations come in the form of seven tent sites, nine RV sites, and 25 cabins. The cabins range from primitive (dry cabins with two double beds, electricity, and refrigerators) to deluxe (two bedrooms with queen beds, a sofa sleeper, electric heat, fireplace, limited cable television, full kitchen, and full bath. None of them cost more than $100 a night. If you want to vacation in style reserve the Grand Cabin for a few dollars more. This rental is a newer two-story home with two queen beds in the loft, a master bedroom downstairs, a large living room with fireplace, and lots of other amenities. With a large deck outside and big bay windows that look towards the lake, this cabin is great for families.

There is a store that has groceries, fishing tackle, and gas (for the cars) as well as propane (for the RVs). A grill inside the store building serves breakfast, lunch, and espresso. Enjoy your food at a small table inside or outside at the lake. DVD rentals are also available in case of a rainy day. Coin-operated laundry machines come in handy if you are low on clean clothes, and a washroom with showers is on site for the tent campers, primitive cabin tenants, and day visitors.

Fortunately, few days are rainy in this part of eastern Washington. This gives you plenty of time to relax outside with a game of horseshoes or volleyball, go splash around at the swimming beach, fish off the dock, or rent a row boat, kayak, or paddleboat to explore the two Twin Lakes. As you paddle along look for wildlife such as deer, bear, elk, or moose along the shoreline. Eagles and osprey soar above the lake, beaver swim in it, and at the far end of South Twin Lake is a protected area where you may be able to spy nesting loons, a rarity in Washington State.

Paddling, water skiing, and power-boat play are popular in the summer, but so are land-based activities like bicycling. Several miles of trails near the lakes and nearby Moon Mountain are used by mountain bikers. If you didn't bring your own bicycle, you can rent one at the store. Staff members will be happy to provide you with a map of the local bike routes.

Even though there is plenty to do here, resort manager Cathy Desautel says the primary reasons people come to the Twin Lakes are to fish and relax. The lake opens for fishing on the second weekend of April. Eastern brook trout often reach 12 inches and rainbow trout commonly weigh a pound. Largemouth bass are also found here. Two-pound bass are said to be the norm, and they reportedly go as big as 8 pounds. Like most lakes, the fishing is best in the spring and again in the fall for trout, though bass fishing holds steady through the summer, especially in the morning and evening. Fourteen-foot aluminum barges with 9.9-horsepower motors can be rented at the resort or you can bring your own boat and launch it here. A tribal permit is required to fish on these lakes and can be purchased at the store.

Fishing season closes on October 31, but a special ice fishing season takes place at the Twin Lakes from New Years Day until March 15 for those willing to brave the elements. If you don't want to sit out on the ice, you can also come to the resort for the cross-country skiing. Plans are in the works to develop several winter trails around the lakes. The store and resort are open all year.

Getting There: Take US Highway 2 to Wilbur. Travel north on State Highway 21, using the ferry to cross the Columbia River, and turn east at Bridge Creek Road. Drive 22 miles to North Twin Lake and follow the signs to the resort.

Waterfront cabins and boats for rent: Two ingredients for a good time at the Rainbow Beach Resort.

Little Pend Oreille Lakes and National Wildlife Refuge

Colville Ranger District
755 S. Main, Colville, WA 99114 / 509-684-7000
www.fs.fed.us/r6/colville/recreation/

Little Pend Oreille National Wildlife Refuge
1310 Bear Creek Road, Colville, WA 99114 / 509-684-8384
www.fws.gov/littlependoreille/index.htm

Lodging Prices

Adventure Pricing

A chain of higher-elevation wooded lakes located between Colville and the Pend Oreille River offer a plethora of outdoor activities. These lakes are fun places to fish, paddle, and see a variety of wildlife. A forest service multi-use trail system in this same region offers miles of opportunities for everyone from hikers to equestrians, ORV enthusiasts, snowmobilers, and cross-country skiers. Several campgrounds and a private resort give you the option of staying awhile to enjoy yourself.

The Little Pend Oreille Lakes are 26 miles east of Colville off of State Highway 20. Feeding the Little Pend Oreille River, the four lakes are named Sherry, Gillette, Thomas, and Heritage. Sherry Lake is the smallest of the four. Surrounded by summer homes, the 26-acre lake has both rainbow and tiger trout in it. Anglers can maneuver small craft into the lake from nearby Gillette Lake.

Gillette Lake is the most heavily-used lake, primarily because there is a Forest Service campground on one side and a resort on the other side off State Highway 20 with several rustic cabins, RV and tent sites, a restaurant, store, and several small boats for rent. The same trout found in Sherry Lake are also found here. One activity worth a go on this 48-acre lake is to paddle a canoe or kayak from here through the narrow gap that widens into adjacent Thomas Lake.

At an elevation of 3,147 feet and 163 acres in size, Thomas Lake is the largest of the four waters that make up the Little Pend Oreille Lakes chain. With far less development than the other two lakes, it is possible to see a variety of wildlife on shore to include deer and the occasional bear or moose. Red-necked grebe and waterfowl paddle through the water near human paddlers and anglers fishing for tiger and rainbow trout. There is a Forest Service campground on the east side of the lake while the northeastern end peters out into a marshy channel connecting to shallow Heritage Lake. This narrow, mile-long lake has not only trout, but bass, perch, and panfish as well.

If you drive further east on Highway 20 from Gillette Lake you'll soon run into Lake Leo. Completely on Colville National Forest property, there are no houses here, just a campground and a place to launch small boats onto a pretty 39-acre lake that is a nice place to cast for trout, row a boat, or paddle a canoe. A short distance down the highway from Lake Leo is Frater Lake. This easily accessible lake has cutthroat trout in it. Like the other lakes mentioned here, it is open for fishing from the last weekend of April through October.

There are a number of multi-use trails in this area to explore. A trail that starts at the parking lot next to Frater Lake is a popular one in the winter for cross-country skiers, many of whom ski to a warming hut a short mile from the lot. Ten miles of trail near Frater Lake and Lake Leo are groomed on a regular basis for skiers in the winter. In the summer, these same trails are used by hikers, mountain bikers, and horseback riders.

This trail system is actually part of the Little Pend Oreille ORV (off-road vehicle) Trail. Covering 67.5 miles, it offers views of the Pend Oreille Lakes and will take you to vistas like Green and Thomas Mountains as well as Granite Peak. The trail can be accessed at Frater Lake, Mill Creek (a quarter mile down County Road 4954 near Gillette lake), and from Clark Creek some 20 miles east of Colville (turn on to Forest Service Road 2389 from State Highway 20).

Closer to Colville, the Little Pend Oreille National Wildlife Refuge encompasses 41,573 acres. Fifty-eight different mammals and over 200 species of birds can be seen in a varied terrain that includes everything from wooded swamps, lakes, and a small river all the way to the top of 5,600-foot Olson Peak. White-tailed deer range here in the winter and turkeys are common in the spring. Other species include black bear, coyote, bobcat, elk, beaver, and the rare Canadian lynx. Two lakes (Bayley and McDowell) are open to catch-and-release flyfishing. The Little Pend Oreille River flows through a portion of the refuge and also provides trout fishing. Six primitive campgrounds provide a place to pitch a tent and are open from mid-April through December. If you want more information, stop by the refuge office that is open weekdays from 7:30am to 4:00pm.

Getting There: Take State Highway 20 east from Colville. The Little Pend Oreille Lakes NWR is 13 miles southeast of town. Continue another 13 miles to Gillette Lake.

You'll find plenty of pan-sized trout in these waters.

Chewelah Mountain and Area Lakes

Washington Department of Fish and Wildlife, Region 1
2315 N. Discovery Place, Spokane Valley, WA 99216 / 509-892-100
www.wdfw.wa.gov/reg/region1.htm

49 Degrees North
3311 Flowery Trail Road, Chewelah, WA 99109 / 509-935-6649
www.ski49n.com

Lodging Prices

Adventure Pricing

Many Spokane residents looking for a weekend getaway outdoors make the short drive north towards Chewelah. The reason is simple. Four lakes in wooded high country offer good fishing, paddling, and water sports from spring through fall, and a ski resort on Chewelah Mountain provides good downhill and Nordic skiing in the winter.

The first lake you reach driving north from Spokane is Loon Lake. It is visible from US Highway 395 some 25 miles north of town. Surrounded by pine trees and summer homes, the deep waters of this 1,100-plus acre lake lure sun worshippers on pontoon boats, personal watercraft enthusiasts, and anglers who catch bass, panfish, sizeable rainbow trout, kokanee, and big mackinaw. You can get on the water from a public launch on the west side of the lake. Two nice resorts with cabins and RV sites offer places to stay and play.

A 5-mile drive from Loon Lake will get you to Deer Lake. This is another large lake that is about a mile in diameter and covers some 1,163 acres. Like Loon Lake, the waters of Deer Lake are home to a variety of fish to include largemouth and smallmouth bass, perch, crappie, stocked rainbow trout, lake trout, and kokanee. Deer Lake also has a good public boat launch on the east side of the lake. A private resort and bed & breakfast provide further lake access and accommodations.

A 35-mile drive north from Spokane brings you to Jump Off Joe Lake. This is a more intimate and scenic place, with far less development. There is a Washington Department of Fish and Wildlife (WDFW) access area along the eastern shore where you can launch small boats. At 105 acres, this spring-fed lake doesn't attract the water sports crowd, making it an ideal place for canoes, rowboats and kayaks. Jump Off Joe is a good place to catch bass, brown trout and brook trout. A small resort has boat rentals, store, and a fishing dock along with cabins and places to park an RV or pitch a tent. The lake is open for fishing from the last weekend of April through October.

Waitts Lake is the final lake north from Spokane, and only a 10-mile drive from Chewelah. Like the other lakes, there is a WDFW access area where you can launch a boat. There are also three resorts offering accommodations, food, boat moorage, and water-oriented recreation. The 455-acre lake is known for kicking out nice brown and rainbow trout along with largemouth bass. If shooting sports are your game, you'll find turkey hunting is very good around here. In the summer, berries ripen for picking on nearby Huckleberry Mountain.

Another place to pick huckleberries in the summer is along the slopes of Chewelah Mountain, 10 miles east of Chewelah. In the winter, visitors head here to visit the 49 Degrees North Ski Resort. While many come for downhill skiing and snowboarding, there is also an area of the resort with 10 miles of backcountry trails dedicated to cross-country skiing (both skate and classic methods) and snowshoeing. A warming yurt, lessons, and rentals (of both skis and snowshoes) make this a good destination once the snow starts falling.

Getting There: You can reach the 49 Degrees North Ski Resort by traveling north on US 395 from Spokane to Chewelah. Turn right (east) on Flowery Trail Road and drive 10 miles to the ski area on Chewelah Mountain. Loon, Deer, Jump Off Joe, and Waitt's Lakes are all accessible from US Highway 395 between Spokane and Chewelah. Loon Lake is 25 miles from Spokane while Waitts Lake is 42 miles away from the city.

SILVER BEACH RESORT

3323 Waitts Lake Road, Valley, WA 99181 / 509-937-2811
www.silverbeachresort.net

Lodging Prices: $ to $$ Adventure Pricing: $ to $$

Great food, nice cabins, fishing, and water play are all on tap at the Silver Beach Resort on Waitts Lake near Chewelah. Silver Beach is one of three resorts on the 455-acre lake but it has some things the others don't. For starters it has Nick's Restaurant. Named after owner Nick Grmolyes, Nick's has been called one of the finest restaurants in Stevens County. Specializing in seafood, steak, and barbeque ribs, they also have an extensive wine list. Penny Grmolyes is Nick's wife and the co-owner of the resort. She says the restaurant's signature dish is a dinner for two that features small portions of Australian lobster tail, shrimp, steak, baby back pork ribs, and wine for around $65. Reservations are recommended at this popular restaurant where dinner is the only meal served.

The resort has 51 RV sites but most are leased out on a seasonal basis. Only nine are available for overnight travelers or vacationers. There are no tent sites on the 13-acre property, but there are six very nice rental cabins. The cabins sleep from four to six people and are well appointed, featuring modern appliances, bathrooms, and knotty pine interiors. All of them are situated on waterfront or water view locations. There is a two-night minimum stay in the cabins, and in July and August they are rented by the week.

In the summer, you can sun yourself on the beach or swim in front of the resort. Renting a canoe or rowboat to exercise and explore the wide 65-foot deep lake is also an option. There is also a large dock providing space for boat moorage and fishing. Fourteen-foot aluminum boats with motors and pontoon boats can be rented if you want to venture farther out onto the lake.

The fishing can be good for German brown trout. The average fish is 18 to 19 inches long and 2.5- to 6-pound brown trout are common. Some are even bigger; according to Nick Grmolyes a 20-pounder was once hauled out of this lake. Rainbow trout also grow large. Penny Grmolyes tells of a 22-pound (non-triploid) rainbow caught here.

If you want to get away from the lake and go for a walk, a trip to nearby Huckleberry Mountain is a good bet. You can wander along the old logging roads and, from late June through July, pick – you guessed it – the huckleberries that grow along the edges of these roads and on the sides of the mountain.

In the spring and fall, turkey hunters stay at the resort and hunt the surrounding area. Merriam's turkeys are prolific, and over 3,000 gobblers are taken from this part of northeastern Washington every spring. The birds often wander close to the resort; the

Grmolyes report a flock of 100 turkeys routinely visit their backyard. A combination of public land and private property (where hunters can enter by permission only) provides plenty of opportunity to bag a turkey and still get back to Nick's in time for dinner.

The Silver Beach Resort is open from mid-April until mid-October. Nick's Restaurant opens up for Memorial Day weekend and stays open for dinner until mid-September.

Getting There: Drive north from Spokane on US Highway 395 towards Chewelah. Turn west (left) at State Highway 232. Travel three miles past the small town of Valley to reach the resort.

Nick's Restaurant at the Silver Beach Resort offers fine dining in a casual lakefront setting.

SHORE ACRES RESORT

41987 Shore Acres Road, Loon Lake, WA 99148 / 509-233-2474
www.shoreacresresort.com

Lodging Prices: $ to $$ Adventure Pricing: $ to $$$

Shore Acres Resort is a cozy, well-kept place on northeastern Washington's Loon Lake. The 1,120-acre lake is a popular weekend destination for Spokane area residents who come here to swim, boat, and fish.

Despite the name of the lake, loons are no longer a common sight. The scarcity of these birds is not for a lack of fish. Rainbow trout that average 12 to 15 inches are abundant, as are kokanee salmon. Lake trout (also known as mackinaw) are also found in good numbers. The average mackinaw reportedly runs 10 pounds or better and the former state record (weighing in at 30 pounds, 4 ounces) was caught here. In the summer, bass, perch, and bluegill offer further opportunities for anglers.

Established in 1946, Shore Acres has 30 RV sites with full hook ups for both RVs and tent campers. They also have 10 cabins overlooking the water, each sleeping from four to eight guests. All of the cabins have showers, kitchens, heat, and cable television.

The resort has a sandy beach with a nice swimming area. Two docks offer boat moorage space and nice fishing platforms for anglers who regularly catch panfish and trout. If you didn't bring your own boat you can rent a canoe, paddleboat, a small aluminum boat with an outboard, or a motorized pontoon boat. Just a few steps away from the beach is a store with an assortment of groceries, gifts, fishing tackle, and snacks. A small but manicured grass playground and picnic area is a popular kid magnet and if you get hungry, Chipper's Restaurant has outside deck seating for a fresh-air dining experience with great views of the lake.

If you want to walk off that meal, there is an abandoned logging road that winds through the woods above the western edge of the lake for 2 miles. The trail starts at the edge of the resort property and ends at the Department of Fish and Wildlife Boat Launch to the north. Along the way you may see deer or turkey, but if you miss them don't worry. Both are known to wander onto the resort grounds on a regular basis.

Shore Acres Resort is open from April 15 until October 15. Chipper's Restaurant serves food from Memorial Day weekend through Labor Day.

Getting There: Head north on US Highway 395 from Spokane for about 26 miles. Turn left at State Highway 291 and drive a short distance to Shore Acres Road. Turn left and travel south 1.6 miles to the resort.

Lake Roosevelt
National Recreation Area

1008 Crest Drive, Coulee Dam, WA 99116 / 509-633-9441
www.nps.gov/laro

Lodging Prices

Adventure Pricing

Encompassing 150 miles of the upper Columbia River from Grand Coulee Dam towards the Canadian border, the Lake Roosevelt National Recreation Area is a fantastic vacation destination that offers great boating, swimming, fishing, paddling, and wildlife watching.

The national recreation area was established in 1946 and the lake was named after President Franklin Delano Roosevelt, whose New Deal program made the construction of Grand Coulee Dam possible. The lower end of the reservoir is primarily a shrub-steppe environment. Sage, bitterbrush, and bunchgrass grow in a region that receives about 10 inches of rainfall a year. A marina at Keller Ferry has boat fuel, a campground, marina, store, and a free car ferry that crosses the river.

The Spokane River flows into the reservoir 43 miles upstream from the dam. Fort Spokane was established here in the latter part of the 19th century. After the military left, the fort became a Native American boarding school. Today, an interpretive center tells the story of the fort and the people who were a part of its history. Marinas at Seven Bays and Two Rivers provide moorage, fuel, and accommodations for campers and RV enthusiasts.

The Columbia River continues north here and as it does, the landscape changes. Ponderosa pine becomes abundant, turning the shrub-steppe into forest. Much of the shoreline remains in a natural state, in large part because the Colville and Spokane Tribes manage much of the lower and middle portion of the reservoir. There is another free car ferry that crosses from Gifford on the eastern shore to the Colville Reservation near Inchelium.

Toward the northern end of the reservoir, the Kettle Falls Marina has moorage space, launch facilities, fuel, a large campground, and a ranger station. This location offers close access to Kettle Falls and Colville, the largest communities near the lake. Also in this vicinity are St. Paul's Mission and the Kettle Falls Historical Center which offer a glimpse into the history of this river when it ran free. Several more campgrounds and boat launches are available on either side of the river in the remaining 25 miles of the recreation area north of Kettle Falls to China Bar near Northport.

The reservoir has become a playground for vacationers interested in water-based fun. Boaters can launch at 23 different places along the reservoir to play under the summer sun, and paddlers in canoes and kayaks will find the reservoir is a wonderful place to explore. There are a number of waterfront campgrounds, to include nine boat-in only sites, conveniently spaced for paddlers working their way downstream. Paddling from one to another is easy enough to do since most of the campsites are separated by less than 10 miles. If you decide to do this, file a float plan with local national park service rangers since weather can be unpredictable and strong winds rapidly change direction along the river.

Another popular way to explore Lake Roosevelt is by houseboat. Rentals are available at the Kettle Falls, Seven Bays, Two Rivers and Keller Ferry marinas. The boats range in length from 52 to 64 feet and are set up for a luxurious waterborne vacation. Separate staterooms, full kitchens, gas barbeques, stereos, televisions, gas fireplaces, and many of the amenities of home are found on the main decks of these boats. Meanwhile the upper decks provide lots of room to enjoy the sunshine, another place to pilot the boat, a waterslide and, in many cases, a hot tub that is perfect for soaking under the stars. Houseboats are generally rented by families or groups for three- to seven-day periods. During the height of the summer a top-of-the-line boat may cost upwards of $7,000 per week, but by booking a late-spring or early-fall trip you can find a more affordable vacation opportunity.

Fishing can be very good on Lake Roosevelt. Rainbow trout are caught throughout the year and the stretch from Grand Coulee Dam to Seven Bays can be very good in the winter. Other species found in the reservoir include good-sized kokanee salmon, smallmouth bass, perch, whitefish, and burbot. Perhaps the most popular species for anglers are walleye. These tasty fish can get very big, and the confluence of the Spokane and Columbia Rivers has long been a hotspot for trophy "marble eyes". The northern end of the reservoir near Northport and mid-lake near Hunters also offers good walleye fishing. Check the state regulations before you drop a line, since there are seasonal closures at the San Poil and Kettle arm and catch limits vary.

Expect to see wildlife whether you are on the water or exploring the shoreline of the recreation area. Deer, coyote, and wild turkey are common, and if you are lucky you may also see a black bear or big lumbering moose. Nighthawks and swallows fly overhead around sunset and during the day you'll likely see bald eagles, several species of hawk, ducks, and Canada geese. If you get the urge to go hunting, you are in luck since it is permitted in many parts of this national recreation area, but you'll want to check both state and national park service regulations first for details.

Getting There: Traveling north from US Highway 2 gets you to a good portion of Lake Roosevelt. From Wilbur a 22-mile drive will get you to the National Recreation

Area Headquarters at Grand Coulee Dam. A 14-mile drive from the same small farming town will put you on the free ferry at Keller. Traveling north from the highway at Davenport or northeast from Creston will get you to Fort Spokane and the Spokane River arm. You can continue north on State Highway 25 from Fort Spokane along the east end of the lake past Kettle Falls all the way to Northport.

A red-necked grebe.

ROOSEVELT RECREATIONAL ENTERPRISES

45751 State Route 21 North, Wilbur, WA 99185 / 800-648-LAKE (5253)
www.rrehouseboats.com

Lodging Pricing: $$ to $$$$ Adventure Pricing: $ to $$$$

If you love exploring the back roads in a luxury RV then you have got to try out a houseboat vacation. Roosevelt Recreational Enterprises (RRE) offers houseboat excursions that last anywhere from a weekend to a week on Lake Roosevelt in northeast Washington. Rent a boat that sleeps up to 13 people and ply the waters of this huge Columbia River impoundment to soak up the sun, play in the water, fish, and watch wildlife.

Roosevelt Recreational Enterprises (RRE) is owned and operated by the Colville Indian Tribe. The company is located at the Keller Ferry landing northeast of Wilbur. They are open year round and have a fleet of houseboats ranging from 59-foot luxury models to 52-foot versions geared for those on more of a budget.

The lavish 59-foot Dreamcatchers feature a hot tub and wet bar on the upper deck, a Bimini top to keep the sun off, and a CD stereo to play your favorite tunes while you pilot the boat. The main floor has three staterooms with queen beds, two small cubby rooms that are great places for kids to sleep and two bathrooms. The main salon has a fully furnished kitchen with modern appliances, a carpeted living area with a propane fireplace, and electronic entertainment in the form of a TV, DVD player, and another stereo. A large dinette and sofa convert to additional sleepers if needed and if you don't want to pilot the boat from the upper bridge, you can do so from this location. An onboard fueling station holds gas for any small boats or personal watercraft you bring along, and a generator provides electricity without running the motors on the boat.

The 54-foot Mirage houseboats offer many of the same bells and whistles as the Dreamcatchers, but at a more affordable price. This model also has a hot tub on the bridge and Bimini top for the skipper. On the main deck are three private staterooms with full beds, two cubby rooms and two bathrooms. The living area is also nice, featuring a fireplace, fully equipped kitchen, stereo system, and a sofa that converts to a sleeper.

The 52-foot Voyager series boats fit the bill if you want to stretch your dollars. There are no hot tubs or fireplaces on board, but there is a lot of room to lie out under the sun (or stars) on the wide-open upper deck. There are also three semi-private staterooms and a sofa/hide-a-bed in the salon. The kitchen is basic but fully furnished. Like the other houseboats, the Voyager has a large gas BBQ on the foredeck, a huge ice chest for your beverages, and a slide that starts on the upper deck and ends with a splash in the water.

Most vacationers are families or groups who rent a boat for three-, four-, or seven-night summer vacations. Many ply the waters of the lake for a few hours each day before stopping at sandy beaches, bays, and coves which offer places to stay the night, play in the water, or fish. With summer temperatures reaching the century mark in this landscape of sandy hills, rocky cliffs, sagebrush, and the occasional pine, frequent soaks in the water and lazy days are the norm for many.

Some boat downstream for three or four hours to visit Grand Coulee Dam. Completed in 1942, this massive dam produces more hydroelectric power than anywhere else in the United States. In the summer, you can moor your boat and walk a short mile to watch the popular Laser Light Show that plays out on the face of the dam every evening from late May through September.

Others motor upstream. Two Rivers is 25 miles from Kellers Ferry, offering a place to dock and take a night off from cooking. A restaurant is available at the marina, as well as a casino run by the Spokane Indian Tribe.

As entertaining as these excursions are, many find the opportunity to watch deer, elk, bear, beaver, and otter along with soaring eagles or osprey, just as interesting. Anglers also have a lot to keep them occupied with walleye, smallmouth bass, tasty kokanee salmon, and rainbow trout all showing up as common catches in this stretch of the Columbia.

If you don't have your own small boat, you can rent a 14-foot motorized skiff or an 18-foot Sea Ray powerboat from RRE to tow behind your houseboat. A mid-summer excursion on a Dreamcatcher houseboat will cost $5,500 or more for a week. On the other end of the spectrum, one of the 52-foot houseboats can be rented for a week in June or September for around $2,000 and mid-week trips on these boats come down towards $1,000. From fall to spring, RRE also rents some of their houseboats as affordable floating cabins for hunters and anglers who come to take advantage of nature's bounty. Even though Roosevelt Recreational Enterprises has 30 houseboats for rent, they are spoken for quickly for the summer. Call in the fall to book a luxury houseboat during a prime mid-summer week.

Getting There: Take US Highway 2 to Wilbur. Turn north on State Highway 21 and drive 15 miles north to the Keller Ferry Marina at Lake Roosevelt.

R/C&S GUIDE SERVICE

Ray Bailey
23463 Curlew Rd. N, Wilbur WA 99185 / 509-647-5801 or 509-721-1010
www.rcguideservice.com

Lodging Prices: N/A   Adventure Pricing: $$ to $$$

He may not do a lot of advertising, but insiders know Ray Bailey as a good guide who draws a steady clientele. Bailey has over 23 years of full-time guiding experience under his belt. He fishes several eastern Washington waters and takes clients out for big game and bird hunting with the help of three other guides (Cecil Woods, Kevin "Spike" Eide, and Dennis Bailey) who make up the R/C&S Guide Service team.

Bailey's home water is Lake Roosevelt, a huge 150-mile long impoundment of the Columbia River that stretches from Coulee Dam to the Canadian border. Bailey stays busy all year on the reservoir fishing for walleye, trout, kokanee, and smallmouth bass. If you want to catch some trophy walleye, try to book a trip on the Spokane Arm of Lake Roosevelt during the last two weeks of March. Bailey is convinced there are giants in these waters. In his words, "One of these days we are going to break the world record here." Bailey tells a story of one walleye he got to the boat that looked like it was 4 feet long. The monster was too big for the net and before they could get it into the boat by hand, the fish bent the hook and got free.

Bailey fishes the Snake River from April through July for other monsters, namely sturgeon and channel catfish, as well as spring chinook when enough of them come back to provide a season. In May and June his guide service takes kids and adults fishing on Long Lake (an impoundment of the Spokane River) for crappie and smallmouth and at times, R/C&S Guides will venture as far south as the Columbia River below McNary Dam to catch big walleye and chinook salmon. As summer transitions to fall the guide service heads back north to battle big salmon on the Columbia near Wells Dam. Come winter, guides and clients bundle up and work Rufus Woods Reservoir in northeastern Washington for huge triploid trout and more walleye.

R/C&S Guides will also take you hunting. Cecil Woods (The "C" part) handles many of these bookings. Bird hunters gun for wild quail, pheasant, duck, and geese on leased land in various locations throughout eastern Washington. Big game hunters head to the Selkirk Mountains in the northeast corner of the state for deer, elk, bear, and cougar. If you are lucky enough to draw a moose permit, they will also help you bag one of these as well. Much of the big game hunting is done through multi-day pack trips, with horses and mules taking you and your gear in and out of the wilderness.

Getting There: Destinations vary.

BULL HILL GUEST RANCH

3738 Bull Hill Road, Kettle Falls, WA 99141 / 877-285-5445
www.bullhill.com

Lodging Prices: $$$ to $$$ Adventure Pricing: Included with lodging

If you want to get away from it all and still remain in Washington, the Bull Hill Guest Ranch is a worthy destination. Located 35 miles northeast of Kettle Falls, you'll find plenty of elbow room and precious little company. Getting to the ranch takes some effort, but upon your arrival you'll find a special place emphasizing both outdoor recreation and relaxation.

Seven ranch cabins make up the accommodations; each with a comfortable bedroom downstairs and in the second story loft. Nice touches include the pine interiors, Pendleton blankets, full bathrooms, woodstoves, and the outdoor or western decorative accents that give each cabin a distinctive feel. If you really want to stay in style, spend a night in the Executive Cabin. This beautiful two-story home features three large bedrooms, two bathrooms, a spacious living room, kitchenette, hardwood floors, a large ceiling fan, fireplace, propane heat, and a big deck overlooking the surrounding hills and valley below.

As nice as the cabins are, the cook house (day lodge) is nothing short of spectacular. Comfortable chairs, sofas, dining tables, and a fully-stocked bar grace this gathering place where game and bull mounts stare out over polished hardwood floors. "Hearty American fare" is how Office Manager Laura Doyle describes the food. Steaks, ribs, chicken, and salmon all frequently appear on the menu. After dinner, feel free to socialize at the bar or soak away your cares in one of the two hot tubs available for guests.

As pleasant as it is indoors, it's the outdoors that attracts people. Brothers Don and Pete Guglielmino own the 50,000-acre ranch that is over 100 years old. Guests enjoy guided trail rides that take them around the ranch, down the hill to Lake Roosevelt for a picnic lunch, north to the Canadian border, or to the nearby China Bend Winery to sample the local chardonnay. A very popular trip involves a ride into the privately-owned Western town of Mooreville. Tie up your steed to the hitching post and swagger into the Crown Creek Saloon for a drink, spend time in the game room, or take in a film at the movie theater. If you want, you can also take part in a cattle drive on this working ranch that boasts over 600 head of cattle.

Hikers and riders alike wander through hilly pastures and forested areas on the ranch. Deer and turkey are very common and elk, bear, and moose are also seen at times. Waterfowl and raptors are frequently viewed as well as more common birds such as robins and swallows (who seem to think the walls of the cookhouse are a great place to nest in the spring).

Another great attraction of Bull Hill is Ansaldo Lake. Named after Peter Ansaldo (who homesteaded the ranch in 1903), the 20-acre lake is stocked with trophy rainbow trout. You'll find a dock and rowboats at the lake, which is surrounded by cow pasture and woodland. Anglers catch and release fish using flies and lures with barbless hooks. On hot summer days, you can also ride a horse here for an afternoon swim. Wingshooters won't find too many upland birds to hunt, but they will enjoy the trapshooting available on the ranch. If you didn't bring your own shotgun, they've got a couple of nice ones you can borrow.

The ranch caters to an upscale clientele and the costs for lodging reflect that. However, the price gets you an all-inclusive vacation that includes meals, beverages, fishing, trail rides, and other activities. While adults from the Interstate 5 corridor are the most frequent guests, children over 8 years old are also welcome and will undoubtedly enjoy their stay. If you don't want to make the two-hour drive from Spokane, there is a 2,400-foot airstrip on the ranch that can accommodate small planes.

Getting There: From Spokane drive north on US Highway 395 to Kettle Falls. Continue through town on the highway and head north after crossing Lake Roosevelt. Turn right at the Kamloops Campground and follow Northport Flat Creek Road 19 miles north to Bull Hill Road. Turn left onto Bull Hill Road and travel up the hill to the ranch.

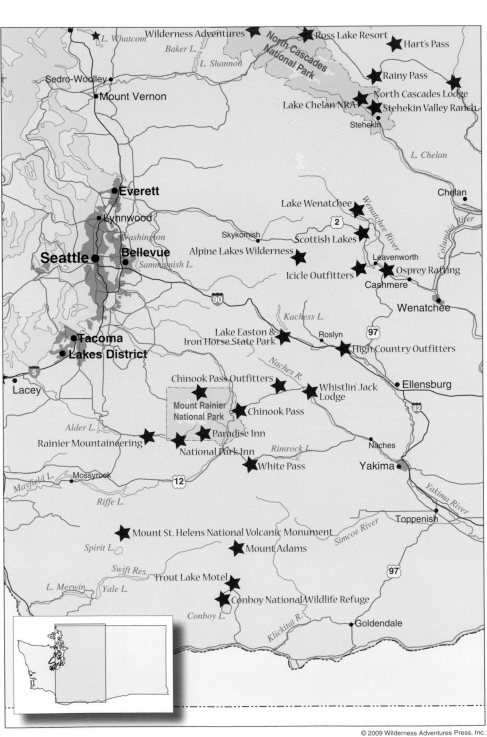

L. Whatcom
Wilderness Adventures
Baker L.
North Cascades National Park
L. Shannon
Ross Lake Resort
Hart's Pass
Sedro-Woolley
Rainy Pass
Mount Vernon
North Cascades Lodge
Lake Chelan NRA
Stehekin Valley Ranch
Stehekin
L. Chelan
Chelan
Everett
Lynnwood
Lake Wenatchee
Washington
Skykomish
Scottish Lakes
Seattle
Bellevue
Alpine Lakes Wilderness
Sammamish L.
Leavenworth
Osprey Rafting
Icicle Outfitters
Cashmere
Wenatchee
90
Kachess L.
Lake Easton &
Iron Horse State Park
Roslyn
97
Tacoma
High Country Outfitters
Lakes District
Ellensburg
Lacey
Naches R.
Chinook Pass Outfitters
82
Whistlin' Jack Lodge
Mount Rainier National Park
Chinook Pass
Alder L.
Naches
Rainier Mountaineering
Paradise Inn
National Park Inn
Rimrock L.
White Pass
Yakima
Mossyrock
12
Yakima River
Mayfield L.
Riffe L.
Toppenish
Mount St. Helens National Volcanic Monument
Simcoe River
Spirit L.
Mount Adams
Swift Res.
97
L. Merwin
Yale L.
Trout Lake Motel
Conboy National Wildlife Refuge
Conboy L.
Goldendale

© 2009 Wilderness Adventures Press, Inc.

The North Cascades

Mount Baker

Mt. Baker – Snoqualmie National Forest – Mt. Baker Ranger District
810 State Route 20, Sedro-Woolley, WA 98284 / 360-856-5700
www.fs.fed.us/r6/mbs/about/mbrd.shtml

Lodging Prices

"Let it snow! Let it snow! Let it snow!" The lyrics from that Christmas classic seem particularly apt for Mount Baker, the volcanic peak visible from much of northwestern Washington that gets an average of 647 inches of the white stuff every year. In fact, in 1999 the mountain set a world record, receiving 1,140 inches (95 feet) of snow. The inordinate amount of snowfall draws thousands of downhill skiers and snowboarders to the Mt. Baker Ski Resort every year, but the mountain and the surrounding area also offer a lot of other fun activities from spring through fall.

There are two main approaches to Mount Baker and its recreation opportunities. The first is along the Mount Baker Highway (State Route 542) from Bellingham, where you drive past the small towns of Maple Falls and Glacier to Heather Meadows, the site of the ski resort in the winter and of a visitor center operated by the US Forest Service during the summer. When planning your trip keep in mind that the parking area may not be accessible (due to snow) until mid-July.

Nonetheless, if you are into beautiful mountain scenery and enjoy hiking, this is a great place to visit. The half-mile Picture Lake Trail is wheelchair accessible and as its name implies, offers very picturesque views of the lake along with Mt. Shuksan. If you want panoramic views of Mt. Baker and several other peaks in the North Cascades, the mile-long trail at Artist Ridge is an option. If you are willing to stretch your legs a bit, hike 6.5 miles along the highly rated Chain Lakes Trail. The route goes past Iceberg, Hayes, and the Bagley Lakes and through meadows full of wildflowers. If you decide to camp at one of these lakes follow the Mount Baker Wilderness regulations

that prohibit the use of campfires. Another reason to visit the Heather Meadows area is the opportunity to pick the mountain blueberries that ripen here in August.

If you want to stay overnight, you can rent a room in nearby Glacier or stay at one of the Forest Service campgrounds between there and Heather Meadows. Douglas Fir Campground is the largest with 30 campsites while Silver Fir Campground has 21 individual sites. Two easy 1.5-mile hikes near Douglas fir are worth noting. The first, the Horseshoe Bend Trail, is a forested loop trail that starts right at the campground. The second hike will get you to Damfino Lake in 0.75 miles, another place known for good blueberry picking. The trailhead for this hike is found towards the end of Canyon Creek Road, accessed a short distance east from the Douglas Fir Campground.

Other recreational activities can be found southeast of Mount Baker in the Baker Lake Basin. To get there, travel east on State Highway 20 from Sedro Woolley some 17 miles and then turn left onto Baker Lake Road. As you drive north, you'll catch several breathtaking glimpses of Mount Baker and Mount Shuksan as well as Baker Lake.

Baker Lake is a good outdoor destination in its own right. The 10-mile-long lake has several Forest Service campgrounds distributed along its west side. The largest, Kulshan, sits at the south end of the dammed reservoir and has 108 camp sites, some with hook-ups for RVs. Heading north, you'll come across Horseshoe Cove (34 sites) and Panorama Point Campgrounds (16 sites), before coming to the Baker Lake Resort. Operated for years by Puget Sound Energy, this rustic resort is closing at the end of 2009 and will be turned into another Forest Service campground. Across the road from the Baker Lake Resort is the Park Creek Campground with 12 individual sites and finally, the Shannon Creek Campground at the northwest end of the lake has 20 campsites.

All of the lakefront campgrounds have boat launches. With great views of Mt. Baker and several other peaks, the lake is a good paddling destination if you want to bring your canoe or kayak along. Anglers troll for kokanee in the late spring and fish for cutthroat and rainbow trout in the summer. Boaters should be careful on this lake when the water is high, since it is often full of wood debris. On the east side, a 14-mile long trail follows the length of the lake and while lengthy, has little elevation gain and passes through some gorgeous old-growth forest.

The forests around Mt. Baker are full of wildlife. Deer, elk, black bear, and mountain goats are some of the larger mammals you may see, and bird watchers can see everything from ptarmigan in the high country to golden-crowned kinglets and chestnut-backed chickadees in the branches of lower elevation firs. Along Baker Lake, keep an eye out for bald eagles, osprey, and common loons.

Finally, a few notes on climbing the 10,781-foot mountain are in order. While Mt. Baker is not known as one of the tougher peaks to climb within the Cascades, novices should be aware that travel across one or more of the mountain's 12 glaciers is required. Therefore, a certain amount of climbing knowledge is helpful before attempting an ascent to the summit. If you are in doubt, give a call to the American Alpine Institute, a longtime climbing service in Bellingham (800-424-2249 – www.aai. cc). Most climbers go up to the flat summit via the Coleman-Deming Route on the west side of Mt. Baker or up the Easton Glacier, which is accessed off the Baker Lake

Road and Forest Service Road 13 to Schreiber Meadows. The prime climbing season is from May to September.

Parking is another thing worth mentioning. A Northwest Forest Pass, or equivalent permit, must be displayed in vehicles parked at trailheads accessible from State Route 542 or the Baker Lake Highway.

Getting There: See above

The placid water of Baker Lake one of the many places in Washington to bring your camera.

North Cascades National Park
(NORTH AND SOUTH UNITS)

North Cascades National Park Service Complex
810 State Route 20, Sedro-Woolley, WA 98284 / 360-854-7200
www.nps.gov/noca

Lodging Prices

If you ask people about what national parks you should visit in Washington, Mt. Rainier and Olympic National Park invariably get mentioned. However, less-visited North Cascades National Park is just as rich in panoramic, unspoiled beauty. Stretching from the Canadian border south to the tip of Lake Chelan, the park complex consists of a North and South Unit as well as the Ross Lake and Lake Chelan national recreation areas. The recreation areas are covered elsewhere in this book, and due to their proximity to modern transportation and lodging, get the lion's share of visitors.

On the other hand, the North and South Units of the national park are a hiker's and climber's paradise from late spring through early fall. The National Park Visitor Center near Newhalem is a great place to stop if you want to orient yourself to the park. In addition to helpful staff who can answer your questions, you can take in a movie about the park and walk around interpretive exhibits that do a fabulous job of describing the different ecosystems found inside the complex. If you come on a clear day, make it a point to walk a few feet outside to take in the view of the spectacular Picket Range to the north. The center is open daily April through October.

After you get your questions answered, it's time to go hiking. There are nearly 400 miles of trails within the park complex. The most famous one is the Pacific Crest Trail in the South Unit. You can access it from Rainy Pass along State Highway 20 just outside of the park. From there, walk south and follow the trail some 15 miles south to the High Bridge Campground at the Stehekin River Road. This is the easy way to make this hike, since by going from north to south you'll descend (instead of ascend) 3,000 feet in elevation and be able to catch the shuttle to Stehekin where a passenger boat can take you to Chelan.

Another popular South Unit hike takes off over Cascade Pass. To get there, cross the Skagit River at Marblemount and follow the Cascade River Road until it ends in the park. From the trailhead, it's 3.7 miles to Cascade Pass, and you'll get to take in awesome views of glaciers and peaks along the way. From the pass, you can head north towards Doubtful Lake or to the Sahale Glacier Camp. Another option is to continue southeast, following the Stehekin River to the High Bridge Campground. Camping is limited to designated sites to protect fragile subalpine meadows and backcountry permits are required.

Yet another popular destination in the South Unit with great views of meadows and peaks is the steep day hike to Easy Pass. Get there from the trailhead at Milepost 151 off of Highway 20 and head south 3.6 miles, gaining 2,800 feet along the way. Snowfields are present in the early summer and an ice axe comes in handy at this time of year. If you want to extend the trip you can continue on from the pass all the way to Colonial Creek Campground, covering a total of 19 miles in the process.

In the North Unit the 12.9-mile Copper Ridge Trail follows a high ridgeline near Copper Mountain while an 18.5-mile trail follows the Chilliwack River to Chilliwack Lake Provincial Park in Canada. Both trails start at Hannegan Pass, accessible from State Highway 542 near Mount Baker.

Another good expedition for backpackers and equestrians alike takes off from the Ross Lake Dam Trailhead at Highway 20. Follow the Big Beaver Trail 24.6 miles through the Ross Lake National Recreation Area to the Little Beaver Trail. Old-growth forests, several active beaver ponds and views of Ross Lake are highlights of this trip. You can turn around and come back at this point (especially if you came in on horseback) or follow the Little Beaver Trail 10 miles back to Ross Lake. If you called Ross Lake Resort in advance they'll meet you at the water's edge in a boat and take you back to the south end of the lake.

Big Beaver is not the only trail available for stock use. In the South Unit, McAlester Pass and Lake provide pleasant riding among hemlock, fir, and larch in an alpine setting. You can get to the pass by hiking or riding 9 miles south from Highway 20 at Rainy Pass or traveling 10 miles from Stehekin. Permits (issued at no charge from ranger stations and visitor centers) are required to camp in the park's backcountry. Groups using pack animals are limited to 12 (that includes animals and humans).

Whether you hike or ride, you can expect to see a wide variety of wildlife. Black bear, deer, skunk, raccoon, opossum, beaver, and various members of the weasel family are found in lower elevations while mountain goat, pika, and hoary marmot can be observed in alpine areas. Two rarely seen mammals – cougars and wolverines – also call the park home. If you are lucky enough to spy either of these animals, let someone know at the nearest ranger station.

Bird watchers will be happy to know there are over 200 different species found in the varied environments of the park. They include everything from colorful harlequin ducks and mournful sounding loons to raptors like osprey, red-tailed hawks, and both golden and bald eagles. Expect to see common spring and summer birds like flycatchers, swallows, chickadees, and red-breasted nuthatches. Other common birds include sparrows, thrushes, warblers, Stellar's jay, and winter wren.

Anglers target trout in the park's alpine lakes or on the Stehekin, Skagit, and Cascade Rivers. In fact, the latter two rivers are some of the only places in Washington where Dolly Varden trout are still present in enough numbers that you can keep them if you choose to.

North Cascades National Park is a popular destination for climbers, who have a number of challenging peaks to scale. The most well-known is 9,131-foot Mt. Shuksan in the eastern end of the park. The glaciers and peaks of the Picket Range offer challenges to serious climbers in the heart of the park complex, while Boston Basin and Eldorado Peak are two popular destinations in the South Unit accessible from trails off the Cascade River Road. All of these destinations require a degree (or great deal) of expertise to reach. If you are unsure of whether you have enough experience, you might want to enlist the service of a guide. American Alpine Institute out of Bellingham (800-424-2249 – www.aai.cc) is one well-established company offering a variety of climbs within the park.

Finally, road cycling is another popular activity in the park (bikes are not allowed on any trails in the park complex). Driving along State Highway 20, you'll see plenty of people pedaling their way uphill (or cruising downhill) from Rainy or Washington Pass. It's a killer ride, covering 42 miles from the visitor center and Newhalem Creek Campground at Mile Post 120 to the overlook at Washington Pass. From there, you have the option of heading back towards Newhalem or continuing east downhill towards Mazama and Winthrop (18 and 31 miles respectively). If you want to break this up into a multi-day expedition, you can camp at Colonial Creek Campground (mile post 130) or the Lone Fir Campground 6 miles east of Washington Pass.

North Cascades National Park is open all year. However, State Highway 20 over Washington Pass is typically closed by heavy snowfall from mid-November through mid-April. Car-accessible and hike-in campsites are both available on a first-come, first-served basis. You'll also need a free backcountry permit from the visitor center if you plan on camping at a hike-in destination. As in other national parks, pets are not allowed on park trails (though they are permitted on leash on the Pacific Crest Trail as well as on trails within the Lake Chelan and Ross Lake National Recreation Areas). There is no entrance fee at this National Park.

Getting There: State Highway 20 is the dividing line between the North and South Units of the National Park. The park's visitor center is located off of Mile Post 120 near Newhalem.

Ross Lake National Recreation Area

North Cascades National Park Service Complex
810 State Route 20, Sedro-Woolley, WA 98284 / 360-854-7200
www.nps.gov/noca

Lodging Prices

Adventure Pricing

It's odd that three dammed lakes supplying electricity to Seattle make up the most visited portion of North Cascades National Park. Much of it has to do with geography. State Highway 20 runs through the Ross Lake National Recreation Area, providing easy access into a park complex largely inaccessible to vehicles.

Coming from the west, you'll enter the recreation area 9 miles west of Newhalem, a company town owned by Seattle City Light. The City of Seattle constructed the dams that formed Gorge, Diablo, and Ross Lakes between 1918 and 1949 to provide reliable hydroelectric power for the city's citizens. A stop in town at the Skagit Tours Information Center offers a good chance to stretch your legs with two short walks along the Skagit River, along the Trail of Cedars or to Ladder Creek Falls. If you are hungry you may want to stop in at the store – it's the last one you'll find until you reach Mazama, 59 miles to the east. Another place worth stopping is the North Cascades National Park Visitor Center west of Newhalem. Check the North Cascades National Park Complex entry in this book for more details.

Traveling east from Newhalem, you'll soon come to a parking area where you can get out and view Gorge Creek Falls or hike a short 0.33-mile paved trail to several overlooks near the falls and Gorge Dam. Continuing east on State Highway 20, you'll next reach Diablo Lake. You can stop at an often breezy overlook above the lake or turn north before reaching the overlook to cross the Diablo Dam and take a boat ride.

The rides in question are offered by Skagit Tours (a subsidiary of Seattle City Light). You can board the Diablo Ferry at 8:30am or 3:00pm aboard the

little Cascadian 3 for a 20-minute trip along the jade colored waters to Ross Dam. The ferry makes the journey back towards Diablo Dam a half-hour later. You'll pay a reasonable price to get to the dam and a little more to get a ride on a truck that will take you above Ross Dam to Ross Lake.

You can also take a tour on 910-acre Diablo Lake aboard the Alice Ross III. This tour boat runs from June through September along the emerald green waters of the lake that are framed by jagged peaks and in many places, narrow channels that wind through rocky cliffs and forested shorelines. During Fridays, Saturdays, and Sundays, you can enjoy the 2.5-hour Diablo Lake Adventure, and on Mondays and Thursdays in July and August you can have a meal during the Diablo Dam Good Dinner excursion. All of these tours depart at 12:30pm from Newhalem. Reservations, especially for the dinner cruise, are highly recommended (206-684-3030 – www.skagittours.com).

There are several car campgrounds in the area. Goodell Creek (21 sites) and Newhalem Creek (111 sites) both accommodate tents and RVs of varying sizes. Little Gorge Lake campground has six campsites while Colonial Creek Campground on the shores of Diablo Lake has 142 sites and a boat launch. None of the sites have hook-ups for RVs and most of them are available on a first-come, first-served basis (some sites at the Newhalem Creek Campground are reserveable in advance through www.recreation.gov).

One popular way to get to Ross Lake is via the ferry from Diablo Lake.

Ross Lake is the crown jewel of the three lakes. You can get there aboard the Diablo Ferry or by hiking a mile from State Highway 20. You can also access it through Canada, traveling south on the Silver-Skagit Road from Hope, British Columbia to the Hozomeen Campground on the U.S. side of the border where there is a boat launch.

Once at Ross Lake, you can boat or paddle its length. If you didn't bring a boat (a tough thing to do from the south end), you can rent a canoe, kayak, or motor boat from the Ross Lake Resort (see their entry for more information). Nineteen different boat-in campgrounds offer paddlers places to stay along the scenic 22-mile lake, making it a great place for a multi-day waterborne expedition. Better still, personal watercraft are not allowed anywhere in the national park complex, something that goes towards a more pristine outdoor experience. If you decide to stay at the boat-in campgrounds you will need a backcountry wilderness permit available from the Wilderness Information Center in Marblemount.

With all of this water, you may want to try your luck fishing. Both Gorge and Diablo Lakes are stocked with rainbow and cutthroat trout and are open all year. Meanwhile, Ross Lake has a short July 1 through October 31 season with several restrictions about where you can fish. Only artificial lures with barbless hooks are allowed. Both rainbow and bull trout are present, but you need to let the bull trout go unharmed and the rainbows have to be at least 13 inches long. You can keep a maximum of three fish per angler at Ross Lake.

Hiking is another activity of note in the Ross Lake NRA. You can follow the East Bank Trail along the lake for 29 miles, all the way from State Highway 20 to Hozomeen, or travel the easy Happy Panther Trail for up to 10.5 miles (round-trip) along the south shore of Ross Lake. On the west side of the lake, the Big Beaver and Sourdough Mountain trails are popular, as is a trek further uplake to the east towards Desolation Peak. It was here that beatnik poet Jack Kerouac once spent a summer working in a fire lookout. If you don't have a boat, you can hop onto a water taxi (operated by the folks at the Ross Lake Resort) that will take you to the trailheads leading to some of these destinations. West of Ross Lake you can also hike to Pyramid Lake (a 4.2-mile round-trip journey of moderate difficulty) from Highway 20 or take in the mountainous views for up to 7.6 miles (round-trip) along the Diablo Lake Trail.

Finally, you can expect to see some wildlife along the way. It may come in the form of spawning salmon in the Skagit River or the bald eagles that feed on them. Chipmunks and squirrels are common near campgrounds, and along the hiking trails you may glimpse a black bear. A variety of other birds and animals may also be seen during a trip here. See the North Cascades National Park and Ross Lake Resort entries for further details.

While the Ross Lake National Recreation Area is technically open all year, State Highway 20 usually closes for the winter near the Ross Dam Trailhead and does not open again for travel until late spring, limiting access. Unlike most national parks, there is no entrance fee required to recreate here.

Getting There: Travel east on US Highway 20 from Burlington/Mt. Vernon to Newhalem. Continue following the Highway past Gorge, Diablo, and Ross Lake.

ROSS LAKE RESORT

503 Diablo Street, Rockport, WA 98283 – 206-386-4437
www.rosslakeresort.com

Lodging Prices: $$ Adventure Pricing: $ to $$

If you are looking for the ultimate outdoor lodging experience in the North Cascades, you've got to go to Ross Lake Resort. It's located in the heart of the North Cascades National Park complex, and the buildings of the resort are not just waterfront – but on the water. Twelve clean cabins and three bunkhouses sit on connected floating docks just off shore at the south end of Ross Lake. The smallest cabins sleep four; several of the nicely furnished Modern Cabins sleep up to six; and two large Peak Cabins with the nicest amenities can handle up to nine guests. Groups may want to rent one of the bunkhouses. Simply furnished, they sleep eight to ten guests. All of the cabins have kitchens for cooking, tables for eating, and private bathrooms. Instead of televisions, two Adirondack chairs sit just outside your door and face across the lake towards Colonial and Pyramid Peaks, a majestic sight in which you can lose yourself for hours.

If staring at the mountains or reading a book to the accompaniment of lapping waves isn't enough entertainment, you can take out one of the 45 boats available for rent at the resort. There's an assortment of brightly colored 17-foot canoes as well as single and double kayaks to choose from. You can sortie out for the day to nearby Cougar Island, take a longer trip to Big Beaver Creek, or paddle along the more sheltered waters of Ruby Arm.

If you want to go farther up the 22-mile lake, rent one of the 14-foot aluminum or hand-built wooden boats powered by 9.9-horsepower motors. One popular destination is Devils Creek, a 30-minute ride from the resort. You'll recognize the outlet of the creek by the hiker's suspension bridge that crosses over it. Go under the bridge and slowly motor up the emerald green waters of the narrow stream that form the base of a narrow, wooded canyon until you can't go any further.

Fishing is another on-the-water option. From July 1 through October 31, you can use single barbless hooks on flies or lures to catch trout. Trolling from boats is the most popular way to hook fish, with rainbow trout up to 17 inches being the predominant catch. Other fish you may see at the end of your line include the occasional cutthroat trout or protected bull trout. Fishing is such a popular activity that the side of an entire building at the resort is full of placards and memorials dedicated to anglers who have fished here over the years.

If you want to get back on land, you can do some hiking as well. Ross Lake Dam is a short walk from the resort; the trail to Big Beaver Creek follows the western shore of Ross Lake; and if you want to go somewhere else, you can hop on the water taxi from the resort and get dropped off (and picked up again) at one of the many trails along the lake.

The season at the resort is relatively short. It opens in the middle of June and closes October 31. Advance reservations by telephone are a must, and the months of July and August are often booked a full year in advance. If you are staying over the weekend, a boat rental is required (and you'll probably want one anyway). Also, you'll need to leave your pets at home, though several dogs and cats live at the resort and are more than willing to be petted.

Getting There: Getting to the resort is an adventure in itself. First, take State Highway 20 towards Newhalem. If you want to hike, there's a parking lot at Milepost 138 and you can backpack 2 miles to the resort. Otherwise, head across Diablo Dam (the turn off is marked with an Environmental Learning Center Sign off the highway) and take the Diablo Ferry to Ross Dam. The staff at the resort will portage you and your gear from there.

Stehekin and The Lake Chelan National Recreation Area

National Park Service – Golden West Visitor Center
P.O. Box 7, Stehekin, WA 98852 / 360-854-7365 (ext. 14)
www.nps.gov/noca

Lodging Prices

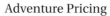

Adventure Pricing

When it comes to the remote community of Stehekin, getting there is half the fun. You can't drive to this small outdoor-oriented hamlet located at the forested inlet of Lake Chelan. However, you can fly in on a floatplane, hike in, or take a cruise 50 miles up the lake from Chelan aboard The Lady of the Lake II or the Lady Express (509-682-2224 – www.ladyofthelake.com). The views along the long narrow lake are both scenic and interesting. Past the 25-mile point, there are no roads to be seen, just green forests, hillsides of grass and rock, and the gray ghosts of timber left standing in the wake of several recent wildfires.

When you arrive at Stehekin, make it a point to walk a few steps from the landing and visit the National Park Service's Golden West Visitor Center for information about hiking, biking, and climbing in the southern portion of the North Cascades National Park complex. If you need a free camping permit (required if you plan on pitching a tent within the park), this is the place to get it. The visitor center is open year round and in the summer rangers offer guided hikes, children's activities, and other educational programs.

Also at the dock is the newly renovated Stehekin Landing Resort (509-682-4494 – www.stehekinlanding.com). Featuring a restaurant, store, and lodging with 27 rooms (all with private baths), the resort is one of two lodging operations currently operated by the Courtney family (the other is at Stehekin Valley Ranch). A lake house rental with four bedrooms, two and a half baths, fireplace, and hot tub is also available through the resort and accommodates up to 12 people. If you want to camp, there are several national park service campgrounds between the landing and the end of the Stehekin Valley Road.

This road – open for 13 miles – follows the Stehekin River from the landing past the High Bridge Guard Station. This area is all part of the Lake Chelan National Recreation Area. Once you cross the High Bridge over the Stehekin River, you enter the South Unit of the North Cascades National Park. The navigable portion of the road continues another 2 miles from the bridge past Tumwater Campground.

Wildlife viewing is a fun activity around here. Mule deer are quite common around Stehekin and black bears are also frequently seen. Waterfowl like colorful harlequin ducks and goldeneye can be seen flying up and down the river, and both blue grouse and pileated woodpeckers call this region home.

Kayakers and rafters come to tackle the Class III rapids of the Stehekin River, paddle the quiet inlet of Lake Chelan, or launch a multi-day canoe or kayak expedition down-lake, stopping at boat-in campgrounds along the way. Flatwater kayaks are available for rent at the Stehekin Landing Resort.

Others come for the fishing. The angling season in this country is short, since snow keeps lakes covered and rivers high for much of the spring and summer. The Stehekin River does have sizeable rainbow and cutthroat trout, and fishing below Agnes Creek from August into October can be productive for anglers casting flies or spinners (selective regulations are in effect, check the Washington state fishing regulations for further details). If you want some lake fishing head towards 9-acre Coon Lake, which has been stocked with trout. However, the lilypad-lined shores of this lake make bank angling tough, so hauling in a float tube may be a good call. Fishing near the upper reaches of Lake Chelan may yield kokanee salmon, lake trout, and cutthroat trout. However, cutthroat caught in this part of the lake or in the Stehekin River must be released.

Hiking is very popular. The Lakeshore Trail starts near the landing and traverses fairly level terrain along the north shore of Lake Chelan as far as Prince Creek (17 miles). A moderate stroll can be found on the 4.4-mile Rainbow Loop Trail, accessed 2.6 miles from the landing. Other walks can be taken after a shuttle ride to High Bridge, 11 miles up the Stehekin Valley Road. After you get off the bus, you can trek along the popular 2.5-mile long trail to scenic Agnes Gorge or follow the 1.3-mile trail from the High Bridge Guard Station to Coon Lake.

Climbers can continue past Coon Lake and head towards 8,149-foot Mt. McGregor. This is a tough hike with a 6,525-foot elevation gain, so an overnight stay at Heaton Camp (6.8 miles from High Bridge) might be a good idea. The summit is 7.7 miles from High Bridge and the trail ends 0.25 miles after leaving Heaton Camp. While no technical climbing skills are needed to reach the summit, you will have to scramble over rocks in a steep, exposed setting. Once at the summit you can enjoy panoramic views of the Stehekin Valley, Lake Chelan, and other mountain peaks within the North Cascades National Park.

If you still want something else to do outside, consider going for a bike ride. You can haul your own bicycle to Stehekin by boat or rent one during the summer from Discovery Bikes (www.stehekindiscoverybikes.com). This business has over 80 different bikes available for rent from their shop near the landing and at the Stehekin

Valley Ranch. Trailer bikes and sit-in trailers for children are also available. Bike helmets are provided free of charge.

One leisurely bike ride takes you from the landing towards Rainbow Falls (a spectacular 312-foot waterfall). Follow this with a stop at the Stehekin Bakery for a pastry, lunch, or ice cream before heading back. If you really want a workout, pedal the entire length of the Stehekin Valley Road from the landing to its end a mile past the Tumwater Campground. The round-trip journey is almost 26 miles. Discovery Bikes also offers a Ranch Breakfast Ride where you are ferried up to Stehekin Valley Ranch for breakfast before cycling at your own pace 8.6 miles back to the landing.

Getting There: See above.

STEHEKIN VALLEY RANCH & STEHEKIN OUTFITTERS

P.O. Box 36, Stehekin, WA 98852 / 800-536-0745
www.stehekin.biz

Lodging Prices: $$ Adventure Pricing: $ to $$

Take a trip to the Courtney family's Stehekin Valley Ranch and you'll get a unique outdoor vacation with lots of activities to choose from. You can hike, bike, raft, kayak, or go horseback riding. Or, you can simply eat, sleep, and relax in the Cascade Mountains. Whatever you decide to do, you'll likely come away satisfied.

The ranch lies along the Stehekin Valley Road – the main arterial that runs from Stehekin Landing through the Lake Chelan National Recreation Area and a short distance into the South Unit of the North Cascades National Park. Your first step in getting to the ranch is to take a boat or float plane from Chelan to the Stehekin Landing. From there, you can take a free shuttle bus or bicycle 8.6 miles to the ranch. Alternatively, you can make your way to the ranch on foot from the nearby Pacific Crest Trail.

The 23-acre Stehekin Valley Ranch is pleasant in more ways than one. There are seven cabins that each sleeps four to six guests. All have clean, comfortable furnishings, pine interiors, electricity, and private bathrooms. There are also seven canvas-topped tent cabins. Sleeping two to four people each, they all have comfy beds, screen windows to let in a mountain breeze, and kerosene lanterns. Bathrooms and showers are located a few steps away in the main lodge.

Guests congregate in the lodge's dining room where three hearty meals are served daily. You eat your food at one of the three 16-foot picnic tables crafted out of Douglas fir. A stoked fire keeps coffee and tea water hot. A sawdust floor and lots of windows looking out towards feeding horses in the pasture complete the ranch ambiance. Upstairs from the dining room is a small library with board games, puzzles, and books ranging from the works of Zane Gray to Audubon Society field guides.

While you may be content to just relax at this wilderness ranch, you should not overlook all the things you can do here. Owner Clifford Courtney describes many of these activities as a series of "Back by Dinner" adventures. One of them is a 9-mile guided rafting trip down the glacial-tinged waters of the Stehekin River. Departing from the ranch at 2:30pm, the three-hour ride takes you through Class II and III whitewater rapids and gets you back to the ranch in time for supper.

If you like your time on the water to be a little more contemplative, you can book a two-hour guided kayak trip. These excursions take place in single and tandem kayaks at the headwaters of Lake Chelan and are suitable for children and novice adult paddlers. One of the highlights of this tour is the chance to view Indian pictographs on the "painted rocks" across the lake from the Stehekin Landing.

Another guided adventure departs from the corral at the ranch. Stehekin Outfitters offers private riding lessons and horseback rides every morning. If you book the guided three-hour ride you'll head to Coon Lake – pretty alpine water that sits at the base of Mt. McGregor. Your steed will be one of the Courtney's Norwegian fjord horses. With a short stocky build and even temperament, they're great for pack trips and riding lessons with children. No riding experience is needed to take part in one of these horse rides, but the small stature of these horses dictates a maximum weight of 200 pounds for riders. Young children are welcome to take a riding lesson at the corral but have to be at least 8 years old to go on a trail ride.

If you are a hunter, Stehekin Outfitters can pack you into three different drop camps for deer and bear hunting in late September during the high hunt season. They also offer base-camp-supported adventures in the summer. Hikers and anglers walk or ride into the Bridge Creek or Cottonwood Campground. From there, you can explore the North Cascades National Park on a series of day hikes and come back every night to a canvas tent, woodstove, cot with sleeping bag, basic food, and a propane stove to cook it on.

Hiking is possible on a number of other trails in the area, and bicycling is also popular along the Stehekin Valley Road. If you didn't bring your own bike, you can rent one at the ranch. Wildlife sightings are frequent. Deer and bear are among the larger animals you may see and birds like colorful yellow and black evening grosbeak gather near the main lodge.

The Stehekin Valley Ranch is open from the first of June through the first week of October. Stehekin Outfitters offers kayaking tours and horseback riding until the end of September. Whitewater rafting is generally available through early August. Contact the ranch in advance to reserve a cabin or an excursion.

Getting There: See above.

Rainy Pass and Hart's Pass

Okanogan-Wenatchee National Forest - Methow Ranger District
24 West Chewuch, Winthrop, WA 98862 / 509-996-4000
www.fs.fed.us/r6/oka

Lodging Prices

Two high mountain passes in the Northern Cascades are great places to begin wilderness expeditions by foot or horseback. The first, Rainy Pass, is easy enough to get to. Simply drive along State Highway 20 from Winthrop in the east or Burlington/Mt. Vernon in the west. You'll reach the pass, at an elevation of 4,855 feet, east of the North Cascades National Park.

Pull into the large parking lot, unload your horses (or lace up your boots) and hit the trail. The primary path from here is the Pacific Crest Trail, which runs south into the national park and north 31 miles to Hart's Pass. If you just want an easy day hike, take off towards Rainy Lake. The trailhead is on the south side of the highway. A level, paved wheelchair accessible trail goes south a mile, ending at the north end of Rainy Lake. Once there you can have a snack and take in the views of the lake and Frisco Mountain. Another lake hike possible from this same trailhead leads to Lake Ann. Start on the trail to Rainy Lake and after a short distance take off on the trail towards 19-acre Lake Ann. You'll reach this alpine water after a 2-mile hike. Both Rainy Lake and Lake Ann have cutthroat trout in them, just in case you decide to bring your fishing rod. Horses are not allowed along the trails to Lake Ann and Rainy Lake.

Farther north, Hart's Pass provides another high-elevation starting point to explore the Cascades. To get there, take the Lost River Road west from Mazama. As you continue west the pavement ends and becomes the Hart's Pass Road, a gravel affair that follows a safe, but steep and narrow path uphill. The only trailers allowed on the road are horse trailers. After an hour or so of driving, you'll reach Hart's Pass, some 20 miles from Mazama. You

can stake out a tent at one of the five sites at the Hart's Pass Campground or at the nearby Meadows Campground, where 14 sites are available. These are basic camping areas, with no water and no garbage service.

The road continues on from the Pass for 3 miles. After a mile and a half, you'll reach a parking lot to access the Pacific Crest Trail and the end of the road brings you to Slate Peak where you can get out and hike a steep 0.25 mile to a sometimes-manned fire lookout.

There is a lot of hiking and horseback riding to be done around here. One trip takes off south from the Meadows Campground to Grasshopper Pass. Thanks to your starting point, it's a relatively easy excursion with little elevation gain. After 2 miles, you'll reach Tatie Peak. Continue on for another 3 miles and you'll get to see the expansive meadows around Grasshopper Pass. Turn around and head back to camp for a well-earned rest after this 10-mile jaunt.

A more difficult trail starts off the road between Hart's Pass and Slate Peak. It goes north from there into the mammoth 530,000-acre Pasayten Wilderness Area to Buckskin Lake. Along the way you'll spend a fair amount of time going up and down and have the chance to stop at Silver Lake near the 3-mile mark. Buckskin Lake, a narrow body of water at the base of a talus slope, has several primitive campsites. Both Buckskin Lake and Silver Lake have trout in them, the Buckskin trout reportedly being larger than the fish at Silver Lake.

Finally, if you are looking for a backpacking trip or more extended ride, follow the Pacific Crest Trail 39 miles into Canada's Manning Provincial Park. The trail starts at the Hart's Pass Guard Station (6,800 feet above sea level) and follows rugged terrain from there. On the way to Canada, you'll pass over five different mountain passes, hike past a number of peaks, and finally descend into Canada. You should bring your passport, though the chances of encountering a customs official on the trail range from slim to none. However, if you get picked up in Canada and want to drive back across the border you will need a passport, or enhanced driver's license and an entry application. You can copy the latter document off the Forest Service's website, mail it in, and upon receipt keep it with you. Look for the application in the trails section of the Methow Ranger District portion of the Forest Service website or give the ranger district office a call.

If you don't want to go all the way to Canada, you can hang a left at Holman Pass and travel west over Deception and Devil's Passes, covering lots of ridges and side slopes in the process, until you drop down to the eastern bank of Ross Lake. The total mileage for this trip is 17.6. At Ross Lake, you can turn around, head uplake, or go south towards Highway 20. You will need a backcountry permit if you plan on camping in the Ross Lake National Recreation Area and you'll want to check with the North Cascades National Park about stock restrictions.

As you might imagine, there is a fair amount of wildlife in this region. Deer are a common sight along the roads to Rainy and Hart's Passes and in this high country, you've got a good chance to see mountain goats while you're on the trail. Pikas, marmots, and other denizens of the high country can also be viewed. If you're lucky, you might even get to see a wolverine. This part of the North Cascades is one of the few places these rare mammals have been seen in recent years. Other rare animals thought to be in this mainly roadless area include bears (definitely black bears – and suspected grizzly bears), lynx, cougar, and perhaps even gray wolves. On the birding side, you can expect to see pine grosbeak, sparrows, grouse, and a number of raptors to include eagles and red-tailed hawks that soar in the thermal currents around Slate Peak and Hart's Pass.

The trails in this rugged high country are often snow covered into early July. Be sure to check trail conditions before heading afield.

Getting There: Both Rainy Pass and Hart's Pass are located in the North Cascades west of Mazama. See above for further details.

The North Cascades Lodge is a great base camp for outdoor adventure.

NORTH CASCADES LODGE

255 Lost River Road, Mazama, WA 98833 / 1-866-617-8632
www.northcascadeslodge.com

Lodging Prices: $$ to $$$ Adventure Pricing: N/A

Coming from the west, the tiny community of Mazama is the first bit of civilization you'll see after crossing the North Cascades on State Highway 20. It's a great place to go for a wide variety of outdoor activities to include cross-country skiing and snowshoeing in the winter and for hiking, bicycling, rock climbing, and wildlife watching in the summer.

The North Cascades Lodge is an excellent place to stay while enjoying any of these activities. Located less than 2 miles from Mazama on Lost River Road, the inviting main lodge has lots of large windows that look out over the lawn (or snow) and woods. Inside are six guest rooms, each sleeping two to four people. Two sun rooms offer a place to gaze outdoors and a living room has comfy chairs and a television with lots of movies to watch if you're in the mood to do so. The dining room is a great place to congregate at meal time, and a sunken room surrounding a woodstove is ideal for warming up after some time in the snow. Another amenity worth mentioning is the hot tub at the lodge; a great place to soak after a long day on the trails. Finally, there are four shared bathrooms in the three-story building and Wi-Fi Internet service if you need to catch up on the news from home.

In the summer, the lodge operates as a bed and breakfast. Breakfast usually includes waffles, pancakes, fruit, pastries, juice, and a great brand of specialty coffee from Whidbey Island. In the winter, guests are fed three meals a day. The dinners are especially tasty. Butternut squash soup is a favorite of many while salmon and pork tenderloin are regular meal entrées. If you would rather cook for yourself and want a little more privacy, there is a cabin you can rent that sleeps up to seven with two bedrooms and two bathrooms. The lodge also hosts reunions and other group events, providing guests three meals a day and the use of the entire property.

It's tempting to spend the day inside, but the 22 acres surrounding the lodge are worth exploring. A pond near the lodge is stocked with hefty rainbow and brown trout that the kids are encouraged to catch and release. Trails used by snowshoers, birdwatchers, and hikers go past several more beaver ponds under a canopy of fir trees, cedar, birch, and cottonwood.

The wildlife viewing is superior. Both mule and white-tailed deer graze around the lodge, Douglas squirrels chatter from the trees, and you may see other mammals like snowshoe hares, black bear, and perhaps even a lynx. Bird watching is so good that this spot is listed on the Washington Audubon Society's Great Birding Trail. Some 39 different species of birds have been seen here, to include colorful western tanager and

American goldfinch as well great horned owls, blue grouse, rufuos hummingbirds, and several different types of warblers.

The most popular trail on the property runs right next to the lodge. Follow it and within five minutes you'll find yourself on a bank of the Methow River. Its part of the larger Methow Valley Sports Trail Association (MVSTA) trail system, a 124-mile set of trails that links the lodge, Mazama, Winthrop, and Sun Mountain Lodge (see the MVSTA entry for further details). In the summer, it's used by mountain bikers, hikers, and trail runners. In the winter cross-country skiers use the groomed trail. Many of the skiers stop off at the Cedar Creek Café that's located in the basement of the lodge. It's open to the public during the winter, serving hot drinks and pastries that warm the soul and fuel the body (or at least give you a reason to take a break for awhile).

Rock climbers are other guests you may run into at the lodge. The popular Fun Rock is a sport climbing spot less than half a mile away. The steep walls of the Goat Wall are more challenging and serve as a scenic backdrop to the lodge that beckons to climbing devotees. If you are just getting into the sport you might want to give North Cascades Mountain Guides a call (509-996-3194 – www.ncmountainguides. com). Located in Mazama, they offer courses and guided trips into the rocks and mountainous crags of the North Cascades.

You can also fish and hike off the lodge property. Anglers head downstream to open waters on the Methow near Winthrop for trout during the summer or head up to alpine waters off of State Highway 20. One such place is Cutthroat Lake near Washington Pass, where trout can be caught after an easy hike of just over 2 miles. Closer to Mazama, a 2-mile walk to Cedar Creek Falls is a nice destination on a summer day. If you want more of a challenge, you can head back towards Mazama and follow the road towards Goat Peak. At the end of the road you'll have yet another 2-mile hike. This one is steep in places, but once you reach the top you'll find one of the few manned fire lookouts left in Washington.

The North Cascades Lodge is open all year except for the months of April and November. Reservations, well in advance, are needed to secure a stay during the winter.

Getting There: Take State Highway 20 west from Winthrop or east from Burlington/ Mt. Vernon to Mazama (this latter route over Washington Pass is closed in the winter). Turn right towards the Mazama General Store and then turn left on Lost River Road. You'll reach the lodge in less than 2 miles.

DELI LLAMA WILDERNESS ADVENTURES

Bob and Mariann Shapiro
17045 Llama Lane, Bow, WA 98232 / 360-757-4212
www.delillama.com

Lodging Prices: Included in most adventures   Adventure Pricing: $$ to $$$

In today's outdoor business landscape, you'll find a number of reputable outfitters using horses in Washington, but you'll be hard pressed to find many llama outfitters that are still around. The concept of trekking into the wilderness with llamas was popular a decade ago, but the novelty has faded in recent years. Fortunately, Bob and Mariann Shapiro's Deli Llama Wilderness Adventures continues to offer llama pack trips into the North Cascades.

Bob started this business in 1984 after becoming intrigued with these South American animals that were originally used by the Incas to haul supplies in Peru's Andes Mountains. Today, he uses up to 8 llamas at a time on his packing trips. The llamas can carry 70 pounds each, to include tents, food, and other items that Shapiro brings along for you. As a guest, the only things you really have to bring are clothes and a sleeping bag. The ability to walk unencumbered while the llamas carry your gear makes a 6- to 9-mile hike a much more pleasurable experience.

That brings up another subject. The name Deli Llama is not just a play on words. On a typical expedition with the Shapiros, you'll get to enjoy some exquisite meals. Asian, Indian, North African, and Middle Eastern dishes are all offered as part of a unique culinary menu. Trip sizes generally range from six to ten people and most of these are custom trips where groups contact Shapiro and arrange dates and itineraries in advance. If a group is interested in wildflowers or wildlife watching, the expedition will accommodate those interests, whereas a group wanting to fish alpine lakes will trek along a route that hits several of these waters.

The trip calendar starts in April with single-day conditioning hikes and clinics that take place at Chuckanut Mountain near Bellingham. For around $75 you can learn about the llamas, go for a walk, and enjoy a nice lunch. In May, Deli Llama Wilderness Adventures offers three-day early-bird specials. These trips generally take place in the lower elevations of the North Cascades National Park. With the arrival of summer, you'll find the route map expanding into the Pasayten Wilderness Area, a scenic favorite of Shapiros. This area is best explored in July and August so if you want to hit the mountains in June or September, you will probably head into North Cascades National Park.

Summertime expeditions are typically four to seven days long. If you want you can travel to a single base camp and strike out on your own from there for days full of hiking or fishing. However, Shapiro encourages you to pick up and move camp every day or two. This nomadic existence allows you to sample more of the wilderness and spend more time on the trail with some very unique animals.

Although the vast majority of trips take place in the North Cascades, Deli Llama Wilderness Adventures also has a permit to operate within Olympic National Park. If you are interested in a trip to the Olympic Peninsula, especially in June or in the fall, give the Shapiros a call.

Getting There: Destinations vary.

Who wouldn't want to spend time on the trail with a llama?

Lake Wenatchee

Lake Wenatchee State Park
21588A State Route 207, Leavenworth, WA 98826 / 509-763-3101
www.parks.wa.gov

Lodging Prices

With a backdrop of pine forest and mountains, 5-mile-long Lake Wenatchee is a great destination if you are looking for easy access to good camping opportunities, lots of outdoor recreation possibilities, and sunny skies that are far more common in eastern Washington than on the west side of the state.

The main magnet is Lake Wenatchee State Park, a 489-acre property that fronts 12,613 feet of water at the southeastern end of the lake. The park is divided by the Wenatchee River that originates here. On the north side of the river is a quiet camping area with 97 hook-up sites for RVs and several hiking trails that run along the river, lake, and through the woods. The heart of the park is on the south side of the Wenatchee River. In addition to 100 campsites (with no hook-ups), there is a good boat launch and a large beach with a swimming area that gets crowded in the summer. There is also a camp store, a playground, and an amphitheatre where several programs are offered in the summer. Near the park's entrance is a horse stable operated by Icicle Outfitters. During the summer you can drop in and go for a trail ride lasting anywhere from an hour to all day (see their entry in this book for more details). Lake Wenatchee State Park is open all year, though utility hook ups are not available in the winter.

If the state park is full, you may want to see if a campsite is available at the adjacent Nason Creek Campground. With 73 sites, this Forest Service property along Nason Creek is a good option, as is Glacier View, a small but popular US Forest Service campground at the southwestern end of the lake. There is a day-use area next to the water, a rough boat launch, and 23 overnight sites, though many are not suitable for RVs.

A very short and easy hike of note takes off from Glacier View Campground and also from a nearby trailhead. The hike goes uphill to Hidden Lake which is less than a mile from either point. When you get there you'll be able to enjoy a small, scenic body of water that is great for dipping your toes, going for a cool summer swim, or watching small brook trout gulp down flies from the surface. With little elevation gain, it's a wonderful opportunity to introduce someone to the beauty of an alpine lake, without the workout that usually goes into getting to most of these mountain jewels.

There are lots of other hiking options in this region. Roads take off from the Lake Wenatchee River towards the Napeequa, White, and Little Wenatchee Rivers west of the lake, and another road runs along the Chiwawa River. One of the more popular hikes is the 11-mile Indian Creek Trail that takes off at the end of the White River Road (past the White River Falls Campground) and links up with the Pacific Crest Trail. The well traveled 3.5-mile trail to Heather Lake is a good day-hiking destination that takes off from Forest Service Road 400 (which connects to the Little Wenatchee Road) and the Lower Chiwawa ORV Trail is a multi-use trail above the Chiwawa River that is known as an easy 11.3-mile route for bicyclists, hikers, and horseback riders alike.

There are several small Forest Service campgrounds along these roads, and wildlife encounters with mammals like black-tailed deer, black bear, coyote, squirrels, and chipmunks are common. This region is also known as a good place to bag a bear or a high mountain buck in the fall.

Angling opportunities, on the other hand, are limited. Most of the rivers are closed to fishing, casualties of the Endangered Species Act that listed bull trout and salmon in this area as protected over a decade ago. There are a few cutthroat trout you may catch in 2,445-acre Lake Wenatchee, but the only time this place gets a lot of action is when enough sockeye salmon return to spawn. This fishery historically occurs every four years or so from late July into August. A better bet is to head to Fish Lake, which has good fishing for perch, bass, and trout all year long. A private resort on the 500-acre plus lake has a boat launch, rentals, a fishing dock, and campsites along with rustic cabins to stay in.

Lake Wenatchee is also a good winter destination, thanks to over 8 miles of groomed cross-country skiing trails within the state park. These trails connect to an additional 5 miles of skiing and snowshoeing trails at nearby Kahler Glen Golf and Ski Resort (800-440-2994 – www.kahlerglen.com). More Nordic opportunities are available at the Chiwawa Sno-Park with three skiing trails (one of which is groomed) covering 9.5 more miles. This Sno-Park is located 1.4 miles away from the state park on the Chiwawa Loop Road.

Getting There: Take US Highway 2 from Monroe or Wenatchee to Coles Corner. Turn north on State Highway 207. Travel north for 3.5 miles and turn left on Cedar Brae Road to reach the State Park.

ICICLE OUTFITTERS

Icicle Outfitters & Guides, Inc.
P.O. Box 322, Leavenworth, WA 98826 – 800-497-3912
www.icicleoutfitters.com

Lodging Prices: Included in some adventures   Adventure Pricing: $ to $$$$

Saddle up and ride into the Cascade Mountains for a few days. That's one popular way to spend some time with Icicle Outfitters. The Wick family has operated this business since 1983, introducing a slew of kids and adults to the joys of horseback riding near Leavenworth.

In the summer, Icicle Outfitters operates stables just outside of Lake Wenatchee State Park and the Leavenworth Fish Hatchery. Guides will take you on trail rides lasting anywhere from an hour to all day on gentle horses that seem so unperturbed by any distractions that some riders have deemed them "bomb proof".

You can also sign up for a multi-day pack trip into the Entiat Mountain Range, an offshoot of the Cascades. The "Family Pack Trip" is a great bonding experience for parents and their children, the "Three Lookouts in Four Days" and "Ride to the Sky" trips takes you to panoramic vistas on horseback, and "Four Lakes in Four Days" is an alpine angler's dream come true. All of these trips are guided and feature evening campfires, tasty Dutch oven cooking, cowboy poetry, plenty of wildlife viewing, and a restful night's sleep in a backcountry campsite. Other options include hiring a wrangler or guide for a custom trip where you hike in with the horses carrying your supplies, ride in to a drop camp, or enjoy a deluxe pack trip where a wrangler attends to your camp and pack needs.

As fall arrives, you can join Icicle Outfitter's on their Outfitter's Horse Drive as they move 50 horses to their Entiat Valley Ranch. This is also the time of year that hunting gets a lot of attention. Deer, elk, and bear hunters can hook up with Icicle Outfitters for a guided or non-guided hunt. The staff will also handle a drop camp for you – packing your gear in and packing you and your game out with horses at a prearranged time.

The outdoor experience continues into the winter with sleigh rides that take place near the Leavenworth Fish Hatchery from December through February. These 30-minute rides along the Icicle River take place against the backdrop of the snow-covered Enchantment Mountains. Start off the trip with a cup of hot spiced cider or hot chocolate from the wrangler's tent before cozying up in a blanket and going for a ride along a 1.5-mile snow covered trail. It's a great way to enjoy the winter or holiday season before heading into nearby Bavarian-themed Leavenworth for shopping and dining.

Getting There: The Lake Wenatchee stables are at the state park off of State Highway 207. The Leavenworth stables are located west of town next to the fish hatchery off of Icicle Road.

Alpine Lakes Wilderness

Okanogan – Wenatchee National Forest
215 Melody Lane, Wenatchee, WA 98801 / 509-664-9200
www.fs.fed.us/r6/wenatchee/

Mt. Baker – Snoqualmie National Forest
2930 Westmore Avenue, Everett, WA 98201 / 425-783-6000
www.fs.fed.us/r6/mbs

Lodging Pricing

Established in 1976, the 362,789-acre Alpine Lakes Wilderness Area boasts some 700 lakes, tarns, and ponds in the Cascade Mountains between Stevens Pass and Snoqualmie Pass. It's easy to get into this region of high mountain peaks, lakes, and conifer forests. The crowded parking lots at trailheads leading into the wilderness area attest to the love people have for this beautiful part of the Cascades. In fact, there are good arguments to be made that the enthusiastic crowds flocking here every summer may be giving it a little too much love.

In an effort to keep the fragile environment of this ecosystem healthy, several restrictions have been put into place. Parties are limited to 12, and if you are bringing in stock, that includes the animals. Campfires are discouraged and are not allowed over 5,000 feet above sea level on the east side of the Cascade Crest and over 4,000 feet on the west side. Stock is limited to certain trails while dogs are not allowed in the Enchantment Peaks portion of the wilderness area and must be kept on a leash on several other trails.

You'll need to display a Northwest Forest Pass at almost all of the 47 trailheads that access the Alpine Lakes, and you must also fill out a wilderness permit at these trailheads as well between June 15 and October 15. These permits are free with the exception of overnight permits for the popular Enchantments near Leavenworth, which cost $5 per person, per day.

Most of the Enchantment area permits are issued shortly after March 1 to people who put in their reservation requests ahead of this date. A few more are available every morning except for Sundays between June 15 and October 15 at the ranger station in Leavenworth (509-548-6977 for more information).

Despite the restrictions, the Alpine Lakes is considered a jewel of the Cascades. There are 615 miles of trails within the Wilderness Area, and on a typical hike you'll pass by small lakes, rushing creeks, and through forests of Douglas fir, cedar, hemlock, and larch trees. A fall hike into the wilderness is worthwhile just to see the larches as their needles turn from green to gold. The color allows them to stand out in a spectacular fashion around the rocky shorelines of pristine lakes. Wildlife includes deer, hoary marmot, black bear, the rare cougar or bobcat, and in higher elevations, mountain goats. Smaller animals like chipmunks and gray jays (also known as camp robbers) will boldly approach for a handout or a chance to steal any food you might have left unattended.

A cutthroat trout caught and released in the Alpine Lakes Wilderness Area.

Within this hiker's paradise are several "can't-miss" hikes. One of them is along the 67-mile stretch of the Pacific Crest Trail that runs between Stevens and Snoqualmie Pass. Another is a 15-mile loop hike at the head of the Cle Elum River that takes in the Hyas Lakes, Deception Pass, Cathedral Rock, and Squaw Lake. An ascent into the high-mountain lakes and tarns of the Enchantments south of Icicle Creek is a tough but also a rewarding experience. All of these multi-day journeys can be broken down into smaller pieces for day hikes or short overnight trips. One easy example is the 2.75-mile hike to Hyas and Little Hyas Lake at the end of the Salmon la Sac Road. Another day-hiking choice can be found in the moderate 4-plus-mile walks to Colchuck Lake or Lake Stuart south of Icicle Creek. Other popular hikes, closer to Seattle, are possible from trailheads off of Interstate 90 and US Highway 2 west of Snoqualmie and Stevens Pass.

If you like to fish, take along a rod and reel. Many of the wilderness area's lakes and streams have fish in them. These are primarily cutthroat and rainbow trout though the occasional brook and rare golden trout are also found here. Most of these waters receive little angling pressure and casting a fly or a spinner are both reliable ways to hook into pan-sized fish or the occasional one up to 17 inches long.

Climbers also find much to like in this Wilderness Area. Dragontail Peak, Mt. Stuart (Washington's 2nd tallest non-volcanic peak) and Prusik Peak are three prominent, granite-walled destinations southwest of Leavenworth while 7,960-foot Mt. Daniel, the highest peak of both King and Kittitas Counties, beckons from a trailhead at the end of Salmon la Sac Road northwest of Cle Elum. The granite peaks near Leavenworth require a significant amount of climbing experience to safely summit while Mt. Daniel can be ascended after a glacier traverse of moderate difficulty and some rock scrambling.

Primitive camp sites abound within the alpine lakes, so please don't make any new ones that may further damage the delicate surroundings. This being a wilderness area, no motorized travel is allowed within its boundaries.

Getting There: There are a number of ways to get into the Alpine Lakes Wilderness but accessing the Pacific Crest Trail off US Highway 2 at Stevens Pass or from Interstate 90 at Snoqualmie Pass are two of the main ones. Other access points can be found off Exit 47 on Interstate 90 west of Snoqualmie Pass; from Salmon la Sac Road east of Snoqualmie Pass; or by following the Icicle River Road south from US Highway 2 at Leavenworth.

OSPREY RAFTING

9342 Icicle Road, Leavenworth, WA 98826 / 800-743-6269
www.shoottherapids.com

Lodging Prices: N/A   Adventure Pricing: $ to $$

The Wenatchee River may be the most popular whitewater rafting destination in Washington. Boasting challenging Class III rapids, sunny skies, and great scenery, it's no wonder a slew of rafting outfitters choose to take their clients downstream from Leavenworth to Cashmere every spring and summer. A typical trip takes you on a whitewater journey that begins beside pine forests, continues along fruit orchards, and finishes below sage-covered hills.

Osprey Rafting Company is located in Leavenworth and calls the Wenatchee River home. They offer half-day trips called "The Main Event" down the most popular section of the river for reasonable prices with fun loving, experienced guides. No experience is necessary to climb on board and start paddling under their direction through Class II and III rapids.

If you really want to get your blood pressure ratcheted up, sign up for the "High Adventure" trip that starts off on the Class IV rapids of the Wenatchee at Tenley Falls before following the "Main Event" route to Cashmere. Prior experience is required for this trip. Another option is a two-hour family float through Class I and II waters on the Wenatchee or a scenic nature float down the Icicle River. Deer, salmon, osprey, kingfishers, and other wildlife can be seen on this hour-long float along the quiet waters of this small stream.

If whitewater kayaking is of interest, Osprey Rafting has several different courses of instruction that take place on the Wenatchee River. They also offer late summer tours in inflatable kayaks down the Wenatchee.

In September, Osprey Rafting moves south to the Tieton River. At this time of year water is released from Rimrock Dam, turning the Tieton into a great Class III whitewater destination for a few short weeks. You can book this as a day trip or let the staff assist you in arranging an overnight stay.

Come winter, Osprey Rafting puts the paddles away and opens up their ski shop. You can rent cross-country skis or snowshoes and explore 16 miles of groomed trails maintained by the Leavenworth Winter Sports Club at three nearby locations. One of them is next to the Leavenworth Fish Hatchery, where you can ski or snowshoe on level terrain next to the Icicle River. Another location is the Leavenworth Ski Hill, offering more varied terrain and 3 miles of lighted trails for night Nordic skiing. Finally, you can snowshoe or ski less than a mile away from the ski shop at the Leavenworth Golf Course and Enchantment Park along the Wenatchee River. Check out the Leavenworth Winter Sports Club website for more information about the trails and obtaining trail passes (www.skileavenworth.com).

Getting There: Take US Highway 2 from Wenatchee or Everett to Leavenworth. Osprey Rafting (and Ski Shop) is located at the corner of Highway 2 and Icicle Road at the west end of town.

Rafting the Wenatchee River – Photo courtesy Ryan Schmitten, Osprey Rafting.

SCOTTISH LAKES HIGH CAMP

High Country Adventures
P.O. Box 2036, Leavenworth, WA 98826 / 509-763-3044
www.scottishlakes.com

Lodging Prices: $$ Adventure Pricing: Included with Lodging

Whether you are a hiker, mountain biker, or cross-country skier, you'll appreciate the rustic luxury of the Scottish Lakes High Camp. Perched at 5,000 feet along the northern edge of the Alpine Lakes Wilderness, High Camp consists of several cabins in the woods that surround a bright and cheery day lodge. There is no electricity at this backcountry camp. However, each cabin has propane wall lamps for light, wood stoves to keep you warm, and propane stoves for cooking. Other amenities at the camp include a wood-fired sauna and hot tub that sits under the stars (great at the end of a strenuous day outdoors) as well as a large campfire pit popular during the hiking season. The cabins house from one to ten people. You can bring your own sleeping bag or ask for bedding when you reserve your stay.

Scottish Lake High Camp opens in August for hikers wishing to explore the nearby Scottish Lakes. With names like Lake Julius, Lake Ethel, Loch Eileen, and Lake McDonald, it's easy to see how this camp got its name. All of these destinations lie within the Alpine Lakes Wilderness Area and are easy day hikes from the camp. Each lake offers fishing for cutthroat trout, and nearby Chiwaukum Lake offers anglers a chance at brook trout as well. The scenery at these lakes and within the wilderness is spectacular, particularly in the fall when the larch trees that grow among the pines turn a beautiful shade of gold.

High Camp is also a great destination if you enjoy pedaling in the backcountry. There are several miles of improved trails to navigate that will appeal to cyclists of differing skill levels. You can't take a mountain bike into the wilderness area, but there are plenty of logging roads and recently improved single track trails that lead to ridgelines and viewpoints through forested terrain.

Despite the charms of autumn, winter is the main reason this camp is around. Cross-country skiers and snowshoers have been coming here for years and for good reason. The owners maintain a 35-mile winter trail system that appeals to skiers of all abilities. Backcountry snowboarders have discovered High Camp too, as have families who enjoy sledding on the hill right outside the day lodge.

Getting to Scottish Lakes High Camp is an adventure unto itself. In the summer, four-wheel-drive vehicles take you from a secure parking lot to the camp, located 8.5 miles up a private road. In the winter, you are driven halfway up the road before transferring to snowmobiles, completing the shuttle trip to your cabin in a unique fashion.

The winter season generally runs from early December through mid-April, depending on snow. The fall hiking season goes from August through mid-October. Reservations are recommended well in advance, especially for winter getaways.

Getting There: Take US Highway 2 to the Nason Creek Rest Area (located between Stevens Pass and Leavenworth). The fenced parking area and meeting point for the Scottish Lakes High Camp is directly across the highway.

Nordic skiing in the Cascades (photo courtesy Scottish Lakes High Camp).

HIGH COUNTRY OUTFITTERS AND CAMP WAHOO

1780 Nelson Siding Road, Cle Elum, WA 98922 / 888-235-0111
www.highcountry-outfitters.com

Lodging Prices: Included with some adventures   Adventure Pricing: $$ to $$$$

Want to give your child some memories that will last a lifetime? Then sign them up for a week long stay at Camp Wahoo, located along the appealing North Fork of the Teanaway River in the Okanogan-Wenatchee National Forest. The camp has been operated since 1982 by High Country Outfitters in partnership with the U.S. Forest Service. Children from 8 to 16 years old come on Sunday, choose a horse and ride every day until Friday. Over the course of the week, the kids will learn to saddle, pack, and care for the horses. They'll also practice a little archery, do a little roping, and even build shelters while learning about wilderness survival. The camp cook serves three meals a day and residents sleep in bunk beds within rustic canvas and wood cabins.

While High Country Outfitters keeps busy from mid-June until the end of August, they also manage to provide a variety of other horse-oriented services. From the middle of May through October, you can go into the Central Cascade Mountains on a variety of different rides. The shortest is the half-day ride, perfect for kids and beginners. Those willing to spend more time in the saddle may be interested in a full-day ride that includes a sack lunch. Finally, you can book a mini-overnight trip. Drive up to Camp Wahoo in the evening, sleep in one of the canvas cabins, and then enjoy a nice Dutch oven breakfast while wranglers get your horse ready. After your meal and a cup of coffee climb onto your horse and enjoy a full day in the saddle. This is a great option for parents who are picking up kids from Camp Wahoo, allowing you to spend a summer Friday and Saturday together. In addition to all of this, owner Stacy Sutton hosts several riding programs just for women. Check the company's website for more information.

High Country Outfitters also offers pack trips within the Cle Elum Ranger District. You can hike or ride in and let the mules haul in your supplies. If you want someone else to do the cooking and camp chores, you can hire a wrangler to stay with you for a few extra dollars. The drop camps remain popular into October as hunters (primarily after black-tailed deer) hire these outfitters to pack their gear in and out of the wilderness, along with (hopefully) some game as well.

Finally, expect to see some nice scenery like pine forests, clear running streams, flower-filled meadows, and stunning high vistas in this country. Wildlife is abundant as well. Deer, black bear, and Rocky Mountain elk all live in this area and within Camp Wahoo you'll get to see lots of chipmunks and a variety of song birds like robins, evening grosbeaks, and pine siskins.

The programs at Camp Wahoo are very popular and you'll want to register your child for a stay by early spring. The majority of trips operated by High Country Outfitters depart from Camp Wahoo. Advance reservations are required for both day and overnight trips.

Getting There: Take the South Cle-Elum Exit (Milepost 85) off of Interstate 90 and follow State Highway 970 towards Wenatchee. Shortly after crossing the Teanaway River take a left on Teanaway River Road. Follow this road for 12 miles until the pavement ends. Then follow a Forest Service Road along the North Fork of the Teanaway for 8 miles to Camp Wahoo.

Hitting the trail for a day ride.

Lake Easton
and Iron Horse State Park

P.O. Box 26, Easton, WA 98925 / 509-656-2586 or 509-656-2230
www.parks.wa.gov

Lodging Prices

If you're looking for an easy-to-reach outdoor getaway, Lake Easton State Park is one place you'll be interested in visiting throughout the year. It's just 16 miles from Snoqualmie Pass off of Interstate 90 and only 70 miles from downtown Seattle. The 516-acre park sits along the shores of Lake Easton at 2,250 feet. The elevation and trees ensure you don't get too warm during the summer and lots of snowfall in the winter provides additional opportunities for fun.

Lake Easton is a 1.5-mile-long reservoir that feeds the Yakima River. Drawn down at the end of September, it fills up again in mid-April, just in time for a fishing season that runs from the Saturday before Memorial Day through October 31. Fish are not stocked in the lake, but there is fair angling for both rainbow and brook trout. Park ranger Colleen Hawley reports the trout can reach impressive weights. In the summer of 2007, one lucky angler pulled a 5-pound rainbow out of the lake. The daily limit is two fish. Other trout fishing is possible in the Yakima River (catch and release only) or in the Easton Ponds off of Exit 71 on the north side of Interstate 90.

Kayaks, canoes, and row boats all do well on Lake Easton where only outboard motors of 10 horsepower or less are permitted. If you are out on the water, you'll probably get to see some of the bald eagles or osprey which nest near the lake. Pileated woodpecker, turkey vulture, little brown and big brown bats are some of the other species you'll see framed against the day (or night) sky. On shore elk, deer, black bear, squirrels, and chipmunks are all regularly seen residents.

The park has 95 tent sites in two loop areas and 45 utility sites with full hook ups for RVs. There are also two hiker/biker tent sites and a group site

accommodating up to 50 tent campers. At the lake is a boat launch with a small dock and a day-use area has an unguarded swimming beach, small playground, and picnic area. Four restroom buildings with showers are dispersed throughout the park.

Rangers put on a variety of interpretive programs in the summer. Some involve bike rides or walks along the 6.5 miles of trail that run through the park and around Lake Easton. All but a half mile of this trail system is accessible to bicyclists. In the winter, these same trails are used by cross-country skiers and believe it or not, dog sledders. A little over 3 miles of the trail near the lake and along the Yakima River are groomed on a regular basis when snow is on the ground.

Part of the groomed trail (used in the summer by hikers, equestrians, and bicyclists) is found on the south side of Lake Easton and is part of the Iron Horse State Park (509-656-2586). This park is different from most parks by being situated along an old 100-mile railroad line also known as the John Wayne Pioneer Trail. The length of the park runs from North Bend east to the Columbia River near Vantage. The wide gravel path is ideal for different user groups, and the gentle grade found along much of the route makes for easy traveling. One unique landmark is the tunnel that goes under Snoqualmie Pass. The 2.3-mile tunnel is navigable with flashlights, headlamps, or lanterns if you are not afraid of an extended walk, bike, or horse ride in the dark.

Unfortunately, this tunnel and several others along the trail were recently closed due to the danger of falling debris. It is not clear when they will open again to the public.

Portions of the Iron Horse State Park are groomed for cross-country skiing in the winter. This includes 1.3 kilometers of trail at the inlet of Lake Easton and 7.6 miles of trail from Hyak near Snoqualmie Pass south to Stampede Pass Road. Other groomed trails are found at Cabin Creek (Exit 63 off of Interstate 90) with 10 miles of groomed trails and Crystal Springs (Exit 62 off of Interstate 90) with 12.5 miles of groomed cross-country ski trails and an additional half-mile snowshoe route. A special sno-park permit is required to use these cross-country trails. They can be purchased at the park or online through the Washington State Parks website.

Lake Easton State Park is open all year. However, the camp sites all close towards the end of October and reopen (depending on snow melt) again in mid-April. Dry camping is available for RVs near the boat launch during the winter.

Getting There: The entrance to Lake Easton State Park is just south of Interstate 90 off Exit 70 between Cle Elum and Snoqualmie Pass. Iron Horse State Park can be accessed at numerous points off the interstate. See the Washington State Parks website for details.

Emily Wollebek and Alex Querin enjoy time with the horses during a family pack trip.

Chinook and White Pass Recreation

Okanogan-Wenatchee National Forest – Naches Ranger District
10237 US Highway 12, Naches, WA 98937 / 509-653-1400
www.fs.fed.us/r6/wenatchee

Lodging Prices

The forests, lakes, and streams along the east slope of the Cascades between US Highway 12 leading to White Pass and State Highway 410 to Chinook Pass provide a plethora of outdoor recreational opportunities. Much of the land lies within the William O. Douglas Wilderness. Highlights include two large reservoirs, several trout streams, lots of hiking, stock and cross-country skiing trails, a popular whitewater rafting river, and a cave worthy of exploration.

The cavern in question is Boulder Cave, located about 30 miles northwest of Naches off of State Highway 410. Three hundred and fifty feet long and 30 feet wide, it was formed some 25,000 years ago by the persistent flow of Devils Creek, a stream that still trickles through it today. To get there follow a gently sloping trail from the trailhead about 0.75 mile to the entrance of the cave. A rough path takes you through the dark cavern, and you'll want a flashlight and sturdy footwear to navigate through it. As you pick your way through the darkness and sometimes slippery rocks, keep your voices down and flashlights pointed ahead so you don't disturb the Pacific western big-eared bats that sometimes use this cave in the spring and summer. From November 1 until April 1, this cave is closed to accommodate the 50-some bats that do hibernate here during the winter. The trail to the cave and picnic area at its trailhead is maintained by a concessionaire who charges $5 to park there.

Another natural point of interest along the Chinook Pass Highway is found at Union Creek Falls, 18 miles west of Cliffdell. A half-mile trail leads to Union Creek. After you cross the stream you can work your way uphill to the top of the 70-foot lower falls or veer left on several rough trails to reach the base of this pretty waterfall.

Fishing is another worthwhile pursuit along the road to Chinook Pass. The Naches, Little Naches, Bumping, and American Rivers all offer fine angling from June through October for cutthroat and rainbow trout. The size of these streams and scenery around them, coupled with the large number of Forest Service campgrounds along these streams, make fishing trips here a pleasure. Throw in the fact that the trout average over 12 inches in some of these waters and you've got the makings of a minor angling nirvana. Selective regulations (lures or flies with single barbless hooks and no bait) are the norm here, and there are closures in certain areas, so be sure to check the fishing regulations beforehand. If you are more in the mood for lake fishing, launch a boat onto Bumping Reservoir. Trolling for kokanee can be decent in the summer, and you may also pick up a trout or two. The best fishing reportedly takes place at the upper end of the lake.

If you want to do some more hiking, there is a 4-mile (one-way) walk along the north side of Bumping Lake Reservoir offering good views of the lake. When you are done with your hike, you can settle in at one of the two Forest Service campgrounds along the reservoir. You can also engage in a 27-mile backpacking or horseback riding expedition along the Pacific Crest Trail from Chinook Pass to White Pass. Mid-July through August is the ideal time for this trek. Yet another hike or ride is possible between trails that link the Hells Crossing, Pleasant Valley, and Lodgepole campgrounds between Chinook Pass and the small community of Cliffdell. The 12-plus-mile trail system is worth mentioning because it is also a popular destination

Colorful evening grosbeaks and a pine siskin (lower right) forage at Camp Wahoo.

for cross-country skiers in the winter. Known as the Pleasant Valley Loop, these winter trails offer skiing options ranging from easy to difficult to match your personal skill and fitness level.

In addition to skiing, horseback riding, and hiking, there is also plenty of mountain biking in the Chinook Pass area. The Lost Creek Trail near Edgar Rock offers a challenging 3.2-mile uphill climb and the Little Bald Trail from the Halfway Flat Campground off of State Highway 410 takes you nearly 11 miles to the Little Bald Mountain Lookout for some awesome views. Both of these trails are within a ten minute drive of Cliffdell. The Gold Creek Trail starts at the end of Gold Creek Road and takes you along the Devil's Slide before accessing 4x4 roads along the Manastash Ridge that offer miles of biking opportunities.

There's also plenty of riding and hiking to do off US Highway 12 east of White Pass. Mountain bikers share the trail with other users for 10 miles along the Russell Ridge Trail System and along the Cow Canyon Trail that follows the Tieton River for 4 miles. Close to White Pass, you can hike the 12.9 mile White Pass Loop. Start at the White Pass Campground near the highway and head north. You'll visit a number of alpine waters along the way, to include Deer, Sand, Dumbbell, Cramer, and Dog Lakes. Most of these waters have trout in them and you'll be hard pressed to find another overnight hike with so many different lakes to explore.

If you don't want to hike for your fish, Dog Lake is located right off the highway and has a campground while Leech Lake (next to the White Pass Campground) is a flyfishing-only trout lake. Both Forest Service campgrounds can accommodate tents and small RVs. If you want additional fishing and camping, there are several private resorts along 2,500-acre Rimrock Reservoir, a popular kokanee fishing spot next to US Highway 12.

If you are a paddler, you can canoe or kayak Bumping and Rimrock Reservoirs. Most paddlers come to this area for rafting though, especially in September when water is released from Rimrock Reservoir, turning the Tieton River below it into one huge stretch of exciting Class III and IV whitewater. The turbulent waters should not be attempted by inexperienced rafters. Fortunately, there are several guide companies that have forest-service-issued permits to raft the Tieton. By going with one of these outfits, you'll be assured you are going with insured professionals who know the river well and have all the proper safety equipment and qualifications. One such company is Osprey Rafting, described elsewhere in this book.

All of these activities are complemented nicely by the wildlife viewing opportunities in this part of the state. From spring through fall, elk, deer, bear, raccoon, and other mammals are found throughout the woods and meadows here. In the fall, elk hunting is very popular both south and north of State Highway 410 and US Highway 12. General seasons for bow hunters take place in September, muzzleloaders give it a shot in early October, and late October to early November is when the general rifle season occurs for these big animals.

Getting There: Take US Highway 12 from Yakima or Morton to reach White Pass. Chinook Pass is bordered by Mt. Rainier National Park to the west and State Highway 410 runs east towards Naches and Yakima from there.

WHISTLIN' JACK LODGE

20800 State Route 410, Naches, WA 98937 / 800-827-2299
www.whistlinjacklodge.com

Lodging Prices: $$ to $$$$ Adventure Pricing: N/A

Taking its name from the moniker given to hoary marmots living in the nearby Cascade Mountains, Whistlin' Jack Lodge has been owned by the Williams family since 1957. This pleasant, well-run resort sits along the Naches River where anglers catch trout right in front of the main lodge. The facility has seven cottages and two bungalows set well apart from each other in a grassy, park-like setting. The relaxing, western-themed cottages sleep anywhere from four to eight and include living rooms, gas fireplaces, kitchens, decks, and hot tubs. A motel with eight units sits above the river and has a hot tub for guests staying there. There are no phones or televisions in the rooms though the staff will be happy to loan you a TV to play some loaner VCR movies. For most people though, the squirrels and chipmunks scampering across the grounds, tall pines bending in the breeze, and the sound of the running river provide more than enough to see and hear.

The main building houses a lobby full of impressive stuffed game animals, a gift shop, a lounge, and a full-service restaurant. The restaurant has a longstanding reputation for well-prepared food with several unique outdoor-themed dishes. Eggs Benedict and blueberry pancakes are favorite breakfast meals. Rainbow trout is served three times a day and dinner specialties include elk steak medallions in a cabernet sauce, seafood shipped from Alaska, and what owner Doug Williams calls "top drawer" quality steaks. Next to the lodge is a gas station with a delicatessen and convenience store.

There is a plethora of outdoor adventures to be had within 30 minutes of the resort. The closest opportunities allow you to explore Boulder Cave or hike to Edgar Rock, named after a frontier scout killed by Indians in the 1850s. A number of other hikes and mountain biking trips are available in the summer while winter visitors enjoy cross-country skiing. In addition to fishing from the resort, you can also catch trout from several nearby streams or cast a line into Bumping Reservoir where kokanee salmon fishing can be good. More details are available in the Chinook and White Pass Recreation entry.

Wildlife is abundant in the area, both for wildlife watchers and for big game hunters. In fact, the lodge is a favorite base camp for hunters in the fall. From September through November, elk, grouse, bear, and deer hunters come here in good numbers. The most popular game are bull elk, though hunting for all of the above species can be good within a 20-mile radius of the lodge. A soak in a hot tub and a good meal after a day of hunting the woods is a good way to recuperate. After hunting season, you can still view the wildlife. The Oak Creek Wildlife Area (described elsewhere in this book) is a short drive away and is a fantastic place to see large herds of elk and bighorn sheep in the winter.

The Whistlin' Jack Lodge is open 365 days a year. Pets are not allowed. Lodging reservations are recommended in the summer and during hunting season. It's also a good idea to call in advance for dinner reservations.

Getting There: Whistlin' Jack Lodge is located 35 miles west of Yakima. Follow US Highway 12 past Naches and then take State Highway 410 towards Chinook Pass. The lodge property is adjacent to the highway.

CHINOOK PASS OUTFITTERS

P.O. Box 1030, Naches, WA 98937 / 509-653-2633
www.chinookpass.com

Lodging Prices: Included with some adventures   Adventure Pricing: $ to $$$$

Paul Wilson's Chinook Pass Outfitters is an established company that sticks to the basics. In the summer, they operate in partnership with the U.S. Forest Service to take riders out on day and overnight trips into the Naches Ranger District of the Okanogan-Wenatchee National Forest, which includes the William O. Douglas and Norse Peak Wilderness Areas. Come fall, the focus shifts to hunters after elk and other big game animals.

Riding season starts on Memorial Day weekend and runs through Labor Day with a variety of day and overnight trips. First-time riders and families with kids as young as six may want to go for a one- or two-hour trail ride. Older kids (12 and up) and adults who are more comfortable on horseback can opt to spend up to six hours in the saddle on a day trip. If you want to camp out, the Outlaw Overnight ride may be the way to go. Very popular with families, you'll mount up and, in the words of Wilson, "Travel light as the outlaws did". Wooded trails lead to camp where wranglers will take care of the horses and dinner, serving up a meal that may feature ham or rib eye steaks. After your belly is full, you can enjoy the evening around a campfire before retiring to your tent or if you prefer, just sleep under the stars. In the morning, start your day with a cup of coffee or hot chocolate, fuel up with a hot breakfast, and then ride back to the trailhead, finishing up by 11:00am.

One nice thing about these rides is they don't all lead to the same destinations. With so much Forest Service land to explore, Wilson has the ability to cater the trip to meet your interests. First decide whether you go on a day ride, overnight trip, or hire Wilson to pack in your gear to a drop camp and pick you up a few days later. Then figure out what you want to do. You can go to a lake that's an ideal swimming hole or one that is known for good fishing. If you like hiking, you can ride to a base camp close to any number of trails and if wildlife or nature viewing is of interest, just say so – they can help you with that too.

September heralds the arrival of hunting season. There are huge trophy bull elk in this part of Washington, along with a good number of spike bulls. Other animals of hunting interest include black bear, black-tailed deer, and mountain goats. Chinook Pass Outfitters packs in – and out – a lot of drop camps until hunting season ends in November. You can have the mules and horses pack in your gear for camp, or enjoy a furnished drop camp from the outfitter that includes a canvas wall tent, tent stove, lanterns, and more. Another decision has to do with whether you ride in on a horse or hike in. The latter choice saves a little money and lets you do some last minute scouting along the way.

If you want to concentrate on hunting, reserve a deluxe camp. Unlike the drop camp where you are on your own, Chinook Pass Outfitters will furnish your food, tents, and gear and provide a cook to feed you three meals a day. If you haven't had time for preseason scouting you might want to engage the services of a guide as well. Not only will they look for your trophy before the hunt, but they'll also be with you to help bag him. If you pay the price for a guided hunt, Paul Wilson guarantees a ratio of one guide for every two hunters and strives to provide a one-to-one ratio whenever possible.

Getting There: Specific destinations vary. Most trips start close to State Highway 410 (the Chinook Pass Highway) west of Yakima and Naches.

Outfitter Paul Wilson saddles up a mule for a pack trip.

Mount Rainier National Park

Mount Rainier National Park
Ashford, WA 98304 / 360-569-2211
www.nps.gov/mora

Lodging Prices

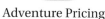

Adventure Pricing

Serving as a beautiful backdrop to the Seattle-Tacoma region, Mt. Rainier towers 14,410 feet above sea level and is the site of the country's fifth national park, established in 1899. Known by early Native Americans as Tahoma, the mountain received its present name after British Captain George Vancouver sighted it during his explorations of the Pacific Northwest in 1792. Today, the busy 378-square-mile park averages two million visitors a year. Most of them come in the summer through the Nisqually Entrance at the southwest corner to drive the road to Paradise where they can check out the visitor center and take in the beautiful views of the summit. Other draws include ample hiking, wildlife viewing, and in the summer, the chance to see alpine fields full of colorful wildflowers. Fishing, horseback riding, and bicycling are possible on a limited basis. In the winter, Nordic skiing and snowshoeing are popular activities.

You don't have to come into the park's main entrance with the summertime masses. Several roads lead to less visited areas. You can get into the park's northwest corner through the Carbon River Entrance. From there, head towards the Ipsut Creek Campground or take the summer road to Mowich Lake, the park's largest standing body of water. If you are coming from the south, you can enter at the Stevens Canyon Entrance and hook up with roads connecting to the more traveled portions of the big park. Finally, the eastern side of the park can be accessed through the White River Entrance via Chinook Pass (State Highway 410). Many visitors coming this way head towards the Sunrise Visitor Center. At an elevation of 6,400 feet, Sunrise is as close as you'll come to the summit in a car. Of all of these entrances, only the Nisqually Entrance is open year round.

Travelers to Mt. Rainier National Park can choose among the five major campgrounds in the park, a number of backcountry campsites for hikers, or two historic lodges (check the National Park Inn and Paradise Inn entry in this book for details about this latter choice). Cougar Rock is the most popular spot to pitch a tent or park an RV. With 200 individual sites and five group camping sites, it sits in a prime location between Longmire and Paradise. Ohanepecosh Campground in the southeast corner of the park also offers lots of camp and RV sites, 205 of them in fact, but you may want to reserve a spot in advance if you are going to either place in the summer, especially during the weekend (log onto www.nps.gov./mora/recreation/camping.htm for details). Both places also have ranger-led interpretive programs throughout the summer, nearby visitor or information centers, and hiking trails that start right at the campground. Other campgrounds can be found at White River (no hook-ups for RVs among 112 sites) in the eastern end of the park, Ipsut Creek near the Carbon River Entrance (also no RV hook-ups, 29 camp sites) and Mowich Lake (a walk-in campground with 30 campsites). A sixth campground at Sunshine Point is closed at this time due to flood damage.

There are numerous hiking trails in the park ranging from easy to strenuous. The longest hike in the park takes you along the Wonderland Trail, a 93-mile journey around Mt. Rainier. If you want to get an easy sample of this long distance trail, walk it as a day hike for a few miles from Longmire, or the Cougar Rock, White River, or Mowich Lake Campgrounds. If you are looking for a strenuous day hike, you can hike 4.5 miles from Paradise to Camp Muir, the 10,188-foot jumping-off point for climbers trying to reach the summit of Mt. Rainier. More moderate hikes in the Paradise and Longmire areas include the 5-mile Lakes Loop that starts at the Reflection Lakes or the 2.5-mile trek to Comet Falls from Christine Falls. An easy walk for the whole family is available on the Trail of Shadows, a 0.75-mile interpretive loop trail around Longmire Meadow directly across the road from the National Park Inn. Kids will love the up-close views of the bubbling mineral springs. If you don't want to work for a great view of a waterfall stop off at Narada Falls between Longmire and Paradise, where a short downhill path leads to a viewpoint made wet with spray from the cascading water.

Another easy summer walk can be had along the Nisqually Vista Trail. The 1.2-mile round-trip walk from the Paradise Visitors Center will give you great views of both the mountain and the wildflowers in the meadows. In fact, the subalpine meadows around Mount Rainier, especially around Paradise, are famous for the explosion of colorful wildflowers that erupt in July and August. White and yellow lilies along with heather, false hellebore, paintbrush, lupine, aster, and more make for a magnificent and natural painter's palette on a green canvas under blue summer skies.

No discussion about Mt. Rainier is complete without talking about a climb to its summit. The first documented ascent of Mt. Rainier occurred in 1870 and since then, several thousand have climbed the summit of Washington's highest mountain. This is no place for the inexperienced to wander alone. The climb is a rough test of endurance and technical skills are necessary to not only reach the top, but to navigate the difficult weather, rocky cliffs, and deep crevasses found in the ice glaciers on the high flanks of the peak. Over the years, some 90 people have died trying to climb this mountain; a stark reminder for anyone contemplating this feat. A permit from the National Park Service is required for anyone wanting to go above Camp Muir, and solo climbers are interviewed before a permit is granted. Those going in groups are well advised to have someone with them with ample experience and current knowledge about the conditions at Mt. Rainier. Those not familiar with the mountain or who lack experience should climb with a National Park Service (NPS) recommended guide service like Rainier Mountaineering, Inc. (see their entry in this book).

Deer are abundant and unafraid, often feeding within a few feet of park visitors. Chipmunks, squirrels, blue stellar jays, and gray jays are also not shy and often found around the inns and campgrounds looking for an easy meal. Mammals as diverse as fox, cougar, black bear, bobcat, beaver, mountain goat, and elk are also common but less frequently seen. Hikers will often see hoary marmot and pika around high-country talus slopes, and birdwatchers may want to stop by the small museum in Longmire or the Ohanapecoh Visitor Center to see a sample of the many avian species found in the park.

In the words of the National Park Service, "Mount Rainier National Park isn't known for its fishing, so don't be disappointed if you fail to catch fish, or if the fish are small." The lakes here have not been stocked since 1973 but at least 27 lakes in the park reportedly contain brook, rainbow, or cutthroat trout. Kokanee salmon are found in Mowich Lake and according to some rangers, the fishing there can be good. If you just have to fish a lake in the park but don't have a lot of time, a short walk to 11-acre Lake Louise may get you into some brook trout.

Several waters are closed for fishing. They include Shadow and Frozen Lakes near Sunrise and Reflection Lake near Paradise. The Ohanapecosh River is open for flyfishing only and no fishing is allowed for Dolly Varden, chinook salmon, or coastal cutthroat trout. One good point about fishing here – no license is required! Check the NPS fishing regulations for further details.

While some people bring bicycles to the park, opportunities to use them are limited. The paved roads are steep and winding, the shoulders narrow, and vehicular traffic heavy, making the use of road bikes challenging. Despite that, some bicyclists will make a counterclockwise loop from Enumclaw that covers over 150 miles and involves a 10,000-foot gain in elevation, while others will make the round trip from Longmire to Paradise and back.

Mountain bicyclists generally head to the Westside Road just east of the Nisqually Entrance. The 13-mile gravel road is open to motor vehicles the first 3 miles but only used by hikers and bicyclists beyond that point. You'll gain 1,120 feet of elevation on this trip that ends at Klapatche Point.

There is bad news if you are a pet owner: They aren't allowed on any of the hiking trails except for the 1-mile Pet Loop Trail near the Sunrise Visitors Center. Stock use is also prohibited in the park except at the Three Lakes Campground at the eastern edge of the park where you can bring in a combination of 12 people and stock animals off of the nearby Pacific Crest Trail. You will need a wilderness permit to camp overnight. You can also take up to five horses, mules, burros or llamas on the Laughingwater Creek Trail. You can park stock trailers near this trailhead or at Chinook Pass.

If you want to visit this national park without the crowds, come during the winter. Snowshoeing and rigorous Nordic skiing on well-used but ungroomed trails is a great way to enjoy the park, and an evening by the fire with a warm drink at the National Park Inn is a great way to finish the day. If you are looking for groomed trails, the Mt. Tahoma Trails Association maintains 50 miles of cross-country skiing trails (20 of them groomed) west of the Nisqually Park entrance off of 92 Road near Ashford and 1 Road east of Elbe. Winter sports equipment is available for rent at Longmire.

Getting There: The Nisqually Entrance, and the road leading to Paradise, is open all year. To get there, take Exit 127 off Interstate 5 in Tacoma. Follow State Highway 512 east to State Highway 7. Turn south on State Highway 7 and follow it to State Highway 706. Take State Highway 706 to the park. There is a $15 entrance fee, good for one vehicle and its occupants for up to seven days. If you enter the park on a motorcycle, bicycle, or on foot, the fee is only $5.

Expect to have several close encounters with deer at Mt. Rainier National Park.

NATIONAL PARK INN & PARADISE INN

Guest Services, Inc.
P.O. Box 108, Ashford, WA 98304 / 360-569-2275
www.guestservices.com/rainier

Lodging Prices: $$ to $$$ Adventure Pricing: N/A

Visitors to Mt. Rainier National Park have several options on where to stay. If you don't mind a commute, you can choose among several inns, motels, or bed and breakfasts in places like Ashford, Elbe, Mineral, or Packwood. However, you may find your experience to be more complete by staying inside the boundaries of the 235,612-acre park. There are a number of places to pitch a tent or park an RV, but if you want to sleep in a bed with a roof overhead, you'll want to reserve a stay at one of the two historic lodges operated by Guest Services, Incorporated.

Paradise Inn is located at 5,400 feet, next to the Paradise Visitor Center. Thousands visit here every summer, drawn by the close-up view of the summit and meadows full of summer wildflowers. Others use Paradise as a jumping off point for summit climbs or shorter day hikes. The lodge, opened in 1917, was built with Alaskan cedar timbers chopped and hewn within the park. The interior has some impressive touches as well. During the lodge's early days a German carpenter, Hans Fraehnke, designed decorative pieces such as cedar tables, chairs, a piano, and a large grandfather clock that can still be seen today.

The inn recently went through significant structural remodeling. Unfortunately, the remodel did not extend to the rooms, best described as "comfortable but rustic". About 20 percent of the 120 rooms have shared bathrooms and two rooms will sleep up to six people (the rest sleep two to four). The lobby, however, is large and features huge cedar tables, lots of places to sit, and two stone fireplaces. The lounge gives you a place to relax with a drink and there is also a large dining room with a fireplace seating up to 200 people for breakfast, lunch, and dinner. Some of the dinner entrées, such as the Buffalo Meatloaf, Sea Scallops in Huckleberry-Lavender Sauce, and Elk Roulade, are both unique and imaginative, and plenty of familiar American fare is also available.

Closer to the park's main Nisqually Entrance is the National Park Inn at Longmire. The smaller 25-room inn was also built in 1917 across the road from a meadow full of mineral springs. The springs were discovered in 1883 by James Longmire. He soon built a hotel catering to tourists who soaked in the springs to "cure" a variety of ailments. The clean and basic rooms are furnished with wood and wicker that fit well with the setting. Eight of the rooms have shared baths and four rooms will sleep up to four people. A small, non-hosted guest lounge offers a place to put together a puzzle, enjoy hot tea and scones, or simply stare into the flames of the lit fireplace.

The inn's restaurant seats about 100 people and serves well-presented Northwest cuisine with the help of a trained chef – something you don't often find at national park eateries. Get ready for your day with a breakfast of Camp Muir French Toast topped with blackberry syrup, go hiking, and then come back to a dinner of Oven Baked Salmon or Orange Pecan Trout. Did you go the extra mile on your hike? If so, reward yourself with a dessert of Apple Crisp or Blackberry Cobbler A la Mode (the outdoors never tasted so good). In the evening, snuggle up in a chair on the large, covered porch and watch the setting sun soften the hues on Mt. Rainier as deer graze on the grass near the inn or go for a contemplative stroll along the interpretive trail across the road from the inn.

Neither Paradise Inn nor the National Park Inn has televisions or telephones in their guest rooms. This is in keeping with many national park accommodations where the emphasis is on getting people outside to see the natural beauty of the parks (and not inside in front of a TV). There are plans, however, to have Internet access at the National Park Inn in the near future. Both inns have gift shops along with nearby ranger stations and small museums.

The National Park Inn is open all year and is a popular place to stay in the winter for Nordic skiers and snowshoeing enthusiasts. The Paradise Inn is open from mid-May until early October. After that, snow (up to 100 feet of it a year) forces the facility to close for the winter.

Getting There: Take Interstate 5 from Tacoma south to State Highway 512 (Exit 127). Follow Highway 512 until it intersects with State Highway 7. Follow State Highway 7 south and turn onto State Highway 706. Follow State Highway 706 to the Nisqually Entrance of Mount Rainier National Park. Continue on this road to the National Park Inn and Paradise Inn.

RAINIER MOUNTAINEERING, INC.

P.O. Box Q, Ashford, WA 98304 / 888-892-5462
www.rmiguides.com

Lodging Prices: N/A   Adventure Pricing: $$$$

If you've ever wanted to climb the tallest mountain in the Pacific Northwest, you'd be wise to book a trip with Rainier Mountaineering, Inc. (RMI). This venerable company (by mountain climbing standards) was founded by climbing legend Lou Whittaker in 1969. Since then, RMI guides have led some 70,000 climbers towards the summit of Mt. Rainier. The company employs a staff of 60 guides and 15 support personnel who work on taking groups of six to twelve climbers to the summit about 110 times a year during their climbing season that starts around May 15 and lasts through September.

A typical trip starts with a phone call to RMI where a staff member interviews you to determine your climbing background. Surprisingly enough, 80 percent of their clients have little to no climbing experience at all. RMI offers 3.5- to 4-day-long sessions culminating in a climb to the summit, as well as a number of mountaineering skills programs.

After signing up, you are asked to get in shape for the summit climb that RMI Operations Manager and former guide Jeff Martin calls a "a tough day". Martin explains that the trip to the top of Mt. Rainier is "considered to be the hardest endurance climb in the lower 48 States". RMI outlines a full training regimen on their website designed to get you ready for your adventure.

On the appointed day, you meet your guides at RMI's office in the little town of Ashford, just outside the Nisqually entrance to Mt. Rainier National Park. A typical group will consist of nine clients and three guides (RMI maintains a one-guide-to-three-client ratio on their trips). After making sure you have the right gear (and getting it if you don't), you're shuttled by bus to Paradise, as far up the mountain as most park visitors go. It is there you'll go through a one-day Mountaineering School where you learn not only the skills you'll need to get up and down the mountain, but also self-care issues to help you make it mentally and physically. Class ends shortly before 4:00pm, at which time you are shuttled back down to Ashford. You are on your own for lodging at this point, though many opt to stay at Whittaker's Bunkhouse (360-569-2439 – www.welcometoashford.com) – a reasonably priced 20-room motel next to the RMI Office.

You meet back at the RMI office at 8:15 the following morning and head back up to Paradise at an elevation of 5,400 feet. From there, you slowly work your way up to Camp Muir at 10,188 feet. The steep 4.5-mile hike typically takes six hours, with the group walking for an hour before taking a 10- to 15-minute "maintenance break". The goal, according to Martin, is to get you up to Camp Muir in the best shape possible.

Once there, you check your gear, eat whatever food you brought with you, and go to bed by 7:00pm in RMI's primitive plywood shelter. Most climbers are too wired to sleep the next few hours, but lying prone in a sleeping bag at least allows the lactic acid you've built up during the day to dissipate.

Somewhere between 11:00pm and 2:00am, you'll rise, shoulder a light pack with food and warm clothing, and start the push to the summit. The climb to the 14,410 foot peak typically takes six to seven hours. Once you make it to the top, you'll only have a short time to savor your success before it's time to head back down. As tough as the climb up is, the walk down is also physically difficult. You'll get back to Camp Muir in around three hours where you'll have a short time to rest and re-pack your gear before descending back to Paradise, arriving there around 5:00pm.

If this sounds like a tough trip, it is – but you'll be happy to know that three out of four people who attempt the trip to the top of Mt. Rainier with RMI make it. For those that don't, weather and/or a lack of physical fitness are the main things that keep them from reaching that literal pinnacle of success (as far as this endeavor goes).

Many people who climb Mt. Rainier with RMI get seriously bitten by the climbing bug. That's okay, because the company also specializes in climbs to Alaska's Mt. McKinley and takes clients to other mountain tops around the world, from South America to Africa to the Himalayas. Within Washington, RMI also offers training and trips to Mt. Adams and Mt. Shuksan. You can find out more about RMI's other offerings by giving them a call or logging onto their website.

Getting There: From Seattle, take Exit 127 off of Interstate 5 and travel east on State Highway 512 for 2.2 miles to State Route 7. Follow State Route 7 south to State Route 706 in Elbe (36 miles). Then take State Route 706 east to Ashford, which is only 6 miles from Mt. Rainier National Park.

RMI climbers work their way towards the summit of Mt. Rainier (photo courtesy RMI).

Mount St. Helens
National Volcanic Monument

Monument Headquarters
42218 NE Yale Bridge Road, Amboy, WA 98601 / 360-449-7800
www.fs.fed.us/gpnf/mshnvm

Lodging Prices

If there is one place you simply have to visit in Washington, Mt. St. Helens is it. The mountain is both a jaw- and summit-dropping experience. This volcano has had several major eruptions, the last one occurring on May 18, 1980 when a devastating blast dropped the elevation of the summit by 1,300 feet, killed 57 people, and scarred the surrounding landscape for miles. The volcano remains active and as late as 2005, it was not unusual to see ash plumes rising from the crater. A series of visitor centers along the Spirit Lake Highway stretching from Silver Lake to Johnston Ridge tell the story of the mountain and what its effect has been on the environment.

The area around Mount St. Helens has been designated as a National Volcanic Monument. The 113,151-acre area administered is by the U.S. Forest Service, but in recent years there has been some interest in giving this mountain a place in the national park system. Such an action would provide more protection for this national resource along with adequate funding for the maintenance of roads and facilities. This discussion gained some momentum in 2007 when a lack of funding forced the closure of the popular Coldwater Ridge Visitor Center.

If you have never been here before, start your visit with a trip to the Johnston Ridge Observatory. Get there by taking Exit 49 off Interstate 5 at Castle Rock. Drive east along the Spirit Lake Highway until it ends at milepost 52 at Johnston Ridge, just 7 miles from the gaping maw of the crater. The observatory is named after geologist David Johnston. His frantic radio transmission "Vancouver, Vancouver, this is it!" were his last words before he was engulfed by the blast that accompanied the opening moments of

the May 18th eruption in 1980. Start off with a visit to the theatre and take in a great audio-visual presentation about the eruption and its impacts. After that, check out the various displays at the observatory and go for a walk on a wheelchair accessible half-mile interpretive trail outside the visitor center. The Johnston Ridge Observatory is open from mid-May to mid-October. You will need to purchase a Monument Pass for a small price to visit here.

Traveling back west along the highway, you can stop off to hike the 2.5-mile Hummocks Interpretive Trail. It is named after the mounds of volcanic debris deposited in this area from the massive landslides that accompanied the 1980 eruption.

The next stop takes you to the southern end of Coldwater Lake. This young lake was formed by debris from the eruption that dammed the creek here. Anglers can catch trout, some of them sizeable, using flies and lures with single barbless hooks. If you are so inclined you can also launch a small boat (electric motors only), canoe, or kayak from the boat launch and explore the 4-mile-long lake. Shore access to the lake is intentionally limited, meant to protect the fragile, developing ecosystem here.

If you are in the mood for a longer hike this is a good place to go. You can walk the length of the lake above its western shore and hook up with trails that take you into the Mt. Margaret backcountry. There are several campsites for hikers in this region, but the easiest ones to reach along this route are found at Shovel, Panhandle, and Obscurity Lakes. All three lakes also have brook trout in them in case you decide to bring a fishing rod along. You can either return the way you came or continue towards Norway Pass at Forest Service Road 26 northeast of Spirit Lake and Mt. St. Helens. A camping permit, which you can obtain in advance from the Monument Headquarters, is required to stay in this backcountry area.

Back on the Spirit Lake Highway, you can drive west past the closed Coldwater Ridge Visitor Center and stop at the Weyerhaeuser Company's Forest Learning Center. This privately operated visitor center focuses on reforestation efforts that have occurred since the eruption. The elk population was also impacted by the eruption and the center talks about the current status of these animals along with others that call this region home. A viewpoint here is a good place to spot some of these elk that are now part of the state's largest herd, with over 10,000 animals. If you are interested in hunting these big mammals, you'll be disappointed to find you can't do so within the monument. However, good elk hunting is possible in the fall outside of its boundaries.

There are also a lot of birds within the monument. Blue grouse are doing well among the new vegetation, as are warbling vireo, northern flicker, hairy woodpecker, Stellar's jay, raven, and several species of warblers. Above the landscape of dead, toppled trees and growing new ones red-tailed hawks and American kestrel hunt for morsels while swallows and swifts swoop low to catch flying bugs.

If you drive farther west, you'll find the Hoffstadt Bluffs Visitor Center at milepost 27 on the Spirit Lake Highway. Operated more as a concession than an educational facility, you can see a glassworks featuring glass blown from volcanic ash, get a meal from the closest restaurant to Johnston Ridge, and even book a ride on board a helicopter that will give you an aerial view of the mountain and surrounding blast zone.

Continue west on the highway along the Toutle River and you'll reach the small town of Toutle, and then Silver Lake. At milepost 5, you can stop in at the Mount St. Helens Silver Lake Visitors Center. Operated by the Washington State Parks Commission, this well-done center has several good interpretive exhibits and also has a short movie that will educate you about the volcanic mountain. If you can't get to the monument itself, this visitor center is just a few minutes drive off of Interstate 5 and is a good place for a quick visit.

Lodging opportunities any closer than Castle Rock are hard to come by. One place that has a motel, cabins, RV spaces, and tent sites is the Silver Lake Resort (see their entry for more information). Seaquest State Park is located across the highway from the Mount St. Helens Silver Lake Visitor Center and is another good place to stay with 55 tent sites, 33 utility sites for RVs, and five yurts (360-274-8633 – www.parks. wa.gov). Both locations are open all year.

Getting There: See above.

Mount Adams

U.S. Forest Service – Mt. Adams Ranger District
2455 State Highway 141, Trout Lake, WA 98650 / 509-395-3400
www.fs.fed.us/gpnf/recreation/

Lodging Prices

Although 12,276-foot-tall Mt. Adams is Washington's second tallest peak, it is often referred to as the "forgotten giant". Despite its size and beauty, the mountain and surrounding wilderness remain surprisingly uncrowded. It seems many prefer to visit Mt. Rainier, Mt. St. Helens, or Oregon's Mt. Hood, leaving those that visit the scenic woods and wilderness here plenty of elbow room.

There is a lot of public land around this mountain, most of which lies within the Gifford Pinchot National Forest. Of particular interest is the 46,353-acre Mt. Adams Wilderness that surrounds Mt. Adams and the Trout Lake Natural Area Preserve on the outskirts of Trout Lake, a small community just south of the mountain.

The Trout Lake Natural Area Preserve is managed by the Washington Department of Natural Resources and is accessible off of Lake Road near the Forest Service ranger station in Trout Lake. Once you get there, you'll find a short, level trail that follows Trout Creek. The trail overlooks the creek and a large marshy wetland surrounded by willows, alder, and cottonwood that has filled in what once was Trout Lake. Bring a camera, because the views of Mt. Adams are spectacular. You'll also want to bring a pair of binoculars to view the wildlife here.

The preserve was established in 1996, primarily to protect the largest population of Oregon spotted frogs known to exist in Washington. However, the preserve also benefits some 200 other avian and animal species. They include uncommon birds such as sandhill cranes, pileated woodpeckers, and bald eagles along with waterfowl such as multi-colored wood ducks and

hooded mergansers. Deer and squirrels are common, and if you are lucky you may get to see river otters playing in the creek below.

The view of Mt. Adams may entice you to climb it. Knowing that technical skills are generally not needed on the main route may tempt you more. If you decide to give it a go, you'll want to start off by getting a climbing permit from the ranger station in Trout Lake. From there, you can decide whether to go for the South Climb (the non-technical route) or the more challenging routes along the North Cleaver or Adams Glacier. Either way, you'll want to be in good shape.

Most summit the mountain by taking the South Climb Trail. You get there by driving to the end of Forest Service Road 8040.5 to the Cold Springs trailhead; park and hike 5.7 miles, going up some 6,700 feet in the process, to reach the summit. Most take six to eight hours to reach the top and, after that obligatory top-of-the-world rest and photo opportunity, you can plan on another four- to six-hour trek downhill back to the trailhead. Ice axes and crampons are recommended for this route, with the prime climbing season taking place in July and August.

If you want some hikes that are not quite as challenging as a summit climb, the 1.4-mile trail to a rock formation known as Sleeping Beauty will take you to the site of an old fire lookout where great views of the Cascade Crest can be found. Even though this is a short hike, you will get a good workout gaining 1,400 feet. You should also be cautious and careful of your footing when you reach the rocky outcropping at the top. Get to this trailhead southwest of Mt. Adams by traveling up Forest Service Road 24 to Road 8810 from Trout Lake and then traveling a short distance on Road 040. Another option that involves little effort is the short quarter-mile walk downhill to pretty Langfield Falls off of Road 88. The 40-foot waterfall is named after the ranger who discovered it. A trail leads towards the stream below it, a perfect place to dip your toes on a warm summer day.

There are several other easily accessible natural points of interest near Trout Lake. One of them, the Ice Cave, is just a few miles east of Trout Lake on Forest Service Road 24. Park your car and climb down a ladder into the hole. It is the entrance into a cave formed thousands of years ago as lava flowed and cooled during eruptions from nearby Mt. Adams. Ice on the floors, walls, and roof near the entrance attracted early settlers in the area who stocked up on this rare natural commodity. If you want to explore further within the cave you can, but watch your step and make sure you bring a flashlight or headlamp.

The Natural Bridges are another geological point of interest that lie a short distance east of the Ice Cave and allow you to see the remnants of lava tube caves from above ground. The lava tube caves collapsed in this area, forming apparent creek bottoms. However, several lava rock bridges that were once the roof of these caves cross over the open floor of the small canyons. A short trail from another Forest Service day-use area takes you around these canyons and bridges.

If you are looking for a place to stay, there are accommodations in Trout Lake (see the Trout Lake Motel entry) and several campgrounds in the area. The closest ones to the mountain are probably the Trout Lake Creek and Morrison Creek Campgrounds, but both are primitive and not recommended for trailers or RVs. More comfortable camping can be found west of Trout Lake at the Peterson Prairie Campground. Located near the Ice Cave and the Atkisson Sno-Park this level, lightly wooded camping area has 30 individual sites and a group site suitable for tents and RVs up to 32 feet long along with potable water. This campground is also a popular base camp in the middle of August. That's when lush, purple huckleberries that grow abundantly around here are ripe for the picking.

If you want to combine camping with fishing continue a few miles west from Peterson Prairie. You can pitch a tent at the Goose Lake Campground (18 sites available, no water) or at the Forlorn Lakes (25 sites, no water, tents and small RVs to 18 feet). North of Trout Lake, the 54-site campground at Takhlakh Lake can accommodate RVs or trailers to 22 feet but has no water. All three places offer trout angling and electric motors are allowed on boats at both 58-acre Goose and 35-acre Takhlakh Lake.

The area around Mt. Adams is also a good winter destination. The Atkisson Sno-Park is not only popular with snowmobilers, but also with cross-country skiing enthusiasts who enjoy several miles of ungroomed trails around the Ice Cave, Natural Bridges, and up to Peterson Ridge. Northeast of Trout Lake, off Road 82, the Pineside and SnowKing Sno-Parks provide over 23 miles of groomed skiing along the Eagle, Big Tree, Hole-in-the-Ground, Pipeline, and Lava Loop Trails.

Getting There: Take State Highway 14 towards White Salmon. Head north 27 miles on State Highway 141 to the Mt. Adams Ranger District Station in Mount Adams.

A white-crowned sparrow enjoys a tasty morsel.

Conboy National Wildlife Refuge

100 Wildlife Refuge Road, Glenwood, WA 98619 / 509-364-3410
www.fws.gov

The Conboy National Wildlife Refuge may be one of the most scenic places to go wildlife watching in Washington. Located southeast of Mt. Adams near the small community of Glenwood, the 6,500-acre refuge has habitat that includes open-floored pine forests, prairie, and a large seasonal marsh called Conboy Lake.

You can get acquainted with the refuge by hiking the 2-mile Willard Springs Loop Trail. You'll find the trailhead a short distance from the headquarters at the northwest end of the refuge. Walk along the level trail amongst ponderosa pine towards Willard Springs, a place that draws both deer and elk. Other mammals you may see are western gray squirrels in trees and beaver or coyote near creeks and areas of standing water. Make it a point to stop at the observation deck where the forest meets the marsh. You'll get a chance to see more wildlife and will also be rewarded with a spectacular view of Mt. Adams.

This area is primarily managed for waterfowl, but a variety of different species call this land home. This includes seven different amphibians, 40 mammals, and 165 different birds. Two unique species found here are the Oregon spotted frog and the sandhill crane. About 18 nesting pairs of these big birds can be seen at the refuge from year to year, sharing the marsh with waterfowl like handsome pintails, brightly colored wood ducks, mallards, geese, and all three types of teal (green-wing, blue-wing, and the striking cinnamon teal). Expect to see raptors too. There is one pair of nesting bald eagles, and red-tailed hawks soar over the marsh with northern harriers. Open up your other senses by listening to the song of the marsh. Not only will you hear a chorus of frogs (that also include bullfrogs and Pacific tree frogs) but also the sweet sound of meadowlarks, a songbird found in good numbers here.

Wildlife watching is best in the spring and early summer, when the marshes still contain plenty of water. However, hiking and wildlife viewing are not the only activities possible. In the fall, you can hunt for black-tailed deer or waterfowl in a designated hunting area consisting of open grasslands, creeks, and a few stands of lodge pole and ponderosa pine. There is also a small fishing area at the northeast corner of the refuge where Frazier and Outlet Creeks meet. Rainbow and brook trout are both reportedly present.

The refuge is open all year during daylight hours. Leashed pets are allowed (except during hunting season, when they can be off leash but must be under voice control). The refuge headquarters and nearby Whitcomb-Cole Log House (an example of a pioneer era home) are open weekdays from 7:30am to 4:00pm. The remainder of the refuge outside of the Willard Springs Trail and designated hunting and fishing areas is closed to the public for the benefit of the species that live here.

Getting There: Take State Highway 141 north from White Salmon to Trout Lake. Follow the Trout Lake Road to Glenwood Road 10 miles and turn right into the refuge where you'll soon find the parking lots for the Willard Springs Trail and the refuge headquarters.

Golden-mantled ground squirrels are often confused with smaller chipmunks.

TROUT LAKE MOTEL

2300 State Highway 141, Trout Lake, WA 98650 / 509-395-2300
http://business.gorge.net/troutlakemotel

Lodging Prices: $$ Adventure Pricing: $

They really ought to rename this place. The Trout Lake Motel has more in common with an outdoor lodge than a bungalow-style motel. Yes, the 13 rooms are laid out in an L-shaped strip and the prices are certainly in line with what you would expect from a motel, but the similarities end there.

Dave and Carley Tipton built their establishment from the ground up in 2002. The exterior and much of the interior is pine and items such as wooden skis, snowshoes, a sled, and maps of the Mount Adams Wilderness decorate the outer walls. A seasonal creek runs through the nicely maintained property, and a small wooden bridge over it leads to a small, grassy park with trees where you can swing on a hammock or barbeque your lunch.

The rooms are spacious, agreeably decorated, and have a lot of amenities. Featuring either a queen bed and a loveseat or two queen beds, they all have log furniture and accents from the Tipton's farm. Each room has a private bath, small refrigerator, microwave, satellite television, Wi-Fi Internet access, and a gas fireplace to take the chill off during the colder months.

There is a laundry room on site to clean dirty clothes and a hot tub where you can soak aching muscles. The big dining area is also furnished in an outdoor lodge motif with wooden tables, chairs, and a bison mount that silently gazes over the room while you enjoy homemade sweet potato waffles and syrup with your complimentary continental breakfast.

The motel is located in the tiny community of Trout Lake at the base of Mt. Adams. There is a plethora of outdoor activities in this region. Bicyclists enjoy traveling along roads bordered by pastures, farmer's fields, and woods. If you don't bring your own bike you can rent a comfortable hybrid bicycle from the motel for a low price. Designed for the casual cyclist, they are perfect for exploring the easy 11-mile loop around Sunnyside Road. More serious cyclists may want to tackle a 50-mile route that takes you from the motel to Glenwood, south to the busy rafting village along the White Salmon River known as BZ Corners, and then back north to Trout Lake.

If you enjoy whitewater rafting there is a public launch at BZ Corners that will get you into challenging whitewater on the White Salmon River. Some interesting geological features in the form of lava tube caves and waterfalls are a short drive away. Wildlife watchers will want to head to the Conboy National Wildlife Refuge (NWR) or the Trout Lake Nature Preserve. Meanwhile, hiking and cross-country skiing opportunities abound in the Gifford Pinchot National Forest and Mount Adams

Wilderness. Speaking of Mt. Adams, the motel is a great place to stay before a summit climb to the peak and an even better place to find a comfortable bed to collapse in once you are done. For more details about these activities, check out the Mt. Adams and Conboy NWR entries in this book.

The Trout Lake Motel is open all year. The Tipton's do have a couple of pet-friendly rooms available. Call in advance if you would like to reserve one of them.

Getting There: Take State Highway 14 towards White Salmon and turn north on Highway 141 Alternate. Follow State Highway 141 north 21 miles to the Trout Lake Motel.

Washington State Bird Species

The Slater Museum of Natural History is located at the University of Puget Sound in Tacoma. The museum has kindly agreed to provide a comprehensive list of birds found within Washington for this book. For more information about the museum, call 253-879-3356 or log onto www.ups.edu/slatermuseum.xml.

ANSERIFORMES

ANATIDAE (waterfowl)

Greater White-fronted Goose	Anser albifrons
Snow Goose	Chen caerulescens
Cackling Goose	Branta hutchinsii
Canada Goose	Branta canadensis
Brant	Branta bernicla
Trumpeter Swan	Cygnus buccinator
Tundra Swan	Cygnus columbianus
Wood Duck	Aix sponsa
Gadwall	Anas strepera
Eurasian Wigeon	Anas penelope
American Wigeon	Anas americana
Mallard	Anas platyrhynchos
Blue-winged Teal	Anas discors
Cinnamon Teal	Anas cyanoptera
Northern Shoveler	Anas clypeata
Northern Pintail	Anas acuta
Green-winged Teal	Anas crecca
Canvasback	Aythya valisineria
Redhead	Aythya americana
Ring-necked Duck	Aythya collaris
Greater Scaup	Aythya marila
Lesser Scaup	Aythya affinis
Harlequin Duck	Histrionicus histrionicus
Surf Scoter	Melanitta perspicillata
White-winged Scoter	Melanitta fusca

Black Scoter	Melanitta nigra
Long-tailed Duck	Clangula hyemalis
Bufflehead	Bucephala albeola
Common Goldeneye	Bucephala clangula
Barrow's Goldeneye	Bucephala islandica
Hooded Merganser	Lophodytes cucullatus
Common Merganser	Mergus merganser
Red-breasted Merganser	Mergus serrator
Ruddy Duck	Oxyura jamaicensis
Order GALLIFORMES	

PHASIANIDAE (partridges, grouses, turkeys)

Chukar	Alectoris chukar
Gray Partridge	Perdix perdix
Ring-necked Pheasant	Phasianus colchicus
Ruffed Grouse	Bonasa umbellus
Greater Sage-Grouse	Centrocercus urophasianus
Spruce Grouse	Falcipennis canadensis
White-tailed Ptarmigan	Lagopus leucurus
Dusky Grouse	Dendragapus obscurus
Sooty Grouse	Dendragapus fuliginosus
Sharp-tailed Grouse	Tympanuchus phasianellus
Wild Turkey	Meleagris gallopavo

ODONTOPHORIDAE (New World quails)

Mountain Quail	Oreortyx pictus
California Quail	Callipepla californica
Northern Bobwhite	Colinus virginianus
Order GAVIIFORMES	
GAVIIDAE (loons)	
Red-throated Loon	Gavia stellata
Pacific Loon	Gavia pacifica
Common Loon	Gavia immer
Yellow-billed Loon	Gavia adamsii

PODICIPEDIFORMES

PODICIPEDIDAE (grebes)

Pied-billed Grebe	Podilymbus podiceps
Horned Grebe	Podiceps auritus
Red-necked Grebe	Podiceps grisegena
Eared Grebe	Podiceps nigricollis
Western Grebe	Aechmophorus occidentalis
Clark's Grebe	Aechmophorus clarkii

PROCELLARIIFORMES

DIOMEDEIDAE (albatrosses)

Laysan Albatross	Phoebastria immutabilis
Black-footed Albatross	Poebastria nigripes

PROCELLARIIDAE (petrels)

Northern Fulmar	Fulmarus glacialis
Pink-footed Shearwater	Puffinus creatopus
Flesh-footed Shearwater	Puffinus carneipes
Buller's Shearwater	Puffinus bulleri
Sooty Shearwater	Puffinus griseus
Short-tailed Shearwater	Puffinus tenuirostris
Manx Shearwater	Puffinus puffinus

HYDROBATIDAE (storm-petrels)

Fork-tailed Storm-Petrel	Oceanodroma furcata
Leach's Storm-Petrel	Oceanodroma leucorhoa
Order PELECANIFORMES	

PELECANIDAE (pelicans)

American White Pelican	Pelecanus erythrorhynchos
Brown Pelican	Pelecanus occidentalis

PHALACROCORACIDAE (cormorants)

Brandt's Cormorant	Phalacrocorax penicillatus
Double-crested Cormorant	Phalacrocorax auritus
Pelagic Cormorant	Phalacrocorax pelagicus

CICONIIFORMES

ARDEIDAE (herons)

American Bittern	Botaurus lentiginosus
Great Blue Heron	Ardea herodias
Great Egret	Ardea alba
Cattle Egret	Bubulcus ibis
Green Heron	Butorides virescens
Black-crowned Night Heron	Nycticorax nycticorax

THRESKIORNITHIDAE (ibises and spoonbills)

White-faced Ibis	Plegadis chihi

CATHARTIDAE (American vultures)

Turkey Vulture	Cathartes aura

FALCONIFORMES

ACCIPITRIDAE (hawks)

Osprey	Pandion haliaetus
White-tailed Kite	Elanus leucurus
Bald Eagle	Haliaeetus leucocephalus
Northern Harrier	Circus cyaneus
Sharp-shinned Hawk	Accipiter striatus
Cooper's Hawk	Accipiter cooperii
Northern Goshawk	Accipiter gentilis
Red-shouldered Hawk	Buteo lineatus
Swainson's Hawk	Buteo swainsoni
Red-tailed Hawk	Buteo jamaicensis
Ferruginous Hawk	Buteo regalis
Rough-legged Hawk	Buteo lagopus
Golden Eagle, Aquila	chrysaetos

FALCONIDAE (falcons)

American Kestrel	Falco sparverius
Merlin	Falco columbarius
Gyrfalcon	Falco rusticolus

Peregrine Falcon	Falco peregrinus
Prairie Falcon	Falco mexicanus

GRUIFORMES

RALLIDAE (rails)

Virginia Rail	Rallus limicola
Sora	Porzana carolina
American Coot	Fulica americana

GRUIDAE (cranes)

Sandhill Crane	Grus canadensis

CHARADRIIFORMES

CHARADRIIDAE (plovers)

Black-bellied Plover	Pluvialis squatarola
American Golden-plover	Pluvialis dominica
Pacific Golden-plover	Pluvialis fulva
Snowy Plover	Charadrius alexandrinus
Semipalmated Plover	Charadrius semipalmatus
Killdeer	Charadrius vociferus

HAEMATOPODIDAE (oystercatchers)

Black Oystercatcher	Haematopus bachmani

RECURVIROSTRIDAE (avocets & stilts)

Black-necked Stilt	Himantopus mexicanus
American Avocet	Recurvirostra americana

SCOLOPACIDAE (sandpipers)

Spotted Sandpiper	Actitis macularia
Solitary Sandpiper	Tringa solitaria
Wandering Tattler	Tringa incana
Greater Yellowlegs	Tringa melanoleuca
Willet	Tringa semipalmata
Lesser Yellowlegs	Tringa flavipes
Upland Sandpiper	Bartramia longicauda

Whimbrel	Numenius phaeopus
Long-billed Curlew	Numenius americanus
Bar-tailed Godwit	Limosa lapponica
Marbled Godwit	Limosa fedoa
Ruddy Turnstone	Arenaria interpres
Black Turnstone	Arenaria melanocephala
Surfbird	Aphriza virgata
Red Knot	Calidris canutus
Sanderling	Calidris alba
Semipalmated Sandpiper	Calidris pusilla
Western Sandpiper	Calidris mauri
Least Sandpiper	Calidris minutilla
Baird's Sandpiper	Calidris bairdii
Pectoral Sandpiper	Calidris melanotos
Sharp-tailed Sandpiper	Calidris acuminata
Rock Sandpiper	Calidris ptilocnemis
Dunlin	Calidris alpina
Stilt Sandpiper	Calidris himantopus
Buff-breasted Sandpiper	Tryngites subruficollis
Ruff	Philomachus pugnax
Short-billed Dowitcher	Limnodromus griseus
Long-billed Dowitcher	Limnodromus scolopaceus
Wilson's Snipe	Gallinago delicata
Wilson's Phalarope	Phalaropus tricolor
Red-necked Phalarope	Phalaropus lobatus
Red Phalarope	Phalaropus fulicarius

LARIDAE (gulls & terns)

Franklin's Gull	Larus pipixcan
Little Gull	Larus minutus
Bonaparte's Gull	Larus philadelphia
Heermann's Gull	Larus heermanni
Mew Gull	Larus canus
Ring-billed Gull	Larus delawarensis
California Gull	Larus californicus

Herring Gull	Larus argentatus
Thayer's Gull	Larus thayeri
Western Gull	Larus occidentalis
Glaucous-winged Gull	Larus glaucescens
Glaucous Gull	Larus hyperboreus
Sabine's Gull	Xema sabini
Black-legged Kittiwake	Rissa tridactyla
Caspian Tern	Hydroprogne caspia
Black Tern	Chlidonias niger
Common Tern	Sterna hirundo
Arctic Tern	Sterna paradisaea
Forster's Tern	Sterna forsteri
Elegant Tern	Thalasseus elegans

STERCORARIIDAE (skuas)

South Polar Skua	Stercorarius maccormicki
Pomarine Jaeger	Stercorarius pomarinus
Parasitic Jaeger	Stercorarius parasiticus
Long-tailed Jaeger	Stercorarius longicaudus

ALCIDAE (alcids)

Common Murre	Uria aalge
Pigeon Guillemot	Cepphus columba
Marbled Murrelet	Brachyramphus marmoratus
Xantus' Murrelet	Synthliboramphus hypoleucus
Ancient Murrelet	Synthliboramphus antiquus
Cassin's Auklet	Ptychoramphus aleuticus
Rhinoceros Auklet	Cerorhinca monocerata
Tufted Puffin	Fratercula cirrhata

COLUMBIFORMES

COLUMBIDAE (pigeons)

Rock Dove	Columba livia
Band-tailed Pigeon	Patagioenas fasciata
Mourning Dove	Zenaida macroura

STRIGIFORMES

TYTONIDAE (barn owls)

Barn Owl	Tyto alba

STRIGIDAE (typical owls)

Flammulated Owl	Otus flammeolus
Western Screech-owl	Megascops kennicottii
Great Horned Owl	Bubo virginianus
Snowy Owl	Bubo scandiacus
Northern Pygmy-owl	Glaucidium gnoma
Burrowing Owl	Athene cunicularia
Spotted Owl	Strix occidentalis
Barred Owl	Strix varia
Great Gray Owl	Strix nebulosa.
Long-eared Owl	Asio otus
Short-eared Owl	Asio flammeus
Boreal Owl	Aegolius funereus
Northern Saw-whet Owl	Aegolius acadicus

CAPRIMULGIFORMES

CAPRIMULGIDAE (nightjars)

Common Nighthawk	Chordeiles minor
Common Poorwill	Phalaenoptilus nuttallii
Order APODIFORMES	

APODIDAE (swifts)

Black Swift	Cypseloides niger
Vaux's Swift	Chaetura vauxi
White-throated Swift	Aeronautes saxatilis

TROCHILIDAE (hummingbirds)

Black-chinned Hummingbird	Archilochus alexandri
Anna's Hummingbird	Calypte anna
Calliope Hummingbird	Stellula calliope
Rufous Hummingbird	Selasphorus rufus

CORACIIFORMES

ALCEDINIDAE (kingfishers)

Belted Kingfisher	Ceryle alcyon

PICIFORMES

PICIDAE (woodpeckers)

Lewis' Woodpecker	Melanerpes lewis
Acorn Woodpecker	Melanerpes formicivorus
Williamson's Sapsucker	Sphyrapicus thyroideus
Red-naped Sapsucker	Sphyrapicus nuchalis
Red-breasted Sapsucker	Sphyrapicus ruber
Downy Woodpecker	Picoides pubescens
Hairy Woodpecker	Picoides villosus
White-headed Woodpecker	Picoides albolarvatus
American Three-toed Woodpecker	Picoides dorsalis
Black-backed Woodpecker	Picoides arcticus
Northern Flicker	Colaptes auratus
Pileated Woodpecker	Dryocopus pileatu

PASSERIFORMES

TYRANNIDAE (tyrant flycatchers)

Olive-sided Flycatcher	Contopus cooperi
Western Wood-Pewee	Contopus sordidulus
Willow Flycatcher	Empidonax traillii
Least Flycatcher	Empidonax minimus
Hammond's Flycatcher	Empidonax hammondii
Gray Flycatcher	Empidonax wrightii
Dusky Flycatcher	Empidonax oberholseri
Pacific-slope Flycatcher	Empidonax difficilis
Say's Phoebe	Sayornis saya
Ash-throated Flycatcher	Myiarchus cinerascens

Western Kingbird	Tyrannus verticalis
Eastern Kingbird	Tyrannus tyrannus

LANIIDAE (shrikes)

Loggerhead Shrike	Lanius ludovicianus
Northern Shrike	Lanius excubitor

VIREONIDAE (vireos)

Cassin's Vireo	Vireo cassinii
Hutton's Vireo	Vireo huttoni
Warbling Vireo	Vireo gilvus
Red-eyed Vireo	Vireo olivaceus

CORVIDAE (crows & jays)

Gray Jay	Perisoreus canadensis
Steller's Jay	Cyanocitta stelleri
Blue Jay	Cyanocitta cristata
Western Scrub-Jay	Aphelocoma californica
Clark's Nutcracker	Nucifraga columbiana
Black-billed Magpie	Pica hudsonia
American Crow	Corvus brachyrhynchos
Common Raven	Corvus corax

ALAUDIDAE (larks)

Sky Lark	Alauda arvensis.
Horned Lark	Eremophila alpestris

HIRUNDINIDAE (swallows)

Purple Martin	Progne subis
Tree Swallow	Tachycineta bicolor
Violet-green Swallow	Tachycineta thalassina
Northern Rough-winged Swallow	Stelgidopteryx serripennis
Bank Swallow	Riparia riparia
Cliff Swallow	Petrochelidon pyrrhonota
Barn Swallow	Hirundo rustica

PARIDAE (tits)

Black-capped Chickadee	Poecile atricapillus
Mountain Chickadee	Poecile gambeli
Boreal Chickadee	Poecile hudsonica

AEGITHALIDAE (long-tailed tits)

Bushtit	Psaltriparus minimus

SITTIDAE (nuthatches)

Red-breasted Nuthatch	Sitta canadensis
White-breasted Nuthatch	Sitta carolinensis
Pygmy Nuthatch	Sitta pygmaea

CERTHIIDAE (creepers)

Brown Creeper	Certhia americana

TROGLODYTIDAE (wrens)

Rock Wren	Salpinctes obsoletus
Canyon Wren	Catherpes mexicanus
Bewick's Wren	Thryomanes bewickii
House Wren	Troglodytes aedon
Winter Wren	Troglodytes troglodytes
Marsh Wren	Cistothorus palustris

CINCLIDAE (dippers)

American Dipper	Cinclus mexicanus

REGULIDAE (kinglets)

Golden-crowned Kinglet	Regulus satrapa
Ruby-crowned Kinglet	Regulus calendula

TURDIDAE (thrushes)

Western Bluebird	Sialia mexicana
Mountain Bluebird	Sialia currucoides
Townsend's Solitaire	Myadestes townsendi
Veery	Catharus fuscescens
Swainson's Thrush	Catharus ustulatus
Hermit Thrush	Catharus guttatus
American Robin	Turdus migratorius
Varied Thrush	Ixoreus naevius

MIMIDAE (mockingbirds)

Gray Catbird	Dumetella carolinensis
Northern Mockingbird	Mimus polyglottos
Sage Thrasher	Oreoscoptes montanus

STURNIDAE (starlings)

European Starling	Sturnus vulgaris

MOTACILLIDAE (wagtails)

American Pipit	Anthus rubescens

BOMBYCILLIDAE (waxwings)

Bohemian Waxwing	Bombycilla garrulus
Cedar Waxwing	Bombycilla cedrorum

PARULIDAE (wood warblers)

Orange-crowned Warbler	Vermivora celata
Nashville Warbler	Vermivora ruficapilla
Yellow Warbler	Dendroica petechia
Yellow-rumped warbler	Dendroica coronata
Black-throated Gray Warbler	Dendroica nigrescens
Townsend's Warbler	Dendroica townsendi
Hermit Warbler	Dendroica occidentalis
Palm Warbler	Dendroica palmarum
American Redstart	Setophaga ruticilla
Northern Waterthrush	Seiurus noveboracensis
MacGillivray's Warbler	Oporornis tolmiei
Common Yellowthroat	Geothlypis trichas
Wilson's Warbler	Wilsonia pusilla
Yellow-breasted Chat	Icteria virens

THRAUPIDAE (tanagers)

Western Tanager	Piranga ludoviciana

EMBERIZIDAE (buntings)

Green-tailed Towhee	Pipilo chlorurus
Spotted Towhee	Pipilo maculatus
American Tree Sparrow	Spizella arborea
Chipping Sparrow	Spizella passerina
Clay-colored Sparrow	Spizella pallida
Brewer's Sparrow	Spizella breweri
Vesper Sparrow	Pooecetes gramineus
Lark Sparrow	Chondestes grammacus
Black-throated Sparrow	Amphispiza bilineata

Sage Sparrow	Amphispiza bellii
Savannah Sparrow	Passerculus sandwichensis
Grasshopper Sparrow	Ammodramus savannarum
Fox Sparrow	Passerella iliaca
Song Sparrow	Melospiza melodia
Lincoln's Sparrow	Melospiza lincolnii
Swamp Sparrow	Melospiza georgiana
White-throated Sparrow	Zonotrichia albicollis
Harris' Sparrow	Zonotrichia querula
White-crowned Sparrow	Zonotrichia leucophrys
Golden-crowned Sparrow	Zonotrichia coronata
Dark-eyed Junco	Junco hyemalis
Lapland Longspur	Calcarius lapponicus
Snow Bunting	Plectrophenax nivalis

CARDINALIDAE (cardinal grosbeaks)

Black-headed Grosbeak	Pheucticus melanocephalus
Lazuli Bunting	Passerina amoena

ICTERIDAE (troupials)

Bobolink	Dolichonyx oryzivorus
Red-winged Blackbird	Agelaius phoeniceus
Tricolored Blackbird	Agelaius tricolor
Western Meadowlark	Sturnella neglecta
Yellow-headed Blackbird	Xanthocephalus xanthocephalus
Brewer's Blackbird	Euphagus cyanocephalus
Brown-headed Cowbird	Molothrus ater
Bullock's Oriole	Icterus bullockii

FRINGILLIDAE (finches)

Gray-crowned Rosy-Finch	Leucosticte tephrocotis
Pine Grosbeak	Pinicola enucleator
Purple Finch	Carpodacus purpureus
Cassin's Finch	Carpodacus cassinii
House Finch	Carpodacus mexicanus
Red Crossbill	Loxia curvirostra
White-winged Crossbill	Loxia leucoptera

Common Redpoll	Carduelis flamme
Pine Siskin	Carduelis pinus
Lesser Goldfinch	Carduelis psaltria
American Goldfinch	Carduelis tristis
Evening Grosbeak	Coccothraustes vespertinus

PASSERIDAE (sparrows)

House Sparrow, Passer domesticus

A yellow-pine chipmunk munches on a snack.

Washington State Wildlife List

The following list is also provided courtesy of the Slater Museum of Natural History, located at the University of Puget Sound in Tacoma.

DIDELPHIMORPHIA (opossum-like marsupials)

DIDELPHIDAE (opossums)

Virginia Opossum	Didelphis virginiana

INSECTIVORA (insectivores)

SORICIDAE (shrews)

Masked Shrew	Sorex cinereus
Preble's Shrew	Sorex preblei
Vagrant Shrew	Sorex vagrans
Montane Shrew	Sorex monticolus
Water Shrew	Sorex palustris
Pacific Water Shrew	Sorex bendirii
Trowbridge's Shrew	Sorex trowbridgii
Merriam's Shrew	Sorex merriami
Pygmy Shrew	Sorex hoyi

TALPIDAE (moles)

Shrew-mole	Neurotrichus gibbsii
Townsend's Mole	Scapanus townsendii
Coast Mole	Scapanus orarius

CHIROPTERA (bats)

VESPERTILIONIDAE (vespertilionid bats)

Little Brown Myotis	Myotis lucifugus
Yuma Myotis	Myotis yumanensis
Keen's Myotis	Myotis keenii
Long-eared Myotis	Myotis evotis
Fringed Myotis	Myotis thysanodes

Long-legged Myotis	Myotis volans
California Myotis	Myotis californicus
Western Small-footed Myotis	Myotis ciliolabrum
Hoary Bat	Lasiurus cinereus
Silver-haired Bat	Lasionycteris noctivagans
Western Pipistrel	Pipistrellus hesperus
Big Brown Bat	Eptesicus fuscus
Spotted Bat	Euderma maculatum
Western Big-eared Bat	Plecotus townsendii
Pallid Bat	Antrozous pallidus

LAGOMORPHA (lagomorphs)

OCHOTONIDAE (pikas)

| Pika | Ochotona princeps |

LEPORIDAE (hares and rabbits)

Pygmy Rabbit	Brachylagus idahoensis
Eastern Cottontail	Sylvilagus floridanus
Nuttall's Cottontail	Sylvilagus nuttallii
European Rabbit	Oryctolagus cuniculus
Snowshoe Hare	Lepus americanus
White-tailed Jackrabbit	Lepus townsendii
Black-tailed Jackrabbit	Lepus californicus

RODENTIA (rodents)

APLODONTIDAE (mountain beaver)

| Mountain Beaver | Aplodontia rufa |

SCIURIDAE (squirrels)

Least Chipmunk	Tamias minimus
Yellow-pine Chipmunk	Tamias amoenus
Townsend's Chipmunk	Tamias townsendii
Red-tailed Chipmunk	Tamias ruficaudus

Yellow-bellied Marmot	Marmota flaviventris
Hoary Marmot	Marmota caligata
Olympic Marmot	Marmota olympus
Piute Ground Squirrel	Spermophilus mollis
Washington Ground Squirrel	Spermophilus washingtoni
Columbian Ground Squirrel	Spermophilus columbianus
California Ground Squirrel	Spermophilus beecheyi
Golden-mantled Ground Squirrel	Spermophilus lateralis
Cascade Ground Squirrel	Spermophilus saturatus
Eastern Gray Squirrel	Sciurus carolinensis
Western Gray Squirrel	Sciurus griseus
Eastern Fox Squirrel	Sciurus niger
Red Squirrel	Tamiasciurus hudsonicus
Douglas' Squirrel	Tamiasciurus douglasii
Northern Flying Squirrel	Glaucomys sabrinus

GEOMYIDAE (pocket gophers)

Northern Pocket Gopher	Thomomys talpoides
Western Pocket Gopher	Thomomys mazama

HETEROMYIDAE (heteromyid rats)

Great Basin Pocket Mouse	Perognathus parvus
Ord's Kangaroo Rat	Dipodomys ordii

CASTORIDAE (beavers)

Beaver	Castor canadensis

CRICETIDAE (cricetid rats)

Western Harvest Mouse	Reithrodontomys megalotis
Deer Mouse	Peromyscus maniculatus
Forest Deer Mouse	Peromyscus keenii
Northern Grasshopper Mouse	Onychomys leucogaster
Bushy-tailed Woodrat	Neotoma cinerea
Gapper's Red-backed Vole	Clethrionomys gapperi
Heather Vole	Phenacomys intermedius
Meadow Vole	Microtus pennsylvanicus
Montane Vole	Microtus montanus
Gray-tailed Vole	Microtus canicaudus

Townsend's Vole	Microtus townsendii
Long-tailed Vole	Microtus longicaudus
Creeping Vole	Microtus oregoni
Water Vole	Microtus richardsoni
Sagebrush Vole	Lemmiscus curtatus
Muskrat	Ondatra zibethicus
Northern Bog Lemming	Synaptomys borealis

MURIDAE (murid rats)

Black Rat	Rattus rattus
Norway Rat	Rattus norvegicus
House Mouse	Mus musculus

ZAPODIDAE (jumping mice)

Western Jumping Mouse	Zapus princeps
Pacific Jumping Mouse	Zaphus trinotatus

ERETHIZONTIDAE (new world porcupines)

Porcupine	Erethizon dorsatum

MYOCASTORIDAE (nutrias)

Nutria	Myocastor coypus

CARNIVORA (carnivores)

Fissipedia

CANIDAE (canids)

Coyote	Canis latrans
Gray Wolf	Canis lupus
Red Fox	Vulpes vulpes

URSIDAE (bears)

Black Bear	Ursus americanus
Grizzly Bear	Ursus arctos

PROCYONIDAE (procyonids)

Raccoon	Procyon lotor

MUSTELIDAE (mustelids)

Marten	Martes americana

Fisher	Martes pennanti
Ermine	Mustela erminea
Long-tailed Weasel	Mustela frenata
Mink	Mustela vison
Wolverine	Gulo gulo
Badger	Taxidea taxus
Western Spotted Skunk	Spilogale gracilis
Striped Skunk	Mephitis mephitis
River Otter	Lontra canadensis
Sea Otter	Enhydra lutris

FELIDAE (cats)

Cougar	Puma concolor
Lynx	Lynx canadensis
Bobcat	Lynx rufus

Pinnipedia

OTARIIDAE (eared seals)

Northern Fur Seal	Callorhinus ursinus
Northern Sea Lion	Eumetopias jubatus
California Sea Lion	Zalophus californianus

PHOCIDAE (hair seals)

| Harbor Seal | Phoca vitulina |
| Northern Elephant Seal | Mirounga angustirostris |

CETACEA (cetaceans)

Gray Whale	Eschrichtius robustus
Fin Whale	Balaenoptera physalus
Sei Whale	Balaenoptera borealis
Minke Whale	Balaenoptera acutorostrata
Blue Whale	Balaenoptera musculus
Humpback Whale	Megaptera novaeangliae
North Pacific Right Whale	Eubalaena japonica

DELPHINIDAE (dolphins)

Striped Dolphin	Stenella coeruleoalba
Common Dolphin	Delphinus delphis
Pacific White-sided Dolphin	Lagenorhynchus obliquidens
Grampus	Grampus griseus
False Killer Whale	Pseudorca crassidens
Short-finned Pilot Whale	Globicephala macrorhynchus
Killer (orca) Whale	Orcinus orca
Northern Right-whale Dolphin	Lissodelphis borealis

PHOCOENIDAE (porpoises)

Harbor Porpoise	Phocoena phocoena
Dall's Porpoise	Phocoenoides dalli

ZIPHIIDAE (beaked whales)

Baird's Beaked Whale	Berardius bairdii
Goose-beaked Whale	Ziphius cavirostris
Bering Sea Beaked Whale	Mesoplodon stejnegeri
Arch-beaked Whale	Mesoplodon carlhubbsi

ARTIODACTYLA (even-toed ungulates)

CERVIDAE (deer)

Elk	Cervus elaphus
Mule Deer	Odocoileus hemionus
White-tailed Deer	Odocoileus virginianus
Moose	Alces alces
Caribou	Rangifer tarandus

BOVIDAE (bovids)

Mountain Goat	Oreamnos americanus
Bighorn Sheep	Ovis canadensis

Selected Fishes

ACIPENSERIFORMES

ACIPENSERIDAE (sturgeon)

Green Sturgeon	*Acipenser medirostris*
White Sturgeon	*Acipenser transmontanus*

CLUPEIFORMES

CLUPEIDAE (herring)

American Shad	*Alosa sapidissima*

SALMONIDAE (trout, whitefish)

Lake Whitefish	*Coregonus clupeaformis*
Pygmy Whitefish	*Prosopium coulteri*
Mountain Whitefish	*Prosopium williamsoni*
Golden Trout	*Oncorhynchus aguabonita*
Cutthroat Trout	*Oncorhynchus clarki*
Pink Salmon	*Oncorhynchus gorbuscha*
Chum Salmon	*Oncorhynchus keta*
Coho Salmon	*Oncorhynchus kisutch*
Rainbow Trout (steelhead)	*Oncorhynchus mykiss*
Sockeye Salmon	*Oncorhynchus nerka*
Chinook Salmon	*Oncorhynchus tshawytscha*
Atlantic Salmon	*Salmo salar*
Brown Trout	*Salmo trutta*
Bull Trout	*Salvelinus confluentus*
Dolly Varden	*Salvelinus malma*
Brook Trout	*Salvelinus fontinalis*
Lake Trout	*Salvelinus namaycush*
Arctic Grayling	*Thymallus arcticus*

OSMERIDAE (smelt)

Longfin Smelt	*Spirinchus thaleichthys*
Eulachon	*Thaleichthys pacificus*

ESOCIDAE (pickerel)

Grass Pickerel	*Esox americanus*
Northern Pike	*Esox lucius*
Tiger Muskellunge	*Esox lucius x Esox masquinongy*

CYPRINIFORMES

CYPRINIDAE (minnows)

Grass Carp	*Ctenopharyngodon idella*
Common Carp	*Cyprinus carpio*

ICTALURIDAE (catfish)

Black Bullhead	*Ameiurus melas*
Yellow Bullhead	*Ameiurus natalis*

Wrangler Fred Duzan can take you to some great alpine fishing destinations.

Brown Bullhead	*Ameiurus nebulosus*
Channel Catfish	*Ictalurus punctatus*
Tadpole Madtom	*Noturus gyrinus*
Flathead Catfish	*Pylodictis olivaris*

GADIFORMES

GADIDAE (cod)

| Burbot | *Lota lota* |

PERCIFORMES

CENTRARCHIDAE (sunfish)

Rock Bass	*Ambloplites rupestris*
Green Sunfish	*Lepomis cyanellus*
Pumpkinseed	*Lepomis gibbosus*
Warmouth	*Lepomis gulosus*
Bluegill	*Lepomis macrochirus*
Smallmouth Bass	*Micropterus dolomieu*
Largemouth Bass	*Micropterus salmoides*
White Crappie	*Pomoxis annularis*
Black Crappie	*Pomoxis nigromaculatus*

EMBIOTOCIDAE (surfperch)

| Shiner Perch | *Cymatogaster aggregata* |

PERCIDAE (perch)

| Yellow Perch | *Perca flavescens* |
| Walleye | *Stizostedion vitreum* |

PLEURONECTOFORMES

PLEURONECTIDAE (righteye flounder)

| Starry Flounder | *Platichthys stellatus* |

Websites

Several websites have proved invaluable while researching this book. I suspect they'll also be good resources for you while planning your next trip outdoors in Washington.

Washington State Parks Commission	www.parks.wa.gov
National Forests of the Pacific Northwest	www.fs.fed.us/r6/r6nf.htm
National Wildlife Refuges – Pacific Region	www.fws.gov/pacific/refuges
National Park Service – Washington State	www.nps.gov/state/wa
Washington Department of Fish and Wildlife	www.wdfw.wa.gov
State of Washington Tourism	www.experiencewa.gov
Washington Audubon Society	http://wa.audubon.org
Washington Lakes.com	www.washingtonlakes.com
Washington Trails Organization	www.wta.org
Washington Outfitters & Guides Association	www.woga.org

Mule deer

Index

David Kruse rode to this alpine lake with Icicle Outfitters.